WAS REVOLUTION
INEVITABLE?

WAS REVOLUTION INEVITABLE?

TURNING POINTS OF THE RUSSIAN REVOLUTION

EDITED BY TONY BRENTON

OXFORD
UNIVERSITY PRESS

OXFORD
UNIVERSITY PRESS

Oxford University Press is a department of the University of Oxford.
It furthers the University's objective of excellence in research, scholarship,
and education by publishing worldwide. Oxford is a registered trade mark of
Oxford University Press in the UK and certain other countries.

Published in the United States of America by Oxford University Press
198 Madison Avenue, New York, NY 10016, United States of America.

© Tony Brenton 2017

First published in Great Britain by Profile Books.

Library of Congress Cataloging-in-Publication Data
is available from the Library of Congress

ISBN 978–0–19–065891–5

1 3 5 7 9 8 6 4 2

Printed by Sheridan Books, Inc.,
United States of America

Русский бунт, бессмысленный и беспощадный
(Russian revolt, mindless and merciless)
A. S. Pushkin

CONTENTS

A NOTE TO THE READER

Prior to February 1918 Russia still used the Julian calendar (so called Old Style, OS) which was thirteen days behind the Gregorian calendar (New Style, NS) to which it then switched, bringing it in line with the West. Throughout this book dates for events in Russia are given Old Style up to February 1918 and New Style thereafter. In case of ambiguity we make clear whether OS or NS.

CHRONOLOGY

1905

9 Jan: Bloody Sunday.

10 Jan: Major wave of strikes and disturbances (continuing through year).

14 May: Battle of Tsushima, culminating Russian defeat in war with Japan.

5 Sept (NS): Treaty of Portsmouth ends Russo-Japanese war.

15 Oct: Witte offers draft political reforms to Tsar.

17 Oct: Tsar announces package of political reforms, including creation of Duma.

1906

16 April: Witte, having lost Tsar's confidence, resigns as Prime Minister.

26 April: New Fundamental laws made public; Stolypin Minister of Interior.

27 April: First Duma opens.

8 July: First Duma dissolved; Stolypin Prime Minister.

Aug–Nov: First round of Stolypin reforms.

1907

20 Feb: Second Duma opens.

March: Stolypin announces further reforms.

2 June: Second Duma dissolved; new electoral law.

7 Nov: Third Duma opens, runs to 1912.

1911

1 Sept: Stolypin shot; dies four days later.

1912

15 Nov: Fourth Duma opens.

1914

29 June: Assassination attempt on Rasputin.
1 Aug (NS): Germany declares war on Russia.
Late August: Major Russian defeats in Germany.

1915

April–July: Germans invade Poland. A number of ministers,
    including Minister of war, replaced.
19 July: Duma reconvened for six weeks.
21 Aug: Unavailing demand from Ministers that Tsar let Duma form
    cabinet.
22 Aug: Tsar takes command of armed forces. Moves to HQ at
    Mogilev. Period of 'Tsaritsa Government' begins.
3 Sept: Duma prorogued.

1916

Jan–Nov: Empress/Rasputin oversee stream of rapid ministerial
    changes, including Minister of War, Interior Minister and Prime
    Minister (twice).
1 Nov: Duma reconvenes. Major attack by Kerensky on Rasputin and
    by Miliukov on top level 'stupidity or treason'.
17 Dec: Rasputin murdered.
27 Dec: Yet another new Prime Minister.

1917

14 Feb: Duma reconvenes.

23–24 Feb: Demonstrations in Petrograd provoked by bread shortage.

25 Feb: Demonstrations turn violent. Tsar (in Mogilev) orders suppression by force.

26 Feb: Army fires on crowd, killing forty. Part of garrison mutinies in protest. Tsar dismisses as panic Rodzyanko's telegraphed demand for new government.

27 Feb: Most of Petrograd in hands of mutinous troops. Duma prorogued, but sets up 'Temporary Committee'. Government dissolving. Tsar orders General Ivanov to proceed to Petrograd and put mutiny down. Organising meeting for Petrograd Soviet.

28 Feb: Tsar sets out for Tsarskoe Selo. First meeting of Petrograd Soviet. Disturbances spread to Moscow.

1 March: Imperial train diverted to Pskov. Arrives in the evening. Tsar, at urging of Alexeev, agrees to Duma based ministry and cancels Ivanov's mission. Meanwhile Duma and Soviet agree principles for establishment of Provisional Government. Formation of Moscow Soviet. 'Order No. 1' effectively strips military officers of most of their authority.

2 March: Provisional Government formed under Prince Lvov. Rodzyanko cables Ruzsky in Pskov to say abdication necessary. In course of morning Alexeev and other commanders endorse that advice. Nicholas accepts this and sends telegrams declaring Alexis Tsar. But with arrival of representatives of Duma changes mind and nominates Grand Duke Michael instead.

3 March: Michael decides not to accept crown. End of Romanov dynasty.

8 March: Nicholas returns to Tsarskoe Selo under arrest.

Late March: Britain withdraws offer of asylum to imperial family.

3 April: Lenin arrives in Petrograd, demands 'All power to the Soviets'.

20–21 April: 'April Days' – Petrograd riots, instigated by Bolsheviks, against Provisional Government, and particularly Foreign Minister Miliukov.

4–5 May: Formation of coalition government including socialist leaders. Miliukov out. Kerensky Minister of War.

16 June: Disastrous 'Kerensky Offensive' launched.

20–30 June: Rising tension in Petrograd as troops ordered to front.

3–4 July: 'July Days'. Military mutiny. Demonstrators occupy Petrograd and threaten to overthrow Government. Lenin fails to give decisive lead. Demonstration fizzles out. Loyal troops arrive.

5 July: Lenin goes back into exile. Other Bolshevik leaders arrested.

7 July: Lvov resigns and names Kerensky as Prime Minister.

18 July: Kornilov appointed Commander in Chief.

31 July: imperial family depart for Tobolsk.

9 Aug: Elections and convocation of Constituent Assembly put back to November.

26–27 Aug: Kerensky secures dictatorial powers, pronounces Kornilov traitor. Kornilov mutinies.

30 Aug: Release of imprisoned Bolsheviks ordered.

1 Sept: Kornilov arrested.

10 Oct: Bolshevik Central Committee, with Lenin present, votes to prepare to seize power.

20–25 Oct: Bolsheviks in effect take control of Petrograd garrison.

24 Oct: Lenin, in disguise, makes way to Smolny in evening. Persuades Bolsheviks to launch coup.

25–26 Oct: 'Storming of Winter Palace'. Kerensky escapes to front to seek support. Other ministers arrested. Non-Bolshevik parties walk out of Congress of Soviets when announcement is made. Bolshevik government (Sovnarkom) with Lenin as chairman set up.

27 Oct: Opposition press outlawed.

28 Oct – 2 Nov: Various anti-Bolshevik strikes and military actions (particularly in Moscow) overcome.

12–30 Nov: Elections to Constituent Assembly. Socialist revolutionaries get 40 per cent, Bolsheviks 25 per cent.

20 Nov (OS): Armistice negotiations begin at Brest-Litovsk.

28 Nov: Demonstration in favour of Constituent Assembly. Constitutional Democrats banned and leaders arrested.

7 Dec: Cheka established.

Late December: Generals Alexeev and Kornilov found 'Volunteer' (ie White) Army.

1918

5 Jan: Meeting of Constituent Assembly. Demonstration in support repressed. Assembly closed down late that night, and locked out the following morning.

15 Jan – 3 March: Conclusion of Treaty of Brest-Litovsk. Lenin presses colleagues for acceptance of punitive terms, but only prevails when Germans renew their military offensive and demand even more concessions.

Early March: Bolshevik government moves to Moscow in face of German threat to Petrograd.

9 March: Allied contingent lands in Murmansk. This is the first of a series of allied interventions, eventually in support of the Whites, in NW Russia, Ukraine and the Far East. Final withdrawal in the West in Aug 1919, and by the Japanese from Vladivostok in Oct 1922.

26 March: Trotsky becomes War Commissar. Over next few weeks overcomes fierce party resistance to recruit former Tsarist officers to Red Army.

12 April: Kornilov killed in action. Denikin takes over command.

26 April: Nicholas and family sent to Ekaterinburg.

9 May: First Bolshevik efforts to requisition grain from peasants.

29 May: Czech Legion in Chelyabinsk refuses to disarm. Align themselves with Whites. Take over Trans-Siberian railroad.

8 June: Czechs occupy Samara. Komuch formed.

12–13 June: Grand Duke Michael murdered in Perm.

16–17 July: Murder of Nicholas II and family in Ekaterinburg.

30 Aug: Fanny Kaplan attempts to kill Lenin.

5 Sept: Red Terror launched. Widespread massacres of prisoners and hostages.

23 Sept: Anti-Bolshevik 'Provisional All Russian Government', notionally answerable to Komuch, formed in Omsk.

11 Nov: Armistice ends World War I. Germany rapidly abandons gains in Eastern Europe, most of which over the next two years are reclaimed by Russia.

18 Nov: Kolchak coup in Omsk effectively makes him military dictator of White cause.

1919

January: 'Razverstka', policy of grain requisition from peasants, formally introduced.

March–May: Kolchak launches offensive in Siberia. Initially successful, almost reaching the Volga. But halted by mid-May and then forced into retreat.

July–Oct: Denikin launches offensive against Red Army in South, and Yudenich in North West. Both initially make good progress, with Denikin approaching Tula and Yudenich almost taking Petrograd, but by October are forced into retreat.

14 Nov: Kolchak retreats to Irkutsk. Yudenich disbands his army.

17 Dec: Kolchak forced to resign, Subsequently he is handed over to the Bolsheviks and shot (7 Feb 1920).

1920

27 March: Denikin abandons command. Vrangel takes over.

August: Tambov rising of peasants against grain requisitioning, followed by a spate of similar risings elsewhere.

7 Nov: White army under Vrangel evacuates via Crimea. End of Civil War.

1921

March: A spate of demonstrations against food shortages culminates in the naval uprising at Kronstadt, brutally put down. The Communist Party bans factions within it, paving the way for total dictatorship, but also abandons grain requisitioning and so initiates the New Economic Policy (NEP).

1922

16 February: Decree on confiscation of church valuables marks start of Bolshevik campaign against Church. Patriarch Tikhon publicly opposes campaign.

3 April: Stalin becomes General Secretary of the Communist Party, the basis for his future dominance.

26 May: Lenin has first major stroke.

June: Metropolitan Veniamin and a number of other priests tried for counterrevolutionary activity and subsequently shot.

Dec: 'League of Militant Godless' established.

1923–24

Lenin, increasingly incapacitated by a series of strokes, dies 21 January 1924. He leaves a testament recommending (with reservations) Trotsky as his successor, and arguing that Stalin should be demoted.

ACKNOWLEDGEMENTS

First and foremost I must thank the contributors to this book. They agreed to take on what for a professional historian was an offbeat, if not suspect, task. They have delivered magnificently.

I owe extra thanks to two of them. Orlando Figes has been encouraging from the start and offered me many useful tips in my search for contributors. Dominic Lieven was kind enough to read through my own draft chapter and offer a professional commentary to remedy my amateurisms. The defects that remain are of course mine alone.

For the Afterword I needed the advice of someone with a deep knowledge of today's Russia. Duncan Allan was exactly the right person to turn to, and could not have been more helpful. Again the remaining faults belong exclusively to me.

The whole team at Profile have been splendid, but I must mention two names in particular. The late Peter Carson enthused about my original concept and was crucial in enabling me to run with it. He is still widely missed, including by me. And Nick Sheerin picked the project up and has worked tirelessly at bringing it to fruition. In many ways he is co-editor of this book.

Finally, my family; Sue, Tim, Kate and Jenny. They have over the years had to put up with a lot because of my obsession with Russia. This book is dedicated to them.

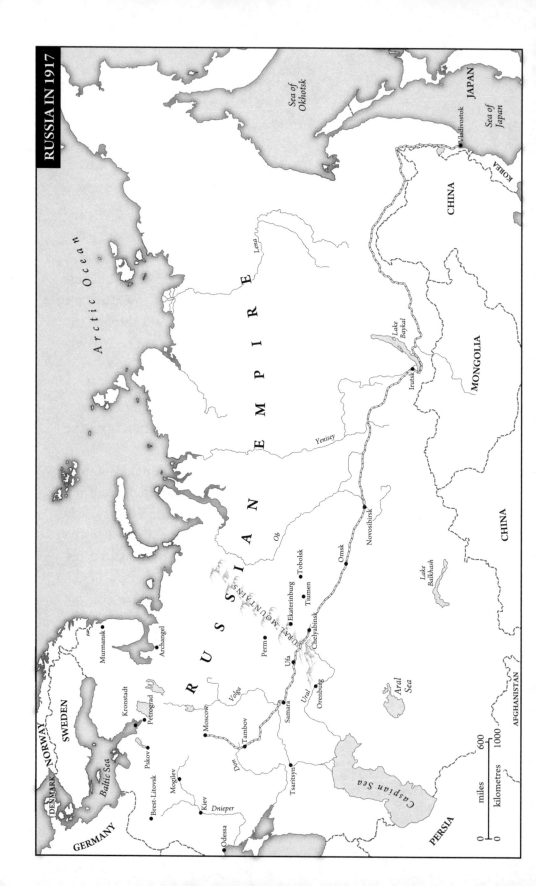

WAS REVOLUTION INEVITABLE?

INTRODUCTION

TONY BRENTON

I

We are approaching the 100th anniversary of the Russian Revolution. If one had to pick the single event which has most shaped twentieth-century history, and so our world in the early years of the twenty-first, this must be it. The Revolution put in power the totalitarian communism that eventually ruled one third of the human race, stimulated the rise of Nazism in the 1930s, and thus the Second World War, and created the great antagonist the West faced for the forty years Cold War balance of terror. It is hard to think of another example where the events of a few years, concentrated in one country, and mostly in one city, have had such vast historical consequences.

The events of 1917 have themselves become a historical battlefield. For seventy years it was a core Soviet belief that the revolution was the triumphant product of ineluctable historical forces. That view may now look quaint but, in a softer version, it has held extensive sway among Western historians. In this view tsarism was rotten and doomed, socialism, even Bolshevism, offered Russia a bright new future, and it was Stalin who corrupted the dream. Others have taken a much less sympathetic standpoint. They argue that there was a liberal alternative to tsarism, which the Bolsheviks strangled at birth, that it was Lenin who created the dictatorship and the terror, and that Stalin was no more than his apt pupil. And there are lots of other variants. In one, tsarism was on the way to modernising Russia, and liberalism would inevitably have followed had the revolution not stopped it in its tracks. In another, Russia's whole historic tradition is of state-dominated tyranny, and the regime made by Lenin just the latest manifestation.

Where you come out on all these grand questions depends heavily on how you view what happened in Russia in the years surrounding 1917. Could things have gone differently? Were there moments when a single decision taken another way, a random accident, a shot going straight instead of crooked (or vice versa) could have altered the whole course of Russian, and so European, and world, history?

This book picks out those moments in the history of the revolution where that feeling of contingency is particularly intense. These are the forks in the road where one senses that there genuinely was a question over which way things would go. For each of these moments a distinguished historian has been invited to describe the background, significance and consequences of the event as it happened, and also to speculate a little as to how things might have gone otherwise. This is not a full narrative history of the revolution (there are plenty of excellent ones already) but rather a series of snapshots that catch a very tangled series of events at key moments and ask whether the story might have been radically different.

II

Before presenting our snapshots it may be helpful to put them in context.

The revolution did not come out of the blue. The problems of a backward-looking autocracy struggling to navigate a period of rapid social and economic change were not unique to Russia. They have produced revolutions before, notably in France in 1789 (an example constantly on the minds of the Russian revolutionaries). In Russia's case, the dress rehearsal for the events of 1917 took place in 1905. The year 1904 had seen a 'perfect storm': military defeat by the Japanese; impoverishment and discontent in the countryside; appalling living and working conditions in the cities; and the spread of socialist and democratic ideas (often in an extremely virulent form) among the intelligentsia. These came together on 'Bloody Sunday' (9 January 1905) when the Imperial Guard in St Petersburg gunned down hundreds of unarmed demonstrators. The result was a mortal blow to the credibility of Nicholas II and his regime. Massive nationwide strikes and demonstrations forced the tsar to accept the first-ever representative assembly in Russian history, the Duma. This concession brought a few years of precarious stability. In our first snapshot, Dominic Lieven looks at how things might have gone if the 1905 revolution had turned into full-scale social collapse, as it in fact did twelve years later.

The next few years saw a bitter tug of war between a Tsar who (encouraged by his uncompromising wife and their resident 'holy man', Rasputin) was intent on maintaining his autocratic power, and a series of Dumas (regularly disbanded and reconstituted by Nicholas in what he hoped would be a more helpful way) demanding economic and political reform. The one statesman of the period who showed any capacity to master these conflicting forces was Pyotr Stolypin, prime minister 1906–11. Stolypin was an 'authoritarian moderniser' – admired in particular by Vladimir Putin – who tried to use the Tsar's authority to bring about the economic reforms which Russia so badly needed. These efforts ended with Stolypin's assassination in 1911. Simon Dixon in his chapter looks at Stolypin's impact, and asks how events might have evolved if he had not gone to the Kiev opera that night.

With the abandonment of serious efforts at reform, the one thing that temporarily allayed rising social disorder and discontent was Russia's entry into the First World War in 1914. As so often happened (and, indeed, still does today), Russian society pulled together in the face of a common enemy. Strikes stopped, agitators were jailed, there were huge patriotic demonstrations. But in the longer term the war, which brought military humiliation and rising economic dislocation, was the final nail in the coffin of the tsarist regime. Douglas Smith looks at the little-known role of Rasputin in talking Nicholas out of entering an earlier Balkan war, and his efforts to dissuade him in 1914 as well. Not only Russia but the world too would be a very different place if he had succeeded.

He of course didn't. The war took Nicholas far away from Petrograd (the new, patriotic, name of St Petersburg) to command his troops.

Government was left in the capricious and incompetent hands of the empress Alexandra and Rasputin, about whom all sorts of scandalous rumours circulated. The standing of the Tsar reached rock bottom; even members of his family were plotting to remove him. Rising popular discontent came to a head with bread riots in Petrograd in February 1917. After some attempts at suppression the army joined the rioters. Nicholas's attempt from his distant headquarters to send in relief forces failed. His generals now advised him that the only way to save the dynasty, and Russia, was for him to abdicate in favour of his son Alexis. Concerned about Alexis' health, Nicholas tried instead to pass the crown to his brother, Michael. But Michael was unacceptable to the civilian politicians in Petrograd who, as the Provisional Government, were to inherit real power. Thus through a chapter of accidents, as described by Donald Crawford, the 300-year-old Romanov dynasty came to an end.

The fall of the Romanovs precipitated the rise of the 'Soviets' (directly elected assemblies of soldiers, peasants and industrial workers) in Petrograd and other cities. As the economic and political situation deteriorated these assemblies were increasingly radicalised. The extremist Bolshevik faction in particular rapidly gained influence. The Provisional Government, drawn from traditional tsarist-era politicians, found itself having to work in uneasy deference to the Petrograd Soviet (which at any time could bring the city to a halt with strikes and demonstrations). In this atmosphere, the German Foreign Ministry, wanting Russia out of the war, arranged the return to Russia of the Bolshevik leader, Vladimir Lenin, in his famous 'sealed train'. He swiftly overcame reluctance among his fellow Bolsheviks and electrified the political scene with his strident (but widely echoed) demands that the Provisional Government be overthrown and the war ended. With German financial help he was able to bolster Bolshevik support and build Bolshevik forces on the streets (the so-called 'Red Guards'). The Bolsheviks set about propagandising and weakening the Russian armed forces, so contributing to a series of Russian military defeats and mutinies. This activity culminated in an attempted Bolshevik seizure of power in July, which failed. Many Bolsheviks were arrested and Lenin went back into exile. Sean McMeekin analyses Lenin's role in these months, and asks what course events might have taken if there had been no sealed train.

The failed Bolshevik coup exacerbated the mutual suspicions between the left (as represented in the Petrograd Soviet) and the right (as represented in the Provisional Government). Alexander Kerensky, a charismatic left-wing politician but with solid ministerial credentials, took over the Provisional Government in July as the only figure acceptable to the two sides. He chose as the new head of the armed forces the respected patriot General Kornilov who was charged with a mission of reimposing discipline and prosecuting the war. But, through a series of disastrous misunderstandings described in Richard Pipes's chapter, Kerensky came to see Kornilov as an aspiring military dictator. He accordingly swung left, engineered a surge of socialist support against the 'counter-revolution' (including having the recently arrested Bolsheviks released – but not readmitting Lenin), and at the end of August 1917 had Kornilov dismissed and arrested. The price he paid was the loss of army support for his government and a leap in the popularity of the Bolsheviks (who at this point became the majority party in the Petrograd Soviet). The way was now open for them to seize power.

The key moment was the evening of 24 October 1917. A congress of all the Soviets from around the country was due to meet in the Smolny Palace the next day. This would duly have thrown the Provisional Government out and replaced it with a coalition of all the socialist parties (not just the Bolsheviks). Lenin, now surreptitiously back in Petrograd, was determined to pre-empt this. He crossed the city in disguise. A police patrol stopped but did not recognise him. Once at the Smolny, he bullied the Bolshevik leadership (who up until this point had been actively engaged in the negotiations for a coalition) into launching an immediate takeover of power. That takeover (including the famous 'storming' of the Winter Palace) took place the following day. It was not a socialist coalition but the Bolsheviks alone who were to rule Russia.

Orlando Figes in his chapter looks at how different history would have been if that patrol had recognised and arrested Lenin.

So far the Bolsheviks only controlled Petrograd and (after a few days fighting) Moscow. But with single-minded brutality (including the establishment in December 1917 of the 'Cheka', the regime's fearsome secret police) they gradually extended their grip. In Moscow (now the capital of Russia) they squeezed rival parties out of the political process and arrested many of their leaders. In the provinces they rapidly found themselves fighting against the 'Whites', a disparate range of anti-Bolshevik forces, led by former tsarist generals and politicians, and enjoying some foreign support. At this point the Bolsheviks saw the danger of the tsar, now living in prison in Siberia with his family, becoming a 'living symbol' around which the counter-revolution could rally. Edvard Radzinsky looks at moments when the Tsar might indeed have escaped and played such a role. Fearing precisely this, the Bolsheviks had him and his family killed in Ekaterinburg in July 1918.

One of the key promises made in February by the Provisional Government, which of course had no electoral mandate, had been to proceed rapidly to the election of a 'Constituent Assembly'. Political hopes had long focused on this as the body that would create a constitution for post-Romanov Russia and install a government with proper democratic credentials. But preparations were slow. The widely anticipated elections (which even the Bolsheviks, although by now in power, could not stop) did not take place until November. The Bolsheviks got only about a quarter of the vote. Lenin condemned the results on the grounds that the interests of the revolution stood higher than 'bourgeois democracy'. The Assembly convened in Petrograd in January 1918, but within a day was closed down by Red Guards. It did not meet again. In my chapter I ask how things might have gone if the Provisional Government had been quicker.

Rising political repression, civil war and economic dislocation inevitably brought opposition to the Bolshevik regime. This received its most dramatic expression in the attempt on 30 August 1918 by a former non-Bolshevik revolutionary, Fanny Kaplan, to assassinate Lenin. She seriously wounded but did not kill him. The attempt was used as the justification for the first 'Red Terror' under which the Cheka arrested and executed tens of thousands of the regime's opponents (and created a precedent for Stalin's 'Great Terror' thirty years later). Lenin's injury probably also contributed to his early death in 1924, clearing the way for Stalin to inherit power. Martin Sixsmith tells the story of the assassination attempt and asks what the consequences could have been if Fanny Kaplan had been more, or less, accurate.

It was by no means inevitable that the Bolsheviks would win the Civil War. While by early 1918 they had established control over most of central Russia, they faced chaos and resistance, including widespread peasant aversion to their rule, in the east and south. Their 'shameful' peace treaty with the Central Powers in March 1918, which handed Ukraine and most of west Russia over to German and Austro-Hungarian occupation, did not add to their standing. The opposition to the Bolsheviks was led by a number of White generals, with some foreign support, but also, importantly, in Siberia by the 'Komuch'. This was a group of politicians, including some who were left-wing, who claimed their legitimacy as the 'All Russian Provisional Government' as former members of the disbanded Constituent Assembly. The Komuch, however, foundered in splits and divisions between its left and right wings. In a coup on 17 November 1918 it was replaced by the dictatorship of Admiral Kolchak. The right wing now dominated all the anti-Bolshevik forces – but with its reactionary political programme it had essentially nothing to offer the peasants. They therefore largely swung behind the Bolsheviks and helped ensure their eventual victory. Evan Mawdsley examines these events and asks if there was any alternative.

One of the by-products of the Civil War was 'War Communism' – the brutal imposition by the Bolsheviks of total control over the Russian economy and population, enforced by mass killings and arrests, which in many ways pre-figured Stalinism. A key feature of this was the 'razverstka' – wholesale seizure of grain from the peasants, often resulting in mass starvation. As the war drew to a close in 1919–20, this led to growing levels of peasant and provincial revolt (including the uprising in February 1921 of the Kronstadt naval garrison, formerly among the staunchest supporters of the revolution). The regime was accordingly forced to abandon the razverstka in 1921. This was the key first step towards the 'New Economic Policy' (NEP), a brief thaw and partial reversion to market economics, which brought the protests to an end and allowed the Russian economy to recover. But a significant proportion of the party detested the NEP on ideological grounds, and in 1928 Stalin as part of his ascent to power ended it and reintroduced grain seizures. Erik Landis asks if the route to Stalinism might have been altered if (as Trotsky proposed at the time) the razverstka had been ended twelve months earlier.

The Bolshevik movement was of course radically and aggressively atheist. A key test of their style of government was their handling of the Russian Orthodox Church (which enjoyed the support of the majority of Russians throughout the Communist period). In fact, while ideological hostility to the Church, and its maltreatment, was constant throughout the Communist years, there was only one real surge of active repression. This started with the confiscation of Church valuables in 1922. Catriona Kelly looks at this episode and asks what it tells us about other features of Bolshevik rule, as well as what might have been the implications of a different approach to church-state relations.

The eventual outcome of the revolution was of course totalitarian communism. Power was confined to a single ruling party: highly centralised; secretly and bureaucratically run; and dependent upon a vast repressive apparatus. Wider public debate, let alone opposition, was rigidly excluded and brutally punished. Many have argued that such an outcome was the inevitable result of the seizure of power by an extremist faction representing a small minority of the populace and driven by an eschatological ideology, which had then to retain power in the teeth of external hostility, domestic civil war and economic collapse. In the early days, however, there were hopes of an alternative under which, even if democracy outside the party was excluded, democracy within it could be maintained. Richard Sakwa looks at these alternatives and asks if they really offered a way of avoiding the totalitarian outcome.

III

It is hard not to see the course of the Russian revolution as deeply tragic. A fitfully, but genuinely, developing country, confronted with forces inspired by the highest hopes for mankind, plunged to quite unprecedented levels of tyranny and mass murder. Even conventional Marxist historians (a vanishing breed) now admit that the road to Utopia went seriously astray. But how 'inevitable' was that tragedy?

Let me explain this book's approach to that question. There is something of a fracas going on in the historical profession on the issue of 'counterfactual history'. Partly in response to a well-received book of counterfactual historical essays edited by Professor Niall Ferguson, Professor Richard Evans has recently written a book dismissing counterfactuals as, mostly, right-wing wishful thinking, often fun, but with virtually nothing to contribute to any real understanding of the past. And indeed as I sought contributors for this book a couple of eminent names declined precisely because they did not wish to play the counterfactual game.

Which is all very well. But in pure logic I find it very hard to understand how the inevitability, or not, of a historical event can be assessed except on the basis of a close look at moments where the road might have taken another direction, and where it might then have led. Contributors to this volume have responded to the challenge in various ways. Some have taken us some way down a route very different from the course history actually did take. Some have focused on moments of extreme contingency when even a very slight change in circumstances might plausibly have led to a dramatically different historical outcome. Some have described the chapter of accidents and misunderstandings leading to a particular outcome, leaving the reader to reflect on how different that outcome might have been. And a significant number have looked at widely touted alternatives to the way things actually went, only to conclude that in fact none of those alternatives was likely. All of these approaches seem to me to be valid. And taken together they ask, from a range of points of view, how unavoidable Russia's tragic twentieth century really was – in a way that a conventional narrative history would find it much harder to do.

It was Hegel who said that 'the one thing we learn from history is that no one learns anything from history'. I hope he was wrong. As a working diplomat I often had no other guide in analysing a particular challenge or situation than whatever relevant history I could lay my hands on. For Russia in particular (a country where I spent a lot of my career), with its famously opaque style of governance, knowledge of Russian history was often a key source of insight into current developments. The Russians, too, rely heavily on history in trying to understand where the world is going. For the revolutionaries of 1917 the key historical precedent, both positive and negative, was the French Revolution. A central aim of all the Russian revolutionaries was to avoid the emergence, as happened in France, of a military dictator – a 'Napoleon'. They succeeded. But they got Stalin instead. Was that inevitable? I leave the reader to judge.

1

FOREIGN INTERVENTION: THE LONG VIEW

1900–1920

DOMINIC LIEVEN

W HEN I FIRST became a historian of late imperial Russia in the 1970s, among Anglo-American historians the field was dominated by the debate between so-called optimists and pessimists. The optimists believed that the constitutional regime established in 1906–14 heralded Russia's move towards Western liberal democracy, a move which would have ended in success had not the First World War intervened and provided Lenin with the opportunity to stage what these historians saw as the Bolshevik coup of October 1917. The pessimists, on the other hand, believed that tsarism was doomed and that Bolshevism was always the likeliest victor in Russia's inevitable revolutionary crisis.

I believed even then that this conception of Russia's fate in 1914 as lying either with democracy or communism reflected much more the Cold War context in which the debate occurred than it did Russian realities in the early twentieth century. The debate was in many ways less Russian history than a battle between rival ideological positions within the Western intelligentsia, which was being fought out on Russian soil. The terms of the debate also illustrated the very powerful hold that the present and its concerns have on historians' thinking, above all in so highly 'relevant' and politically explosive a field as Russian history in the Cold War era.

The idea that Russia could have made a peaceful transition to liberal democracy is very wishful thinking. Russia was a great multinational empire, one of many that dominated the globe in 1900. None have survived and none have disappeared without serious conflict. Russia was also a country on Europe's poorer and less developed periphery, where middle classes and states were weaker and property less secure than in the continent's core. Confronting the onset of mass politics was much more dangerous and frightening for elites on Europe's periphery than for those at its centre. I call this periphery the Second World. Most of the countries of this world lived under authoritarian regimes after 1918 from which some of them were freed in 1945 less by their own efforts than by Anglo-American victory in the Second World War. If Spain and Italy, where liberal institutions and values were much deeper rooted than in Russia, adopted authoritarian and even semi-totalitarian regimes in the 1920s, what chance did Russian democracy have?

A Bolshevik victory in early twentieth-century Russia was likelier than a liberal democratic one but nevertheless not the likeliest outcome. For this there are many reasons. Of these perhaps the most important is the international context: it seems to me a fantasy to imagine that in peacetime the European great powers would have allowed any Russian regime to secede from the international system, set itself up as the headquarters of international socialist revolution, and repudiate today's equivalent of trillions of dollars of foreign debt, most of it owed to citizens of these great powers.

Here immediately one comes to the core of this chapter, which stresses the crucial influence of the international context on the Russian Revolution and suggests a number of possible outcomes that would have been strongly influenced by the 'international factor'. To develop this theme we must begin our story in 1905–6.

In these years Russia was rocked by a revolution that came very close to bringing down the monarchy. If one looks at events from the perspective of revolutionaries or liberals this may seem an exaggeration. The regime appeared only too durable. But that is not the view you get when you study the higher reaches of the regime from the inside and through the eyes of many of its leading officials. In these circles deep fear existed that the regime would crumble. The worst months of crisis came between October 1905 when Nicholas II granted a constitution and July 1906 when he successfully dissolved the first Duma.

The promise of a constitution in the manifesto of 17 October in no way satisfied the majority of Russian liberals. Their party, the Constitutional Democrats (Kadets), continued to call for universal male suffrage, a government responsible to parliament, the expropriation of much gentry land and an amnesty for all political prisoners. The revolutionary socialist parties were totally irreconcilable from the regime's (correct) perspective and they enjoyed great support among urban workers. Meanwhile much of the countryside was in uproar as peasants burned manor houses, expropriated crops and terrorised landowners and their agents. Worst of all for Russia's rulers, its own forces were in disarray. After the October 1905 manifesto the Police Department of the Ministry of Internal Affairs, which guided and coordinated repression, was in a state of confusion with officials losing confidence and unclear how to act, and their agents and informants beginning to scurry for cover. Most of the navy and much of the army were unreliable as agents of repression. Even in the army, mutinies were frequent and units of the armed forces might easily become servants of the revolution rather than of the regime. Loyalty hung by a thread in many regiments, which were capable of suppressing riots one day and going on strike the next. The government knew what hopes the peasants, whose sons filled the army's ranks, placed in the first Duma: at the centre of these hopes was the expropriation of all gentry land. As the time to dissolve the Duma approached, fears mounted. On 11 June 1906 the First Battalion of the Preobrazhensky Guards, the senior unit in the Russian army, mutinied. General Alexander Kireev, usually a great optimist, wrote in his diary, 'this is it'.[1]

What would have happened had the army's loyalty disintegrated, with most of its other ranks refusing to obey orders or even joining the revolution? A spiral of radicalisation would have occurred similar to that which happened in France in 1789, but it would have been more radical and more rapid. There was no chance that Russia's liberal leaders of the Kadet Party would have been able to control or channel this process. Unlike in the French Revolution, socialist doctrines and revolutionary socialist parties now existed, and indeed had put down deep roots in the Russian intelligentsia. In their determination to eliminate gentry landowning most peasants were unconscious socialists, and many workers were attracted to the socialist vision articulated by the revolutionaries. Mayhem would have been at its worst in the non-Russian areas: the Trans-Caucasus slipped largely beyond the government's control even as things turned out in the winter of 1905–6. Had the regime fallen, the process of disintegration would have gone further, with social revolution quickly taking on the additional aspect of inter-ethnic war. Elsewhere, movements for full-scale independence would only have developed in Poland and perhaps Finland, but in other non-Russian areas there would have been demands for varying degrees of local autonomy. Inevitably extremes of revolution would have caused a counter-revolutionary response, as indeed happened in 1905–7 when there was widespread support for the so-called Black Hundreds. If this process of domestic conflict had been allowed to reach its denouement it is very difficult to know when it would have stopped or which forces would ultimately have emerged victorious.

But in reality, external forces were certain not to allow a disintegrating Russia to decide its own fate and their intervention would probably have been decisive, at least in the short run. The leadership in intervention would almost necessarily have to come from Germany since it was a neighbouring power and had Europe's most formidable army. It is true that the German Chancellor, Bernhard von Bulow, dreaded having to intervene. He recalled the effect of foreign intervention in 1792–93 in uniting French nationalism with the revolution and pushing the latter to extremes. He knew too that intervention on behalf of counter-revolution in Russia would be deeply unpopular with German socialists. But the hands of Bulow and other European leaders were almost certain to be forced as Russia spiralled towards anarchy and socialism. Presumably no Russian regime in peacetime would have taken the suicidal path of repudiating debts and thereby inviting foreign intervention. But as revolution spread, the economy crashed, and capital fled, Russia would have been forced to default on its international obligations. Pre-1914 capitalists and the great powers that supported them had a tough response to defaulters. The pressure of foreign bondholders on their governments to protect their investments by backing the re-creation of a stable non-socialist regime in Russia would have been intense, especially in France, the country most affected. The thought of the German army spearheading intervention in Russia in order to protect French bondholders might have caused some unusual Franco-German solidarity for a time but in Paris this would have been far outweighed by fear that Russian power, the guarantee of French security and the European balance, was gone for the foreseeable future.

Default would spark some version of foreign intervention but the spreading violence against foreign persons and property in Russia would likely result in more immediate and drastic action. Even as it was, in the winter of 1905–6 the British consul in Riga (to take one of many possible examples) was howling for Royal Naval landing parties to protect British subjects in what we now call Latvia. Here above all, however, it would be the Germans who must lead. There were far more ethnic Germans in Russia than there were French, English, Italians or Austrians. Many of these Germans were subjects of the tsar. The most prominent were the landowning, business and professional elites of the Baltic provinces. Many of the Baltic landowning nobility in particular possessed powerful connections in Berlin. At the height of the Russian Revolution of 1905 Emperor William II told Professor Schiemann, the best-known professional middle-class Balt in Berlin, that if the tsar fell and anarchy spread in the Baltic provinces then the German army would intervene. Of course the Kaiser's promises were not government policy but in this case it is hard to see how any German government could have stood aside as ethnic Germans in neighbouring provinces were stripped of their property, saw their manor houses burned over their heads and in many cases were killed. This was already happening in the Baltic provinces but the process was stopped in its tracks by the brutal intervention of punitive Russian military expeditions from early 1906. Had the Russian monarchy fallen and its army disintegrated then arson, mayhem and murder would have become near universal and German military intervention surely unavoidable.

What would have been the result of foreign intervention? Would it, as in France in 1792–93, have led to an alliance of radicalism and nationalism in the revolutionary cause? Maybe, but it is very hard to imagine Russian property-owners allying themselves with any social-ist regime committed to their expropriation. Perhaps the Russian counter-revolution would have allied itself to foreign intervention as Franco did in 1936, for all the nationalist ideology at the core of his counter-revolutionary cause. Possibly a better parallel is with Russian intervention in Hungary in 1849. The dominant ideology of Russian conservatism by 1900 was nationalism, and the Russian elites were imbued by a strong commitment to their country's power, status and honour. If restored to power on German bayonets their humiliation would have been extreme. Perhaps like Austria after 1849 a conserva-tive Russia would have turned on its German saviour, astonishing the world – in the words of Felix Schwarzenberg – by its ingratitude.

But one must not forget the traumatic impact of Russia's collapse and German intervention on international relations in Europe and on the European balance of power. The Russian ambassador in London in 1903–16, Count Alexander Benckendorff, believed that the result of Russian disintegration and German intervention would probably be an immediate Franco-British alliance and very possibly a European war soon after. It is impossible to say whether he would have been proved correct. The one certain point is that it would have taken Russia signifi-cantly longer to recover from disintegration and foreign intervention than it actually took to restore Russian power after 1906. In that period Germany's relative power would have been greatly enhanced. If a Russian recovery was combined with nationalist anti-German frenzy (of which there was a good deal in 1906–14 even without foreign inter-vention) then the temptation for Berlin to seize the opportunity and go to war in order to ensure its hegemony in Europe and its security for the foreseeable future might have proved irresistible. At which point the reader might ask whether this scenario differs greatly from what actually happened. War did after all come in 1914. The key difference would have been that in my counterfactual narrative Germany almost certainly would have won the war.

It may seem that a counterfactual essay on early twentieth-century Russia that concentrates on the international context should focus on the key event of the era, namely the outbreak of the First World War. After all, endless exam questions have asked the question, 'No War, no Revolution?' This might seem all the more pressing because the current trend in historiography of the First World War's causes is to stress contingency and suggest that the war could well have been avoided. I agree up to a point. If Franz Ferdinand had not been assassinated then war would probably not have occurred in 1914. The initial decision for war was made in Vienna. Facing geopolitical decline and growing nationalist challenges, Austria's rulers reacted with a combination of desperation, arrogance and miscalculation. One can find parallels with other imperial elites in similar circumstances. In many ways the Suez crisis was the '1914 moment' for the British and French empires. The key difference between 1914 and 1956 was that, whereas Washington vetoed London's adventure, Berlin not merely allowed but encouraged Vienna to strike. Once the Germans had given their 'blank cheque' to Austria on 22–23 June 1914 then war was the probable outcome.

The deeper background to the war was the struggle of empires and nationalisms, which in various forms was one of the key elements in twentieth-century history. In that sense the First World War was by no means the bolt from the blue depicted in much of the literature. At the very moment in 1914 when this struggle was spilling over into war in south-eastern Europe, it was also paralysing British government and threatening civil war in Ireland. The First World War erupted as a result of the huge and very difficult issues raised by the decline and possible fall of the Ottoman and Habsburg empires. The only way that

this process could have been managed peacefully was through cooperation between Russia and Germany. The so-called 'pro-Germans' in
the Russian leadership urged a return to alliance with Berlin but the
growing antagonism between Germany and Russia before 1914 had
many causes and would have been difficult to withstand.

A war avoided in 1914 could have occurred in the following years but
it could also very easily have been a different war, with Britain remaining neutral. By 1914, there were many signs of growing British détente
with Berlin, and growing distrust of Russia. All of which brings us back
to a big counterfactual question: what if Germany had won the war?
Had Britain remained neutral, as is likely in this scenario, Germany
probably would have done so. But to imagine this, it's not necessary to
envisage Britain staying out of a European conflict since Germany very
nearly won the First World War in any case.

The winter of 1916–17 was a decisive moment in history. Had the
Germans not brought the United States into the conflict at the very
moment when revolution was heralding the disintegration of Russian
power then they would have had every chance of winning the First
World War, with enormous implications for Russia, and Europe. So
a key counterfactual question is: what if the German leadership had
not opted for unrestricted submarine warfare in the winter of 1916–17
thereby bringing the United States into the conflict? The key point to
bear in mind is that in order to win the First World War the Germans
did not need outright victory on the western front. All that was required
was stalemate in the west and victory in the east. Victory would have
boiled down to something like the pre-war status quo in the west and
the survival of the peace treaty of Brest-Litovsk in the east, which ended
the Russo-German war in March 1918. If the Germans had not brought
the Americans into the war then this outcome was almost certain.

Without American or Russian assistance the French and British
could never have defeated Germany. By the winter of 1916 there was
a strong chance that the United States would not continue to allow
Britain and France to finance their war effort by floating ever-greater
loans on the American market. On its own that might not have forced

a compromise peace with Germany but combined with the disintegration of Russia it would have made Allied victory impossible. American
intervention made a huge difference to Allied finances but also to Allied
morale in the dark days of 1917 and early 1918. By the second half of
1918 the American army was playing a major role on the western front.
Even more important, the knowledge that an almost unlimited flow of
American manpower would join the fight if it continued beyond 1918
was crucial to the decisions made by the German high command in
1918 and to growing German pessimism about the war's outcome.

The Treaty of Brest-Litovsk created a 'German order' in east-central
Europe. This had huge implications for all Europeans. In the twentieth
century Germany and Russia were always, at least potentially, conti-
nental Europe's greatest powers. The two world wars in Europe more
than anything revolved around their competition. If either Germany or
Russia were decisively weakened then the other power must dominate
all of eastern and central Europe unless – as happened after 1945 but was
unthinkable before then – the Americans remained fully committed to
sustaining the European balance of power. In 1918 Russia's disintegration allowed Germany to dominate east-central Europe and therefore
inevitably become by far the most powerful state in Europe. In 1945 the
pattern was reversed. In 1989–91 a second collapse of Russian power
led to German reunification. Partly as a result we are now facing – for
the moment still in less dangerous circumstances – the task of feeling
our way towards adapting to a German leadership in Europe which
will be moderated by other powers and acceptable to Europeans and
to the German people too. For reasons of both history and contemporary political economy this is a very difficult challenge and this explains
many of contemporary Europe's problems.

The Treaty of Brest-Litovsk took from Russia all the territories it
had acquired since the reign of Peter the Great. In other words it was
confined to its present-day borders. But the key to Brest-Litovsk lay
much less in Russia's loss of the lands acquired by Peter and his successors than in the independence of Ukraine, which had become tsarist
territory already in the seventeenth century. Without Ukraine, early

twentieth-century Russia would cease to be a great power. Ukraine furnished most of the empire's exported grain at a time when the Russian Empire was competing with the United States to be the world's greatest grain exporter. Grain exports were the key to Russia's favourable trade balance and to the government's strategy of economic development, which in the short to medium term relied on importing foreign capital and technological know-how in exchange for grain exports. Ukraine also produced most of the empire's coal and iron, and was the centre of its metallurgical industry. Ukraine's vital economic role was enhanced by the fact that the Urals region, which Peter the Great had developed as the centre of Russia's metallurgical and defence industries, had been in decline for a century and would not recover until Stalin's industrialisation drive of the 1930s.

If Russia lost Ukraine then Germany must become Europe's hegemon. This was all the more certain because any notionally independent Ukraine could only exist as a German satellite. No Russian government would willingly tolerate Ukrainian independence and only Germany could protect Ukraine against its eastern neighbour. On top of geopolitical vulnerability Ukraine also suffered from great internal weaknesses. An independent Ukraine confronted by Bolshevik Russia could be sure of the disloyalty of Communists, Russian workers in the eastern cities and mines, and most Jews. This constituted a very sizeable part of the population, and in many eastern regions even a majority. Still worse, Ukrainian nationalism was very much a minority cause even in core central areas of Ukraine. Most of the region's peasants had no sense of Ukrainian identity. In most cases they thought of themselves as belonging to their village and to the Orthodox Church. Traditionally, to the extent that they possessed a wider sense of political identity and loyalty, this was to the tsar as protector of the Orthodox community. In the pre-war decades an increasingly bitter conflict was waged among the region's intelligentsia over the question of whether Ukrainians were a separate nation or a branch of the greater Russian community. This conflict was fought on both sides of the Russo-Austrian border since over one quarter of what we now call Ukrainians were subjects of the Habsburg emperor. The heartland of Ukrainian nationalism was in Austrian Galicia. Both Vienna and Petersburg understood the immense potential geopolitical importance of this struggle to define Ukrainian identity and to instil this definition into the Ukrainian masses as they evolved from illiterate villagers into modern citizens. The Ukrainian issue was an increasing thorn in Russo-Austrian relations, though one very little noticed in English-language historiography on the origins of the First World War.

To say that Ukraine could only exist as a German protectorate might seem to claim that the new Ukrainian state was illegitimate. I do not mean that. Given time a Ukrainian state could have used its control over the educational system to inculcate a sense of Ukrainian identity into most of its people. Independent Ukraine was certainly a more real country than, for example, the Iraqi state that Britain carved out of the carcass of the Ottoman Empire, in part to guarantee its access to oil. A basic problem for many post-imperial states is that empires by definition are made up of many peoples entwined by history and geography. Unravelling them is a tricky and often brutal business. No polity is worse equipped to do this than one that combines a Westphalian insistence on absolute sovereignty with European nationalism's obsession with language, history and blood. So an independent Ukrainian state would have been weak and conflict-ridden in its early decades but, granted German protection, by no means unviable.

The big question was whether a German-Ukrainian alliance, and more broadly a German order in east-central Europe, could have endured. In general terms one has to remember that creating the military basis for empire or even hegemony is only the first stage, and usually the easier one. For empire to last, a second and often more challenging stage of political consolidation is required and this entails the creation of both institutions and of legitimacy. Napoleon learned this to his cost. So did the British when they conquered an empire in North America in 1763 only to lose most of it within twenty years. Even after winning the First World War the British faced problems in consolidating their existing empire. In Egypt and India they succeeded, albeit at the cost of concessions. In Ireland they mostly failed. Though the post-war settlement allowed the de facto incorporation of much of the Middle East into the British Empire, here too there were great difficulties: in Iraq, London was forced to retreat towards indirect rule in the face of local revolt and limited financial resources. Attempts to control Constantinople and the Caucasus proved to be examples of imperial over-stretch and British forces had to be withdrawn.

So the question is, could Germany successfully have met the challenge of the second stage of empire-building in eastern Europe, namely political consolidation? If one looks at the German record of empire-building in 1917–18 then it is hard to be optimistic. This does not mean that German rulers were necessarily stupid or inhumane. The chief civilian administrator in Ukraine, for example, was a decent and intelligent man who tried to apply in Ukraine the lessons he had learned before the war from studying British land reform in Ireland and from his own experience in managing Japanese railways in Korea. This places the German effort in eastern Europe in its proper imperial context. But on the whole, German administration alienated local populations by its rigidity and authoritarianism, and clashes between the Germans and local nationalists were frequent. Only on the outer edges of their empire in Finland and Georgia was German intervention often both successful and popular. In Finland they were a shield for the Finnish elites and middle classes against the Russian Bolshevik neighbour and its native allies. In Georgia, a similar equation applied, but the Germans were also a welcome shield against the advance of their allies, the Turks, into the Trans-Caucasus.

But one has to remember the context in which the Germans were working. It takes some time to establish a stable basis for empire. In Iraq, for example, in 1918–22 the British had to crush a major revolt and re-think their whole political strategy before a stable imperial order acceptable both to themselves and local elites could be created. In 1917–18 Germany in eastern Europe was working under extreme pressure. All other considerations had to be subordinated to winning the war and this war must be won quickly before the German civilian population began to starve and before American reinforcements handed victory to the Allies. To a great extent German rule in the east boiled down to a vast and not very successful foraging expedition. Take out American intervention and add a peace born of stalemate on the western front and the situation would have been very different. At that point a German empire in the east would have been able to deploy not just military but also economic and cultural power to buttress its rule. In much of the region Germany was a natural economic partner and cultural model. On the other hand, reconciling some key German interests to policies essential to garner support in east-central Europe would sometimes have been very hard: as always the German agrarian lobby would have been among the most vocal and obstructive of these lobbies.

Success would have depended on the intelligence or otherwise with which the Germans went about building their empire. Most of the German civilian statesmen and the great majority of the leaders of the centre and left-of-centre political parties realised that a successful empire in the east had to be 'informal', must take local nationalisms into account, and had to operate through deals with local elites. The military leadership was cruder and both it and some of its civilian allies had far-reaching annexationist schemes. It is very hard to predict the results of the interplay between political groupings within a victorious Germany and between the German leadership and the realities it encountered on the ground in east-central Europe. Once the immediate wartime crisis was over some of the steam ought to have been taken out of the military leadership. Nevertheless, where German strategic interests or German minorities clashed with the locals – as in Latvia, Estonia and Poland – a particularly hard line was likely to prevail in Berlin.

Would a German informal empire in eastern Europe have been acceptable to the local populations? Merely to ask the question is sufficient to inspire apoplexy in local nationalists and often with good reason. For the Poles a German-dominated eastern Europe would have been a huge setback for their national cause, not least if German hegemony rested partly on backing Ukrainians in the venomous Polish-Ukrainian dispute over ownership of eastern Galicia. For the Latvians and Estonians, anxious to throw off the rule of Baltic German elites, German victory would also have been insupportable. Given population losses among Latvians due to war and emigration, a determined policy of German colonisation might actually even have succeeded in turning this small country into a German-majority land. In most of the Austrian Empire, German victory would have strengthened Austrian-Germans' power and boosted their claims that the German language must have priority in administration and education. But so long as the Habsburg monarchy survived (which it would have done in the event of victory) it would never have allowed any extreme version of German nationalism to prevail within its borders because to do so would undermine the dynasty's raison d'être. Moreover, for some of the peoples of eastern Europe, most notably the Jews, German informal empire could have had great attractions.

When contemplating a possible German empire in eastern Europe after the First World War it is important to make comparisons not with the situation in the region today but rather with eastern Europe's fate for most of the twentieth century. The basic point was that 1918 was only a truce, not a true peace settlement. This was partly because the Allied coalition that had won the war and built the Versailles order promptly disintegrated, thereby removing the power-political foundations on which that settlement rested. Above all, this meant the retreat into isolation of the United States and Britain's refusal to sign a military alliance with France or preserve the conscript army that would have made such an alliance real. These were elementary errors that would have made the statesmen who met in Vienna in 1815 cringe. But even without this foolishness the Versailles settlement was very vulnerable. As already noted, the First World War emerged in eastern Europe and revolved around Germanic competition with Russia to dominate that region. Both the Germans and Russians ended up as losers and the Versailles settlement was made at their expense. But Russia and Germany remained potentially the most powerful countries not just in eastern and central Europe but in the continent as a whole. For that reason the Versailles order was very unlikely to survive, especially since it included the large geopolitical hole left by the disappearance of the Habsburgs.

For all these reasons a second great war in eastern Europe was always a likely outcome of 1918. That war brought terrible suffering for the region's peoples and ended in most of them falling under the rule of Stalin's Russia. Would German victory in 1918 have led to a stable east-central Europe and spared the region a second great war? One cannot know but the chances were probably better than those of the Versailles settlement. Would German rule have proved less awful than that of Stalin? Again, it is impossible to say but one should certainly refrain from making glib comparisons between Wilhelmine and Nazi Germany, and never more so than where policy in eastern Europe was concerned. The Kaiserreich contained thoroughly unpleasant authoritarian, nationalist and racist elements and victory might have encouraged them. But it could hardly have warped them more completely than did the bitterness of defeat. During the First World War the Germans were responsible for some atrocities and many infringements of international law. But no belligerent was entirely innocent in this respect and German misbehaviour did not match Russian treatment of the Jews in the eastern war zone, Austrian repression of the Serbs or – at the ultimate extreme – Ottoman destruction of the Armenians. Not even remotely can German policy in the east in 1914–18 be compared to the insane and genocidal savagery of 1941–5.

How should we relate the broader international context in 1914–18 to Russia's fate and specifically to the outcome of the Russian Revolution? Clearly it was crucial and equally clearly it was highly contingent. As I wrote above, had the Russian monarchy fallen in 1906 then Germany would probably have led an international intervention that may well have helped counter-revolution to triumph in Russia, for a time at least. Instead during the First World War Germany bent all its efforts to furthering the cause of revolution in Russia. Lenin entered Russia thanks to the famous 'sealed train', which Berlin allowed to cross German-occupied Europe. Once he had arrived in Petrograd the

√ Germans continued to do everything they could to foster the revolution in order to undermine the Russian war effort. Lenin was extremely fortunate that his gamble at Brest-Litovsk paid off. Germany's defeat on the western front forced Berlin to abandon the treaty and allowed Bolshevik Russia to move back into Ukraine and thereby to preserve the foundations of empire, albeit in renewed and socialist form. The half-hearted intervention of the Western Allies and their unwilling armies on the margins of Russia's Civil War was a very pale reflection of what peacetime European intervention spearheaded by the German army would have entailed. In any case the war, Berlin's support and then German disintegration had allowed the Bolsheviks a crucial year in which to organise their rule and consolidate their hold on Russia's geopolitical core where most of its population, its military supplies and its communications hubs were concentrated. This was probably the single most important factor in Bolshevik victory in the Civil War. In peacetime, foreign intervention in support of domestic counter-revolution would probably have denied a revolutionary government this breathing space. Without the First World War it is possible that something like the Bolshevik-Left Socialist Revolutionary government of 1917 could have come to power but barely conceivable that it could have survived.

A very interesting question concerns relations between a victorious Germany and Russia. Inevitably, in wartime geopolitical interests conquered the ideological distaste of the Wilhelmine elites for Bolshevism. If Germany had won, however, it is a moot point whether it would have continued to tolerate Bolshevism in power in Moscow. The calculation would have been difficult. Germany would have had more than enough on its plate in recovering from the war at home and consolidating its hold on eastern Europe. The last thing it would have needed was renewed war in Russia. Berlin would also have needed to re-integrate itself into the international economy. An intelligent German government would not merely have abandoned all idea of annexations in France and Belgium but even made minor territorial concessions in Alsace to appease the French. With all eastern Europe in its grasp it could well have afforded such gestures, though in the aftermath of war it is very unlikely to have made them. But if the United States had remained neutral in the war then the resumption of trans-Atlantic and global commerce should have been rapid, with enormous consequent benefits to Germany.

In time the French and British would probably have reconciled themselves to German hegemony in the east. In reality, in the twentieth century neither Britain nor France has ever had the power or even (in the British case) the inclination to involve itself decisively in the affairs of the region. The fiasco of Western 'assistance' to the Poles in 1939 and 1944–45 emphasises this point. A consequence of a 'compromise' peace with Germany would probably have been an Anglo-French defensive alliance but Germany would have had no reason to seek to change its western borders once its hegemony in the east was secure. Why run after French coal or iron ore when you have the resources of eastern Ukraine at your disposal?

The only possible challenge to German hegemony in the east could come from Russia. If the Germans succeeded in consolidating their rule in eastern Europe and in particular if a stable pro-German regime established itself in Kiev then it would be a long time, if ever, before any Russian regime could restore their country's power to a level where it could challenge Germany. In 1918 the Germans preferred Bolshevism to the Russian counter-revolution because the latter was pro-allied and was pledged to continuing the war against Germany. After victory Germany would have had the luxury of playing both sides in Russia off against each other. A victorious Germany need have little fear of domestic revolution and could, if necessary, tolerate Bolshevism in power in Moscow. It could also threaten a Bolshevik regime that misbehaved towards Germany with German support for the Russian counter-revolution. The Germans believed that a Bolshevik regime would always be weak. That proved a mistake. But they were correct in believing that it would be far harder for France and Britain to ally with a Bolshevik Russia than with a victorious Russian counter-revolution. So probably for the foreseeable future they would have tolerated

Lenin's rule. The German order in Europe that would have emerged from victory might well have avoided a second world war and would probably have spared Europe from Hitler. But it would probably not have spared the Russians from Stalin.

Like all counterfactual arguments this conclusion is no more than informed guesswork. Counterfactual debates are to some extent just an amusing possibility to give flight to the imagination but they do also have more serious uses. Nothing is more fatal than belief that history's course was inevitable. Not only is this untrue, it is also an invitation to moral abdication and political inaction. In this chapter, I have addressed a number of counterfactuals in the international arena that might have radically changed both Russian and European history in the era of the Russian Revolution. This exercise is of special value because it illustrates the manner in which the history of Russia and that of Europe were tightly entangled. The struggle to become and remain a European great power was probably the single most important factor driving the evolution of imperial Russia. At the same time one cannot understand European or global history if one ignores imperial Russia's vital impact on both. At no time was the connection between Russia's fate and that of Europe more closely entwined than in the years 1900–1920.

2

THE ASSASSINATION OF STOLYPIN

September 1911

SIMON DIXON

EVER SINCE PYOTR ARKADYEVICH STOLYPIN was shot at the Kiev Municipal Theatre on 1 September 1911, his assassination has provoked debate. Among the few aspects of the case that remain beyond dispute is the identity of the prime minister's killer. Dmitry Bogrov, a twenty-four-year-old lawyer on the fringes of the Socialist Revolutionary movement, fired twice at Stolypin from point-blank range. But why did he do it? Was the assassination an exculpatory gesture of loyalty demanded by fellow terrorists, shocked that he had betrayed them to the police in order to repay his student gambling debts? Or was he still a double agent in the pay of shadowy forces on the right who despised Stolypin's land reforms as a sell-out to Jewish speculators? Was Bogrov on the contrary defending his own Jewish family's interests in the face of Stolypin's increasingly strident Great Russian nationalism, as Alexander Solzhenitsyn suggested in his fictionalised treatment of the assassination in *The Red Wheel*? More fundamentally still, posterity has wondered whether history could have turned out differently had Stolypin lived. Might his ambitious programme of reform have averted the revolutions of 1917? Could his celebrated 'wager on the strong' – an attempt to transform the impoverished Russian peasantry into a flourishing agrarian bourgeoisie – have laid the foundations for the stable era of peace and prosperity that so cruelly eluded the Bolsheviks?

The obvious ideological significance of such questions has helped to give them lasting contemporary relevance. In the West, Stolypin's reputation first became a political punchball during the Cold War, when it divided the minority of historians unsympathetic to the left. While a handful of so-called optimists argued that revolution had been far from inevitable in Russia, a larger number of sceptics – including some of those who advised Margaret Thatcher in advance of her meeting with Mikhail Gorbachev in Moscow in spring 1987 – insisted that Stolypin was a transient figure whose failure demonstrated just how impervious Russia could prove to root-and-branch reform.[1] In Russia itself, it was the collapse of the Soviet Union that converted Stolypin's legacy into a prominent part of the search for a useable political past. Since 1991, he has been rehabilitated as the progenitor of the sort of patriotic, conservative consensus yearned for by many Russians in the early twenty-first century: an economically plausible way of restoring national pride without resorting to the atrocities associated with Stalin. In an opinion poll to find the greatest Russian in history – organised by the state-controlled television station Rossiya in December 2008 and answered by more than fifty million people – Stolypin came second only to the medieval warrior, Prince Alexander Nevsky. Stalin was pushed into third place; Pushkin, Peter the Great and Lenin also ran.

How did a tsarist prime minister, ignored and reviled for much of the Soviet period, suddenly come to be so widely admired? Some small part of the answer may lie in the flood of documents, biographies and monographs published by historians over the course of the last twenty-five years.[2] Present-minded concerns certainly seem to lie close to the surface of many scholarly attempts to portray Stolypin as a consensual conservative moderate rather than the Bonapartist counter-revolutionary denounced by Lenin or the precursor of Mussolini admired by self-styled Russian Fascists in the 1920s. Still, even the herculean efforts of the academic Stolypin industry can hardly have generated the level of popular adulation registered by the 2008 opinion poll, in which Stolypin garnered 523,766 votes. Neither can such widespread acclaim be attributed to debates in the public sphere, extensive as they have been, for these too have been targeted primarily at the intelligentsia. Not all contemporary Russian commentators have looked favourably on Stolypin's legacy. Indeed, Sergei Kara-Murza, an idiosyncratic critic of progress in both its Marxist and liberal capitalist guises, believes that his reforms had a fatally destabilising effect. First published in 2002, Kara-Murza's *Stolypin: Father of the Russian Revolution* was re-issued at the centenary of the assassination under a still more explicit title: *Stolypin's Mistake: The Prime Minister who Overturned Russia.*[3] His, however, is a minority view. A far greater weight of opinion has come down in favour of Stolypin's prophetic abilities in the manner of a monk at the Trinity St Sergius Monastery at Sergiev Posad whose brief popular biography, published in 2013, presents Stolypin as the victim of 'dark forces' who 'hated' him: 'orphaned' by his assassination, Russia fell 'into the hands of the destroyers' – 'only he knew what had to be done for the prosperity of Russia.'[4]

Like the occasional note of dissent, much of this popular support can be traced to the consistent self-identification with Stolypin of another self-styled man of destiny: Vladimir Putin. Keen to burnish his own image as a conservative moderniser, and no less anxious to underplay Stolypin's authoritarian instincts, Mr Putin reportedly keeps a picture of the former prime minister on his office wall (Angela Merkel apparently prefers Catherine the Great) and has repeatedly underlined his respect for Stolypin's patriotism, stamina and sense of responsibility. Already in 2000, during his first term as president of the Russian Federation, Putin drew explicit parallels between his own aspirations towards stable economic development and Stolypin's attempts to reconcile civil liberties and political democratisation with the virtues of a strong national state. This was no passing fancy. When plans were afoot to commemorate the 150th anniversary of Stolypin's birth in 2012, Putin exhorted every member of his government to donate at least a month's salary in support of a memorial to be placed outside the Russian Parliament building. So it is not merely an intellectual parlour game to wonder what might have transpired had Stolypin's reforms succeeded, and to consider their chances of success had he survived Dmitry Bogrov's attempt on his life.

Stolypin travelled to Kiev at the end of August 1911 to attend the inauguration of a statue to Alexander II (r. 1855–81) by his grandson, Nicholas II (r. 1894–1917). Superficially, such a ceremony might seem unremarkable, and indeed at one level it was merely the latest in a series of commemorations held in the wake of the fiftieth anniversary of the emancipation of Russia's serfs on 19 February. At a deeper level, however, it was no easy matter for Nicholas II to celebrate the legacy of the 'tsar-liberator', whose vision of national greatness varied sharply from his own. In an attempt to recover from the humiliation inflicted on the Romanov dynasty by the Crimean War, Alexander II had taken Russia down the path of Western-inspired reform based on Western-style institutions such as trial by jury. But hopes for the peaceful growth of civic nationalism in Russia were blown to smithereens along with the tsar himself, when terrorists, disillusioned by the slow pace of change, assassinated him on 1 March 1881. Nicholas II stubbornly maintained a very different set of values incorporated in the Muscovite revival begun by his father, Alexander III (r. 1881–1894). After 1881, Russia's last two tsars not surprisingly insisted on the maintenance of order, a virtue instilled into each of them by their tutor, K. P. Pobedonostsev. But Nicholas went further than Alexander III by insisting on the restoration of pure autocracy, sanctioned directly by God and underpinned by a vision of Russian history that reached back beyond the European-ised empire launched by Peter the Great (r. 1682–1725) to venerate the Muscovite tsardom that had gone before. Visual representations highlighted the contrast. At the costume ball to celebrate the bicentenary of St Petersburg in 1903, Nicholas II dressed not as the new capital's irreverent westernising founder, but as his pious Muscovite father, Tsar Alexei Mikhailovich. Indeed, had he not been deterred by the expense, Nicholas would have abandoned Western-style uniforms altogether and clothed his whole court permanently in Muscovite costume.[5]

The biggest political question facing the Russian old regime at the beginning of the twentieth century was whether these two rival world views could be reconciled. Stolypin's appointment as minister of internal affairs in April 1906, and his assumption of the additional office of prime minister in July, offered a glimmer of hope to those who believed that they might be. No man was more closely associated with the restoration of order than Stolypin, who had impressed the tsar since 1903 as governor of the notoriously turbulent province of Saratov. However, although his unflinching resort to force in the face of revolutionary unrest had given his name to the hangman's noose, the progenitor of 'Stolypin's necktie' was no ordinary reactionary. In fact, he was not a reactionary at all. Close to his fortieth birthday in 1902, he had become the empire's youngest provincial governor in Grodno on the strength of his innovative solutions to some of Russia's most intransigent social and economic problems. Born in the year after the serfs were freed, he had studied natural sciences at the University of St Petersburg – an unusual choice for a young nobleman – and eighteen months after starting work at the Ministry of Internal Affairs in 1885 had volunteered for the Ministry of Agriculture's Department of Statistics, where he developed his interest in private farming. In 1889, at the point when he might have launched a conventional bureaucratic career in the capital, he opted instead to return to his native Kovno province (present-day Kaunas in Lithuania), where he learned to manage his own expanding estates, to resolve complex land disputes as chairman of the local peace arbitrators, and to consider wider political questions first as district marshal of the nobility and ultimately as provincial marshal. Presiding at a banquet to commemorate the emancipation in February 1911, Stolypin could plausibly claim that he had been dealing with the institutions of peasant government for most of his conscious life. Here, it seemed, was exactly the sort of dynamic agrarian technocrat dreamed of by those who yearned for a Russian Bismarck.[6]

There were, nevertheless, significant underlying differences between the tsar and his new prime minister that helped to destabilise their relationship.[7] Whereas Nicholas II believed in the divinely consecrated union of tsar and people, Stolypin wanted to make the impersonal state the focus of national unity. This ambition led him to seek to reconcile the two westernised social groups that the tsar distrusted most: the bureaucracy and 'educated society' (*obshchestvennost*) – publicly engaged professionals who had benefited from the civic freedoms granted by Alexander II and who now saw an unprecedented opportunity for political influence in the Duma, the elective chamber created in response to the revolution of 1905.[8] In the cause of national unity, Stolypin also strove to dissolve the boundaries between the congeries of ethnic groups that made up the multinational Russian Empire and between the social estates (*sosloviia*) into which most of the empire's subjects had been legally ascribed at birth.

Of these estates, Stolypin regarded the immiserated peasantry as the Russian nation's weakest link. He had been convinced by his experiences in Saratov, where the peasantry was especially poor and the link between poverty and insurrection inescapable, that if the common people were ever to form a reliable bedrock for the tsarist regime, then they must be enriched by the spread of private property and must be granted the political freedom denied to them by the terms of the emancipation of 1861. This had isolated peasants from most of the new civic institutions that governed the rest of Russian society by keeping them tied to the commune. The cornerstone of Stolypin's programme as prime minister was therefore the decision to permit heads of peasant households to leave the commune at any time under the terms of the agrarian reform of 9 November 1906. In the following year, local Land Settlement Commissions were created to make it easier for peasants to consolidate into private farms their share of the narrow strips of land hitherto widely distributed across their villages under communal cultivation. There was also a significant political dimension to this fundamental economic change. In addition to offering favourable terms in the form of easier credit from the Peasant Land Bank, Stolypin repeatedly justified his policies by stressing that peasant prosperity was inseparable from enlightenment and freedom. So his agrarian reform was flanked by legislation to allow peasants to escape the supervisory institutions he knew so well from Kovno and Grodno, and to gain unprecedented legal independence and freedom of movement.

These provisions alone were sufficient to disconcert Nicholas II, and tensions between him and Stolypin were clearly apparent by the time that the imperial suite travelled to Kiev. For Nicholas, such provincial visits served to signal his detachment from the alien values he associated with cosmopolitan St Petersburg and to emphasise his spiritual closeness to the common people. Kiev was particularly receptive territory for such a strategy because an exceptionally well-organised nationalist movement had developed there, divided though not debilitated by splits between the elite Kiev Club of Russian Nationalists and the populist Union of Russian People (URP), two groups who competed in their efforts to host the tsar.[9] For Stolypin, by contrast, the highlight of the visit was a gathering of deputies from the empire's six western provinces, where, expressly against the wishes of the tsar and the State Council, he had insisted in spring 1911 on the establishment of zemstvos – the elective local authorities created by Alexander II in 1864, but hitherto kept out of the western borderlands in case they became dominated by Polish landowners.

Stolypin had no truck with Polish influence. Indeed, his proposed electoral law incorporated a complex system of ethnic voting blocs designed to emasculate it. Had he been certain of finding a way to ensure Russian dominance there, the zemstvos would also have been extended to three more provinces in his native north-west: Vitebsk, Grodno and Kovno. Nevertheless, his scheme remained suspect in the eyes of Russian noble landowners because the prime minister's way of counteracting the Polish elite was to enfranchise large numbers of Russian peasants – an unprecedentedly democratic scheme that Stolypin evidently intended as a Trojan horse for the further democratisation of local government elsewhere in the empire.

Tensions within the elite could to some extent be masked in Kiev because the pattern of such Russian royal visits, established by Peter the Great and embellished over the course of the following two centuries, prescribed all manner of diverting pomp and circumstance ranging from military manoeuvres to religious ritual. Of all these ceremonial occasions, grand opera was the one on which the imperial party could most readily agree: it bored them rigid. So it was more in the cause of social duty than of artistic anticipation that they trooped into the Kiev Municipal Theatre on the evening of 1 September for a performance of Rimsky-Korsakov's *The Tale of Tsar Saltan*.

Stolypin sat in the front row of the stalls, not far from Baron Frederiks, the minister of the court, and General Sukhomlinov, the minister of war. Stretching their legs at the intervals, they stood with their backs to the orchestra, relaxing with their neighbours. Suddenly, in the second interval, a young man whose evening dress stood out against the overwhelmingly uniformed audience walked coolly down the aisle, drew a revolver from his programme and fired twice at the prime minister. One bullet caught his right hand; the other hit him just below the right ribs (though fully aware of being a terrorist target – his daughter had been crippled by the bomb that destroyed their house in August 1906 – he had characteristically refused to wear a bullet-proof vest). Turning to Nicholas II and his daughters, who had returned to their box having heard the shots from a neighbouring reception room, Stolypin made the sign of the cross (some thought he was blessing the tsar) and collapsed into his seat. Tall, strong and resilient, he initially seemed likely to survive: doctors saw no reason to remove the bullet and declared his condition satisfactory; his wife came to visit him at the hospital; so did the minister of finance, Vladimir Kokovtsov, with whom he talked animatedly about government business. But by nightfall on 3 September, an infection had set in and Stolypin's condition deteriorated. In between bouts of hallucination and unconsciousness, the only word heard clearly from his lips was 'Finland' – the borderland grand duchy whose political autonomy he had done most to undermine in the cause of imperial integration. By the evening of 5 September, Stolypin was dead.

First published in a heavily redacted selection as early as 1914, the documents relating to his assassination have recently appeared in a volume covering more than 700 closely printed pages.[10] Even so, much of the mystery surrounding the event remains unresolved. Since his guilt was obvious, Bogrov was rapidly tried and hanged. But what was his motive? Solzhenitsyn's insistence on the significance of his Jewish roots is easily dismissed: the Bogrovs were a wealthy Kievan family, long since assimilated into the Russian elite. Rumours of a conspiracy on the right are harder to disprove because Stolypin certainly had enemies in the tsarist regime and one of them, his own deputy as minister of internal affairs, was in charge of security in Kiev. Pyotr Kurlov had been responsible for imperial security since 1909, when the tsar made his first official journey after the 1905 revolution in order to celebrate the bicentenary of Peter the Great's victory over the Swedes at Poltava. As a result, Kiev's governor general, who might traditionally have expected promotion or decoration after a successful imperial visit, was mortified to discover that the sole task entrusted to him was the purchase of a car for out-of-town trips – a commission made all the more humiliating when the allocated budget of 8,000 roubles turned out to be insufficient and he had to draw on emergency local funds. Yet although Kurlov persistently intrigued against Stolypin at court, the balance of probabilities points not to a conspiracy but to stunning incompetence on the part of the secret police. Most culpable of all was Colonel N. N. Kulyabko, the head of the Kiev Okhrana (secret police) to whom Bogrov had personally reported as an agent provocateur. The credulous Kulyabko granted Bogrov a ticket for the theatre having believed his promise to identify two (fictional) fellow terrorists, who were themselves allegedly plotting to kill Stolypin. Though subsequent investigations left no doubt of the lapses of Kurlov and Kulyabko, they almost certainly escaped punishment not because the tsar sympathised with their schemes against the prime minister, even if he did, but because it was too embarrassing for Nicholas to publicise their failings.[11]

It is not difficult to see the attractions of Stolypin's 'wager on the strong' for Russian conservatives at the beginning of the twenty-first century. The formation of a prosperous agrarian bourgeoisie in Russia might not have sufficed to dissolve all the underlying tensions between rich and poor peasants a hundred years ago, and rural dwellers would doubtless still have been tempted to hoard grain rather than release it for consumption in the towns. Nevertheless, allowing for the avoidance of extreme shortages and the development of more sophisticated means of distribution in years when the harvest was poor, there would have been no need for the vicious war of peasant against peasant that ravaged the Russian provinces between 1918 and 1920, no need for Stalin's destructive collectivisation of agriculture at the end of the 1920s, and no need for extravagant (and ultimately wasteful) fantasies such as Khrushchev's Virgin Lands campaign thirty years later. More fundamentally still, there would have been no need for either Stalin or Khrushchev, because a thriving class of yeoman farmers of the sort envisaged by Stolypin might conceivably have been reconciled to the monarchy by being granted a meaningful stake in Russia's government and administration. Had such conservative allegiances solidified consistently over the longer term, it would have been much more obvious in both world wars what the Russian populace were fighting for, rather than merely what they were fighting against. Whether a predominantly agrarian regime could have developed the military resources that stemmed from Stalin's forced industrialisation in the 1930s is naturally a moot point. But provided that its borderlands had been secured by the kind of integrationist policies Stolypin urged in Finland and elsewhere, a politically and economically stable Russian Empire might in any case have presented a much less inviting target to any potential invader than the multinational Soviet Union, where many inhabitants of the western regions were by no means wholly hostile to the Germans in 1941. In short, it is possible to imagine that the realisation of Stolypin's dream could have led to the emergence of a strong, stable, more or less autarkic regime, daunting to its international rivals, and securely entrenched in the huge landmass stretching from the Far East to the German borderlands – a phenomenon not so different in outline from the nirvana envisaged by Eurasian philosophers in the 1920s and by neo-Eurasians in the 1990s, but stripped of their overt hostility to European civilisation.

The problem with such a vision is that social and economic change on the scale envisaged by Stolypin would have taken generations to come to fruition wherever it had been planned, and in Russia the conditions were singularly unpropitious. In a newspaper interview in 1909, Stolypin himself suggested that twenty years of peace would be needed if his reforms were to succeed. Considering the underdeveloped state of Russia's economy and society, that sounds like an underestimate: when Stolypin came into office in 1906, the empire was still reeling from both internal revolution and international humiliation. Thanks to the severity of the climate, no one has ever found it easy to make money out of Russian agriculture. In the imperial period, profits were made largely by exporting grain even in time of famine – not a popular policy among Russian peasants – or by converting grain to vodka, which is less expensive to transport by unit weight. Even twenty years of consistent development was a Utopian prospect in a state whose history has notoriously been characterised by extreme political 'zigzags' of the sort that followed Alexander II's assassination. Although he was not yet fifty at the time of his death, Stolypin can hardly have expected to remain in office for much longer. Already five years long by 1911, his tenure as the tsar's chief minister exceeded that of many of his predecessors. And there was no guarantee that any of his successors would have been sufficiently strong or intelligent to sustain his direction of reform.

For all these reasons, the further we move forward from 1911, the more hazardous predictions become. Even in the short term, they are necessarily hedged about with an alarming range of 'ifs' and 'buts'. Pointing to Stolypin's consistent emphasis on Russia's need for peace, his American biographer, Abraham Ascher, speculates reasonably enough that he would have tried to prevent Russia from going to war in July 1914.[12] Whether war would thereby have been aborted is another matter. Growing international rivalries pointed increasingly towards a major European conflict, and since all the great powers knew from their intelligence gatherers that the military reforms spearheaded by Sukhomlinov after the Russo-Japanese War were due to be completed by 1917, Russia's rivals had every incentive to pounce before then. Whenever war broke out, Russia would still have faced the geopolitical difficulties it had experienced in all its armed conflicts with the West since the seventeenth century, when the sheer distances involved in mobilising its troops had repeatedly caused the tsar's armies to start slowly and unsuccessfully. Here, one might think, is a classic case where the power of any single 'great man' to influence events was almost certain to be limited.

As it happens, however, there is no need to speculate, because there is ample evidence to show that Stolypin's political capital had already been exhausted long before his assassination. The crucial question is therefore not what might have happened between 1911 and 1914, but what *did* happen between 1906 and 1911.

In the first place, peasants themselves never showed much enthusiasm for Stolypin's reforms.[13] Except to the extent that land consolidation on the part of even a small number of households sometimes generated a domino effect for a larger range of neighbours, the decision to privatise was voluntary. Only in the Baltic provinces, where German influence ran deep, and in neighbouring parts of Stolypin's north-western stamping ground, did significant numbers of households opt to establish the *khutora* that he envisaged as his ideal: small private farmsteads, no more than three times as long as they were wide, owned by a single head of household, and comprising a single parcel of land surrounding the farm buildings. There was wider support for the *otruba* – a compromise between communal and private tenure in which the farmhouse was separated from its consolidated landholding. But none of these choices necessarily signalled that the peasantry shared Stolypin's commitment either to individual landownership or to the wider responsibilities and opportunities that came with it. Resourceful as ever, many peasants simply exploited his legislation as a means of settling old scores either with their own relatives or with members of rival families. So, although Stolypin's admirers can point to the fact that during the first decade of his agricultural reform some two and a half million peasant households (rather more than a fifth of the total in 1916) received title deeds to land that they had formerly held communally, critics retort that the rate of privatisation had already slowed significantly even before the reform retrospectively passed the Duma in summer 1910. Furthermore, over half the land sold through the agency of the Peasant Land Bank was bought not by individual heads of household but by village communes and cooperatives. In 1916, 61 per cent of all households still held their land in communal tenure and, given a choice in 1917, over 95 per cent of peasants opted to return to it – clear testimony to the resilience of the small-scale collectivist ideal in Russian peasant culture.

A second level of problems arose in the arena of national politics when Stolypin attempted to legislate for the wider consequences of his agrarian reforms. There was no hope of collaboration between government and parliament so long as the first two Dumas remained dominated by two parties on the centre-left. One was the liberal Kadets (Constitutional Democrats), who had been a thorn in Stolypin's side in Saratov province, where they formed an unusually strong alliance with the radical intelligentsia. The other was the Trudoviks (Labourers), whose electoral success exposed the hollowness of the tsar's expectations of a loyalist peasantry. Initially, therefore, Stolypin relied largely on the repressive methods that had served him well in Saratov.

The prospects of more peaceful reform revived only when he engineered a new franchise via the electoral law of 7 June 1907. The third Duma, which met for the first time on 1 November, was dominated by 154 conservative Octobrists (a threefold increase at 35 per cent of the total) and 147 rightists of various degrees of extremism. Kadet representation was halved and Trudovik numbers plummeted to a tenth of their former strength.[14] Yet even from this superficially more pliable constellation of forces, generated almost entirely by his own gerrymandering, Stolypin was unable to secure a working majority. That was partly because the Octobrists and rightists were less politically cohesive than their numbers imply, but mainly because each of the prime minister's projected reforms offended a variety of powerful interest groups who had more to lose than they had to gain from a state governed by the rule of law and from the creation of a new class of peasant smallholders.

Religious reform was a striking case in point. Toleration for the avowedly conservative Old Believers had been under discussion since the late 1850s and was in theory confirmed in the toleration edict of 17 April 1905: a symbolic date, Easter Sunday. For the first time in Russian history, this made confessional allegiance a matter of individual conscience. However, Stolypin's efforts to confirm the concession once the threat of revolution had abated were virulently opposed by Orthodox bishops in the State Council. Other measures proved equally controversial, not so much because they were new – like the religious reforms, most of them had been under discussion for some years – but because Stolypin's drive and determination threatened to shape them into unprecedentedly subversive constellations. Nobles derailed his proposed changes to local government, fearing that their own influence would be squeezed between that of a growing peasant democracy and enhanced powers for the provincial governor. By preventing peasant democratisation, the nobility effectively slowed down the whole process of land reform. The prospect of new local courts with jurisdiction over the whole population, including the peasantry, was equally unpalatable to nobles alarmed by the prospect of judges drawn from the liberal intelligentsia: in the end, the State Council approved a purely peasant court, with peasant judges, to deal with the peasantry, ensuring that they remained as isolated as ever from mainstream institutions of government and justice. Any attempt to conciliate the landowners nevertheless risked opposition from industrialists who were themselves determined to frustrate Stolypin's attempts to introduce accident and sickness insurance for factory workers: the legislation that finally emerged on this subject was not only delayed (in the case of sickness insurance until after the prime minister's assassination), but a good deal more expensive for the consumer than he had intended.[15]

To navigate a consistent course between such incompatible lobbies required greater powers of persuasion and flexibility than Stolypin could readily muster. Though conscious of the need to mobilise public opinion behind his reforms, he was fundamentally a bureaucrat rather than a politician. Using subsidies granted by Stolypin's own government, extremists on the right proved to be masters of the sensationalist tabloid journalism that did much to undermine him. More conventional political parties, profiting from the relaxation of censorship after 1905, could each count on the support of sophisticated broadsheet newspapers. Stolypin, by contrast, conceived the press largely as an organ of government information and never contemplated the creation of a party of his own. That was only one of the many ways in which he differed from Mussolini: he was the opposite of a charismatic leader. His prose was disfigured by the strangulated constructions of Russian 'officialese'. Neither was he a good speaker: his voice was too metallic and his body language awkward. After hearing Stolypin address the Duma, one of Russia's most influential and idiosyncratic columnists, Vasily Rozanov, commented that it was like watching 'a catfish swim through jam'.[16]

Temperamentally ill-equipped to cope with the onset of mass politics, Stolypin was particularly bemused by extra-parliamentary agitation. The charismatic young monk, Iliodor (Trufanov), danced rings around him, denouncing the prime minister as Pontius Pilate at the Fourth Monarchist Congress in 1907 and in 1911 leading a populist crusade on the Volga that dominated the national headlines between the anniversary of the emancipation and Stolypin's assassination. When Iliodor began a widely publicised hunger strike in Tsaritsyn, surrounded by thousands of female admirers, Stolypin responded by besieging his monastery with troops.[17] The same authoritarian instincts were still more fatal to his dealings with the Duma and the State Council. Even his two most significant measures – the agrarian reform of 9 November 1906 and the Western Zemstvo legislation of 1911 – had to be pushed through under Article 87 of the Fundamental Laws promulgated on 23 April 1906, a provision intended to be used only *in extremis*. The dissolution of the second Duma in May 1907 and the promulgation of the electoral law of 7 June were equally flagrant violations of the principle that all new laws must be subject to prior approval by parliament.

In the eyes of even the most respectful of elite liberals, Stolypin's repeated willingness to flout basic constitutional conventions deprived him of all authority. Count Ivan Tolstoy, the only member of Witte's cabinet who had supported full toleration for the Jews in 1905, 'completely refused' to recognise Stolypin as 'a "talented" statesman'. 'For me,' he wrote shortly after the prime minister's assassination, 'he always was, and will always remain, a favourite, i.e. a careerist, with all the shortcomings that brings.' Stolypin's energy and decisiveness therefore had to be set against 'incomparably more serious shortcomings: the absence of a critical mind, narrowness of political outlook'. Such a verdict may catch Stolypin's streak of ambition, but it surely underestimates his independence of mind and the sophistication of his grasp, unrivalled by any contemporary, of the interplay between society, economics and politics. Nevertheless, Tolstoy's hostility indicates the depth of the Kadets' resentment of the prime minister's equally unrelenting contempt for them. Tolstoy was surely not the only liberal who believed that if Stolypin's successors chose to continue his policies, which had allegedly benefited only 'spongers' and 'scoundrels', they would succeed merely in restoring the discredited 'template' of the era before 1905. Nothing could be worse than that.[18]

While liberals were alienated by Stolypin's increasingly desperate attempts to woo the right by supporting chauvinist nationalism, the right itself, and particularly its more radical elements such as the rabble-rousing URP, thought that he had betrayed the tsar by consorting with an illegitimate parliamentary regime. The controversial archbishop of Volhynia, Antony (Khrapovitsky) – a URP sympathiser who liked to rhyme 'constitution' with 'prostitution' – could never trust Stolypin because, for all his many conflicts with the Duma, he persisted in regarding it as an integral part of the Russian legislative process. Doubts on the right set in early. The St Petersburg salon hostess Alexandra Bogdanovich was convinced of Stolypin's duplicity as soon as he became a minister. 'Apparently,' she noted on 29 April 1906, 'Stolypin is both on our side and on yours; in the morning, he is liberal, and in the evening – the opposite.'[19] Over the next five years, a galaxy of disgruntled rightist leaders trooped through her salon to denounce Stolypin as 'two-faced'. Even the veteran general Alexander Kireev, who had more respect for him than most, rapidly lost confidence. At their first meeting in May 1906, the newly appointed minister of internal affairs 'made a *fine* impression' – 'sober-minded, favourably disposed, understands the state of affairs … Our opinions are very close.'[20] Six months later, Stolypin still struck Kireev as 'a real *gentleman*. (And that is important!)' But there was no longer a meeting of minds. The following exchange, recorded in the general's diary shortly before the promulgation of the agricultural reform, reveals a chasm that was to separate the prime minister from many of his potential supporters on the right, obsessed as they were by the spectre of Jewish speculators:

S[tolypin]: Do you rebuke me for the rights given to the schismatics and Old Believers?
Me [Kireev]: No, not at all. I rebuke you for the destruction of communal agriculture.
S: It is impossible not to abolish it! I have seen it, I know – and I know, too, the difference between it and landholding by *khutor*. Russia will immediately become richer.
Me: You have forgotten that it is not only a question of finances, but of politics (you are creating a mass of agricultural proletarians). All the peasants' land will be bought up by Jews.
S: So long as I am in post, that will not happen. The pale of settlement will not be abolished.
Me: Are you eternal, then?[21]

Stolypin was not eternal. Indeed, as Alexander Guchkov remarked, his political death long preceded his assassination. As the scion of a prominent Old Believer dynasty, the Octobrist leader had good reason to admire Stolypin's promotion of civil rights for religious dissenters. Guchkov became the prime minister's closest parliamentary ally, at least until the crisis over the Western Zemstvos in March 1911 when the Octobrists finally lost confidence in him and he came to rely almost entirely on the Nationalist Party. Already in 1909, Stolypin's growing alignment with the Nationalists, a group committed to the protection of Russian interests in the imperial borderlands, had signalled a shift away from his earlier emphasis on economic and political reform. Neither the Octobrists nor the Nationalists offered a sufficiently stable foundation on which to build the wider consensus required for fundamental change. Virulent personal animosities made it more difficult still. As a provincial 'outsider', Stolypin had always aroused resentment and suspicion in St Petersburg. Pyotr Durnovo, his predecessor as minister of internal affairs, hated him from the start; Witte – brilliant, arrogant and permanently embittered by the circumstances of his resignation as prime minister in 1906 – pursued a relentless vendetta against his successor that reached its zenith in 1911 during the State Council debacle over the Western Zemstvos. Characteristic of the increasingly fetid atmosphere of Russian high politics, enmities such as these served primarily to unsettle Stolypin's relationship with the man who mattered more than any other: the tsar.

It was Nicholas II who did most to undermine his own prime minister. While Stolypin's reforms might have strengthened the Russian monarchy, the tsar rightly saw them as a threat to his own autocratic status – a status that he was determined, against all odds, to preserve. Ministers could stomach the idea of autocracy if it meant only that the tsar was divinely sanctioned. But for Nicholas it signalled nothing less than his own undivided sovereignty. So, while educated society greeted the October Manifesto as the dawn of a new constitutional era, the tsar himself regarded it as a personal (and far from inalienable) grant to his people. By the same token, he saw the Duma promised in the Manifesto as an extension of his own autocratic will. Consistently mistrustful of strong ministers, Nicholas ensured that neither Witte nor Stolypin ever became a Russian Bismarck. Instead, the tsar preferred to rely on informal advice from a variety of shadowy figures at court – above all from the empress, who shared his political instincts and was capable of articulating them in a way that he could not, and through her from Rasputin, the antithesis of a westernised official and the incarnation of the idealised Russian peasant who haunted her husband's mind. It was the tsar – egged on by Rasputin and the URP, and more subtly influenced by Pyotr Kurlov – who ensured that the insubordinate monk Iliodor repeatedly escaped censure, humiliating Stolypin in the process. Guchkov believed that by the time of the visit to Kiev in August 1911, Nicholas's support for the fanatical Iliodor had driven Stolypin to contemplate resignation.

All of which helps to explain why few tears were shed for Stolypin even in the immediate aftermath of his death, and why his name rarely passed the lips of his immediate successors. The new premier, Kokovtsov, told the council of ministers that it was their 'moral duty' to 'preserve, continue, and embody the elevated principles' with which Stolypin's 'whole work had been imbued'. But by this he meant no more than a belief in 'the good of Russia and a strong faith in her power and her great future'.[22] There was no commitment to reform and Kokovtsov was in no position to achieve it, being far from the dominant prime minister that Stolypin had once been.

Few incidents in Russian history have attracted as much attention from counterfactualists as Stolypin's assassination. Certainly no event has contributed more to the re-evaluation of Russia's imperial past in the early twenty-first century. And yet, paradoxically enough, this seems to be a case where the level of attention has been inversely proportionate to the plausibility of the results. There are many points in Russia's past at which history might have turned in a different direction. Stolypin's assassination is not one of them.

3

GRIGORY RASPUTIN AND THE OUTBREAK OF THE FIRST WORLD WAR

June 1914

DOUGLAS SMITH

H E MISTOOK HER for a beggar when she first approached.
It was early on the afternoon of 29 June 1914. Grigory Rasputin, recently returned from the capital to his village of Pokrovskoe in western Siberia, had just finished lunch with his family and was on his way to send a telegram. He had opened the gate and was stepping out into the road when there she was at his side. As Rasputin reached in his pocket for his coin purse, the woman drew a long dagger from under her garment and thrust it into Rasputin's belly. He buckled over in pain, moaning, 'I'm hurt! She stabbed me!' and then set off running down the street trying to escape. After about twenty paces he turned to look back. She was dressed all in black with a white kerchief over her face covering everything but her eyes. In her right hand she held the bloody dagger aloft. And she was chasing after him. Rasputin kept running in the direction of the village church, then he stopped and picked up a large stick from the road. As she came near he raised the stick and brought it down hard over her head, knocking her to the ground. The villagers came out at the commotion, grabbed the woman, and dragged her back up the road to the Pokrovskoe district administration building.[1]

Rasputin was helped back to his home and laid down on a bench. His family was in hysterics. A local medical orderly was fetched, and he bandaged the wound to stop the bleeding. Meanwhile, Alexander Vladimirov, the senior doctor in Tyumen, the closest large city some fifty-two miles away, was summoned by telegram, and he immediately set out for Pokrovskoe. Rasputin drifted in and out of consciousness. At one point he called for a priest. It seemed to those gathered around Rasputin that there was little hope he would survive.

Vladimirov and his assistant arrived in the early hours of 30 June. After a brief examination, he decided that they would have to operate immediately for there was no chance of getting Rasputin back to Tyumen alive. Rasputin was put under with chloroform, and the doctor made a three-and-a-half-inch incision between the wound and the navel. Sections of Rasputin's small intestine had been sliced and had to be sutured. The wound was extremely serious; the threat of infection was great. It would be some time before they could be certain that Rasputin was out of danger.[2]

Her name was Khionya Guseva. She was thirty-three years old, single, and a resident of the city of Tsaritsyn (Volgograd), where she worked as a seamstress. The white kerchief she wore served to hide a grotesque deformity: Guseva was lacking a nose. She was questioned for two days. From the start she confessed to her crime, saying that Rasputin was 'a false prophet, slanderer, a rapist and a molester of young maidens'. It soon became known that she was a follower of the radical right-wing priest Iliodor, once one of Rasputin's most prominent supporters, now among his greatest foes. Guseva claimed she had acted alone and that the attempt to kill Rasputin had been entirely her own, although it was clear to the police, and to Rasputin, that Iliodor had played some role in the crime. Before they could track him down, however, Iliodor, disguised as a woman, fled his home and escaped abroad. As for Guseva, after a year-long investigation she was found irresponsible for her actions due to insanity and placed in the Tomsk

Regional Clinic for the Insane, where she would remain until March 1917 when she was released by the Provisional Government, her attack interpreted by Russia's new rulers as an act of patriotic heroism.[3]

Almost immediately after the attack Rasputin's daughter Matryona sent a telegram to Nicholas and Alexandra describing what had happened and how her father had miraculously survived.[4] The royal family was sailing in the Finnish skerries on *The Standard* when they got the news. Alexandra cabled back: 'Deeply disturbed. We grieve with you and are praying with all our hearts.'[5]

The attack was a terrible blow to the ruling family who had drawn close to Rasputin after he first appeared at court in November 1905. Born in Pokrovskoe in January 1869 into a simple peasant family, Rasputin by 1914 was the second most famous (if not infamous) man in Russia after the tsar. His early years are largely unknown. After what appears to have been a rather rowdy youth, sometime in the 1890s Rasputin had a religious awakening. He left his wife to join the ranks of Russia's holy pilgrims (*stranniki*) spending many months away from home wandering across the vast country from monastery to monastery in search of enlightenment. With time, word of a Siberian holy man of profound Christian spirituality and with a mysterious gift for healing and prophecy reached St Petersburg. Rasputin came to the attention of clerics at the capital's Theological Academy and then made the acquaintance of the so-called Black Princesses, the sisters Militsa and Anastasia, daughters of the king of Montenegro, who introduced Rasputin to Nicholas and Alexandra.

The couple, and particularly Alexandra, had long been interested in mystics and popular holy men, an interest shared by many in the Petersburg elite, and over time they came to see Rasputin as one of their few true friends, someone who could be counted on to speak honestly about all matters, could convey to them the transformative beauty of Orthodoxy, and could ease the suffering of Alexis, the haemophiliac tsarevich, through the power of his prayers. As the years passed, Alexandra also came to believe that Rasputin possessed unmatched insight into practically all matters, be it faith, politics and even warfare.

Yet for the majority of Russians, Rasputin was an intensely controversial figure. Although almost no one knew the truth of his relationship with the royal family, still everyone had an opinion. To most, Rasputin was a conniving fake, a bogus holy man, a dangerous sectarian and vulturine womaniser craftily using his influence at court to enrich himself and destroy his enemies. In a word, he was an unforgivable stain on the Romanov throne.[6]

Guseva's attempt on the life of Rasputin was international news. The story was followed by papers across Europe and Britain; the *New York Times* carried the story on its front page.[7] In Russia, the attack filled the papers for weeks and, for a time, even eclipsed the story upon which all of Europe was focused, namely the assassination on 28 June of Archduke Franz Ferdinand in Sarajevo by the Serbian nationalist Gavrilo Princip.

The closeness of the attacks on Rasputin and the archduke has created a good deal of regrettable confusion and outright mendacity among historians and biographers. At first glance it does seem odd that both men were attacked only a day apart – 28 and 29 June. But any chronological (or other) connection is a mirage, for the archduke was murdered on 28 June of the Gregorian (New Style) calendar, then used in the West, which was a full thirteen days ahead of the Russian (Old Style) Julian calendar. Thus, Franz Ferdinand died on 15 June in Russia, exactly two weeks before Guseva's attack on Rasputin.

But this hasn't stopped conspiracy theorists from seeing some larger international plot. To contemporary Russian nationalist historians the attacks were part of a conspiracy by international 'Jew-Masonry' to kill the only two men who could have prevented war, the goal being to push the world into a war that would destroy the Christian empires of Europe and Russia and ignite world revolution. (Others add a third figure: the French socialist and leading anti-militarist Jean Jaurès, assassinated in Paris at the Café du Croissant on 31 July [New Style].[8]) Indeed, some of the more extreme proponents of this notion go so far as to claim (against all reason and facts) that the two attempts on the men's lives happened not only on the same day but at the same hour. In his 1964 biography of Rasputin, Colin Wilson, claiming to be the first person to notice the suspicious timing of the attacks, wrote: 'Ferdinand's death made war probable; Rasputin's injury made it certain, for he was the only man in Russia capable of averting it.'[9]

In fact, Rasputin was still in Petersburg at the time of Franz Ferdinand's assassination. Asked his thoughts about it by a reporter for the *Stock Exchange News*, he said:

Well, brothers, what can Grigory Efimovich say? He's dead. Cry and shout as much as you want, it won't bring him back. Do what you will – the result will always be the same. It's fate. But our English guests in Petersburg can't help but be glad. It's good [for them]. My peasant mind tells me it's a big event – the beginning of friendship between the Russian and the English people. It's a union, my dear, of England with Russia, and if we find friendship with France as well, that's no trifle but a powerful force, really good.[10]

Rasputin, however, did have his worries. He told an Italian journalist: 'Yes, they say there will be war, and they are getting ready for it. May God grant that there will be no war. This troubles me.'[11] On 1 July, the newspaper *Day* published an article by Vladimir Bonch-Bruevich, an expert on Russian sects as well as a Bolshevik and future secretary of Lenin, titled 'On Rasputin':

'It's easy for you to talk,' he once, being genuinely angry, scolded a person of high position, 'if you're killed, you'll have a funeral with music, newspapers will praise you, your widow will get a pension of thirty thousand, your children will be married to princes or counts, but look here: They must go to beg for minuscule alms, their land has been taken away, their house has been emptied, tears and woe, and if you're alive but have lost your legs, you'll limp along Nevsky on your hands or crutches and listen to every street cleaner telling you off: 'You, this and that, go to hell, get out of here! Out to the lane with you!' ... I've seen how Japanese war heroes are scared away off Nevsky. Have you? This is it, this is war! But you can't be bothered! You'll wave your handkerchief to the train taking the soldiers off to war, you'll prepare lint, you'll make five new dresses ... but you should see what terrible wailing there was in the village when the husbands and sons were taken off to war ... Remember that and even now there is sadness and a burning feeling here,' and he pressed as if he wanted to pull the heart out of his chest. 'There will be no war, no war, right?'[12]

Whatever his faults, Rasputin was a man of peace. He had an innate antipathy to bloodshed and his devout Christian faith taught him that war was a sin.

At times he spoke like a pacifist, as in this interview for *Smoke of the Fatherland*, again published before the war in 1914:

The Christians are preparing for war, preaching it, tormenting themselves and everyone else. War is a bad thing, and Christians instead of practicing humility are marching right into it. [...] In general, people shouldn't fight, shouldn't deprive each other of their lives and life's pleasures, one shouldn't violate Christ's testament and so destroy one's own soul prematurely. What will I get if I destroy you, enslave you? I would need to guard you and be afraid of you after that, and you will still be against me. That's when I use the sword. But with godly love, I will take you and will fear nothing. Let the Germans, the Turks fight each other – it's their misfortune, their blindness. They will find nothing and would sooner do each other in. But we shall act with love, peacefully, looking inside ourselves, and so shall we raise above them all.[13]

For this he was attacked on the pages of *Responses to Life*, the publication of the rabidly anti-Rasputin archpriest Vladimir Vostokov:

Gr. Rasputin, judging from his publication *Smoke of the Fatherland,* is the worst enemy of Christ's holy Church, the Orthodox faith, and the Russian state. We don't know what influence this traitor of Christ's teaching has on Russia's foreign policy, but during the war of liberation of the Balkan Christians against Turkey [in 1912] he did not support Christ but instead the pseudo-prophet Mohammed. [...] He preaches non-resistance to evil, advises Russian diplomacy to make concessions in every issue, being fully convinced, as a revolutionary, that the lost prestige of Russia and the refusal to perform her age-old tasks will cause the destruction and decay of our country. [...] Rasputin is not only a sectarian, a crook and a charlatan, but a revolutionary in the full sense of this word, working to ruin Russia. He does not care about Russia's glory and might, but aims to diminish its dignity and honour; he is fine with betraying our spiritual comrades and leaving them to the Turks and Swabians. He is prepared to welcome various misfortunes brought upon our fatherland through the disposition of Godly Providence because of the betrayal of our ancestor's legacy. And yet this enemy of God's ultimate truth is hailed as a saint by some of his followers.[14]

The mention of Rasputin's opposition to the Balkan Christians' 'war of liberation' refers to his position during the Balkan crisis of 1912, specifically the war launched by Montenegro and Russia's other client states in the region (Serbia, Bulgaria and Greece) against the Ottoman Empire in October of that year. As the armies of these 'small nations' marched on Constantinople, war hysteria swept across Russia. Demonstrators marched through the streets of Petersburg under the banner 'A Cross for Holy Sophia'. The Russian press called for war in defence of their fellow Slavs against the infidel, as did Mikhail Rodzyanko, president of the Duma, who told the tsar in March 1913, 'A war will be joyfully welcomed and it will raise the government's prestige.'[15]

Several people have insisted that it was indeed the counsel of Rasputin that kept Nicholas from going to war. Anna Vyrubova, his most devoted disciple after the empress, later wrote: 'I remember only one incident when Grigory Efimovich truly exercised influence on Russia's foreign policy. It was in 1912, when Grand Duke Nikolai Nikolaevich, grandson of Tsar Nicholas I, a cousin of the Emperor, and husband of Anastasia, daughter of the king of Montenegro, tried to talk the Emperor into taking part in the Balkan war. Rasputin practically got on his knees before the Emperor and begged him not to do this, saying that Russia's enemies are waiting for nothing but Russia getting involved in this war, which will lead to inescapable misfortune for Russia.'[16]

Count Sergei Witte, the former prime minister, concurred, noting that Rasputin 'spoke decisive words at the time of the Balkans War. One must consider him therefore a fact of life.'[17] Witte was even quoted on the matter by the German *Vossische Zeitung* on 5 May (18 May New Style) 1914: 'The entire world disparages Rasputin, but did you know that Rasputin saved us from war?'[18]

Convinced of Rasputin's power at court, the German press was keen to divine his opinion on war in the Balkans. The *Frankfurter Zeitung* ran a story titled 'Russia and the Balkans', claiming that Rasputin had been heard to say that 'the Bulgarians have repaid the Russians for their love with ingratitude and hate, and so we must now think of ourselves and not take care of matters for these unworthy people.'[19]

Rasputin had travelled through the Balkans on his way to the Holy Land in 1911. What he saw did not please him.

'But perhaps the Slavs are not right, perhaps they are being put to some sort of trial?! Look, you don't know them,' he told the press, 'they are haughtier than the Turks and they hate us. I journeyed to Jerusalem, I've been to old Mount Athos – there's great sin there due to the Greeks and they don't live properly, not as monks should. And the Bulgarians are even worse. How they made fun of us Russians when they brought us there. They're a bitter people, their hearts are hard. The Turks, on the other hand, are more religious, more polite and peaceful. But if you look in the newspapers you'd think just the opposite. But I'm telling you the absolute truth.'[20]

With this Rasputin went well beyond simply announcing his

opposition to pan-Slavism, daring to state at a moment of heightened xenophobia that Muslims were actually more truly religious than the Russians' Slavic brothers.

While Rasputin's position against the war is beyond doubt, the effect he had on Nicholas's decision is less clear. There is no record to suggest that Nicholas even listened to Rasputin's views at the time. Moreover, Rasputin was not alone in speaking out against getting dragged into the Balkans. Foreign minister Sergei Sazonov, having done much to embolden the Balkan nations and so make the war possible, was against involvement, and so, too, was Nicholas himself. He had told his ambassador to Sofia at the beginning of 1911 never to forget for a moment that Russia could not go to war for at least another five years. The mere thought of it was out of the question.[21]

Nicholas's words show that he and Rasputin approached the problem from somewhat different perspectives. For the emperor, war itself was not wrong, and Russia, so he suggests, would possibly go to war, but not until the country was fully prepared. For Rasputin, the matter was a bit more complicated. On one hand he suggested war was inherently wrong for a Christian, although his damning comments about the Bulgarians (and by extension other Slavs) implied that war might be a necessary evil, but only if fought for true friends.

A year after the outbreak of the war against Turkey, during which the allied Balkan states had ended up turning against each other, a vindicated Rasputin expressed his views publicly on the pages of the *Petersburg Gazette* on 13 October 1913.

What have our 'dear little brothers', about whom writers screamed so loudly that we must defend them, shown us? ... We have seen the deeds of our dear little brothers and now we understand ... Everything [...]

So there was a war in those Balkans. And all the writers began to scream in the newspapers: let there be war, let there be war! And, it seems, we, too, must then fight ... And they called us all to war and stoked the fire ... And so I would ask them [...] I would ask the writers: 'Dear Sirs! Exactly why are you doing this? Is this really the right thing? One must calm the passions if there is some discord, for then there will be true war, and not stoke discord and hatred. [...]

We should do away with the fear and discord of war and not encourage discord and hostility. We Russians should avoid conflict and build a monument to peace – a real monument I say – to those who work for peace. A peaceful policy against war should be considered lofty and wise.[22]

In the days before Guseva's attack Vyrubova telegraphed Rasputin while en route to Pokrovskoe to keep him abreast of the opinions of Nicholas and Alexandra on the international crisis.[23] After the attack Rasputin tried to follow the unfolding events from his hospital bed in Tyumen and to offer his advice to the emperor. The reporters there sought out his opinion about the ever-graver situation in the Balkans.[24] According to his daughter Matryona, Rasputin was beside himself with worry during those days that Nicholas would go to war. He supposedly said as he lay recovering: 'I'm coming, I'm coming, and don't try to stop me. [...] Oh, Lord, what have they done? Mother Russia will perish!'[25] Rasputin wrote to Nicholas telling him to 'stay strong' and not heed the voices calling for war. Such was his worry that his wound opened up and began to bleed again.[26]

On 12 July (25 July New Style), Rasputin wired to Vyrubova: 'A serious moment, there's a threat of war.'[27] The next day he cabled again, urging her to tell the tsar to avoid war at any cost.[28] On the following day, 14 July, he received an unsigned telegram from Peterhof most likely from Vyrubova, asking him to change his mind and support the calls for war: 'You are aware that our eternal enemy Austria is preparing to attack little Serbia. That country is almost entirely made up of peasants, utterly devoted to Russia. We shall be covered in infamy should we permit this shameless violence/reprisal. If the occasion arises, use your influence to support this just cause. Get well soon.'[29]

More pleading telegrams followed:

16 July 1914. From Peterhof to Tyumen. Rasputin.
Bad news. Terrible moments. Pray for him. No more strength to
fight the others.

17 July 1914. From Peterhof to Tyumen. Rasputin.
The clouds threaten ever more. For our defence we must openly
prepare ourselves, suffering terribly.

From Petersburg to Rasputin's secretary Lapshinskaya.
Should the health of the starets allow, immediate arrival is
necessary to help Papa in light of imminent events, his loving
friends advise and fervently request. Kisses. Awaiting your answer.[30]

But Rasputin did not follow Vyrubova's advice and stuck to his position. He sent the emperor a telegram urging him not to go to war. The
telegram has been lost, but Vyrubova, who claimed to have seen it,
said it read: 'Let Papa not plan for war, for war will mean the end of
Russia and yourselves, and you will lose to the last man.' Nicholas was
reportedly furious at the telegram, resentful at Rasputin's interference
in affairs of state that, as he saw it, did not concern him.[31]

Once it became clear that his telegram had failed, Rasputin
made one last attempt to stop Nicholas. He requested pen and
paper and from his hospital bed wrote a remarkable and prophetic
letter:

Dear friend I'll say again a menacing cloud is over Russia, lots of
sorrow and grief, it is dark and there's not a ray of hope. A sea of
tears, immeasurable, and as to blood? What can I say? There are no
words, indescribable horror. I know they all want war from you, evidently not realizing that this means ruin. Hard is God's punishment
when he takes away reason, it's the beginning of the end. You are the
Tsar, Father of the people, don't allow the madmen to triumph and

destroy themselves and the people. Yes, they'll conquer Germany, but what of Russia? If one thinks then truly never for all of time has one suffered like Russia, drowned in her own blood. Great will be the ruin, grief without end.

Grigory[32]

Remarkably, the letter has survived. Although it may well not be true that Nicholas carried the letter on his person through the war, as has been asserted, nonetheless he most definitely placed great value on it, and for this reason took it with him into exile in August 1917 when the entire family was sent away from Tsarskoe Selo. It was while the Romanovs were being held in Tobolsk in early 1918 that Nicholas managed to secretly pass the letter on to Matryona Rasputin's husband, Boris Soloviev, then in Siberia trying to organise a plot to save the family. Later, after fleeing Russia, Matryona ended up in Vienna, where she apparently sold the letter to a Prince Nikolai Vladimirovich Orlov in 1922. It then changed hands at least two more times (including those of Nikolai Sokolov, investigator of the murder of the Romanovs in Ekaterinburg) before coming into the possession of one Robert D. Brewster, who donated it to Yale University in 1951.[33]

Rasputin's letter makes for one of those powerful 'What if ... ?' moments. What if Nicholas had heeded Rasputin's words, what if the image Rasputin presented with these few charged words had opened the tsar's eyes to the horror and great danger facing Russia in the summer of 1914? Had Nicholas followed Rasputin's advice, the course not only of Russian history, but indeed world history would have been radically different. Had Russia stayed out of the war, it is hard to imagine there would have been a revolution or at least one so violent and catastrophic. The suffering that would have been avoided is unimaginable. And without the Russian revolutions of 1917, it is difficult to conceive of the rise of Hitler's Nazi Germany. But again, Nicholas ignored Rasputin's words, words that would have saved his reign, and his life and those of his family, and words that more than compensated for the harm Rasputin had caused, and would later cause, the prestige of the throne.

Later, once he was healed and back in Petersburg, Rasputin liked to say that had he been in the capital at the tsar's side he would have been able to convince him not to go to war.[34] Count Witte, repeating his comments on the Balkan crisis, said nearly the same thing.[35] It is impossible to know whether this was indeed the truth. It makes for a nice story, but ultimately it doesn't seem convincing, for as of 1914 Nicholas had rarely ever taken Rasputin's advice on important matters and when he did, it was restricted to religious affairs. It was not until much later, after Nicholas had taken up supreme command of the armed forces in 1915 and was away at Stavka, that he showed any willingness, and then reluctantly and rarely, to follow Rasputin's advice communicated to him via Alexandra's letters, the best example of this being the appointment of Alexander Protopopov as minister of the interior in September 1916.

It must also not be forgotten that Rasputin's was not the lone voice for peace. Former ambassador to the US Baron Roman Rosen, Prince Vladimir Meshchersky (publisher of *The Citizen* and a long-time friend of both Alexander III and Nicholas), and Witte, all spoke out against the war. After Rasputin, no one was as explicit with the tsar about the catastrophes certain to befall Russia should the country go to war than Pyotr Durnovo, former minister of the interior, which he laid out in a famous memorandum in February 1914.[36]

While Rasputin was writing to Nicholas, the press was wildly speculating on just what he was making of the international situation. The *St Petersburg Courier*, for example, noted on 16 July how Rasputin was 'extremely depressed' upon receiving a telegram from the capital about Austria's declaration of war against Serbia the day before.[37]

As it had during the Balkan crisis, the European press, too, ruminated on just what Rasputin was thinking. Axel Schmidt of the *Hamburger Fremdenblatt* wrote on 21 June 1914 (New Style) that the 'former apostle of peace' was now supposedly speaking the language of the pan-Slavists and calling for the unification of all Slavs and Orthodox believers under the Russian sceptre. If this were indeed true, he noted, this would present a great danger to peace in Europe, for it was only religion that could get the Russian masses to go to war. 'Whatever the case,' he concluded, 'it is simply ridiculous to think that peace in Europe now depends on the murky wishes and the will of a cunning mystic or a simple adventurer. But in the land of unlimited impossibilities all is possible.'[38]

The speculation ran wild. A newspaper in Toulouse expressed the view that Witte had been able to use Rasputin to convince the tsar to align Russia with Germany against that 'godless country' of France.[39] German papers (*Vossische Zeitung, Berliner Tageblatt*) opined that whereas in the past Rasputin had been powerful enough to keep the tsar from going to war, he could just as easily now use this same power to make him go to war. And yet another German paper – *Deutsche Warte* – wondered (when in the first days after Guseva's attack it was believed that Rasputin had been killed) whether he had been assassinated by those very forces in Russia who had opposed his politics of peace and now wanted to push Russia to war.[40]

Back in St Petersburg, Nicholas was inclined not to make too much of events unfolding in the capitals of Europe. He sent his condolences to Emperor Franz Joseph of Austria upon learning of the assassination and then moved on to other matters. Even after Austria delivered its humiliating, and unacceptable, ultimatum to Serbia on 10 July (23 July New Style), Nicholas described the development as nothing more than 'disturbing'. But several of his ministers were a good deal more animated by events. 'C'est la guerre européenne,' foreign minister Sazonov remarked. The following day at a meeting of the Council of Ministers, Sazonov stressed upon the tsar the need to defend Russia's honour in the Balkans and to boldly respond to Austria's threat of invading Serbia. Not to act forcefully, he warned, would reduce the country to a second-rate power in Europe. The other ministers fell in behind the bellicose Sazonov.

Nicholas, however, refused to be pushed into going to war. He reached out to Kaiser Wilhelm, begging him in a number of telegrams to stop Austria from going to war and stressing the necessity of a peaceful resolution of the crisis. The signals coming from the Germans were contradictory, and the tsar's ministers continued to press the case for war. Adding their voices to Sazonov's were now General Vladimir Sukhomlinov, minister of war, General Nikolai Yanushkevich, chief of the general staff, minister of agriculture Alexander Krivoshein, as well as Duma president Rodzyanko. Eventually the tsar broke down and gave in. On 17 July, he ordered full mobilisation of the Russian army for the following day. War was now inevitable. When Alexandra learned of this she rushed to Nicholas's office, where they argued for half an hour. The empress had been caught off guard by the move and was beside herself. She raced back to her room, threw herself on to her couch and started to cry. 'It's all over,' she said to Vyrubova, 'we are now at war.' As for Nicholas, Vyrubova noticed he seemed at peace. The agonising question that had been hanging in the air had now been answered.[41]

On 19 July (1 August New Style), Germany declared war on Russia. Rasputin telegraphed Vyrubova a message for Nicholas and Alexandra: 'My dear darling ones! Don't despair!'[42] The following day he sent a cable directly to Nicholas:

'My dear and darling, we treated them with love while they were preparing their swords and misdeeds for us for years, I am convinced: everyone who has experienced such evil and cunningness will get a hundredfold punishment; God's mercy is powerful, we will remain under its cover.'[43]

On 24 July, Austria-Hungary declared war on Russia. Rasputin wired a message of hope to Alexandra: 'God will never take His hand from your head, He will give you consolation and strength.'[44]

As insistent as Rasputin had been for peace, now that war had begun he committed himself to victory and never again did he question the righteousness of Russia's cause nor waver in the need to fight until she was victorious over her enemies.[45]

He wired to Vyrubova on 26 July:

Everyone, from the east to the west, has come together with the same spirit for the Motherland, this is a great joy.[46]

Rasputin again wrote of his confidence of Russia's victory in war to Nicholas in the middle of August:

God is wise and shows us glory through the cross, you will win with this cross. The time will come. God is with us, the enemies will tremble with fear.[47]

A week later Rasputin was released from the hospital and left straight-away for the capital. On 22 August he was received by Nicholas.[48] With his return came the usual salon gossip. The French ambassador Maurice Paléologue recorded that Rasputin had told the empress how his miraculous survival was further proof of God's care for him. And there was a good deal of speculation on what stance Rasputin had taken with regard to the war. Paléologue, for one, thought that Rasputin had been urging Nicholas to seek an alliance with Germany, although, like a good many members of the upper classes at the time who couldn't imagine a peasant having his own ideas, the ambassador was certain that Rasputin had not come to this notion on his own, but was simply repeating the phrases fed to him by Prince Meshchersky.[49]

As for the press, the *St Petersburg Courier* now reported that Rasputin not only endorsed the war, but was planning on enlisting himself and heading to the front. Such was the word at the salon of Countess Sophia Ignatieva, and when Rasputin's female followers heard of this they raised a cry of worry, insisting he not place himself in any danger.[50]

The story in the *Courier* so upset one government official, a certain I. A. Karev serving in Dagestan, that he felt he had to write to Rasputin himself:

I learned from the newspapers the other day that you are planning on leaving for the field of battle, and as every Russian must sacrifice himself for the defence of the Fatherland, so is your intention of the greatest merit, but please stop and think – this terrible war and its horrors have already devoured a great many lives and you too shall not escape this fate, yet by remaining where you are, so shall you still bring a great benefit to humanity. If your wish to leave for the war is steadfast and you nonetheless want to go there, then go with God, many will be praying to God for you [...].[51]

Needless to say, Rasputin never did go off to war, nor did he ever have any intention to.

Rasputin never wavered after this point in his support of Russia's war effort. His notes and telegrams to Nicholas and Alexandra for the next two years convey one and the same message: that if the tsar remains firm and resolute, God will bless Russia with victory.[52]

It is one of the strange ironies of Rasputin's life that regardless of his actual commitment to the war, in the eyes of a great many Russians he came to be seen as an agent of the Germans secretly working to secure a separate (and, to most, traitorous) peace. There never was, nor is there now, any evidence of this outlandish claim, but to contemporaries the existence of 'Dark Forces' led by Rasputin and the empress Alexandra selling out the country to the Huns was taken as indisputable fact.[53] Russians would have been amazed to have known that by the final months of Romanov rule Rasputin was in fact trying to save the dynasty. One of his chief preoccupations by the autumn of 1916 was the food crisis in Russia's major cities, the danger of which – for the regime – he intuitively sensed, and he repeatedly urged the tsar to act on the matter, even offering specific steps to alleviate the problem.[54]

But by then Rasputin's days, and those of the dynasty, were numbered. Early in the hours of 17 December (30 December New Style) Rasputin was murdered in cold blood in the Petrograd mansion of Prince Felix Yusupov. His killers insisted they had acted solely out of patriotism, as if the assassination of a Siberian peasant might save the regime. Alexandra would go to pieces at his death, Yusupov believed, and would be shut up in either a convent or asylum, while the tsar, finally liberated from the influence of the 'Dark Forces', would lead Russia to victory on the battlefield and stem the tide of chaos sweeping the country.[55] The reasoning is stunning for its naïveté.

Although news of the murder was initially met with euphoria, soon notes of concern could be heard.

Pavel Zavarzin, the former head of the Moscow Security Bureau (aka Okhrana), recalled travelling in a train across central Russia soon after the murder. He was reading about the details in the newspaper along with his fellow passengers in the restaurant car when one man, a middle-aged Siberian merchant, broke the silence: 'Thank God that they've killed that bastard.' With that, everyone began to speak at once. 'A dog's death for a dog,' he heard some state. But others saw something wrong in the affair. One man was heard to say that a true nobleman doesn't invite a man into his home to kill him, and another that the murder by men so close to the throne amounted to a knife in the back of the Russian sovereign. 'It's a sign of chaos and the inevitable revolution,' said a bearded Siberian man in glasses, and with that sharply stood and left the car.[56]

The fact that Rasputin's murderers were aristocrats was not lost on the common folk. A society lady in Petrograd overheard wounded soldiers in a military hospital complaining, 'Yep, only one peasant managed to make his way to the Tsar, and so the nobles killed him.' It was a fairly common opinion among the masses and helped fuel the hatred of Russia's upper classes that was soon to erupt with white-hot fury.[57] A peasant from Pokrovskoe told Sergei Markov while travelling through Rasputin's village in early 1918 that the 'Burschujs' had killed Rasputin since he had defended the interests of the poor folk before the tsar.[58]

Not only had Yusupov and his fellow conspirators failed to save the monarchy, they had helped to hasten its demise. As Alexander Blok famously, and correctly, noted, the bullet that felled Rasputin 'struck the very heart of the ruling dynasty.'[59]

4

THE LAST TSAR

March 1917

DONALD CRAWFORD

AT THE TURN of 1917 there was no one in Russia, or anywhere else for that matter, who could have credibly foreseen that within the year the Russian state would have disintegrated – the Romanov dynasty swept aside and its successor, the forerunner of what had appeared its future as the new socialist republic, brought down in the disorder. There was nothing in this to justify any claim to 'historical inevitability', but everything to remind the world that cometh chaos, there is only hindsight to explain the outcome.

True, the enforced abdication of Emperor Nicholas II could be seen as inevitable, given that he had by then alienated almost the entire political establishment as well as a large part of the wider Romanov family. In the midst of a disastrous war with Japan he had survived the revolution of 1905 by reluctantly yielding to demands for an elected parliament, the Duma, albeit with ministers answerable to him. In the midst of a war with Germany he stubbornly ignored demands for a government appointed by and responsible to that same Duma. Autocracy not constitutional monarchy was to remain the model for imperial Russia.

Much of the blame for his downfall could rightly be placed at the door of his interfering and dominating German-born wife, Empress Alexandra. When Nicholas took over as Supreme Commander in 1915 and removed himself to the Stavka, his front-line headquarters over 400 miles away at Mogilev, he gave his wife control of the ministers left behind in the capital Petrograd. Progressively over the next couple of years the government became *her* government, with ministers appointed only with the approval of her hated 'holy man', Grigory Rasputin. His hold over the empress stemmed from her belief that only his 'divine spirit' could protect the life of her haemophilic son Alexis. However, since the boy's disease was a secret kept from the world, it saved neither from the contempt of both society and the political establishment.

In consequence, the news in mid December 1916 that Rasputin had been murdered – not by political terrorists but by Prince Felix Yusupov and Grand Duke Dimitri Pavlovich, both members of the imperial family – was cheered across the country. That was followed by wild talk of a palace coup led by the three Vladimirovich brothers, Grand Dukes Kirill, Boris and Andrei, which envisaged Alexandra being taken away and confined in some far-distant convent. Nothing came of it but it served to confirm opinion in the capital's salons that the days of 'that woman' were numbered.

But there was no intent to bring down the Romanov dynasty itself: the consensus was that Nicholas, forced from the throne, would be succeeded by his twelve-year-old son Alexis, in accordance with the law, and with Nicholas's younger brother Michael Alexandrovich as regent. Michael was a war hero, a cavalry commander holding Russia's two highest battlefield awards, and was known to be sympathetic to constitutional monarchy on the British lines; the army held him in high regard and he would also be a popular choice in the Duma where he was widely trusted and respected.

Of the several political conspiracies emerging the most serious was headed by one of the Duma's most influential party leaders, Alexander Guchkov, who feared that without change there was high risk of left-wing extremists taking to the streets and facing Russia with a second revolution.

His alternative was to be a bloodless palace coup – to capture the tsar's train while it was travelling between the capital and the army headquarters at Mogilev, and thus present the country next morning with a fait accompli. Guchkov was confident that popular support would then oblige the tsar to concede his throne.

A second and unrelated plot went to the heart of the Stavka itself where General Mikhail Alexeev, the chief of staff, supported it. One of the principals was Prince Lvov, the popular leader of the civic and volunteer organisations across Russia. Their intention was to arrest Alexandra on one of her regular visits to Stavka, and compel the tsar to remove her to Livadia; if he refused, as they knew he would, then he would be compelled to abdicate – with the same result as in the Guchkov plot: a boy emperor with his uncle Grand Duke Michael as regent. Although plans had not been finalised and there was much work to be done, the conspirators in both camps felt certain of success. For the Guchkov plotters, believing they would be ready to strike in March, what was clear was that removing this weak tsar and his dangerous wife was both a necessity and inevitable if tsarist Russia was to be saved from itself.

History, as is so often the case, had other ideas. The future of Russia was not to be determined by an elite few but by the clamour of a street mob that as yet had no idea that it might have any role at all.

It was a spontaneous uprising, with no master plan or even a decisive leader who could be identified afterwards. Unrest became disturbance, disturbance grew into rebellion, and then in turn into revolution. And yet all this was in large part confined to the capital, with the rest of the country unaffected, at least in the beginning, and with some regions unaware of events until they were all over.

The ostensible cause was fear of a bread shortage; although supplies were adequate the fear was self-fulfilling in that housewives hoarded, creating the shortage. But that was only one of many factors. There had been large-scale strikes, following a lockout of workers at the giant Putilov factories, with an estimated 158,000 men idle by late February.

Petrograd itself was a vast military camp, with 170,000 armed troops in barracks, many of them susceptible to agitators – among them

German agents actively fomenting resentment in the hope of bringing about a revolution that would remove Russia from the war.

Suddenly, on Saturday 25 February (10 March New Style), that threat of revolution turned into reality. It was not just that six people had died that day but that one of those killed was a police inspector who, intent upon seizing a protestor's red flag, was killed by a Cossack trooper as he rode into a crowd of demonstrators. The Cossacks were the traditional scourge of rioters and demonstrators – and if they were no longer reliable, no one was.

By the next day, Sunday, the number of dead had risen to 200. More ominously, a company of the elite Pavlovsk Guards had mutinied in their barracks, attacked their colonel, and cut off his hand. With that, it was revolution or the hangman's noose.

A desperate Mikhail Rodzyanko, leader of the Duma, telegraphed the tsar. 'The capital is in a state of anarchy. The government is paralysed... General discontent is growing. There is wild shooting in the street... There must be a new government, under someone trusted by the country,' he urged, adding that 'any procrastination is tantamount to death...'

Reading that, Nicholas dismissed it as panic. 'Some more rubbish from that fat Rodzyanko.' However, he did decide to put together a loyal force and despatch it to the capital, with he himself returning to his home at Tsarskoe Selo, thirteen miles south of Petrograd. That should settle matters. The rebel soldiers were no more than an armed rabble. They would never stand against proper front-line troops.

That complacent view was easier held in Mogilev than in the streets of Petrograd. The rebels indeed were not front-line soldiers but depot reservists, many of them new recruits, the scrapings of the military barrel. Military discipline was a thin veneer that was easily stripped away, turning such troops into a uniformed mob. Nevertheless, they had guns and were as well armed as any soldiers being sent to face them. By noon on Sunday, only some twenty-four hours into the disorders, 25,000 troops had gone over to the side of the demonstrators; the bulk of the available forces, however, simply stayed in their barracks as the rebels and the mob took command of the streets.

The Arsenal on the Liteiny was captured, putting into the hands of the rebels thousands of rifles and pistols, and hundreds of machine guns. The headquarters of the Okhrana, across the Neva and opposite the Winter Palace, as well as a score of police stations, were overrun and set on fire. The prisons were opened and their inmates freed, criminals as well as political detainees. By the evening of that second day, only the very centre of the city, around the Winter Palace, could be said still to be in government control. Guchkov's plan to pre-empt any such uprising had been overtaken by events. As the tsar's brother Grand Duke Michael noted in his diary that night, it was 'the beginning of anarchy'.

At its home in Petrograd's Tauride Palace the Duma was in uproar. Just thirteen days after the start of its new session, deputies arrived to find that the Duma had been shut down again. Prince Golitsin, the third prime minister in the past year, had used a 'blank' decree from the tsar to prorogue the Duma, thinking it would defuse tension by silencing the more radical elements.

He was wrong. The deputies refused to disperse, adjourned to another chamber, and set up a 'temporary committee' that then claimed to be the de facto government. That said, it had no idea of what might happen next, and nor did its leader, Duma president Rodzyanko. 'What shall I do? What shall I do?' Rodzyanko cried out in vain hope of any answer.

So Rodzyanko turned to the only man he thought could rescue them. He slipped out of the chamber and telephoned Grand Duke Michael at his home in Gatchina, twenty-nine miles south, urging him to come to the capital immediately.

Michael did just that. His special train left at 5 p.m. and an hour later in Petrograd he was whisked away to the Marie Palace on St Isaac's Square to join an emergency conference attended by the prime minister, Golitsin, and his chief ministers, together with Rodzyanko and other leading members of the Duma's new 'temporary committee'.

In the government there was only resigned defeatism. That evening the hated interior minister Protopopov had been persuaded to resign and as he shuffled off into the night he muttered that there was nothing now left to him 'but to shoot myself'. No one cared what he did and no one bothered to say goodbye to the man so trusted by the empress, so despised by the nation.

Yet his departure was also its own signal that the government was no more. Golitsin accepted that his ministry was finished, but admitted that he did not know how to write out the death certificate. He hoped that Grand Duke Michael would do that for him.

As the conference agreed, with Golitsin having thrown in the towel, the only hope now was that Michael would take over control in the capital, and rally loyal troops to his side, including the relief force the tsar had promised Rodzyanko. He was a famous general, and the army would do as he demanded. He would also need to form a new government, which in turn meant the tsar formally appointing his brother as regent in the capital.

Rodzyanko confidently expected that he would be the obvious new 'strong man' premier and was visibly dismayed when instead Michael proposed Prince Georgy Lvov – the preferred choice of the leading Duma men and its own evidence that Michael knew more about what was going on among the key political leaders than the surprised Rodzyanko.

Lvov was not a member of the Duma, but as long-time head of the powerful union of local authorities, the zemstvos, he was the best-known civic leader in the country and more popular and more trusted among the radical elements than the authoritarian bull-voiced Rodzyanko. The majority Progressive Bloc in the Duma had already opted for Lvov, and now, named by Michael, it was Lvov who was endorsed at the two-hour conference.

In the event they were all wasting their time. Leaving the Marie Palace for the War Ministry across the square, Michael began his despatch to his brother on the Hughes apparatus, a primitive form of telex. He set out succinctly what had been agreed at the conference, and that the situation had become so serious that every hour counted. The reply came forty minutes later, passed on through chief of staff General Alexeev. Almost dismissive, it ignored Michael's proposals, but said that the tsar would return next day to Tsarskoe Selo and also send four infantry and four calvary regiments to restore order. Then, at 11.35 p.m., snubbing Michael, Nicholas telegraphed Golitsin to say that 'I personally bestow upon you all the necessary powers for civil rule.'

But by then it was too late. Golitsin and his ministers had drifted away into the night and there was no prime minister and no civil rule. Later, Michael would sum up the story of those futile hours with one word in his diary: *Alas.*

At 5 a.m. in the pre-dawn of Tuesday, February 28, the train carrying the tsar back to Tsarskoe Selo left Mogilev, its windows darkened, its passengers asleep. The start time had moved forward because it had been decided to take a roundabout route back, so as to leave the direct line to Petrograd clear for the relief force that had been ordered. The change would mean that he would arrive home at around 8 a.m. the following morning, Wednesday.

'Every hour is precious,' Michael had told his brother on his wire on Monday night, urging him not to leave Mogilev at all so that he could be in direct communication throughout the crisis. On his train, Nicholas would be virtually incommunicado. Russia no longer had a government and over the next crucial twenty-seven hours or more it would, for all practical purposes, be without an emperor. Nevertheless, when he reached Tsarskoe Selo the next morning the tsar expected to hear that General Nikolai Ivanov and his 6,000 front-line troops were in place to crush the rebellion. He could sleep easily. His train was on schedule and at 4 a.m. the next morning he was less than 100 miles from Tsarskoe Selo, having covered 540 miles since leaving Mogilev.

It was then that the train abruptly stopped, at the town of Malaya Vishera, with the alarming news that revolutionaries had blocked the line ahead. Since the train had only a few guards aboard, fighting their way forward was out of the question. There was only one choice for them: to go back to Bologoe, halfway between Petrograd and Moscow, and then head west for Pskov, headquarters of General Nikolai Ruzsky's Northern Army. It was the nearest safe haven, though it would still leave Nicholas 170 miles from home and worse off than if he had stayed in Mogilev where he could command the whole of his armies. His journey had been entirely wasted.

'To Pskov, then,' he said curtly and retired back to his sleeping car. But once there he put his real feelings into his diary. 'Shame and dishonour', he wrote despairingly. The journey to Pskov meant that for the next, and decisive, fifteen hours – until about 7 p.m. that Wednesday evening – the Emperor of All the Russias would once again vanish into the empty snow-covered countryside, a second day lost.

In consequence, with no government and a nomadic tsar lost in a train, power in Petrograd passed on Tuesday 28 February to the revolution, with the Tauride Palace home of a Duma that was no more. Instead, it now housed a noisy mass of workers, soldiers and students, joined together in a new organisation, a Soviet on the lines of the 1905 revolution. The few hundred respectable deputies who backed the Temporary Committee of the Duma now jostled for places in rooms and hallways packed with excited street orators, mutineers and strike leaders. It was chaos and would remain so for days to come.

In that crush, the young man beginning to stand out as the dominant figure was Alexander Kerensky, a member of the Temporary Duma Committee but also vice-chairman of the new 'Petrograd Soviet of Workers' and Soldiers' Deputies'. Bestriding both camps, his power was enormous, with the Duma deputies recognising him as their only bridge to the new Soviet, the master if it chose to be. The Temporary Committee of the Duma had the better claim to government, but its members knew that in this revolution they could only lead where Kerensky was willing to follow.

At the same time, the Soviet had the sense to know that they were in no position to form 'a people's government' – their authority did not extend beyond the capital, and they had few if any among them with the experience to act as ministers. There had to be a deal, and for the Duma men that meant securing the tsar's abdication while preserving the monarchist system itself, by the same means earlier intended by the plotters in their ranks: Nicholas would be replaced by his lawful successor, his son Alexis, with Grand Duke Michael as regent.

But Nicholas had first to be compelled to give up the throne – and trundling around Russia in his train, he had, as yet, no idea that that was what was being demanded of him.

As the tsar had hoped, his train did eventually reach Pskov at around 7 p.m. that Wednesday evening, after travelling 860 miles in total but still almost 200 miles from his intended destination of Tsarskoe Selo. However, at least he was back in contact with the world, albeit one very different to that he had left thirty-eight hours earlier.

Not knowing what time his train was to be expected, there was no one at the station to meet him, though shortly afterwards the army commander, General Nikolai Ruzsky, turned up, his manner unwelcoming.

He did not bring good news. What of those relief troops that Nicholas had sent to the capital? The answer was that with no orders, no tsar, and no one in authority, General Ivanov had simply abandoned his task and turned back. The capital was lost and would stay lost.

In the tsar's study aboard the train, Ruzsky believed that Nicholas now had no option but to grant the concessions demanded of him and he said so, doggedly, over a gloomy dinner. As stubborn as ever and still blind to his own peril, Nicholas refused to give up his autocratic powers, though he conceded that he was willing to appoint Rodzyanko as prime minister, albeit with a cabinet responsible to the tsar.

Ruzsky was getting nowhere until a telegram arrived from General Alexeev at Mogilev, urging the same concessions. Nicholas, now in an uncomfortable corner, sought compromise. He insisted that, whatever else, the ministers for war, navy and foreign affairs should continue to be accountable to him. Ruzsky would not even concede that.

Nicholas went to his sleeping car a rattled man. In refusing the demands of politicians and dismissing the pleas of his brother and others, he had assumed the absolute loyalty of his senior military commanders. Now they, too, seemed to be against him. At 2 a.m. he called Ruzsky to his carriage and told him that he had 'decided to compromise'; a manifesto granting a responsible ministry, already signed, was on the table. Ruzsky was authorised to notify Rodzyanko that he could now be prime minister of a parliamentary government.

However, that proved only how little the tsar knew of what had happened in the capital since Michael had wired him at 10.30 p.m. on Monday night, a little more than forty-eight hours earlier. When, at 3.30 a.m., Ruzsky got through to Petrograd on the direct line, Rodzyanko's reply was shatteringly frank: 'It is obvious that neither His Majesty nor you realise what is going on here ... Unfortunately the manifesto has come too late ... and there is no return to the past ... demands for an abdication in favour of the son, with Michael Alexandrovich as Regent, are becoming quite definite.'

When Ruzsky finished his painfully slow discussion on the direct wire, it was 7.30 a.m. that Thursday morning, 2 March. It was only then that Ruzsky knew that the crisis in Petrograd had moved beyond demands for a constitutional monarchy to that of the abdication of Nicholas. He therefore sent on Rodzyanko's taped message to Alexeev at Supreme Headquarters and at 9 a.m. on the same morning Alexeev cabled his reply: 'My deep conviction that there is no choice and that the abdication should now take place ... but there is no other solution.'

Having made his own views clear, at least to Ruzsky, Alexeev – less pained than he pretended – sent out his own telegrams to his other army commanders and to the admirals commanding the Baltic and Black Sea fleets. Russia had a war to fight and Alexeev was determined that the revolution in Petrograd should not undermine the front-line armies waiting to begin their spring offensive.

'The dynastic question has been put point-blank,' he told his commanders. 'The war may be continued until its victorious end only provided the demands regarding the abdication from the throne in favour of the son and under the regency of Grand Duke Michael

Alexandrovich are satisfied. Apparently the situation does not permit another solution …'

His cables went out at 10.15 a.m. Four hours later, at 2.15 p.m., he wired the emperor at Pskov giving him the first three replies. They would prove decisive.

The first, from 'Uncle Nikolasha', the former Supreme Commander sacked in 1915 and now commander on the Caucasus front, could not be more frank: 'As a loyal subject I feel it my necessary duty of allegiance in the spirit of my oath, to beg Your Imperial Majesty on my knees to save Russia and your heir … and hand over to him your heritage. There is no other way …'

The second, in like terms, was from Brusilov, Michael's former commander-in-chief, and the most successful fighting general in the army: 'The only solution … is the abdication in favour of the heir Tsarevich under the Regency of Grand Duke Michael Alexandrovich. There is no other way out; otherwise it will result in incalculable catastrophic consequences.' The third was from General Alexei Evert, the commander on the western front: 'abdication is the only measure which apparently can stop the revolution and thus save Russia from the horrors of anarchy'.

Nicholas rose and went to the window, staring out unseeingly. He could not defy his generals and they had just passed a vote of no confidence in him, both as tsar and Supreme Commander. He could not sack them, nor could he argue with them. Suddenly he turned and said calmly: 'I have decided. I shall renounce the throne.' He made the sign of the cross and Ruzsky, realising the enormity of what had just been said, followed suit.

Two short telegrams were drafted for Nicholas – the first to Rodzyanko.

> There is no sacrifice which I would not bear for the sake of the real welfare and for the salvation of our own dear Mother Russia. Therefore I am ready to abdicate the throne in favour of my son, provided that he can remain with me until he comes of age, with the Regency of my brother the Grand Duke Michael Aleksandrovich.

That was the response that was hoped for by the Duma men – Nicholas gone, a boy emperor, Michael as regent. His second telegram, to Alexeev, was in similar terms. At 3.45 p.m. Nicholas told Ruzsky to send them out.

At that moment, Nicholas ceased to be tsar, Alexis was the new emperor and Michael was regent. Or so it was assumed when an excited Rodzyanko spread the word in the Duma. Indeed, the abdication was so generally known that in London Nicholas's cousin King George V that night wrote in his diary: 'Heard from Buchanan [the British ambassador] that the Duma had forced Nicky to sign his abdication and Misha had been appointed Regent...' The king was in no doubt about the reason: 'I fear Alicky [the empress] is the cause of it all and Nicky has been weak.'

That was exactly the verdict of the relieved Duma men as they began their negotiations with the Soviet over ending the revolution and forming a responsible government. The 'historically inevitable' had, it seemed, stepped in to save Russia. In fact, Nicholas was just about to demonstrate yet again that history only happens afterwards.

Before Nicholas's signed abdication had been signalled to Petrograd, two leading Duma men had boarded a train for Pskov, thinking they would only obtain that abdication by facing him directly. They were Guchkov, the architect of the earlier plot to arrest the tsar and compel him to go, and his co-monarchist Vasily Shulgin. For the next seven hours they would be out of touch with events, and arrive in Pskov at around 10 p.m. not knowing that in Petrograd the matter was taken as already settled.

But what as yet no one knew was that in those same hours Nicholas had changed his mind: yes, he would abdicate, but in so doing he would also remove his son from the succession. It would be his brother Michael not the boy Alexis who would be emperor.

Petulance? *If you won't have me, then you won't get my son.* That may have been the thinking in Nicholas's embittered mind, but behind it was a real worry that without the care of his family the fragile haemophilic Alexis could die, a possibility confirmed by Professor Sergei Fedorov, the court physician travelling with him. The professor could have no idea about the future plans for caring for the boy, but whatever these may have been, Alexis was always at risk. And in stating the obvious Fedorov gave Nicholas the excuse he was looking for.

Guchkov, expecting a fierce row, was stunned to find that Nicholas had not only already abdicated but had drawn up a second abdication manifesto removing Alexis from the succession. At a stroke it demolished a key aspect of the Duma men's argument – an innocent boy lawfully inherits the throne and a new responsible ministry is protected by Michael as regent.

Guchkov and Shulgin recognised the problem as they retired to discuss it with Ruzsky and two other generals. Could an emperor remove a lawful successor for health reasons? No one knew the answer, except perhaps that as an autocrat Nicholas could do as he liked. And neither of the Duma men welcomed the prospect of returning empty-handed to Petrograd; they decided therefore that they had no choice but to accept the second abdication as it stood. Filing back into the saloon they told him that they had agreed to his terms.

With that Nicholas took the manifesto into his study for amendment and signature. With the removal of Alexis, it now read: 'We have judged it right to abdicate the Throne of the Russian state and to lay down the Supreme Power. Not wishing to be parted from Our Beloved Son, We hand over Our Succession to Our Brother Grand Michael Aleksandrovich and Bless Him on his accession to the Throne of the Russian state ...' A sealed copy of the abdication was handed over to Guchkov and another to Ruzsky for transmission to the army commands and to Petrograd and other key centres.

It was then 11.40 p.m. but it was agreed that the manifesto should be timed as of three o'clock that afternoon – as stated on the draft sent from the Stavka when Nicholas had first decided to abdicate, albeit with Alexis as his successor. That made this second abdication appear to have been signed at the same time as the first – and thus to seem its equal and not a belated substitute.

Just after midnight, when Guchkov and Shulgin, with their precious signed manifesto, headed back to the capital, the text of that second manifesto was being broadcast overnight to the world at large. Nicholas, in his turn, left Pskov for Mogilev, the headquarters from which he had departed with such confidence just forty-four hours earlier. Throughout the formalities he had given no sign of distress but within himself he was anything but calm. On the train he went to his diary and revealed his private agony: 'At one o'clock this morning I left Pskov with a heart that is heavy over what has just happened. All around me there is nothing but treason, cowardice, and deceit!'

As always with Nicholas, everyone was to blame but himself.

As news reached the Tauride Palace in the early hours of Friday morning that Nicholas had removed both himself and his son from the throne, panic set in among the Duma leaders. The deal which they had thought settled with a reluctant Soviet had depended in great degree on persuading them that the new tsar would be a harmless boy – not a tough battlefield commander with a high reputation in the army. Among the throng of mutineers, fearful enough that Michael would be regent, the immediate reaction was that, with Michael as emperor, their necks were more at stake than ever. Talk of a general amnesty would not save those who had killed their own officers.

But fear worked in two directions and Rodzyanko was one of those as scared of the revolution as the revolution was scared of the monarchy. Pavel Milyukov – a resolute monarchist and the newly-appointed foreign minister in what was now called the Provisional Government – would describe him as being in 'a blue funk'. But in that sense so was the new premier Prince Lvov, who sided with Rodzyanko's alarmist predictions. Emperor Michael would have to be abandoned; Nicholas had done for the Soviet what the Soviet did not dare to do on its own.

To save itself the new government would have to persuade Michael to give up the throne. The Duma men knew where he was. Kerensky, appointed justice minister, picked up a copy of the Petrograd telephone directory, flicked through the pages and ran his finger down the column to the name of Princess Putyatina. Her number was 1–58–48. A few moments later, at 5.55 a.m., the telephone rang in 12 Millionnaya Street.

Although the new ministers hoped to meet Michael even before he knew he had become emperor – and possibly had started acting as one – there was never any chance of it remaining a secret. At first light, thousands of troops in front-line units were cheering his name and swearing an oath of allegiance to Emperor Michael II. At Pskov itself, with Nicholas gone, a Te Deum was ordered for the new emperor in the cathedral. Even in far-off Crimea, people celebrated Michael's succession. Princess Cantacuzène, one of Petrograd's leading hostesses, remembered that Nicholas's portraits disappeared 'from shop windows and walls within an hour after the reading of the proclamation; and in their place I saw by the afternoon pictures of Michael Aleksandrovich. Flags were hung out, and all faces wore smiles of quiet satisfaction.'

In Moscow, where the garrison had also gone over to the revolution, although without any of the excesses in Petrograd, the succession of Michael was greeted by the rebels with 'wooden indifference', with no sign of the resistance so feared by Rodzyanko in the hothouse of the Tauride Palace – indeed, the opposite seemed true elsewhere in the capital.

Guchkov and Shulgin, arriving back from Pskov, cried 'Long live Emperor Michael' as they hurried from their train, cheered by the people as they went by. After Shulgin read out the manifesto, a transit battalion of front-line troops and the surrounding crowd responded with cheers that 'rang out, passionate, genuine, emotional'.

Shulgin suddenly became aware of an urgent voice telling him that he was wanted on the telephone in the station-master's office. When he picked up the receiver it was to hear the croaking voice of Milyukov.

'Don't make known the manifesto,' barked Milyukov. 'There have been serious changes.'

A few moments later the telephone rang again – the new Railway Commissioner was sending his own man to the station. 'You can trust him with anything ... Understand?' Shulgin understood perfectly. A few minutes later a messenger arrived and Shulgin slipped him the envelope bearing the manifesto. Taken to the transport ministry offices, it was hidden under a pile of old magazines.

In the Tauride Palace, such was the confusion among the 'Council of Ministers' that it was not until 9.30 a.m. that they were assembled, though without Guchkov and Shulgin who had been delayed in a confrontation with the rebel-supporting railwaymen.

By then one question had settled itself: the news was such common knowledge that the Soviet now also knew that Michael was emperor, and the resulting clamour among the mutineers left the Duma majority in no doubt what that meant for them. They had no choice but to insist upon Michael's immediate abdication – their own necks depended on it.

They would take a hastily drafted manifesto with them to Millionnaya Street, and with luck bring it back signed by lunchtime. That should quieten the Soviet. The majority also agreed that Michael should be told that if he refused to sign, no one of them would serve as his ministers. He would be tsar with no government. It was him or us.

The apartment first-floor drawing room had been prepared to provide an informal setting. The settees and armchairs were arranged so that Michael, when he took the meeting, would be facing a semicircle of delegates. Lvov as premier and Rodzyanko as Duma president would lead the majority call for Michael's abdication, while Milyukov argued the minority case for preserving the monarchy, futile though that would be.

At 9.35 a.m., the delegates deciding that they could no longer wait for Guchkov and Shulgin, the drawing room door opened, ministers and deputies rose to their feet, and in walked the man being hailed across the country as His Majesty Emperor Michael II. He sat down in his tall-backed chair, looked around the men facing him, and the meeting began.

For Michael the first reality was to find that everyone addressed him not as 'Your Imperial Majesty' but as 'Your Highness' – thus, not as emperor but as grand duke. It was intended as intimidation, and they thought it would also speed up the clock.

Michael, looking around the room, could see that the Duma men were exhausted, unshaven, bedraggled and, as Prince Lvov would put it, unable even to think straight any more. Many were also clearly frightened, and that dread of the Soviet would be heightened by Kerensky, the only man in the room who could claim to speak for the mob. A master of the theatrical posture, Kerensky also claimed to be 'terrified', and that at any moment a gang of armed men might break in and murder the new emperor, if not the rest of them.

Rodzyanko also used fear as the excuse for abdication. 'It was quite clear to us that the grand duke would have reigned only a few hours, and that this would have led to colossal bloodshed in the precincts of the capital, which would have degenerated into general civil war. It was clear to us that the grand duke would have been killed immediately ...'

Milyukov, with Guchkov not yet arrived, was the sole spokesman for those who believed that Rodzyanko and Lvov were leading the government to ultimate ruin, as would prove the case. Rousing himself, he argued that it would be immeasurably more difficult in the long term if the established order was simply abandoned, for in his reasoning the 'frail craft' of the self-elected Provisional Government, without a monarch, would soon be sunk 'in the ocean of national disorder'.

During all this shouting and argument, Michael had sprawled in his chair saying nothing. To Kerensky he seemed 'embarrassed' by what was going on and 'to grow more weary and impatient'. He had heard quite enough, and saw no point in hearing more.

He rose and announced that he would consider the whole matter privately with just two of the men in the room. To general surprise his choice fell on Lvov and Rodzyanko and not his principal supporters Milyukov and the recently arrived Guchkov. It could only mean that he had given in. Instead, what he wanted was reassurance that the new government was in a position to restore order and continue the war, and that they could ensure that the promised elections for a democratic Constituent Assembly would not be blocked by the Soviet. The answers were confidently 'Yes'.

Rodzyanko and Lvov returned to the drawing room, their faces barely concealing their triumph as they nodded to the others that all was settled. Michael hung back, talking to his long-serving personal lawyer, Alexei Matveev. When he too returned to the room, his face expressionless, no one took a note of what he said, and no one could afterwards remember what he said. Nevertheless it was enough to settle minds that he was abdicating.

There were sighs of relief. Nekrasov fingered the abdication manifesto in his pocket: *We, by God's mercy, Michael II, Emperor and Autocrat of all the Russias* ... After that preamble the rest could be filled in simply enough. It would need a few flourishes, perhaps, to give the required sense of occasion, but essentially 'abdicate' was the word that mattered. Allowing five minutes or so for regretful comments and funereal courtesies, Michael's manifesto could be in the Tauride Palace by lunchtime, with the Soviet obliged to hail their success. By late afternoon it could be posted all over the city.

In fact, it would turn out to be rather more complicated than that. Michael was not going to give them 'abdicate'. And, as if on cue, the drawing room door opened and the smiling figure of Princess Putyatina appeared to ask those who could to join her for lunch.

In their surprise no one seemed able to voice a protest. Unsure what to do, about half the men in the drawing room accepted the invitation and shuffled in to sit at the lunch table. They included Prince Lvov, Kerensky, Shulgin, Tereshchenko and Nekrasov, his unsigned abdication manifesto tucked back in his pocket. Princess Putyatina sat at the head of the table, with Michael at her right hand; lawyer Matveev and Michael's private secretary Johnson sat together at the end of the table.

Rodzyanko and the other ministers and deputies, confused, left the building and went back to the Tauride Palace, their victory delayed.

Since the Soviet was still unaware that there was a meeting with Michael, and as yet the returning delegates could not wave his abdication manifesto, there was nothing they could do but keep out of the way and fend off questions.

At the lunch table, conversation was polite, with no mention of the reason for their all being there, until lunch was finished and Princess Putyatina rose from the table and withdrew. The delegates then looked at Michael, waiting for the moment when he would formally provide his abdication; Nekrasov fingered again the manifesto in his pocket.

Matveev, having sat throughout lunch in silence, then asserted himself, asking Nekrasov to let him see what he had written down. Nekrasov handed it over, and Matveev read through it, then returned it with the air of a man who had found it wanting. Nekrasov glanced down at the paper: he had no experience of drafting a manifesto of this kind; had he missed something? Michael clearly thought so for he then suggested that Matveev 'should help set down in proper form what had taken place'.

Nodding towards Nekrasov, Matveev announced to the table that in order to prepare a proper manifesto for Michael's signature they would first need to have a copy of the original abdication manifesto signed by Nicholas, as well as a copy of the Fundamental Laws.

An embarrassed Prince Lvov knew from Shulgin that he had handed the manifesto over to some man from the transport ministry, but had no idea what had happened to it thereafter – that it was still hidden under a pile of old magazines. As for the Code of Laws – where could they get a copy of those?

The lunch table was now in disarray, any thought of a quick exit with a signed manifesto abandoned. Somehow, the lawyers were going to have to take over and since Michael had his own in Matveev they were going to need one themselves. The man they settled on was Vladimir Nabokov, and Prince Lvov volunteered to call him. For Michael he was a welcome choice: Nabokov's sister was a close friend of his family and her daughter a playmate of his seven-year-old son George.

With that, Kerensky and the Duma men, with the exception of

Lvov and Shulgin, decided to return to the Tauride Palace. There was nothing they could do here, and it was clearly going to be a long afternoon. Assured by Prince Lvov that they would be told as soon as the manifesto had been signed, they left looking rather more subdued than they had done on arrival almost six hours earlier. They were not sure how it had happened, but somehow Michael now seemed to be in charge.

At almost that very moment a telegram was sent to Michael from Sirotino, a railway station some 275 miles from Pskov. Nicholas, having 'awoken far beyond Dvinsk', had suddenly remembered that he had neglected to mention to his brother that he was the new emperor. He hastily scribbled out a telegram, despatched at 2.56 p.m. and addressed to 'Imperial Majesty Petrograd'. It read:

> To His Majesty the Emperor Michael: Recent events have forced me to decide irrevocably to take this extreme step. Forgive me if it grieves you and also for no warning – there was no time. Shall always remain a faithful and devoted brother. Now returning to HQ where hope to come back shortly to Tsarskoe Selo. Fervently pray God to help you and our country. Your Nicky.

As so often during the past days, Nicholas had acted when it was too late to matter. However, at least it was delivered, unlike the last telegram sent to him, and returned *Address Unknown*.

Nabokov reached Millionnaya Street just before 3 p.m. After briefing him, Prince Lvov explained that 'the draft of the Act had been outlined by Nekrasov, but the effort was incomplete and not entirely satisfactory, and since everyone was dreadfully tired ... they requested that I undertake the task'.

With the original manifesto lost Nabokov argued that they could manage without it since the whole country knew what it said; however, he agreed with Matveev that they could not proceed without the Code of Laws and that it was essential that they had the Fundamental Laws in front of them. The man they could count on for those was the constitutional jurist Baron Nolde in nearby Palace Square. He arrived ten minutes later.

As they retreated into a bedroom, the immediate problem which confronted the two lawyers was precisely that which had exercised Michael on first learning that he had been named emperor: was Nicholas's abdication manifesto lawful?

Nabokov and Nolde did not need any prompting on that issue: both recognised from the outset that Nicholas's manifesto contained 'an incurable, intrinsic flaw'. Nicholas could not renounce the throne on his son's behalf and as Nabokov would say, 'from the beginning Michael must necessarily have felt this'. Rightly, he judged that 'it significantly weakened the position of the supporters of the monarchy. No doubt it also influenced Michael's reasoning.'

That said, Nabokov and Nolde were left in the same position as everyone else: the political fact was that Alexis had been bypassed and could not be restored in any practical sense. There would be civil war, and the collapse of any responsible government.

When Nabokov and Nolde began their task, handing out drafts of the manifesto to Matveev for perusal and approval by Michael, they began with the same preamble used by Nekrasov: *We, by God's mercy, Michael II, Emperor and Autocrat of all the Russias* ... They started off therefore on the premise that Michael was lawful emperor, and that in abdicating he 'commanded' the people to obey the authority of the Provisional Government in which he was vesting his powers until a Constituent Assembly determined the form of government.

This formula gave legitimacy to the new government, which otherwise was simply there by licence of the Soviet. No one had elected the Provisional Government which represented only itself, and in that regard it had arguably less authority than the Soviet which could at least claim to have been endorsed by elected soldier and worker delegates.

Michael could make the new government official and legal, as no one else could, and therefore it was important that his manifesto be issued by him as emperor. If he was not emperor, he had no power to vest, and no authority to 'command' anyone. Of political necessity the new government needed Michael to give up the throne, but first they needed him to take it.

However, it was not going to be that simple. Michael was clear in his own mind about the position in which he had found himself. He had not inherited the throne. Alexis had been unlawfully bypassed and Michael proclaimed emperor without his knowledge or consent. He had not willingly become emperor and Nicholas had no right to pass the throne to him. At the same time, there was nothing that could be done about that. The wrong could not be righted; it was far too late. The only issue therefore was how best to salvage the monarchy from the wreckage Nicholas had left in his wake.

That the government were demanding his abdication in order to appease the Soviet was a serious complication, but even so, he was not going to abdicate. Besides, if he did, who was going to succeed him? The throne 'was never vacant' – the law said that – and it followed therefore that if he abdicated, someone else would immediately become emperor in his place. The next in line, the Grand Duke Kirill?

Nobody that morning seemed to have thought of it, but Nabokov and Nolde understood perfectly his argument. The problem was how to express all of it in a manifesto. Tearing up their first draft, and thereby consigning Nekrasov's manifesto to the dustbin, they started again, with Michael darting in and out of the schoolroom to make sure that their new draft stayed in line with his wishes.

There was not much time, but fortunately they were both very good lawyers, and with Matveev they worked as a team that knew the difference between the small print and the telescope to the blind eye. The result was a manifesto which would make Michael emperor without it saying that he had accepted the throne; that as emperor he would vest all his powers in the new Provisional Government; and with that done he would wait in the wings until a future Constituent Assembly voted, as he hoped, for a constitutional monarchy and elected him. Meanwhile, he would not reign, but neither would he abdicate.

Despite the intense pressure on Michael and the lawyers in Million-naya Street as evening drew in that day, his final manifesto said exactly what he wanted it to say, and it bore no resemblance whatsoever to the manifesto which Nekrasov had drafted that morning and which he had handed over after lunch. It said:

> A heavy burden has been thrust upon me by the will of my brother, who has given over to me the Imperial Throne of Russia at a time of unprecedented warfare and popular disturbances.
>
> Inspired like the entire people by the idea that what is most important is the welfare of the country, I have taken a firm decision to assume the Supreme Power only if such be the will of our great people, whose right it is to establish the form of government and the new basic laws of the Russian state by universal suffrage through its representatives in the Constituent Assembly.
>
> Therefore, invoking the blessing of God, I beseech all the citizens of Russia to obey the Provisional Government, which has come into being on the initiative of the Duma and is vested with all the pleni-tude of power until the Constituent Assembly, to be convoked with the least possible delay by universal suffrage, direct, equal and secret voting, shall express the will of the people by its decision on the form of government.

MICHAEL

By this manifesto Michael made clear that the throne had been 'thrust upon me' not inherited, and that he was passing all his powers to the new Provisional Government until the future status of Russia was decided by a democratically elected Constituent Assembly. He had changed the imperious word 'command' in the first version to 'beseech' and had removed all use of the imperial 'We', as well as the description of him as 'Emperor and Autocrat', but he had signed with the imperial Michael, rather than the grand ducal Michael Alexandrovich.

There was no precedent for a manifesto in these terms, and the Code of Laws, seemingly so essential a few hours earlier, had been closed and put aside as irrelevant to the necessity of the moment. But as Nabokov later commented, 'we were not concerned with the juridical force of the formula but only its moral and political meaning'.

In so saying, the credit for that went to Michael and his refusal to do what he was told by the new government. As for the 'abdication manifesto' itself, curiously, for those who took the trouble to read it carefully, of the 122 Russian words meticulously written by Nabokov 'in his beautiful handwriting' the one word which did not appear, unlike Nicholas's manifesto, was 'abdicate'.

The final manifesto, as Nolde would recall, 'was in essence the only constitution during the period of existence of the Provisional Government'. Nabokov also recognised it as 'the only Act which defined the limits of the Provisional Government's authority'. When the British ambassador later asked Milyukov where the government derived its authority, he replied: 'We have received it, by inheritance, from the Grand Duke.' No, not the grand duke but the emperor, since only an emperor was empowered to act as he did.

Nabokov, as Michael came into the room and took up the pen, thought he was 'under a heavy strain but he retained complete self-composure'. Nolde was also impressed, declaring Michael to have 'acted with irreproachable tact and nobility'. Shulgin thought to himself 'what a good constitutional monarch he would make'. The theatrical outburst, predictably, was left to Kerensky. 'Believe me,' he cried out, 'that we will carry the precious vessel of your authority to the Constituent Assembly without spilling a drop of blood.' In fact, he would spill it all, but that no one could then foresee.

It was only after the delegation returned to the Tauride Palace that the arguments began over the meaning of the manifesto. At Millionnaya Street there had been no time to study it. Professor Lomonosov had turned up from the transport ministry, belatedly bringing with him the original Nicholas manifesto hidden there; the intention was that it be published jointly with Michael's. But should these be presented as Acts of two Emperors? Since the word 'abdicate' was missing from Michael's, how was his manifesto to be described?

Because it was a political rather than a legal document, at midnight there was still no clear answer to the question. However, Milyukov and Nabokov argued that the answer was obvious. Since the majority who wanted it said that Michael had abdicated then that in itself meant he had been emperor. At 3.50 a.m. Nabokov's final manifesto was taken away to the printers. But since it did not mention 'abdicate' the Provisional Government gave it that meaning by claiming it as an abdication. That was simple. It said so in the newspapers. People could understand that, and one of them that evening was Michael's brother in Mogilev.

He had just returned from Pskov when Alexeev came in with Rodzyanko's wired version of what had happened in Millionnaya Street. Afterwards, Nicholas wrote in his diary: 'Misha, it appears, has abdicated. His manifesto ends up by kowtowing to the Constituent Assembly, whose elections will take place in six months. God knows who gave him the idea of signing such rubbish.'

Given the wreckage that he had mindlessly left behind him and the impossible position in which he had placed his brother, his effrontery had an epic quality about it. Certainly, when he said much the same to his brother-in-law Sandro a few days later, Sandro confessed himself to be 'speechless'.

Nicholas would never understand what he had done – that the consequence of his 'father's feelings' – his own explanation for removing Alexis – would destroy the Romanov dynasty itself. No one, including the Soviet, had expected that, nor demanded it. 'Historical inevitability'? After all, as history itself knows only too well, Nicholas doesn't deserve that as his excuse.

5

ENTER LENIN

April–July 1917

SEAN MCMEEKIN

The [Germans] transported Lenin in a sealed truck like a plague
bacillus from Switzerland into Russia

Winston Churchill.[1]

T HE OUTBREAK OF THE FEBRUARY REVOLUTION found V. I.
Lenin in Zurich, where he and his wife Krupskaia had lived, in
a single-room apartment in the Spiegelgasse across the street from a
sausage factory, since February 1916. While Lenin's wartime residence
in Zurich is widely known – his presence even features in a Tom Stop-
pard play, *Travesties* (1974) – not everyone knows the reasons he was
there. When war between Russia and the Central Powers opened in
1914, Lenin had been living in Vienna, where he was arrested on 8
August (along with Grigory Zinoviev) as an enemy alien. Nine days
later, however, Lenin was released on the express orders of the Austro-
Hungarian military, on the grounds that he had endorsed Ukrainian
independence – one of the key war aims of Vienna and Berlin. On 1
September 1914, Lenin and Krupskaia were sent to the Swiss border
aboard an Austrian military mail train, in an eerie foreshadowing of the
famous 'sealed train ride' under German military escort in 1917.[2]

Lenin had not wasted his time in Switzerland. Like dozens of other
political exiles disgusted by the 'betrayal of 4 August [1914]', which
had seen socialist and labour parties in Belgium, Britain, France,

Germany and Austria-Hungary vote for war credits in violation of pre-war pledges to sabotage any 'imperialist war', Lenin participated in the peace congresses held at Zimmerwald (1915) and Kienthal (1916). Unlike most other delegates, Lenin had opposed the majority resolutions penned by Trotsky (then still a Menshevik) and others, which expressed a principled opposition to the war and summoned 'the working class' to 'begin the struggle for peace' – without specifying how this might be done. Lenin's 'Zimmerwald Left' fraction argued that, rather than opposing the war on pacifist grounds – counselling draft resistance and the like – socialists should flood the armies with socialist recruits who could later use the weapons given them to 'turn the imperialist war into civil war'. Further, Lenin articulated the belief, in his treatise on *Socialism and War* (1915), that true socialists should root for their own countries to lose the war so as to weaken the ruling regime, a doctrine known as 'revolutionary defeatism'.[3] Although these views were seen as divisive by other Marxists, Lenin was arguably closer to the spirit of Eugène Pottier's socialist anthem 'Internationale', which openly endorsed army mutiny.[4]* It was to promote his new strategy of 'turning the armies red' – that is, encouraging young socialists across Europe to volunteer for service, Trojan-horse-style – that Lenin moved from Bern to Zurich in 1916, where he began collaborating with Willi Münzenberg, secretary of the Socialist Youth International. So far from expecting a revolution to break out that winter, Lenin told Münzenberg's youth socialists, at a meeting in the Zurich Volkshaus on 22 January 1917 (4 February New Style), that 'we old-timers may not live to see the decisive battles of this coming revolution'.[5]

---

* The kings intoxicate us with gunsmoke,
Peace between ourselves, war on the tyrants.
Let us bring the strike to the armies,
fire into the air and break ranks!
If they insist, these cannibals,
On making us into heroes,
They'll know soon enough that our bullets
Are for our own generals!

The news of the February Revolution came as just as much a surprise to Lenin as to everyone else in Europe: he read about in the Zurich
papers only on 2 March 1917 after Order No. 1 had already been issued
by the Executive Committee of the Petrograd Soviet (Ispolkom).
But this is not to say that he was unprepared to take advantage of it.
Lenin had been quietly receiving subsidies from the German Imperial
Government since 1916 at least (for this we have unimpeachable documentary evidence) and probably since 1915, when the socialist agent
Alexander Israel Parvus-Helphand had first advised Berlin to give
Lenin and his Bolsheviks financial support.[6] Lenin's apologists later
made a meal out of the agonies he supposedly went through before
'allowing' the Germans to send him back to Russia. As Münzenberg
dubiously recalled, Lenin told him that he had finally resolved to
return to his homeland even if forced to travel 'through hell itself' (i.e.
Germany). But this was balderdash. In fact, the initiative came from
the German Foreign Office, with the express authorisation of German
Chancellor Theobald von Bethmann Hollweg. After some brief and
not terribly contentious negotiations over terms, Berlin appropriated
five million gold marks to finance Lenin's journey and initial operations
in Russia. Five days later, Lenin boarded a train at Zurich's Hauptbah-
nhof bound for the German Baltic port of Sassnitz, accompanied by
Krupskaia, Radek, Zinoviev, Fritz Platten, as well as Lenin's long-time
mistress, Inessa Armand. After a brief stopover in Stockholm, Lenin's
party arrived at Petrograd's Finland Station on 3 April 1917 just past
11 p.m., in a train car now encased in glass to commemorate the historic
moment.[7]

It did not take long for Lenin to make an impression. Whisked
away to Bolshevik headquarters, he launched into a fiery speech
denouncing party backsliders who had foolishly offered support to
the Provisional Government, outlining a revolutionary programme so
extreme that the Bolshevik party organ *Pravda* initially refused to print
it. This programme, later revised into the so-called 'April Theses', is best
remembered for the slogan 'All Power to the Soviets' (meaning that the
party should offer no support to the Provisional Government, nor any

elected parliamentary regime to follow) but it was equally extreme on foreign policy, disavowing any support for the war against Germany and advocating the abolition of the tsarist army (along with the police and state bureaucracy). Little wonder Nikolai Sukhanov, a Menshevik member of Ispolkom who had gone to listen to Lenin's speech, recalled the experience as akin to being hit by 'lightning … it seemed as if all the elemental forces had risen from their lairs and the spirit of universal destruction … circled above the heads of the enchanted disciples'.[8] A bit more soberly, Georgy Plekhanov, the founder of the Russian Social Democratic Party and now an elder Menshevik statesman, penned a wry response 'On Lenin's Theses and Why Deliriums Are Occasionally Interesting'.[9]

Still, we should be careful not to exaggerate the impact of Lenin's arrival on Russian politics, at least in the short run. As an exile, Lenin had been free to devise a policy line unconstrained by concern for comity with fellow Russian socialists or any other practical considerations, unlike those Bolsheviks already in Russia, like Lev Kamenev and Joseph Stalin. Kamenev, speaking for the Bolshevik Central Committee, said that it would defend the current party platform, which offered qualified support for the Provisional Government and the war, 'against the demoralizing influence of "revolutionary defeatism" and against Comrade Lenin's criticism'.[10] Stalin denounced Lenin's 'down with the war' slogan as 'useless' in the pages of *Pravda*.[11] The April Theses were voted down soundly in the Petrograd Committee on 8 April 1917 by 13 to 2 against. Despite his later reputation for infallibility, Lenin had not won over his own party yet, and remained unable to do so for months afterwards, losing votes in the Central Committee in October 1917 (on a resolution to overthrow the government without the pretext of a gathering of the Soviets, 10 to 2) and in a national party conference in January 1918 (on whether to sign a separate peace immediately with the Germans, 48 to 15).[12]

Nevertheless, Lenin had laid down an unmistakable declaration of intent that could not be ignored. Unlike the Mensheviks led by Nikolai Chkeidze, who chaired Ispolkom, and the Social Revolutionaries of

Alexander Kerensky, who commanded the loyalty of most Russian peasants, the Bolsheviks now had a spokesman (if not yet a leader) willing to abandon the world war altogether in order to further the revolution. With the Western allies – including now, after 6 April 1917 (19 April New Style), the United States as an 'associated power' – expecting Russia to stay in the war and carry out her promised diversionary strike on the eastern front before summer, Lenin's anti-war stance had potentially explosive political and strategic implications. True, he was not alone in this stance: Viktor Chernov, the SR party leader in exile who had arrived in Petrograd just five days after Lenin, took a similarly uncompromising (though not identical) line on the war. It was Chernov, not Lenin, who first singled out the liberal Kadet foreign minister, Pavel Milyukov, for abuse over his refusal to renounce Russia's imperialist war aims – including, especially, the conquest of Constantinople and the Ottoman Straits – at a press conference on 22 March 1917 (4 April New Style). Denouncing the 'saturnalia of predatory appetites' expressed in the 'secret treaties', Chernov called for Milyukov's head.[13] (As Milyukov explained his own view in a private letter to a friend, 'it would be absurd and criminal to renounce the biggest prize of the war … in the name of some humanitarian and cosmopolitan idea of international socialism'.[14]) Chernov was, however, no Lenin. Instead of declaring war on the Provisional Government, he went to work for it as agriculture minister in May 1917, allowing Lenin to appear as the leader of the anti-war opposition, untainted by any connection to the Provisional Government.

The Milyukov crisis was the first test of Lenin's mettle after he arrived in Russia, and deserves a closer look. The issue of war aims was arguably *the* political question opened up by the February Revolution, even if it had been initially obscured in the popular euphoria over the fall of the tsar and his secret police. For what purpose, after all, were all those millions of wretched muzhiks fighting, bleeding and dying on fronts stretching from the Gulf of Finland to the Black Sea? While few in Russia, or anywhere else, yet suspected the full extent of the secret Ottoman partition plans agreed between then-foreign minister Sergei

Sazonov, Mark Sykes and Georges Picot in 1915–16, rumours were running hot, and getting hotter all the time. On 2 December 1916, then-chairman of the Council of Ministers A. F. Trepov, to quiet the usual mob of hecklers that had greeted his first Duma address, had revealed publicly for the first time that Britain and France had promised Russia Constantinople and the Straits.[15] Realising the political potency of the issue, Kerensky had reportedly rifled through the Foreign Ministry archives after the tsar had abdicated in March for copies of these 'secret treaties', and then instructed the Provisional Committee of the Duma to 'Hide them!' Suspecting that the Provisional Government was indeed hiding something, Bolshevik factory committees in Petrograd had issued a series of resolutions demanding the publication of the secret treaties.[16]

The Bolsheviks were not wrong to be suspicious. Back on 24 December 1916, Tsar Nicholas II had authorised the creation of a special amphibious 'Black Sea division', crowned by a 'Tsargradsky regiment', to spearhead the conquest of Constantinople ('Tsargrad' being the name favoured by Russian chauvinists for the Ottoman capital).[17] As late as 21 February 1917, before the February Revolution broke out, the last foreign minister of tsarist Russia, N. N. Pokrovsky, had submitted a memorandum to Stavka recommending a Bosphorus strike be carried out as soon as possible, to ensure that Russia not be deprived of her prize by her allies if the war ended later that year.[18] On 26 February 1917, at the height of the revolutionary chaos, Russia's chief of army staff, Mikhail Alexeev, huddled with political advisers, including ex-foreign minister Sazonov and former chairman of the Council of Ministers Boris Stürmer, to discuss Pokrovsky's request in light of the disturbing news from Petrograd. Stürmer, who knew all about popular mobs after being demonised for his German name, expressly advocated that the seizure of Constantinople was now 'essential in order to calm public opinion in Russia'.[19] One day after this, the French government solemnly reaffirmed its commitment to 'settling at the end of the present war the question of Constantinople and the Straits in conformance with the age-old vows of Russia'.[20]

On the very day Milyukov first got in hot water over his refusal to renounce these war aims – 22 March 1917 – a squadron of Russia's Black Sea fleet arrived at the mouth of the Bosphorus in 'grand style', comprised of 'five or six destroyers', two battle cruisers and three sea-plane carriers. Although news of this reconnaissance probe was little reported in politics-obsessed Petrograd, there were real dogfights in the air, as the Germans and Turks scrambled seven of their own sea-planes into action to send Russian pilots back to their carriers before they could surveille the city's defences.[21] The very next day, undaunted by the firestorm of opposition stirred up by his press conference, the diplomatic liaison at Russian military headquarters reported to Milyu-kov that two full divisions would be ready to sail for the Bosphorus by mid May, and, hopefully, a third by later that summer.[22] More even than the Bolsheviks knew, Milyukov was dead serious about conquer-ing Constantinople.

Lenin, for his part, was just as serious that Russia's 'imperialist war' must be stopped in its tracks. Shortly before he had returned to Russia, Milyukov had been pressured by Kerensky and the Petrograd Soviet, on 27 March 1917, into issuing a revised 'declaration of war aims' which stated that 'the purpose of free Russia is not domination over other nations, or the seizure of their national possessions or forcible occupa-tion of foreign territories, but the establishment of stable peace on the basis of self-determination of peoples' – while also pledging Russia, in a glaring contradiction, to observe fully 'all obligations assumed towards our Allies'.[23] In an interview with Morgan Philips Price of the *Manchester Guardian*, Milyukov had been similarly equivocal, hinting that Russia might be willing to renounce her sovereign claim on the Ottoman Straits, so long as she retained 'the right to close the Straits to foreign warships', which was 'not possible unless she possesses the Straits and fortifies them'.[24] To clear up the resulting confusion Mily-ukov had then, on 11 April, declared that, while he understood the appeal of a 'peace without annexations', Russia and her allies remained committed to projects such as 'the reunification of Armenia' (i.e. the ongoing carve-up of Ottoman Asia Minor by the Russian Army of the

Caucasus) and the 'reunification of Poland' and 'the gratification of the national aspirations of the Austrian Slavs' (i.e. the Russian conquest of Habsburg Galicia). Livid, Lenin published these remarks in *Pravda* on 13 April 1917 while exhorting all 'comrades, workers and soldiers' to 'read this statement of Milyukov at all your meetings! Make it understood that you do not wish to die for the sake of secret conventions concluded by Tsar Nicholas II, and which are still sacred to Milyukov!'[25]

The battle for the soul of Russian foreign policy now came to a head. On 13 April 1917, the same day Lenin was calling proletarians to the barricades against Milyukov in the pages of *Pravda*, Kerensky tried to placate the Bolshevik opposition by announcing that the government was preparing a note to Russia's allies in the spirit of the 9 April 1917 statement on war aims, now referred to generally (though inaccurately) as the 'peace without annexations' declaration. This was untrue, but it did force Milyukov's hand. Under ferocious pressure, the beleaguered foreign minister agreed to hand over to Entente diplomats the 9 April declaration, with a note appended to it reaffirming Russia's intention to stay in the war against the Central Powers and 'fully to carry out [her] obligations' to her allies. It is still not clear whether Kerensky, in arranging this compromise, meant to save Milyukov or destroy him. In the event, it was partly the timing that did in the foreign minister. The two 'notes to the Allies' were cabled to Russian embassies abroad on 18 April 1917 – that is, on May Day, still celebrated by most Russian socialists according to the western Gregorian calendar.[26]

Their blood now up, the Bolsheviks moved in for the kill. Although both Lenin and his party handlers later took great pains to deny that he advocated toppling the government during the 'April Days' rioting of 20–21 April 1917, the circumstantial evidence we have suggests that he must have done so at least tacitly. The two surviving party resolutions passed between 18 April and 22 April, of which Lenin's authorship was later confirmed, both denounced the Provisional Government in no uncertain terms; the first called for power to pass to the Soviets, and the second advocated fraternisation with the Germans at the front.[27] Whether on Lenin's cue or spontaneously, Bolshevik agitators fanned out across Petrograd and Moscow carrying banners that read 'Down with the Provisional Government', 'Down with Milyukov' and 'All Power to the Soviets'. In Petrograd, the rioting grew quite serious on 21 April after N. I. Podvoisky, head of the Bolshevik Military Organisation, summoned sailors of the Kronstadt Soviet, widely known as enthusiastic street brawlers, into town. When the Bolshevik agitators approached the Kazan cathedral, shots were fired (to this day it is unknown by whom), and three people were killed. Once the failure of the putsch (if that is indeed what it was) had become clear, the Bolshevik Central Committee disowned further anti-government agitation in a resolution passed on 22 April. Lenin himself stayed mostly indoors during the rioting, uncertain, as he put it in his own postmortem, 'whether at that anxious moment the mass had shifted strongly to our side'.* Whatever Lenin's real role in the April Days, the pro-government counter-demonstrators had few doubts who was responsible, as many of their banners read 'Down with Lenin!'[28]

In scarcely two weeks, Lenin had utterly radicalised the Russian political landscape. To be sure, Chernov and other Social Revolutionaries shared Lenin's opposition to the 'imperialist war', and there were plenty of labour and socialist radicals who remained wary of the Provisional Government and Milyukov in particular. But until Lenin's arrival on the scene, these sentiments had remained inchoate and largely unexpressed. Whether or not activists and politicians agreed with him, Lenin's uncompromising views had become impossible to ignore. Judging by the aftermath of the April Days, which saw both Milyukov and Alexander Guchkov, the minister of defence, resign their posts, the Leninist opposition had established a kind of veto power

---

* Confusingly though revealingly, Lenin later insisted that the Bolsheviks had 'merely wanted to carry out a peaceful reconnaissance of the enemy's strength, not to give battle'. But he also admitted, as if nonchalantly, that it had been the first Bolshevik 'attempt to resort to violent means'.

over Russian foreign policy, if not yet outright control. Lenin was not alone responsible for the fall of Russia's liberals in May 1917, but he had a lot to do with it. In terms of political marketing, Lenin had established a powerful brand as the leader of the anti-war, anti-government opposition. All he had to do was stand firm on principle, and wait for Russia's leaders to flounder while prosecuting an increasingly unpopular war.

It was no easy task to square the circle of a post-imperialist foreign policy – certainly not with Lenin waiting to pounce on any mistake. In a new declaration of war aims dated 5 May 1917, the revamped, post-liberal cabinet vowed to 'democratise the army' and disowned imperialist war aims, while also asserting, a bit less convincingly, that 'a defeat of Russia and her Allies would be a great misfortune for all peoples, and would delay or make impossible a universal peace'.[29] On 15 May 1917, the post-Milyukov Foreign Ministry tried to reconcile the Ottoman partition terms of Sazonov-Sykes-Picot with the Soviet's 'peace without annexations' principle. As if to confirm that the ghosts of Russian imperialism were not easily buried, the new statement of revolutionary Russia's war aims referred to 'provinces of Asiatic Turkey taken by right of war' before asserting, in an apparent contradiction, that the former Ottoman vilayets of Van, Bitlis and Erzurum would be 'forever Armenian'. Trying to blend together the old imperialist paternalism with the new idealism, the memorandum stipulated, awkwardly, that these 'Armenian' provinces would be administered by Russian officials, who would help repatriate Armenian, Kurdish and Turkish refugees.[30]

All across the lands of the former tsarist empire in May and June 1917 and especially on the military fronts, furious and fractious debates were conducted over the war and whether to pursue it, over war aims and their meaning, and over Lenin himself. Alexander Kerensky, Guchkov's successor as minister of war, went on a barnstorming tour of the European fronts prior to the planned Galician offensive of June, trying to rally troops behind the idea that they were the vanguard of a new Russia, fighting no longer for the wretched tsar and his secret treaties but for democracy and the allies, socialism and the people. Most accounts seem to agree that these pep talks were well received, although the effect 'evaporated as soon as Kerensky left the scene'.* In Tiflis, headquarters of the Army of the Caucasus, which had dealt Turkey a series of near-death blows in 1916, mutinous sentiment was virtually non-existent. 'The membership of the soldiers' committees,' reported the new commander-in-chief Nikolai Yudenich (who had replaced the Romanov Grand Duke Nicholas), resolved 'to conduct the war to a victorious end'.[31] In the Black Sea port from which Russia's amphibious operations against the Bosphorus were to be launched, morale had likewise remained generally robust after the February Revolution. 'Of course there are extremists here as well as in other parts,' G. W. Le Page, a British naval liaison officer, reported from Sevastopol on 29 April 1917, 'but the general feeling is that the war must be pushed on until the military power of the Central Powers is crushed.'[32] In mid May, the sailors' soviet of Sevastopol debated the question of whether to invite Lenin – already notorious for his advocacy of ending the war immediately – to town. The vote was 342 to 20 against.[33]

A closer examination of the Black Sea fleet provides a fascinating case study of the impact of Lenin's doctrine of revolutionary defeatism on the Russian Revolution. While mutiny had spread through the ranks here as elsewhere after the proclamation of Order No. 1, costing the lives of about twenty naval officers in all, fleet commander Alexander Kolchak claimed to have restored discipline by the end of April.[†] While a more egalitarian ethos prevailed on shore, with the saluting of 'bluejackets' frowned upon, once on board most men obeyed orders.

---

* In the David Lean epic *Doctor Zhivago*, a like-minded officer stands atop a beer barrel exhorting the men to defend their homes, their women – not to shamefully surrender to the Germans. The men cheer: until the barrel gives way and the commissar falls into the beer. The men laugh, and shoot him.

† Bad as this sounds, mutinies in the Baltic fleet in spring 1917 were far more serious, costing at least 150 lives.

Even as chaos was spreading through the armies, Russian warships continued operating with impunity up and down the Black Sea littoral. As late as 10 and 14 August 1917, Russian squadrons landed troops ashore on Turkey's northern coastline near Trabzon. Right up to the Bolshevik seizure of power, what remained of a functioning officer corps at Black Sea command continued planning for a major amphibious landing at Sinop.[34]

By contrast, after the Bolsheviks seized power in October, what remained of Russia's Black Sea fleet – two (below-strength) dreadnoughts, the *Volya* and the *Svobodnaia Rossiya*, five destroyers, some transports and torpedo boats, a few submarines – was sent to anchor at Sevastopol. Within weeks these ships had been rendered all but useless, as any officers opposed to Bolshevism had been lynched. By early April 1918, German intelligence estimated that its striking power had been reduced by 99 per cent.[35]

In the armies on the European fronts, the destructive wages of Leninism were felt more quickly than in the Ottoman theatre. Much, to be sure, still remains murky about the mutinies and desertions that ensued in the wake of the February Revolution, beginning with the scale of both. According to Russian military files, between March and May 1917, the Northern Army (facing the Germans) and the Western (facing the Austro-Hungarians in Galicia and Romania) saw about 25,000 desertions apiece, of which roughly three quarters occurred in rear areas. Plenty of eyewitnesses reported seeing 'AWOL' soldiers milling about the towns of European Russia in large numbers, suggesting that the official numbers may be low. Nonetheless, the fact remains that the vast majority of front-line troops stayed loyal (and even some of those who 'deserted' later returned to their units). As late as June 1917, prior to the so-called 'Kerensky offensive' launched in Galicia, the Russian armies in Europe remained largely intact.[36]

The drumbeat of Bolshevik propaganda, however, was beginning to take its toll. *Soldatskaia Pravda*, aimed at the army, and *Okopnaia Pravda*, distributed directly to front-line troops, ramped up to a combined print-run of some 100,000 in May and June 1917, enough to 'supply one Bolshevik daily per company,' even while *Soldatskaia Pravda* churned out some '350,000 pamphlets and broadsheets'.[37] Contemporaries had no way of knowing – as we do today – that funds for this anti-war propaganda came from the German Foreign Office, wired in to Petrograd by way of Olof Aschberg's Nya Banken in Stockholm (the record of at least one of these wires was preserved on the Russian side; German sources are voluminous and entirely backed up by Aschberg's own confessions both under interrogation and in his memoirs).[38] Still, it was obvious to everyone that, as Allan Wildman wrote in *The End of the Russian Imperial Army*, 'Bolshevik publications ... were now reaching the front in massive quantities.'[39] It is impossible to know precisely what effect this propaganda had on the men, but letters from troops on the Galician front, collected by military censors, suggest that it may have gravely undermined Kerensky's famous barnstorming tour prior to the June offensive.[40]

On 16 June 1917, Russia's armies opened a two-day artillery barrage against the Austrians in Galicia. Diversionary offensive feints were opened on German positions further north. The bombardment was effective, at least in Galicia. Austrian positions were quickly abandoned: Russian troops marched forward for nearly two days without encountering resistance. But the Russian advance stopped even before any serious counter-attacks commenced, because most of the men – whether out of exhaustion or the effects of Bolshevik propaganda – had no desire to see combat, certainly not of the offensive variety. As soon as German reinforcements arrived, the Russian advance turned into headlong flight. There is an extraordinary photograph of Russian soldiers fleeing after they learned that the Germans were in Galicia. The original caption, as published in the *Daily Mirror*, tells the story elegantly: 'Soldiers running away, leaving their arms. The enemy was still 12 miles distant.'[41]

Whether or not Lenin's peace propaganda had played any role in Kerensky's ill-fated offensive, the Bolsheviks lost no time in capitalising on the fallout. To shore up faltering morale in Galicia, the First Machine Gun Regiment, largest unit of the Petrograd garrison, was ordered to the front on 30 June. Unbeknownst to Kerensky and the generals, this unit had been powerfully infected with Bolshevik defeatist propaganda. Its men refused to obey the summons, instead holding a series of protest meetings.

Capitalising on the disarray, the Bolsheviks denounced the government and Kerensky's Galician offensive. Curiously, Lenin was nowhere to be found (it emerged later that he had gone into hiding in Finland). Instead, Trotsky, who had recently arrived from New York City and converted to Lenin's cause (although he had not yet formally joined the Bolshevik party), led the charge. The Bolshevik boss from the naval base of Kronstadt, the appositely named Raskolnikov, rallied radical sailors (many of them anarchists) behind the slogan 'Beat the bourgeois'. Kronstadt provided the striking power for the impending coup: some 5,000 armed men, who disembarked in Petrograd at 11 a.m. on 4 July (17 July New Style). Pro-Bolshevik factory workers and mutineers from the First Machine Gun Regiment surrounded the Tauride Palace, which housed the Petrograd Soviet. Lenin now surfaced, almost certainly to take personal command of the putsch. Raskolnikov's sailors marched down Nevsky Prospekt before turning on to Liteinyi Street – into a hail of gunfire. Raskolnikov's men hit the ground; some were killed, in the first violence in the capital since the February Revolution. Behind the scenes, the Bolsheviks drew up a shadow cabinet for their would-be government. Teams of 'ten to fifteen men in trucks and armored cars lorded it over the city', seizing whatever buildings, bridges and strongpoints they felt like taking. Several anti-Bolshevik newspapers were forcibly shut down, including the old pre-revolutionary *Novoe Vremya*. Thus far only Raskolnikov's Kronstadt brawlers had met serious resistance: but they recovered to seize the Tauride Palace, seat of both the Provisional Government and Ispolkom, just past 4 p.m. With most of the city already in the control of pro-Bolshevik factions of one kind or another, and with the combined forces of the Provisional Government and Ispolkom amounting to about six outmatched bodyguards, all eyes turned to Lenin. A petition, signed by Bolshevik factory committees, had already been prepared demanding that the Petrograd Soviet take power.

Demonstrators outside the Tauride Palace were growing impatient; one even shouted at Chernov, the Left SR agriculture minister, 'Take power, you son of a bitch, when it's given you!' Would Lenin mount the rostrum to announce as promised, 'all power to the Soviets'?[42]

He never did. Curiously, Lenin lost his nerve just as history's stage beckoned, making only a few brief remarks to the Kronstadt sailors before disappearing from view. To this day we do not know why Lenin backed down in what appeared to be his moment of political triumph: was it stage fright? Cowardice? Or his analysis of the balance of forces, which suggested that the Bolsheviks had not yet won over enough soldiers and workers in Petrograd to legitimise a putsch? Or was it – as Richard Pipes has suggested – Lenin's fear of being caught in an overt act of treason, now that rumours were swirling that the government would publish a dossier of his dealings with the Germans?[43]

Lending credence to Pipes's argument was the fact that Pavel Pereversev, Kerensky's minister of justice, published the first bit of treasonous evidence against Lenin on the afternoon of 4 July 1917, even as the final showdown was brewing at the Tauride Palace. Although Pereversev, ostensibly in order to hold back his 'smoking guns' for an upcoming treason trial, released only the least damaging material in the government's possession, the revelation was still enough to 'electrify' the Petrograd garrison. Regular army troops rapidly blanketed the capital, throwing Bolshevik forces into disarray. The Tauride Palace was retaken by government loyalists, mutineers from the First Machine Gun Regiment were disarmed, the *Pravda* printing plant was destroyed, and some 800 insurrectionists – including Trotsky and Kamenev, though not Lenin – were arrested.

Next day, the government ordered Lenin's arrest for 'high treason and organizing an armed uprising'. 'Now they are going to shoot us,' Lenin told Trotsky – before shaving his beard and fleeing for Finland. The Justice Ministry began preparations for a show trial to discredit Bolshevism for ever. It seemed that Lenin's moment had come and gone. Politically, the Bolsheviks, as suspected German agents, appeared to be finished.[44]

Lenin was, however, fortunate in his enemies. For his own mysterious reasons, Kerensky never went ahead with the treason trial against the Bolsheviks, and most of those arrested had been released by the end of summer. Lenin, from the safety of Finland, was thus left free to flood the armies with more defeatist propaganda while he plotted the next Bolshevik attack on the government. In a kind of backhanded compliment to Lenin, Kerensky, who now took over as prime minister (he was also war and naval minister), ordered the removal of the Romanov crown jewels from Petrograd after the attempted Bolshevik putsch, shipping them to Moscow to be hidden in the Kremlin armoury.[45]* He also decreed the deportation of the Romanovs from Tsarskoe Selo to Tobolsk in Siberia on 7 July 1917, for similar reasons of security.

In the three months following his German-sponsored return to Russia, Lenin had utterly radicalised the Bolshevik party line, engineered two abortive putsches against the Provisional Government, and put such a scare into its outstanding figure that Kerensky had evacuated the Romanov family, and its illustrious treasures, from Petrograd to keep them from falling into Bolshevik hands. These were considerable achievements. But Lenin was just getting started.

What might the Russian political and strategic landscape have looked like in July 1917, without Lenin's arrival? If the Germans, that is, had not sent Lenin, Krupskaia, Radek, Zinoviev et al. to Russia in April – nor wired funds from Stockholm to Petrograd for Leninist propaganda? While it is impossible to know for sure, certain key factors call out for attention. First, without German funds the Russian armies in Europe would not have been bombarded with anywhere near the level of defeatist propaganda they were that fateful spring. While mutinous sentiment in the Petrograd garrison, which reached critical levels by

---

* So well did Kerensky hide the Romanov treasure in the Kremlin that the Bolsheviks did not find it until March 1922.

the end of February, developed largely independently of Germano-Bolshevik influence, the mood at the front seems to have been far less poisonous at the time of the February Revolution, and might have remained so. Without the April Days rioting, mainstream liberal figures like Milyukov and Guchkov might have remained at the helm through June and possibly July, taking some of the political pressure off Kerensky as he tried to alleviate the worst tensions surrounding Order No. 1 and square the circle between the Petrograd Soviet and the army. Had a Galician offensive still been ordered in June, it is likely that Russian morale would still have cracked as soon as German reinforcements arrived, with a concomitant political crisis back in the capital. The man of the hour, however, would likely have been Chernov instead of Lenin: and Chernov was not a wrecker. With Chernov's mediation, some kind of compromise could have been reached, with the Soviet accepting a restoration of officers' authority in exchange for a pledge from Alexeev, Brusilov or Kornilov – or whoever emerged as the most acceptable commander-in-chief to the men – not to order more futile offensives. The disintegration of the Russian army would then have followed the French model following the Chemin-des-Dames mutinies of May 1917, which saw Philippe Pétain emerge as a man ordinary soldiers trusted not to waste their lives unnecessarily.

Because Russia was a far less cohesive country and society than France, we should not be overly optimistic about her political prospects in this counterfactual. Still, without a towering personality like Lenin to channel anti-war sentiment in the most nihilistic possible direction, it is easy to imagine a less destructive course in 1917.

Much would still have depended on the Germans. Not having Lenin wreaking havoc behind the front line, the German high command might have resumed the offensive more quickly on the eastern front, dealing Russia a decisive blow and discrediting the mainstream politicians – Milyukov, Guchkov and Kerensky – who had chosen to continue the war. Still, at some point the Germans would have stopped in order to impose their peace terms and free up forces for the west. Had statesmen of the calibre of Milyukov been involved, it is not hard to imagine a much less harsh treaty than Brest-Litovsk, which, because not negotiated by reputed German agents like the Bolsheviks, would also have had a better chance of being accepted as legitimate by the Western powers. Armistice talks in the east might even have turned into the general peace conference the Germans desperately wanted Brest-Litovsk to be. Without the 'poisoned chalice' of a Bolshevised Russia tempting them into prolonging the world war into 1918 with vistas of eastern 'Lebensraum', the Germans might even have accepted mediation from the United States (still an aloof 'Associate Power' whose troops had not yet seen combat) to broker a compromise peace. Russia would still have lost a great deal of territory in the post-war settlement and forfeited any chance at conquering Constantinople. But this would have been a small price to pay for avoiding all the horrors to come.

6

THE KORNILOV AFFAIR: A TRAGEDY OF ERRORS

August 1917

RICHARD PIPES

T HE INCIDENT KNOWN IN RUSSIAN HISTORY as the 'Kornilov affair' – the feud between the prime minister, Alexander Kerensky, and the head of the armed forces, General Lavr Kornilov, in August 1917 – virtually assured the success of the Bolshevik coup two months later. But it also had a deeper significance. It demonstrated that critical historical events could be caused not only by determination and force but also by confusion and misunderstanding. None of the participants in this affair desired what turned out to be its outcome. Yet they made it all but inevitable.

In early July 1917, after some hesitation, the Bolsheviks in Petrograd attempted to take advantage of the mutiny of a Machine Gun regiment whose men refused to go to the front, to seize power in the name of the Soviet. The attempt failed after the government released information about Lenin's dealings with the Germans. This intelligence angered the troops and ended their mutiny. Many Bolsheviks were arrested and Lenin once again had to flee. The challenge to the Provisional Government from the left seemed contained.

It was replaced by a challenge from the right that Kerensky considered to be far more dangerous. As he would write after the events, 'It was only from that quarter [the right] that we faced any real danger at that time.'[1] Indeed, then and afterwards, he was absolutely convinced that the military were involved in a 'conspiracy' to remove him from power and install a dictator.[2] This judgement, based on no evidence, was to prove a fatal miscalculation. It led to a needless conflict with General Kornilov that opened to the Bolsheviks the door to power.

Kornilov, who was forty-seven years old at the time, was born into a family of Siberian Cossacks. In 1915, while commanding a division, he was wounded and taken prisoner by the Austrians. He managed to escape and make his way back to Russia. A man of legendary courage, he watched with dismay the disintegration of Russia's armed forces and the helplessness of the Provisional Government in dealing with it. In late summer 1917 he concluded that this government had become a captive of socialist internationalists and enemy agents planted in the Soviet.

Although he was not a political man, this judgement made him receptive to suggestions that he assume dictatorial authority.

After the abortive Bolshevik putsch, Kerensky turned to Kornilov to restore discipline in the armed forces. On 19 July he offered him the post of commander-in-chief. Kornilov, however, wanted major reforms before he would accept the appointment: restoration of army discipline, reintroduction of the death penalty for desertion or mutiny, the imposition of discipline in defence industries. These conditions placed Kerensky in a quandary for he was dependent on the Soviet, which was unlikely to consent to these stipulations. Kornilov informed Kerensky on what conditions he would be prepared to accept command over Russia's armed forces: (1) he would owe responsibility only to his conscience and the nation; (2) no one would interfere with his operational orders or command appointments; (3) the disciplinary measures which he had mentioned would apply also to the troops in the rear; and (4) the government would accept his previous requests.[3]

Kerensky was so incensed by these demands that he considered withdrawing his command offer to Kornilov but then thought better of it, attributing them to the general's 'political naïveté'. In fact, Kornilov's demands were directed at the Soviet and its Order No. 1, which gave it the authority to countermand military instructions. The negotiations between the two parties dragged on and Kornilov assumed command only on 24 July, after receiving assurances that his conditions would be met.

Unfortunately, Kerensky could not keep his promises to Kornilov. For one, he was entirely dependent on the Executive Committee of the Soviet, which regarded all attempts to restore military discipline, especially in the rear, as 'counter-revolutionary'. To carry out his promises to Kornilov would have forced him to break with the socialists, his principal supporters. Furthermore, he came to view the general as a rival who wanted to replace him. So, instead of cooperating with Kornilov by honouring his pledges, he steadily retracted them: on 7 August he stated that he would not, under any circumstances, agree to introducing the death penalty for soldiers serving in the rear of the front. And eleven days later the Soviet passed by a virtually unanimous vote a resolution proposed by the Bolsheviks to abolish the death penalty for front-line troops.

In the person of the prime minister and the general, two Russias confronted each other: the Russia of international socialism and the Russia of patriotism. There could be no conciliation between them.

On 3 August, Kornilov came to Petrograd to brief a closed cabinet meeting on the military situation. While he was describing the balance of forces, Kerensky leaned over and in a whisper warned him to be careful. Kornilov assumed that the warning concerned the minister of agriculture, V. M. Chernov.

This incident had a shattering effect on him for he interpreted it to mean that at least one minister was suspected of leaking military secrets. He came to regard the Provisional Government as disloyal and incompetent.

On 6 or 7 August, Kornilov ordered three badly undermanned divisions to move up to a position roughly equidistant between Moscow and Petrograd. When asked to explain this order he said that he wanted these troops to be in a position to suppress a potential Bolshevik coup in either city, with or without the government's consent. Russia, he felt, desperately needed 'firm authority'. 'I am not a counter-revolutionary,' he explained,

I despise the old regime, which badly mistreated my family. There is no return to the past and there cannot be any. But we need an authority that could truly save Russia, which would make it possible to end the war honorably and lead her to a Constituent Assembly ... Our current government has solid individuals but also those who ruin things, who ruin Russia. The main thing is that presently Russia lacks authority and that such an authority must be created. Perhaps I shall have to exert some pressure on the government. It is possible that if disorders break out in Petrograd, after they had been suppressed I will have to join the government and participate in the establishment of a new, strong authority.[4]

On 8 August, the Ministry of War presented Kerensky with two lists, one of left-oriented persons, the other of right-oriented ones, all of whom should be arrested. Kerensky agreed to the arrest of all conservative politicians but hesitated to sign the list of radical ones.[5]

On 14 August, Kornilov made an appearance at the State Conference, which Kerensky had convened in Moscow to rally public support. When Kornilov turned up at the Bolshoi Theatre he was cheered and carried aloft by the crowd; the right-wing delegates gave him a riotous welcome. Kerensky felt thoroughly threatened by this reception of his rival. As he testified subsequently 'after the Moscow conference it was clear to me that the next attempt at a blow would come from the right and not from the left'.*[6]

In mid August, Boris Savinkov, the man in charge of the Ministry of War, received from French intelligence information that the Bolsheviks were planning at the beginning of September an all-out effort to seize power. Kerensky disbelieved this information but he realised that it could be useful in neutralising Kornilov. So he asked Savinkov to proceed to Mogilev, the locale of the military headquarters, in order

---

* Kerensky told this author in private conversation that his actions at the time were strongly influenced by the experience of the French Revolution when indeed the threat came from Bonaparte.

to liquidate the suspected officer conspiracy and to despatch the Third Cavalry Corps to Petrograd for the purpose of imposing martial law and defending the Provisional Government from any and all assaults, and, in particular, the assault of the Bolsheviks, who had rebelled on 3–5 July and who, according to information from foreign intelligence, were once again preparing to rise.[7]

Later, Kerensky would accuse Kornilov of sending the same cavalry corps, commanded by General Alexander Krymov, to the capital in order to unseat him.

Savinkov arrived in Mogilev on 22 August and stayed there for two days. He told Kornilov that the government had information of an impending Bolshevik putsch and that in order to deal with it Kerensky wanted to withdraw Petrograd and its suburbs from the Petrograd Military district and place it under his personal command. Kornilov was not pleased with this proposal but consented. Then Savinkov added that the prime minister wanted the Third Cavalry Corps to be moved to the capital where it would also come under government control. If necessary, he added, the government would carry out a 'merciless' operation against the Bolsheviks and, should it side with them, also the Petrograd Soviet. All this was prevarication for, as mentioned, Kerensky did not believe the Bolsheviks would act.

Kornilov responded as follows:

I must tell you that I no longer believe in Kerensky and the Provisional Government. In the Provisional Government serve such people as Chernov and such ministers as Avksentiev. The only salutary measure for the country is firm authority. This the Provisional Government is unable to provide … As concerns Kerensky, he is not only weak and indecisive but also insincere.[8]

Kornilov took the prime minister's instructions at face value. As they were parting, he told Savinkov that he supported Kerensky because the country needed him.[9]

Following Savinkov's departure, Kornilov issued the following order to General Krymov:

> In the event that you receive from me or directly on the spot information that the Bolshevik uprising had begun, you are to move without delay with the Corps to Petrograd, occupy the city, disarm the units of the Petrograd garrison that have joined the Bolshevik movement, disarm the Petrograd population, and disperse the Soviet. [10]

This instruction implemented Kerensky's order.

Savinkov reported to Kerensky on 25 August that all his commands would be carried out.

At this point a well-meaning but bumbling individual threw a monkey wrench into a situation already teeming with misunderstanding. He was Vladimir Nikolaevich Lvov, a man of burning ambitions but few talents with which to realise them. A member of the Duma as a conservative Octobrist, he had served for several months after the February Revolution as Procurator of the Holy Synod but in July 1917 Kerensky dismissed him from this post. In August, he joined a group of conservative intellectuals in Moscow who were eager to save Russia from collapse. He and his friends believed that the Provisional Government needed to be strengthened with the inclusion of representatives of business as well as the armed forces.

According to Lvov's recollections, in mid August he heard rumours of conspiracies at Kornilov's headquarters to proclaim the general dictator. He felt it his duty to alert Kerensky to these rumours, and duly met with him on 22 August. Kerensky paid attention to what Lvov told him, namely that it was necessary to include in the cabinet persons enjoying close relations with the military, but later denied that he had authorised him to travel to Mogilev and negotiate with Kornilov. Lvov nevertheless interpreted Kerensky's interest in his opinions as giving him licence to act as an intermediary between the prime minister and the commanding general. He travelled to Mogilev, arriving there on 24 August, just as Savinkov was about to leave.

According to Kornilov's testimony given shortly after the event, Lvov announced to him 'I am coming to you from Kerensky with a commission.' He said, in Kerensky's name, that if in Kornilov's opinion Kerensky's further participation in the government was undesirable then Kerensky was prepared to resign.

Every word of this of course was an outright lie. [11]

Carelessly, without asking for Lvov's credentials, Kornilov entered with him into a highly sensitive conversation. According to Kornilov's testimony, he responded that the only escape from the difficult situation in which the country found itself was the introduction of a dictatorship and placing the country under martial law. He further said (according to Lvov's testimony given on 14 September 1917):

It is expected that between August 27 and September 1, the Bolsheviks will act. Their plan is to overthrow the government, to install themselves in its place, at once to conclude a separate peace and to disclose it to the front in order to demoralise the army and to deliver to Germany the Baltic fleet ... During the Bolshevik uprising there will occur a clash of all ... forces, there will take place incredible bedlam in the course of which the Provisional Government, without a doubt, will collapse. [12]

Kornilov further said that he was not striving for power and would subordinate himself to a dictator but if the Provisional Government were to offer him dictatorial powers he would not refuse. He asked Lvov to warn Kerensky that since the Petrograd Bolsheviks were making preparations for a rising his life was at risk and hence it would be prudent for him to come to the headquarters. Once there, Kornilov intended to discuss with him the reorganisation of the government. [13]

The interview over, Lvov left for Petrograd. On 26 August, he met with Kerensky. As in the interview with Kornilov he had pretended to represent the prime minister, so he now affected the role of an agent of the general. He told Kerensky that Kornilov demanded dictatorial powers. According to Kerensky, on hearing this, his first reaction was to burst into laughter. But laughter soon yielded to alarm. He asked Lvov to put Kornilov's demands in writing. This is what Lvov wrote down:

General Kornilov proposes:

1. That martial law be proclaimed in Petrograd.
2. That all military and civil authority be transferred into the hands of the commander-in-chief.
3. That all ministers, not excluding the Prime Minister, resign and that provisional executive authority be transferred to deputy ministers until the commander-in-chief had constructed a cabinet.

Petrograd, August 26, 1917 V. Lvov [14]

None of which, in fact, Kornilov had demanded.

As soon as he had read these words, Kerensky recalled, everything became clear: a military coup was in the making. But to make absolutely certain that this was indeed so, he decided to contact Kornilov directly by telegraph and invited Lvov to come to the office of the minister of war at 8 p.m. to participate in the conversation. Lvov was late and after half an hour's wait, Kerensky initiated the discourse in the course of which he would impersonate Lvov. The following is the complete text of the exchange as recorded on the telegraphic tapes:

Kerensky: Prime Minister on the line. We are awaiting General Kornilov.
Kornilov: General Kornilov on the line.
Kerensky: How do you do, General. V. N. Lvov and Kerensky are on the line. We ask you to confirm that Kerensky can act in accordance with the information conveyed to him by Vladimir Nikolaevich [Lvov].

Kornilov: How do you do, Alexandr Fedorovich. How do you
do, Vladimir Nikolaevich. To confirm once again the outline
of the situation in which, I believe, the country and the army
find themselves, an outline of which I sketched out to Vladimir
Nikolaevich with the request that he convey it to you, let me
declare once more that the events of the last few days and those
already in the offing make it imperative to reach a completely
definite decision in the shortest possible time.

Kerensky [impersonating Lvov]: I, Vladimir Nikolaevich, am
inquiring about this definite decision which has been taken, which
you have asked me to inform Alexandr Fedorovich strictly in
private. Without such confirmation from you personally, Alexandr
Fedorovich hesitates to completely trust me.

Kornilov: Yes, I confirm that I asked you to transmit my urgent
request to Alexandr Fedorovich to come to Mogilev.

Kerensky: I, Alexandr Fedorovich, take your reply to confirm the
words reported to me by Vladimir Nikolaevich. It is impossible for
me to do that and leave today, but I hope to leave tomorrow. Will
Savinkov be needed?

Kornilov: I urgently request that Boris Viktorovich [Savinkov]
come along with you. What I said to Vladimir Nikolaevich applies
equally to Boris Viktorovich. I would beg you most sincerely not to
postpone your departure beyond tomorrow …

Kerensky: Are we to come only if there are demonstrations,
rumours of which are circulating, or in any event?

Kornilov: In any event.

Kerensky: Goodbye. We shall meet soon.

Kornilov: Goodbye.[15]

The two men were talking at cross purposes. Kerensky now was
certain that Kornilov wanted him at his headquarters in order to place
him under arrest and proclaim himself dictator. But it is known from
eyewitnesses that when their conversation was over Kornilov heaved
a sigh of relief, interpreting Kerensky's agreement to come to Mogilev

to mean that he was willing to work jointly on the formation of a new and strong government.

On the basis of such flimsy evidence, Kerensky decided on an open break with Kornilov. When Lvov belatedly turned up, he had him arrested. Later that night he convened a cabinet meeting. After telling the ministers what had transpired, he asked and obtained full dictatorial powers to deal with the emergency. The cabinet resigned, never to meet again: the Provisional Government, in effect, ceased to exist. Next, Kerensky sent a wire to Kornilov in which he dismissed him from the post of commander-in-chief and ordered him to report at once to Petrograd. The dismissal, according to Savinkov, was unlawful, because only the Provisional Government had the right to issue such an order.[16]

Kornilov, ignorant of Kerensky's interpretation of their telegraphic exchange, proceeded to help the government suppress the anticipated Bolshevik power grab. At 2.40 a.m. he cabled Savinkov:

> The [Cavalry] Corps is assembling in the environs of Petrograd toward evening August 28. Request that Petrograd be placed under martial law August 29.[17]

The receipt on the morning of 27 August of Kerensky's cable dismissing Kornilov threw the generals into utter confusion.

Their initial reaction was to treat it as a forgery not only because it made no sense in terms of the conversation the two men had had the previous night but also because it was improperly formatted. On second thoughts, the generals decided that the cable was perhaps genuine but sent under duress, possibly because the prime minister was a prisoner of the Bolsheviks. Kornilov, therefore, decided to ignore the cable's orders and commanded General Krymov to accelerate the advance of his cavalry corps to the capital.

That afternoon Savinkov contacted Kornilov who told him he was convinced that Kerensky's order dismissing him had been issued under the pressure of the Soviet: he further said that he would not leave his post and asked to meet Kerensky and Savinkov to clear up what he called a 'misunderstanding'.

Kerensky, in the meantime, issued to the press a communiqué over his signature of the following contents:

> On August 26, General Kornilov sent to me Duma Deputy Vladimir Nikolaevich Lvov to demand that the Provisional Government transfer to General Kornilov full civil and military authority with the proviso that he himself, at his own discretion, would appoint a new government to administer the country. The authority of Duma Deputy Lvov to make such a proposal was subsequently confirmed to me by General Kornilov in a direct wire conversation.[18]

Kerensky's accusation threw Kornilov into uncontrollable rage. After reading it, he no longer thought of the prime minister as a captive of the Bolsheviks but as the initiator of a despicable provocation intended to discredit him and the armed forces. He responded by sending to all front commanders a counter appeal:

> The telegram of the Prime Minister … in its entire first part is an out-and-out lie. I did not send Duma Deputy Vladimir Lvov to the Provisional Government – he came to me as a messenger from the Prime Minister … Thus, there occurred a grand provocation which gambles with the destiny of the Fatherland …
>
> Russian people: our great homeland is dying!
>
> The moment of death is near!
>
> Compelled to speak out openly, I, General Kornilov, declare that the Provisional Government, under pressure from the Bolshevik majority in the Soviet, acts in full accord with the plans of the German General Staff …
>
> I, General Kornilov, the son of a Cossack peasant, declare to each and all that personally I desire nothing but to save Great Russia. I swear to lead the people through victory over the enemy to the Constituent Assembly, where it will decide its own destiny and choose its new political regime.[19]

This, at last, was open mutiny. Kornilov later stated that he had decided on an open break with the Provisional Government because this government had accused him of rebellion.

Kerensky responded to this challenge by enjoining military commanders to ignore orders from Kornilov and by lying about the reason the Third Cavalry Corps was approaching Petrograd, namely that he himself had requested it. He ordered Krymov to stop his advance – an order which the general obeyed because he realised that the capital was not in Bolshevik hands. Kerensky invited him to a meeting during which Krymov explained that he had moved his cavalry units to help him: as soon as he had learned of a misunderstanding between the government and headquarters he ordered his men to halt. Kerensky went into no explanations. Refusing to shake hands with the general, he ordered him to report to a military-naval court. Krymov instead went to a friend's apartment and put a bullet through his heart.

During the days that followed, Kornilov tried but failed to rally public support for his cause. Confused by disinformation spread by Kerensky, which depicted the general as a mutineer and traitor, the public ignored his pleas. On 29 August, *Izvestiia* reported that Pavel Milyukov, the leader of the liberal Constitutional Democrats (Kadets), offered his services as an intermediary between Kerensky and Kornilov but the prime minister rejected this offer on the grounds that 'there can be no talk of reconciliation'.[20]

Despondent, Kornilov did not resist when he was placed under arrest. He escaped his prison and helped found the Volunteer Army. Half a year later, in April 1918, he was killed by an artillery shell that struck his headquarters. When the Bolsheviks occupied the region where he was buried they dug out his corpse, dragged it on the streets and then tossed it on the local dump.

Was there a Kornilov 'conspiracy'? All the evidence indicates that there was none. The term implies secrecy and Kornilov did everything above board. Rather there was a Kerensky 'conspiracy' whose aim was to discredit the popular general and elevate the prime minister to a position of unrivalled popularity. The source of the problem was Kerensky's obsessive conviction that the threat to his regime and democracy in Russia came from the right, not the left. As he would tell a commission appointed to investigate the Kornilov affair on 8 October 1917, that is, some two weeks before the Bolsheviks would seize power in Petrograd, and which they would hold for most of the century, 'I knew for sure there would be no Bolshevik campaigns [*vystuplenia*].'[21] This commission exonerated Kornilov. It concluded that Kornilov's military initiatives had been intended not to topple the Provisional Government but to defend it from the Bolsheviks. The commission accused Kerensky of 'deliberately distort[ing] the truth in the matter of Kornilov from lack of courage to admit guilt for the grandiose mistake' he had committed.[22] This author may add his opinion that, had Kerensky retired and bestowed dictatorial powers on his commander-in-chief, there is a good chance Kornilov would have crushed the Bolshevik coup of October.

There is no evidence that Kornilov craved personal power: he was prepared to serve Kerensky or assume authority, whichever would save Russia from the Germans and their Bolshevik allies. In the words of an English journalist who observed these events at first hand:

[Kornilov] wanted to strengthen the Government, not to weaken it. He did not want to encroach upon its authority, but to prevent others from doing so … He wanted to emancipate it from the illicit and paralyzing influence of the soviets. In the end, that influence destroyed Russia, and Kornilov's defiance of the Government was a last desperate effort to arrest the process of destruction.[23]

Peter Struve, an outstanding Russian intellectual who over the course of his career progressed from socialism to liberalism, and from liberalism to conservatism, in a speech delivered in Prague on the fifth anniversary of Kornilov's death had this to say:

With criminal thoughtlessness [the Provisional Government], instead of supporting the only force capable of joining the battle against Bolshevism, repelled and repulsed him, to face alone the Bolsheviks and its own weakness. The accusation that Kornilov and his associates were guilty of state treason was not only singular infamy but also the grandest political stupidity.[24]

What is incontrovertible is the fact that Kerensky's quarrel with his commander-in-chief made the Bolshevik seizure of power all but inevitable.

7

THE 'HARMLESS DRUNK': LENIN AND THE OCTOBER INSURRECTION

October 1917

ORLANDO FIGES

A T AROUND 10 P.M. on 24 October 1917, Lenin left his hiding place on the Vyborg side of Petrograd disguised in a wig and worker's cap with a bandage wrapped around his head. Accompanied by the Finnish Bolshevik, Eino Rakhia, he set off for the Smolny Institute, the Soviet headquarters, to urge his party comrades to launch an insurrection before the Soviet Congress the next day. Lenin rode through the Vyborg district in an empty tram. He badgered the conductress with questions on the latest situation in the capital, where Red Guards and soldiers were fighting for control of the railway stations and the streets. Discovering that she was a leftist, he harangued her with advice on revolutionary action. From the Finland Station the two men continued their journey on foot. Near the Tauride Palace they were stopped by a government patrol, but Kerensky's policemen mistook Lenin for a harmless drunk and let him pass.[1]

Lenin reached the Smolny shortly before midnight. The building was ablaze with lights. Trucks and armoured cars rushed to and fro laden down with troops and munitions. Machine guns had been set up outside the gates, where Red Guards on alert for 'counter-revolutionary forces' loyal to Kerensky's government checked the passes of those entering. Without a pass, Lenin only succeeded in gaining entry by squeezing past the Red Guards in a crowd. He went at once to Room 36, where the Bolshevik caucus to the Soviet Congress met. He bullied them into convening a meeting of the Central Committee, which gave the order for the insurrection to begin.

What might have happened if the government patrol had arrested Lenin on his way to the Smolny? Counterfactual ('what if?') history is only really meaningful if it hinges on a single chance event that could demonstrably have changed the course of history. That is clearly the case here. Had Lenin been arrested, we can say with reasonable certainty that the Bolsheviks would not have launched an insurrection on 25 October; that Soviet power would have been proclaimed by the Congress; and a government of all the parties in the Soviet would have been established as a consequence. In the following weeks and months there would no doubt have been bitter conflicts between the socialists. Soviet power would have been opposed by military forces on the right. But not for long: the Soviet forces would have been too strong. There would not have been a military conflict on the vast scale of the Civil War that engulfed Russia in the four years after October 1917 – a civil war that shaped the violent culture of the Bolshevik regime under Lenin and Stalin.

I

Lenin's arrival at the Smolny changed the course of history. Historians are agreed on that. Without him, the Bolsheviks would not have launched an insurrection on 25 October. There was no need to. Until Lenin's intervention, the majority of the Central Committee had not envisaged the overthrow of the Provisional Government before the opening of the Soviet Congress, and this view was shared by the Military Revolutionary Committee (MRC). Formed on 20 October to defend the Petrograd garrison against Kerensky's order to transfer the bulk of its Bolshevised troops to the northern front, the MRC became the leading organisational force of the Bolshevik uprising.

There was no need for an insurrection to establish Soviet power. Kerensky's power had collapsed. 'Nobody wants the Bolsheviks, but nobody is prepared to fight for Kerensky either,' wrote his firmest supporter, the poet and salon hostess Zinaida Gippius in her diary on 24 October.[2] After the Kornilov fiasco, bourgeois and rightist groups would have nothing more to do with the Provisional Government, and even welcomed its demise. Many preferred to let the Bolsheviks take power in the belief that they would bring the country to such ruin that *all* socialists would be discredited, whereupon the rightists would impose a military dictatorship. The Western Allies, who had backed Kerensky in the summer, also turned against him after the Kornilov crisis, partly based on rumours that he was about to make a separate peace with Germany.

With the MRC in control of the Petrograd garrison, Kerensky had lost effective military control of the capital a full five days before the armed uprising began. Belatedly, on the evening of the 24th, he tried to summon loyal troops from the northern front. His order was despatched with the forged signature of the Soviet leaders, because Kerensky feared the soldiers would not recognise the authority of the Provisional Government. By the following morning, there was still no sign of the troops, so he resolved to go off in search of them. With the railways in Bolshevik hands, he was forced to travel by car. But such was the utter helplessness of the Provisional Government that it did not have one at its disposal. Military officials had to seize a Renault from outside the American Embassy, which later launched a diplomatic protest, while a second car was found at the War Ministry, although it had no fuel and more men had to be sent out to 'borrow' some from the English Hospital. At around 11 a.m. the two cars sped out of the Winter Palace and headed out of the city. Kerensky was seated in the second car, flying the Stars and Stripes, which helped him past the MRC pickets already forming around Palace Square.

Meanwhile the Soviet delegates were arriving for the opening of the Congress in the Great Hall of the Smolny. From their composition it seemed highly likely that there would be a solid majority in favour of Soviet power. Following the Kornilov affair, there had been a sharp leftward turn in the mood of the soldiers and workers. The mass of the soldiers suspected that their officers had supported Kornilov. For this reason there was a dramatic deterioration in army discipline from the end of August. Soldiers' assemblies passed resolutions calling for peace and Soviet power. The rate of desertion rose sharply: tens of thousands left their units every day. Most of the deserters were peasants, eager to return to their villages, where the harvest season was now in full swing. Armed and organised, these peasant soldiers led the attacks on the manors that became more frequent as of September.

In the big industrial cities there was a similar process of radicalisation in the wake of the Kornilov crisis. The Bolsheviks were the principal beneficiaries of this, winning their first majority in the Petrograd Soviet on 31 August – adding to their control of the Soviets in Ivanovo-Voznesentsk (the 'Russian Manchester'), Kronstadt, Ekaterinburg, Samara and Tsaritsyn. The Soviets of Riga, Saratov and Moscow itself fell to the Bolsheviks soon afterwards. The rising fortunes of the Bolsheviks were due mainly to the fact that they were the only major political party that stood uncompromisingly for 'All power to the Soviets'.

This point bears emphasising, for one of the most basic misconceptions about the October Revolution is that the Bolsheviks were swept to power on a tide of mass support for the party. They were not. The October insurrection was a coup d'état, actively supported by a small minority of the population, but it took place in the midst of a social revolution, which was focused on the popular ideal of Soviet power. After the Kornilov crisis there was a sudden outpouring of resolutions from factories, villages and army units calling for a Soviet government, by which they understood a social revolution of their own making, led by all the parties in the All-Russian Soviet. It was to be a government specifically without the parties of the bourgeoisie, the Kadets in particular, which had been discredited by their involvement in the Kornilov movement. But almost without exception these resolutions called on all the socialist parties to participate in a Soviet government.

On the evening of 24 October, it looked as if an all-socialist government would come into being at the Soviet Congress the next day.
While Lenin was making his way towards the Smolny, Kamenev was
rushing round inside trying to win the support of the other socialist
parties for a resolution calling on the Congress to form a Soviet government. The SRs and Mensheviks, whose congress delegates met late
into the night, were coming round in favour of the plan.

Until Lenin's arrival on the scene, the Bolshevik leaders planned to
wait for the Soviet Congress, arming their supporters on the streets
to make sure it convened by defending it, if necessary, against any
'counter-revolutionary' forces attempting to close it down. Trotsky,
who in Lenin's absence had effectively assumed the leadership of the
party, repeatedly stressed the need for discipline and patience. On the
morning of the 24th, when Kerensky ordered the closure of two Bolshevik newspapers, Trotsky refused to be drawn by this 'provocation':
the MRC should be placed on alert; the city's strategic installations
should be seized as a defensive measure against any further 'counter-
revolutionary' threats; but, as he insisted at a meeting of the Bolshevik
Congress delegates in the afternoon, 'it would be a mistake to use even
one of the armoured cars which now defend the Winter Palace to arrest
the government ... This is defence, comrades. This is defence.' Later
that evening, in the Petrograd Soviet, Trotsky declared – and had good
reason to believe – that 'an armed conflict today or tomorrow, on the
eve of the Soviet Congress, is not in our plans'.[3]

2

An insurrection had not been in the Bolsheviks' immediate plans at
any point since July. The uprising of 3–4 July had ended in disaster for
the party, with hundreds of Bolsheviks arrested and Lenin forced into
hiding in Finland rather than face trial for high treason in the courts.
But Lenin disagreed with his comrades. In his view these repressions showed that the Provisional Government had been taken over
by the 'military dictatorship' – the Civil War had started – and that

meant that the party was obliged to fight or die in an armed uprising for the seizure of power. 'It is not a question of "the courts", but of *an episode in the Civil War* ... All hopes for a peaceful development of the Russian revolution have vanished for good,' he wrote on 8–10 July.[4]

After the Kornilov crisis, when the Mensheviks and SRs both moved to the left, Lenin was prepared to consider the idea of a compromise with them. Not that he gave up on his basic aim of a Bolshevik dictatorship. 'Our party,' he wrote in his article 'On Compromises' on 1 September, 'is striving after political domination *for itself*.'[5] The leftward move of the Soviets – in which the Bolsheviks were rapidly becoming a dominant force – opened up the prospect of moving once again towards Soviet power through peaceful agitation, as Lenin had proposed before the July Days. During the fortnight leading up to the opening of the Democratic Conference, on 14 September, when the power question was to be resolved, Lenin supported Kamenev's initiative to persuade the Mensheviks and SRs to break with the Kadets and join the Bolsheviks in a socialist government based on the Soviets. If the SR and Mensheviks agreed, the Bolsheviks would renounce an armed uprising and compete for power within the Soviet movement itself. But Lenin's implication remained clear: if the Soviet leaders refused, the party should prepare for the seizure of power.

The Democratic Conference failed to break the coalition of the Mensheviks and SRs with the Kadets. On 24 September, Kerensky named a new cabinet, which looked much like the old one of July–August, with the socialists technically holding a majority of the portfolios but the Kadets in several key posts. With Kamenev's plan for a socialist coalition undermined by the outcome of the Democratic Conference, Lenin reverted to his campaign in the party for an immediate uprising.

He had already begun to advocate this in two letters to the Central Committee written from Finland on the eve of the Democratic Conference. The Bolsheviks, Lenin had argued, 'can and must take state power into their own hands'. Can – because the party had already won a majority in the Moscow and Petrograd Soviets, which was 'enough to carry the people with it in any civil war', provided the party in power proposed an immediate peace and gave the land to the peasants. Must – because if it waited for the convocation of the Constituent Assembly, 'Kerensky and Co.' would take pre-emptive action, either by giving up Petrograd to the Germans or by delaying the convocation of the Constituent Assembly. Reminding his comrades of Marx's dictum that 'insurrection is an art', Lenin concluded that 'it would be naive to wait for a "formal" majority for the Bolsheviks. No revolution ever waits for that … History will not forgive us if we do not assume power now.'[6]

These two letters reached the Central Committee on 15 September. They were, to say the least, highly inconvenient for the rest of the Bolshevik leaders since the Democratic Conference had just begun and they were still committed to Kamenev's conciliatory tactics. It was decided to burn all but one copy of the letters, lest they fall into the hands of the rank-and-file Bolsheviks and spark a revolt. The Central Committee continued to ignore Lenin's advice and printed instead his earlier articles, in which he had endorsed the Kamenev line. Lenin was beside himself with rage. Afraid to return to Petrograd (Kerensky had ordered his arrest at the Democratic Conference), Lenin moved from Finland to the resort town of Vyborg, eighty miles from Petrograd, to be closer to the capital. He assaulted the Central Committee and lower-level party organisations with a barrage of impatient letters, full of violent and abusive phrases heavily underlined, in which he urged them to start the armed insurrection at once. Lenin condemned the 'parliamentary tactics' of the Bolshevik leaders and welcomed the prospect of a civil war, which they were trying to avert on the false assumption that, like the Paris Communards, they were bound to lose. On the contrary, Lenin insisted, the anti-Bolshevik forces would be no more than those aligned behind the Kornilov movement, and they were bound to win.

On 29 September, at the high point of his frustration, Lenin scribbled an angry tirade against the Bolshevik leaders, in which he denounced them as '*miserable traitors* to the proletarian cause'. They had wanted to delay the transfer of power until the Soviet Congress, whereas the moment was already ripe for the seizure of power and any delay would merely enable Kerensky to use military force against them. The workers, Lenin insisted, were solidly behind the Bolshevik cause; the peasants were starting their own war on the manors, thus ruling out the danger of an Eighteenth Brumaire, or a 'petty-bourgeois' counter-revolution, like that of 1849; while the strikes and mutinies in the rest of Europe were 'indisputable symptoms ... that we are *on the eve of a world revolution*'. To 'miss such a moment and "wait" for the Congress of Soviets would be utter idiocy, or *sheer treachery*', and if the Bolsheviks did so they would 'cover themselves with shame and destroy themselves as a party'. As a final ultimatum, he even threatened to resign from the Central Committee, thereby giving himself the freedom to take his campaign for an armed uprising to the Bolshevik rank and file, scheduled to meet at a party conference on 17 October. 'For it is my profound conviction that if we "wait" for the Congress of Soviets and let the present moment pass, we shall *ruin* the revolution.'[7]

Returning to Petrograd, where he lived under cover in the flat of a Bolshevik activist in Serdobolskaya Street on the Vyborg side, Lenin convened a secret meeting of the Central Committee on 10 October. The decision to prepare for an armed uprising was taken at this meeting, which, ironically, was held in the apartment of the Menshevik memoirist Nikolai Sukhanov, whose wife, Galina Flakserman, was a veteran Bolshevik. Of the twenty-two Central Committee members only twelve were present (the most important resolution in the history of the party was thus taken by a minority of the Central Committee). By ten votes against two (Kamenev and Zinoviev) they recognised 'that an armed uprising [was] inevitable, and the time for it fully ripe', and instructed party organisations to prepare for it as 'the order of the day'.[8]

An armed uprising had thus been put on the Bolsheviks' agenda.

But a date for it had not been set. 'The resolution of 10 October is one of the best resolutions the Central Committee has ever passed,' declared Mikhail Kalinin, 'but when the uprising will take place is uncertain – perhaps in a year.'[9] The ambivalent mood of the streets was the leaders' main concern. It was not at all clear whether the Petrograd workers and soldiers would 'come out' for an uprising. Many remembered the failure of the July uprising and the loss of workers' jobs and repressions that had followed it; they were reluctant to risk another defeat. The Bolshevik Military Organisation, which favoured an uprising, warned that the workers and the soldiers were not yet ready to come out on the party's call, though they might take to the streets if the Soviet was in danger from a 'counter-revolutionary' threat.

The same conclusion was suggested by the evidence presented to a meeting of the Central Committee on 16 October. The representatives of the Bolshevik Military Organisation, the Petrograd Soviet, the trade unions and factory committees who attended this meeting all warned of the risks involved in staging an uprising before the Soviet Congress. Krylenko stated the view of the Military Organisation that the soldiers' fighting spirit was weakening: 'they would have to be stung by something, such as the break-up of the garrison, to come out for an uprising'. Volodarsky from the Petrograd Soviet confirmed the 'general impression ... that no one is ready to rush out on to the streets but that everyone will come out if the Soviet calls'. Massive unemployment and the fear of dismissal held the workers back, according to Shmidt of the trade unions. Shliapnikov added that even in the metalworkers' union, where the party's influence was dominant, 'a Bolshevik rising is not popular and rumours of this even produce panic'. Kamenev drew the logical conclusion: 'there is no evidence of any kind that we must begin the fight before the 20th [when the Soviet Congress was due to convene]'.[10]

But Lenin was insistent on the need for immediate preparations and saw no reason to hold back in the cautious reports on the mood of the Petrograd masses: in a military coup, which is how he conceived of the seizure of power, only a small force was needed, provided it was well armed and disciplined enough.* Such was Lenin's domination of the party that he got his way. A counter-resolution by Zinoviev prohibiting the actual staging of an uprising before the Bolshevik delegates to the Soviet Congress had been consulted was defeated by 15 votes to 6, though the closeness of the vote, compared with the 19 to 2 majority in favour of Lenin's vaguer call for an uprising in the immediate future, suggests that several Bolshevik leaders had serious apprehensions about the wisdom of an insurrection before the Soviet Congress, albeit not enough to make an open stand against Lenin. Only Kamenev and Zinoviev found the courage to do that.

At the end of the meeting Kamenev declared that he could not accept its resolution, which in his view would lead the party to ruin, and submitted his resignation to the Central Committee in order to make his campaign public. He also demanded the convocation of a Party Conference, which Lenin had managed to get postponed: there was little doubt that it would oppose the call for an uprising before the Congress. On 18 October Kamenev aired his views in Gorky's newspaper, *Novaia zhizn*. 'At the present,' he wrote, 'the instigation of an armed uprising before and independent of the Soviet Congress would be an impermissible and even fatal step for the proletariat and the revolution.' This of course was to let the cat out of the bag: rumours of a Bolshevik coup had been spreading for weeks, and now the conspiracy had finally been exposed. Trotsky was forced to deny the rumours in the Petrograd Soviet, but for once his performance was less than convincing. Lenin was furious and, in a sign of the sort of purges to come, denounced Kamenev and Zinoviev in the Bolshevik press. 'Strike-breaking', 'betrayal', 'blacklegs', 'slanderous lies' and 'crime' – such terms were littered throughout the angry letters he sent on 18 and 19

---

* During September he had even thought of organising the Petrograd uprising as a military invasion from the Baltic region, where he had spent the summer and had been impressed by the revolutionary mettle of the Latvian Riflemen (who would make a substantial portion of Lenin's personal bodyguard in the early days of Soviet rule). 'It seems to me,' he had written to Smilga, 'that we have completely at our disposal only the troops in Finland and the Baltic Fleet and that only they can play a serious role.'

October. 'Mr Zinoviev and Mr Kamenev' (this was the ultimate insult – they were no longer even 'comrades') should be 'expelled from the party'.[11]

With the Bolshevik conspiracy public knowledge, the Soviet leaders resolved to delay the Soviet Congress until 25 October. They hoped that the extra five days would give them the chance to muster their supporters from the far-flung provinces. But it merely gave the Bolsheviks the extra time they needed to make the final preparations for an uprising. Moreover, it lent credibility to Lenin's claim that the Soviet leaders were planning to ditch the Soviet Congress altogether. He had always based his argument for a pre-emptive seizure of power (before the Soviet Congress) on the danger – which he either overestimated or (more likely) invented – that the Provisional Government might not allow the Congress to convene. All the local party reports had made it clear that, while the Petrograd workers and soldiers would not come out on the call of the party alone, many would do so if the Soviet were threatened. The postponement of the Congress was the provocation he needed.

3

Why was Lenin so insistent on the need for an armed uprising *before* the Soviet Congress? All the signs were that time was on the side of the Bolsheviks: the country was falling apart; the Soviets were moving to the left; and the forthcoming Congress would almost certainly endorse the Bolshevik call for a transfer of power to the Soviets. Why run the risk of civil war and possible defeat by staging an uprising that party activists in Petrograd believed was premature? Other senior Bolsheviks stressed the need for a transfer of power to coincide with the Soviet Congress. This was the view of Trotsky and many other Bolsheviks in the Petrograd Soviet executive, and since they were closely informed about the mood in the capital and would have to play a leading role in any uprising, their opinion was important. While these leaders doubted that the party had enough mass support to justify an insurrection in its name, they thought that it might be successfully carried out in the name of the Soviets. Since the Bolsheviks had conducted their campaign on the slogan of Soviet power, it was said that they needed the Congress to legitimise such an uprising and make it appear as the work of the Soviet as a whole rather than of one party. By taking this line, which would have delayed the uprising by no more than a few days, Lenin could have won widespread support in the party against those, such as Kamenev and Zinoviev, who were flatly opposed to an uprising. But Lenin was adamant – the seizure of power had to be carried out before the Congress.

Lenin justified his impatience by the notion that any delay in the seizure of power would enable Kerensky to organise repressive measures against it. Petrograd would be abandoned to the Germans. The seat of government would be moved to Moscow. The Soviet Congress would be banned. This of course was nonsense. Kerensky was quite incapable of such decisive action and, in any case, as Kamenev pointed out, the government was powerless to put any counter-revolutionary intentions into practice. Lenin was exaggerating the danger of a clampdown by Kerensky to strengthen his own arguments for a pre-emptive insurrection. There were rumours in the press that the government was planning to evacuate the capital. These no doubt reinforced his conviction that a civil war had begun, and that military victory would go to the side that dared to strike first. 'On s'engage et puis on voit.'

But there was another motive for wanting the insurrection before the Soviet Congress, quite apart from military tactics. If the transfer of power took place by a vote of the Congress itself, the result would almost certainly be a coalition government made up of all the Soviet parties. The Bolsheviks might gain the largest share of the ministerial places, if these were allocated on a proportional basis, but would still have to rule in partnership with at least the left wing – and possibly all – of the SR and Menshevik parties. This would be a resounding political victory for Kamenev, who would no doubt emerge as the central figure in such a coalition. Under his leadership, the centre of power would remain with the Soviet Congress, rather than the party; there might even be a renewed effort to reunite the Bolsheviks with the Mensheviks. As for Lenin himself, he ran the risk of being kept out of office, either on the insistence of the Mensheviks and SRs or on account of his own unwillingness to compromise with them. He would thus be consigned to the left-wing margins of his own party.

On the other hand, if a Bolshevik seizure of power took place before the Congress, then Lenin would emerge as the political master. The Congress majority would probably endorse the Bolshevik action, thereby giving the party the right to form a government of its own. If the Mensheviks and SRs could bring themselves to accept this forcible seizure of power, as a fait accompli, then a few minor places for them would no doubt be found in Lenin's cabinet. Otherwise, if they could not accept an armed seizure of power, they would have no choice but to go into opposition, leaving the Bolsheviks in government on their own. Kamenev's coalition efforts would thus be undermined; Lenin would have his Dictatorship of the Proletariat; and although the result would inevitably be to plunge the country into civil war, this was something Lenin himself accepted – and perhaps even welcomed – as a part of the revolutionary process. Civil war, in Lenin's view, was a necessary and vital phase in any social revolution, the deepening of the 'class struggle' in a military form. Since July he had been arguing that the Civil War had been started by the forces of the right, and that the seizure of power should be seen as the joining of the fight by the proletarian side. The 'class struggle' could not be resolved by political means. Russia was split into warring camps – the 'military dictatorship' and the 'Dictatorship of the Proletariat' – and it was a question of which side would prevail. 'Kto kogo,' as Lenin liked to say.

In this Leninist scenario the armed insurrection was a provocation to the Mensheviks and the SRs. It was as much against the other Soviet-based parties – and those in his party who would compromise with them in a Soviet government – as it was against the Provisional Government.

4

Lenin's arrival at the Smolny had a decisive effect. In Room 36 the mood changed dramatically, according to the Bolsheviks who were present. From defence they shifted to the offensive, issuing the order for the insurrection to begin, and getting out the maps to plan the main lines of attack. By lunchtime they had seized control of the railway stations, the post and telegraph, the state bank, the telephone exchange, police stations, and the central zone around the Winter Palace and St Isaac's Square. But the assault on the Winter Palace, where the remnants of Kerensky's cabinet were bunkered without hope of salvation in the Malachite Hall, was delayed by technical problems and postponed until 3 p.m., then 6 p.m., whereafter the MRC ceased to bother with any set deadlines at all. For Lenin these delays were infuriating: it was vital for him to have the seizure of power completed before the opening of the Soviet Congress. At around 3 p.m. he told a packed session of the Petrograd Soviet that the Provisional Government had already been overthrown. It was of course a lie but that was not the point: the fact of the seizure of power was to be so important to his political strategy over the next few hours that he was prepared to invent it. As afternoon turned into evening, he screamed at the MRC commanders to seize the Winter Palace without delay. Podvoisky recalls him pacing around in a small room in the Smolny 'like a lion in a cage. He needed the Winter Palace at any cost … he was ready to shoot us.'[12]

The assault began with a signal blast from the guns of the Baltic cruiser *Aurora* anchored in the Neva River near the Winter Palace. Just as the bombardment was getting under way, at 10.40 p.m., the Soviet Congress finally opened in the Great Hall of the Smolny. The majority of the delegates were workers and soldiers in their tunics and great-coats; their unwashed and dirty look contrasted sharply with the clean suits of the old executive members, the Mensheviks and SRs, seated on the platform for the final time. Sukhanov remarked that the 'grey features of the Bolshevik provinces' had a clear preponderance among the Congress delegates.[13] The Bolsheviks did not have an absolute majority, although with the support of the Left SRs they could push through any motion they liked. The Credentials Committee reported that 300 of the 670 delegates were Bolsheviks, 193 SRs (of whom more than half were Left SRs), while 82 were Mensheviks (of whom 14 were Internationalists). The mandates of the delegates showed an overwhelming majority in favour of a Soviet government. It was up to the Congress to decide how this should be formed. Martov proposed the formation of a united democratic government based upon all the parties in the Soviet: this, he said, was the only way to stop civil war. The proposal was met with torrents of applause. Even Lunacharsky was forced to admit that the Bolsheviks had nothing against it – they could not abandon the slogan of Soviet power – and the proposal was immediately passed by a unanimous vote.

But just as it looked as if a socialist coalition was about to be formed, news arrived of the violent storming of the Winter Palace and the arrest of Kerensky's ministers. Denouncing this 'criminal venture', which they said was bound to throw the country into civil war, a large number of the Menshevik and SR delegates walked out of the hall in protest, while the Bolshevik delegates stamped their feet, whistled and hurled abuse at them. Lenin's planned provocation – the pre-emptive seizure of power – had worked. By walking out of the Congress, the Mensheviks and SRs undermined all hopes of reaching a compromise with the Bolshevik moderates and of forming a coalition government of all the Soviet parties. The path was now clear for the Bolshevik dictatorship, based on the Soviet, which Lenin had no doubt intended all along. In the charged political atmosphere of the time, it is easy to see why the Mensheviks and SRs acted as they did. But it is equally difficult not to draw the conclusion that, by their actions, they merely played into Lenin's hands. Writing in 1921, Sukhanov admitted as much:

We completely untied the Bolsheviks' hands, making them masters of the whole situation and yielding to them the whole arena of the Revolution. A struggle at the Congress for a united democratic front might have had some success ... But by leaving the Congress, we ourselves gave the Bolsheviks a monopoly of the Soviet, of the masses, and of the Revolution. By our own irrational decision, we ensured the victory of Lenin's whole line.[14]

The effect of their walkout was to split the opposition forces, leaving Martov and the other left-wing advocates of a Soviet coalition isolated against Lenin's drive towards dictatorship. Martov made one more desperate appeal for an all-democratic government. But the mood in the hall was changing. As the mass of the delegates saw it, the Mensheviks and SRs had proved themselves to be 'counter-revolutionaries' by walking out of the Congress. They were now ready to follow the lead of the Bolsheviks in opposing the whole idea of a compromise with them. Trotsky seized the initiative and, in one of the most often-quoted speeches of the twentieth century, denounced Martov's resolution for a coalition:

> The masses of the people followed our banner and our insurrection was victorious. And now we are told: Renounce your victory, make concessions, compromise. With whom? I ask. With those wretched groups who have left us or who are making this proposal ... No one in Russia is with them any longer. A compromise is supposed to be made between two equal sides ... But here no compromise is possible. To those who have left and to those who tell us to do this we say: You are miserable bankrupts, your role is played out; go where you ought to go – into the dustbin of history.[15]

In a moment of rage, which he must have agonised over for the rest of his life, Martov shouted, 'Then we'll leave!' and walked out of the hall – and into the political wilderness. It was past two o'clock in the morning and it only remained for Trotsky, who was now clearly doing the work of Lenin, to propose a resolution condemning the 'treacherous' attempts of the Mensheviks and SRs to undermine Soviet power. In effect, this would be to give a Soviet stamp of approval to a Bolshevik dictatorship. The mass of the delegates, who probably did not grasp the political import of what they were doing (weren't they in favour of Soviet power?), raised their hands in support of Trotsky's resolution.

5

There was one more chance to force Lenin to accept a united government based on all the parties in the Soviet. On 29 October (11 November New Style), as forces loyal to Kerensky's government fought against the Red Guards on the outskirts of Petrograd as well as in the centre of Moscow, the leaders of the railwaymen's union (Vikzhel) issued an ultimatum demanding that the Bolsheviks begin talks with the other socialist parties to form an all-socialist government, threatening to bring the railways to a halt if they did not. Lenin's government could not survive if food and fuel supplies to the capital were cut. It depended on the railways for its military campaign against Kerensky's forces in Moscow and Petrograd. Without victory in Moscow, even Lenin recognised that the Bolsheviks could not stay in power on their own. The inter-party talks would have to go ahead. Kamenev was authorised to represent the party in the negotiations on the basis of Soviet power, as passed at the Congress. The right wings of the Menshevik and SR parties were unlikely to accept this, and confident that the Bolshevik regime could not last long, set exacting terms for their involvement in any government: the release of Kerensky's ministers; the abolition of the MRC; the transfer of the Petrograd garrison to the control of the Duma; and the involvement of Kerensky in the formation of the government, which was to exclude Lenin. They softened their position when Kerensky's offensive in Petrograd collapsed, offering to take part in a coalition with the Bolsheviks, provided that the leadership of the Soviet was broadened. Kamenev agreed, suggesting, in a moment of naive credulity, that the Bolsheviks would not insist on the presence of Lenin or Trotsky in the cabinet.

Lenin and Trotsky had different ideas. They had always been opposed to the Vikzhel talks: only the prospect of military defeat had brought them to negotiations. With the defeat of Kerensky's troops, and the fight for Moscow moving towards victory for the Bolsheviks, they set out to undermine the inter-party talks. At a meeting of the Central Committee on 1 November Trotsky condemned the compromise agreed by Kamenev and demanded at least 75 per cent of the cabinet seats for the Bolshevik party. There was 'no point organis-ing the insurrection if we don't get the majority,' he argued.[16] Lenin advocated leaving the talks altogether and demanded the arrest of the Vikzhel leaders as 'counter-revolutionaries' – a provocation meant to wreck the talks. Despite the objections of Kamenev, Zinoviev and others, the Central Committee agreed to present Trotsky's demand as an ultimatum to the inter-party talks and abandon them if it was rejected. The Mensheviks and SR would never accept this, as Lenin and Trotsky knew only too well. The seizure of power had irrevocably split the socialist movement in Russia, and no amount of negotiation could hope to bridge the gap. The Vikzhel talks broke down.

Perhaps there had never been much chance of a coalition Soviet government. There was a brief period in the wake of the Kornilov crisis when that might have been achieved – if only the Mensheviks and SRs had broken off emphatically from the Kadets. This was a time when Lenin was prepared to go along with Kamenev's conciliatory politics towards the other socialists. But that chance did not last long. From the middle of September Lenin was determined to seize power in an insurrection whose ulterior motive was to drive a wedge between the Bolsheviks (as the defenders of 'the Revolution') and those social-ists who opposed them (as 'counter-revolutionaries') along with the Kadets, the monarchists and the White Guards.

Without an insurrection by the Bolsheviks, Martov's resolution would have stood and a government made up of all the parties in the Soviet would have been established on 25 October. Bitter polit-ical differences between the socialists would have made this coalition unstable and difficult. No doubt there would have been many conflicts over the relationship between the Soviet government, the Constitu-ent Assembly, and other democratic bodies such as the Dumas. Lenin would have been opposed to any coalition with the Right SRs and Mensheviks, which might have split the Bolsheviks. In all probability, there would still have been a civil war, albeit one not on the scale of the military conflict that engulfed Soviet Russia between 1917 and 1921. While Kerensky and the White Guards were bound to organise a military force against a Soviet government, their resistance was unlikely to last long.

From the October insurrection and the establishment of a Bolshevik dictatorship to the Red Terror and the Civil War – with all its consequences for the evolution of the Soviet regime – there is a line of historical inevitability. But Lenin's victory on 25 October was itself the outcome of an accident. For if that 'harmless drunk' had been recognised by the government patrol, history would have turned out differently.

8

THE SHORT LIFE AND EARLY DEATH OF RUSSIAN DEMOCRACY: THE DUMA AND THE CONSTITUENT ASSEMBLY

January 1918

TONY BRENTON

THE BACKGROUND

Russia does not have a rich democratic tradition. The 'Mongol Yoke' (1237–1480) imposed thoroughgoing despotism on the Russian lands even while contemporary Western Europe saw the emergence of embryonic consultative and representative institutions. The most cited example of a medieval Russian city whose civic liberties approached those of its Western analogues, Novgorod the Great, lost those liberties as soon as it fell under the sway of Muscovy in 1478 (and the city's still insufficiently subservient inhabitants were then massacred a century later by Ivan the Terrible). Throughout the tsarist period the full title of the ruler began 'By the grace of God, Tsar and Autocrat of all the Russias...' This was no mere verbal flourish. Russian Tsars exercised genuinely autocratic authority. They had, and used, the power of life and death unmediated by any independent judicial or legislative authority. Early Western visitors of the sixteenth and seventeenth centuries were astonished at the readiness of the most powerful aristocrats to abase themselves before their ruler. Those who wanted to modernise

Russia, notably Peter the Great, saw autocracy as the means to do it. Peter made the peasants serfs and the nobility state servants. Society became a barracks, the Orthodox Church a department of state. Even Catherine the Great, an enlightened modern-minded German princess, abandoned her thoughts of constitutionalism with the weary observation 'I will be an autocrat; that is my job. The Good Lord will forgive me; that is his.'[1] The prevailing metaphor, right up to the end of the regime, was of the tsar as father to his often unruly and in need of discipline, but essentially loving, children.

Russia's official ideology for much of the nineteenth century was explicitly 'Orthodoxy, Autocracy and Nationality'. Only in the middle of that century was the 'Liberator Tsar', Alexander II, able to abolish the system under which the vast majority of Russians were directly owned either by the state or by the land-holding class, and to introduce a limited form of representative local government. In one of history's more fascinating might-have-beens, he was also in 1881 moving towards introducing a very limited representative element into Russian central government. He had no compunction about describing this plan as a 'constitution' – implying real legal limits on the tsar's power. But his assassination that year cut the initiative off, and confirmed his successor in the view that autocracy was the only way to rule Russia. Thus, when Alexander's grandson, Nicholas II, became tsar in 1894, he inherited the title and power of 'Unlimited Autocrat'. His war minister nicely summarised the regime view of the world when he wrote, 'Only before God and History are sovereigns responsible for the paths they choose to take for the wellbeing of their people.'[2]

As the nineteenth century progressed however, the rising demand throughout Europe for more representative government and rights for the people threatened to infect Russia too. But while elsewhere these demands made some progress, in Russia they met deep regime resistance born of the autocratic principle. Russia had Europe's toughest regimes of censorship (through which, interestingly, all the great works of Russian literature had to pass) and political control. There was an extensive repressive apparatus that dealt out copious Siberian

exile and occasional execution. The result was the extreme radicalisation of the opposition, for which the country was to pay dearly in 1917.
A deeply disaffected intelligentsia became hostile to the regime and all
it stood for, and a small proportion of them turned to terrorism. It was
in fact the terrorist movement 'Narodnaya Volya', which assassinated
Alexander II in 1881, that began the call for an 'All People's Constituent
Assembly', a freely elected body of representatives of all the people
which would create a democratic constitution for Russia. The model,
as with so much else through the Russian Revolution, was explicitly
drawn from the French revolutionary assemblies of 1789–91.[3]

The idea of such an assembly became common currency among the
opposition in the last years of the nineteenth century, even if with some
nuances. The liberal right were more willing to see gradual evolution
towards parliamentary government in cooperation with the monarchy,
while the extreme left (notably the early Marxist leader Georgy Plekhanov) made it clear that such an assembly was only justified as long as
it supported the cause of the socialist revolution (thus providing a text
from which Lenin subsequently preached).

It was on 'Bloody Sunday' that the demand for a Constituent
Assembly became talismanic for those seeking change. Russia had
seen a growing political crisis over the past year. Military defeat by
Japan, hunger in the countryside, and appalling working conditions
for the growing industrial labour force came together to give real force
to demands for reform, including for some representational element in
the way Russia was governed. In December 1904, Nicholas turned this
demand down saying to one of his ministers 'I shall never, under any
circumstances, agree to a representative form of government because
I consider it harmful to the people whom God has entrusted to my
care.'[4] A few days later, on Sunday 9 January 1905, a huge demonstration by unarmed workers and their families, many of them dressed
in their Sunday best, gathered in St Petersburg. They carried banners
asserting that they were 'suffocating in despotism' and demanding a
Constituent Assembly. Government troops, unprepared for the size
and determination of the crowd, opened fire and killed hundreds.

At that moment the image of Nicholas as the 'father of his people' took a blow from which it never recovered. In the eyes of many he became no more than a cruel tyrant. At the scene, the leader of the demonstration (a priest) declared 'There is no longer a God. There is no Tsar.'[5] Hundreds of thousands went on strike. The universities had to be closed down. There were uprisings in Poland, peasant violence in much of the countryside and, more ominously for the security of the regime, mutinies in the armed forces. Nicholas was forced into major concessions. The censorship was abolished. Personal and political rights were guaranteed. And, as a surrogate for the Constituent Assembly, Russia was given its first-ever national representative assembly, the State Duma.

THE DUMA

Russia's first experiment with giving the people a voice in government faced huge difficulties from the start. The gap between the reformers and the regime was almost impossibly wide. Nicholas was determined to concede none of his prerogatives. The 'Fundamental Law' establishing the Duma described him as 'Supreme Autocrat', and carefully avoided the explosive word 'constitution'. In his view the very existence of the Duma depended on his autocratic whim. While the Duma did notionally have some serious powers, notably over government finance, the tsar retained control over the appointment of ministers, the power of veto, the power to dissolve the Duma, and the power to pass emergency laws while it was not sitting. Moreover, the electoral arrangements were rigged to produce a supportive assembly with one gentry vote worth that of forty-five workers or fifteen (supposedly more loyal) peasants. Nevertheless shrewd commentators attached real hopes to it. Sergei Witte, Nicholas's most able minister (who indeed had pushed the tsar into agreeing to the Duma on the grounds that otherwise there would be revolution), confidently expected to see it evolve over time into a genuine Russian legislature.[6]

The elections took place in April 1906. They were boycotted by the left-wing parties, which did much to encourage regime expectations of an acceptable result. The outcome was a huge shock. More than half the members of the new body were 'semi-educated' peasants, rough, rude and showing none of the class deference which the smooth Petersburg bureaucracy had confidently predicted. One horrified aristocratic observer described them as 'A gathering of savages. It seemed as if the Russian land had sent to St Petersburg everything that was barbarian in it, everything filled with envy and malice.'[7] And the Duma, instead of focusing on government business as intended, devoted its time to demands for radical reform including wholesale expropriation of non-peasant land, control of the government, and universal male suffrage. These demands fed into a countrywide atmosphere of crisis, including an upsurge in rural violence and terrorism. In late June even the nation's elite regiment – the Preobrazhensky Guards – mutinied. Many concluded at this time that the regime was doomed. On 8 July Nicholas sent in the troops to close the Duma down. It had sat for seventy-two days. At the same time he appointed the 'authoritarian moderniser', Stolypin, as prime minister.

After reimposing civil order by extensive use of 'Stolypin's neckties', the gallows, Stolypin set about the fundamental reform of Russian agriculture, which he saw as the key to modernising Russia. For this he felt he needed wider political support to keep the unreliable and easily swayed tsar on board. He also needed the international financial confidence in Russia that had been shaken by the dissolution of the first Duma. He accordingly arranged for the election of a second Duma in February 1907, and worked hard to influence the result. He failed. This time the radical parties did not boycott the poll. They were elected in large numbers on the explicit programme of making the Duma unworkable so as to clear the way towards a proper Constituent Assembly. In what became known as 'Stolypin's coup' this second Duma was dissolved in June 1907 after sitting for just three months. In a clear breach of Nicholas's own Fundamental Law a new franchise was introduced two days later, still further tilting the electoral process in Nicholas's, and Stolypin's, favour.[8]

The third Duma, elected in 1907 on this much more restrictive franchise, was entirely dominated by gentry and landowners (and was thus dubbed the 'Duma of Lords and lackeys'). It nevertheless briefly played a more significant role in formulating policy than either of its two intransigent predecessors. Stolypin, not least through bribery and press manipulation, set out to generate support in the Duma to offset the influence of reactionaries in the regime. In the early days this tactic proved successful, and helped him carry through a range of reform measures. But later attempts at reform bogged down among rival regime factions. And Stolypin's appeal to a body that many around Nicholas believed should never have been created at all, and certainly should be conceded no real power, played a large role in his loss of influence with Nicholas before his assassination in 1911.[9]

After Stolypin's death, efforts to use the Duma to influence government policy ended. The third Duma (which ran its full five-year term to 1912) and the fourth (which immediately succeeded it) drifted into a role of grumbling subservience. They obediently passed the government bills that were sent to them while engaging in (widely reported) debate on the deficiencies of the tsarist regime. It was, for example, a Duma debate following a massacre of strikers in Siberia in 1912 that helped provoke a nationwide wave of protests that May Day. In this period there was active discussion around Nicholas of closing the Duma down or making it purely consultative – ideas not followed through because of fears of popular disturbances. Even at this unproductive time, however, the Duma did play one crucial (and ultimately disastrous) role. Its steady drumbeat of patriotic and anti-German rhetoric helped build the public atmosphere of aggressive nationalism that was the background to Nicholas's decision to go to war with Germany in August 1914. The Duma then underlined its role as loyalist eunuch by proroguing itself so as not to burden the tsar with 'unnecessary politics'.[10]

The war both made and ultimately destroyed the Duma as a real force in Russian government. There was plenty to criticise in the way Russia's inadequate and backward administration managed the needs of modern war. As the months passed without the promised quick victory, so the volume of Duma attacks rose. The body was briefly reconvened in 1915 to approve the budget, and then swiftly dissolved to curb such criticism. But as the year proceeded, and the news from the front got worse, so it became clear that the regime needed wider political support to remedy the problems of manufacturing and supply that were a large part of the weakness of the Russian military effort. Accordingly, in July 1915 a number of boards were set up, including Duma members, to tackle these problems. The government seemed finally to be on a route to accepting the Duma as a legitimate, even useful, part of Russian governance.

At the same time, however (19 July 1915), Nicholas decided to reconvene the whole Duma. This brought the roof down.[11] The Duma was united in its criticism of the regime's inability to conduct the war effectively, and in its determination to take a greater grip on matters itself. It demanded (and on this had the support of most of Nicholas's ministers) that Nicholas appoint a 'Ministry of National Confidence' answerable to the Duma. Nicholas, crucially influenced by Alexandra (who detested the Duma, and endlessly insisted that he should assert his autocratic authority), dismissed the Duma in September. Now things slid badly downhill. In one of his worst decisions (there is a rich choice) Nicholas had taken himself off to the front to command the army, leaving government in the hands of the 'German' tsarina under the shadowy influence of Rasputin. Rumours of treason at the top, and worse, proliferated. Government was a shambles. The period of 'Tsarina Government', September 1915 to February 1917, saw four prime ministers, five ministers of the interior and three ministers each of foreign affairs and of war. Rasputin was said to be taking huge bribes and debauching all the upper-class womanhood of Petrograd. The most lurid of the rumours were of course false, but deeply corrosive of support for the regime.[12]

By November 1916 the situation was so bad that Nicholas felt obliged to let the Duma reconvene. The result was a storm in which Pavel Milyukov, leader of the Duma liberals, famously demanded to know whether official policy was 'treason or stupidity' and the Duma, in the most substantial display of teeth of its whole existence, forced the resignation of the prime minister.[13] Indeed, the Duma had now taken on many of the aspects of a real parliament. Its members were protected by guarantees of parliamentary immunity, so it was able to become the public echo chamber for criticism of the Romanov regime, entirely subverting the tsar's credibility among the elite, the public and the armed forces. Nicholas made minor concessions, such as appointing a few ministers from among the Duma membership, but nowhere near enough to stem the growing torrent of demands for change.

The final collapse came in mid February in Petrograd. A bread short-age (largely caused by very cold weather) led to street demonstrations on 13 February. Coincidentally the Duma reconvened on 14 February and renewed its assaults. Over the next three days the situation deterio-rated dramatically. The demonstrations grew larger and turned violent. For the first time since Bloody Sunday, twelve years before, the troops were ordered to fire on the crowds. Nicholas (far away in army HQ in Mogilev) declared the Duma dissolved. Then on 28 February much of the army garrison in Petrograd mutinied and joined the rioters. A huge crowd gathered outside the Tauride Palace, where the Duma met, demanding in effect that it take over the government.

This was the moment when the Duma as an institution met its destiny. It had come a long way from its inauspicious and neutered start. In the course of the past six months it had become the cockpit of national debate and had acquired real authority over the actions of the government. It now faced a historic test. Would it pick up the reins of national authority so visibly no longer held by the distant Nicholas, or would it leave them for others to seize?

This was a test it only half passed. With the mob gathered outside, Duma moderates prevaricated. Their formal reasoning was that since the tsar had dissolved the Duma they could take no further action without his permission. But the reality was sheer fear in the face of the drunken 'dark people' on the rampage outside. Radical members of the

Duma on the other hand, led by the brilliant left-wing lawyer Alexander Kerensky, insisted that this was their moment. The Duma should defy the tsar and lead the revolution. The upshot was an untidy compromise; the coming together, without formal Duma endorsement, of a 'Provisional Committee of Duma members for the Restoration of Order in the Capital and the Establishment of Relations with Individuals and Institutions' – a body whose very name underlines the hesitations of many in the Duma leadership, paralysed as they were by fear of the street, about taking on governmental responsibility.

Kerensky, much later in exile, wrote that the Duma 'wrote its own death warrant at the moment of the revolutionary renaissance of the people … The Duma died on the morning of 28 February, the day when its strength and its influence were at their highest.'[14] Kerensky, who became the last leader of pre-Leninist Russia, of course had his own axe to grind about the course events took between February and October 1917. But there is a real counterfactual lurking here. If the Duma had indeed convened and declared itself in charge on the evening of 27 February how might events have gone?

It is not entirely impossible that, courageously and cunningly led, the Duma leadership could indeed have placated the Petrograd street long enough to establish an effective claim to national authority on the grounds that they were the only institution left with any basis for such a claim. They had one important advantage; precisely because of their unrepresentative make-up they were trusted by the officer class and bureaucracy. The key reason why the army chief of staff, Alexeev, did not obey Nicholas's command on 1 March to send troops into Petrograd to put down the rising is because the chairman of the Duma, Rodzyanko, assured him that they would inherit power.[15] And if indeed the Duma had been able to establish such a claim to authority the subsequent history of Russia would undoubtedly have been very different.

But there are strong reasons for doubting that any such claim to Duma authority would have survived very long. Already, as the Duma havered, a serious competitor for power was emerging in the form of the 'Petrograd Soviet', a chaotic and ad hoc assembly of representatives from local factories and regiments, powerfully fuelled by class anger, revolutionary venom, and (among the soldiers) aversion to being sent to the front. The Soviet was dominated by an assortment of left-wing parties, with the initially outnumbered Bolsheviks rising in influence as the only party demanding immediate peace. It of course had no real democratic legitimacy, but had one crucial source of power. In the anarchic months after February, it represented, and where necessary deployed, the fearsome Petrograd mob in a way the respectable bourgeois of the Duma could not. The Duma leadership didn't have the backbone to come out on top in any sustained tussle with these forces. A sympathetic commentator later described it as a struggle that set 'those public elements that were sensible and moderate but – alas – timid, unorganised, accustomed only to obeying and incapable of commanding' against 'organised rascality with its narrow-minded, fanatical and frequently dishonest ringleaders'.[16]

In fact, fearful of the mob, the Provisional Committee felt the need to negotiate the terms of its assumption of power with the Soviet, and thus visibly placed itself in a position of dependence on it. The upshot was the creation on 2 March of the 'Provisional Government' of mostly liberal Duma politicians – 'provisional' because it was seen as a temporary arrangement until something more legitimate could be brought into being. And indeed right from the start it faced two huge disabilities. The real power on the streets in Petrograd and other population centres lay with the Soviet and its analogues (which swiftly sprang up all over Russia). And the Provisional Government had little formal legitimacy. It was the irregularly born child of a thoroughly unrepresentative and now dissolved Duma (which, in Rodzyanko's words, now simply 'faded away' because its members were 'unprepared for energetic resistance'[17]). When Prince Lvov was announced as Head of the Government a soldier in the crowd shouted 'You mean all we've done is exchange a Tsar for a Prince?'[18] And when the new minister of foreign affairs appeared before the crowd he met the demand 'Who elected you?'[19]

THE CONSTITUENT ASSEMBLY

The response to this question lay in the eight-point programme the Provisional Government had hammered out with the Soviet. All parties agreed that Russia needed a properly elected basis for legitimate government as soon as possible. So point four of the programme called for 'immediate preparations for the convocation of the Constituent Assembly, to be elected on a universal, secret, direct and equal ballot'. The thirty-year-old dream of an assembly to endow Russia with a proper modern democratic constitution looked at last as if it was about to be realised.

The central role anticipated for the Constituent Assembly very quickly became clear. Over the past few days, while the real power politics of the future of Russian governance was being played out in Petrograd, a rather sad sideshow had been underway at various railway stops in western Russia. The Tsar, blocked by transport dislocations from getting back to his capital, and in only imperfect contact with it, was on 2 March advised by Rodzyanko that he had to abdicate. His key generals swiftly endorsed this advice, leaving him little choice. The legal heir was his twelve-year-old haemophiliac son, Alexis. But Nicholas, caring family man and obtuse politician to the end, was worried about Alexis' health and instead settled the crown on his own brother, Michael Alexandrovich. While the shakily installed new rulers in Petrograd might have gone along with the throne falling to the legal heir, a sickly boy, his arbitrary replacement by a mature, militarily experienced Romanov prince was a very different prospect. And there was a very real question as to whether the mob was in any mood for the monarchy to survive at all. Michael quickly decided to dodge the bullet, and on 4 March issued a manifesto putting off all decisions on the future of the Romanov dynasty, including who, if anyone, should wear the crown, to the Constituent Assembly.

From the start, preparation for the Constituent Assembly was seen as both central to the work of the Provisional Government and urgent. Major governmental decisions were either themselves deemed provisional or simply put off until the Assembly convened. The head of the

Provisional Government described the establishment of the Assembly as 'our essential sacred task',[20] and at an early coordination meeting between the Soviet and the Provisional Government both sides underlined the need for the earliest possible meeting of the Assembly. In the 'March mood' of euphoria after the February Revolution there was huge enthusiasm for the Assembly with all political parties pressing for work to be speedily carried forward. The hope at that stage was that the Assembly could be convened in three to four months. That is by June.

But political and organisational complexities were already making themselves felt. In a vast country, still at war, simply compiling an electoral law, putting together a voting register, and organising polling – all on the basis of organs of local government which were themselves being radically reformed – were a sufficiently formidable challenge. And all of this offered pretexts for delay to political factions which themselves had reasons for wanting to put things off. The Socialist Revolutionary Party (SRs) who principally represented the peasants did not want elections until the autumn when the harvest would be over. Meanwhile the right-wing parties were happy to see some delay to allow the 'raging sea of revolution' to calm down. Ironically, in view of subsequent events, it was the Bolsheviks who pressed most stridently for early progress, accusing the other parties of going slow on democracy.[21]

So things bogged down. It took until May for the political parties to agree on general principles for organising the elections (secret ballot, proportional representation, universal suffrage). But they then set up an extraordinarily cumbersome, almost parliament-sized, special council of lawyers to turn all this into electoral law. The timetable, set in June, was for elections to take place on 17 September and for the Assembly to meet on 30 September. But, as a newspaper noted in June under the headline 'The Last Chance': 'Two principles are struggling here: the principle of the greatest possible perfection and the principle of the greatest possible speed. Two months ago the first principle was undoubtedly prevailing. Now the prevalence apparently is leaning towards the second one.'[22] As the February Revolution slid increasingly into the past, and crisis succeeded crisis on the Petrograd political scene, so popular enthusiasm for the Assembly faded. At the same time another newspaper was expressing the worries of many when it asked, 'Will the ship of state reach the port of the Constituent Assembly? Will the Provisional Government, together with the Democracy, succeed in maintaining the unity of the state before the arrival of the Master?'[23]

The so-called 'July Days', in which the Provisional Government very nearly fell to a Bolshevik uprising, both set back progress and gave added urgency to convening the Assembly. The government responded in mid July by pressing the various bodies to redouble their efforts to meet the timetable, and indeed the Socialist parties demanded that the elections be accelerated. But by now it was becoming apparent that even this timetable was impossible. The sequence of getting local elections out of the way and then publishing the electoral list forty days before the Assembly elections, as required by the emerging draft statute, simply couldn't be done by mid September.[24] The liberals were relatively relaxed about this as the growing radicalism of the revolution made it clearer and clearer that they would not do well in the elections whenever they were held. The Socialist parties took more persuading, but on 9 August finally, fatally, agreed that the elections should be put back to 12 November, with the Assembly due to convene on 28 November.[25]

The Provisional Government, having staggered from crisis to crisis over the eight months of its existence, and seen its authority increasingly leach to the Soviet, was finally put out of its misery by the Bolshevik coup on 27 October. It was replaced by an entirely Bolshevik 'Soviet of People's Commissars' (Sovnarkom), headed by Lenin, whose authority at the start looked very precarious. For the opposition parties the coup reinforced the significance of the forthcoming elections to the Assembly as the moment when there would be a democratically elected body able to take authority from the unelected Bolsheviks. Among the Bolsheviks themselves there had, prior to the coup, been some debate about their attitude to the Assembly – with Lenin in particular very clear that maintenance of Soviet power must always take priority over 'bourgeois democracy'.[26] But their public position had always been firm support for the Assembly, and indeed an insistence that only they could be relied upon to convene the Assembly in a way that the 'counter-revolutionary' Provisional Government could not. Conscious of the precariousness of their situation, the Bolsheviks, despite some opposition from Lenin, maintained this position after the coup. Sovnarkom in fact decreed that it would only hold authority until the Assembly was convened.

So preparations for the elections went ahead, while the Bolshevik regime gradually consolidated its hold on power. The elections started on 12 November. Due to the size of the country the voting took the next two weeks. There were some minor irregularities and the occupied territories could not vote (the country was still at war). But it was a remarkably clean and well-organised procedure. It was the first free national election in Russian history, and the last for the next seventy years. More than forty million voters (about 50 per cent of those qualified) turned out.

Following the October coup many of the opposition parties tried to turn the election into a referendum on the Bolshevik regime. To the extent that they succeeded, it was a referendum that the Bolsheviks lost. They took about a quarter of the votes (although a huge preponderance in some key places: in particular more than 70 per cent of the military vote in both Moscow and Petrograd). The big winners, unsurprisingly given the social make-up of the country, were the peasants' party – the SRs – who got 40 per cent. The big losers were the right-leaning liberals, the Constitutional Democrats (Kadets), who got less than 8 per cent, but were seen by the Bolsheviks as a key threat because of the relatively large numbers they gained in the cities.

The Bolshevik regime now faced a real problem. The Constituent Assembly would have the democratic legitimacy they lacked. Having barely arrived in power were they now on the way out? They certainly weren't going to go quietly. Already, before the count was complete,

Sovnarkom announced the indefinite postponement of the opening of the Assembly (due on 28 November) and demanded an investigation into electoral 'abuses' that could serve as a basis for 're-elections'. The vast majority of the non-Bolshevik opposition responded by setting up a 'Union for the Defence of the Constituent Assembly'. On the originally planned opening day, 28 November, they organised a large demonstration, and staged a symbolic opening of the Assembly in the Tauride Palace, its intended home.

The Bolsheviks responded brutally. The Tauride Palace was closed off with troops. The demonstrations were denounced as counter-revolutionary. And, in a foretaste of a lot that was to come, the leading right-wing party, the Kadets, was banned, its leaders arrested, and its printing presses smashed. It is no coincidence that at this time (in fact 7 December) the 'Cheka' was established – the Soviet secret police – which operated entirely outside the law and which was the direct antecedent of the KGB.

But this did not solve the problem of what to do about the Assembly, which, in the words of a contemporary observer, was to the Bolsheviks 'like a bone in the throat'.[27] The Bolsheviks were still too precariously placed (and internally divided) to set aside the product of more than thirty years of expectation and forty million votes. Lenin came up with his solution on 12 December. He claimed that the elections were invalid. Popular opinion had shifted since they took place. The counter-revolutionary nature of support for the Assembly must be stamped on. The Assembly could meet but its members would be subject to recall by their local Soviets (a licence for opposition deputies to be gradually excluded). A quorum was set of 400 out of 800 members (which meant that, now that the Kadets had been banned, the Bolsheviks could render the Assembly inquorate by withdrawing). And it could only pursue policy lines set out for it by the (Bolshevik-dominated) Soviets.[28]

The day for convening the Assembly was set for 5 January 1918. The preceding four weeks saw intense propaganda campaigns by both the supporters of the Assembly and its opponents. The Union for the

Defence of the Constituent Assembly agitated in the barracks and the factories and turned out leaflets and newspapers by the hundreds of thousands underlining the democratic credentials of the Assembly and arguing that it was not anti-Soviet. The Bolsheviks headlined the danger of the Assembly being taken over by counter-revolutionaries and, more practically, placed Petrograd under martial law and made sure they had sympathetic troops in place for 5 January.

On 5 January Petrograd was like an armed camp. In particular the area around the Tauride Palace was swarming with troops. Supporters of the Assembly had organised a large demonstration whose members began to march towards the Palace but quickly found themselves under fire – the first time the Bolsheviks turned troops on unarmed demonstrators. Meanwhile Lenin – described by a colleague as 'excited and pale like a corpse … his eyes distended and a flame burning with a steady fire'[29] – was in the Palace directing operations. Once it was clear that the demonstration had been dispersed he allowed the Assembly to convene. The atmosphere was close to chaotic. The Bolshevik deputies unitedly jeered anyone else who spoke. The corridors and balconies swarmed with soldiery, often drunken, who for amusement regularly pointed their guns at the speakers. The Bolsheviks introduced a resolution which would in effect have made the Assembly subject to the Soviets, and, when it failed, walked out (making the Assembly inquorate). The Assembly was nevertheless allowed to run on with interminable speeches from respectable revolutionaries until the small hours. At 2 a.m. Lenin, satisfied that he had the situation under control, left. At 4 a.m. the commander of the guard approached Chernov, the chairman of the Assembly, and told him to close the session 'because the guard is tired'.[30] Meanwhile additional contingents of menacingly armed men were arriving. Chernov managed to struggle on for twenty minutes and then adjourned the Assembly until the following day. But the following day the Palace was closed and surrounded by troops. The single fully democratic body in all of Russia's history up to that point had lasted for less than thirteen hours.

This was not quite the end of the story. Opposition members of the

Assembly reconstituted themselves in the cities of first Samara, then Omsk, claiming to be the rightful government of Russia. The ultimate inglorious fate of this so-called 'Komuch' is recounted by Evan Mawdsley in this volume. But the reality was that the long-standing dream of a democratically elected assembly to decide the government of Russia died (or was murdered) in Petrograd on 5/6 January 1918. A prominent historian has argued that this, rather than the October coup, was the real turning point of the revolution.[31] This was the moment when the unscrupulous, brutally repressive and anti-democratic character of the Bolshevik regime came fully into view. Russia was now on the road to Stalinism.

How did they get away with it? Enthusiasm for the Assembly on close examination was very much an elite phenomenon. The vast majority of Russia's population, the peasants, had achieved their revolution. They had their local soviets and were busy seizing land. Why worry about what was going on in distant Petrograd? Even in the cities, popular support was lukewarm. At the symbolic launch on 28 December a leading socialist ruefully noted that 'the people were certainly not as convinced of the Constituent Assembly's power of salvation as its supporters had reckoned'.[32] The demonstrations that day and on 5 January were much smaller and more middle class than had been anticipated. The Petrograd proletariat after ten months of continuous insecurity and turmoil were not about to take on men with guns in pursuit of yet another political innovation, however theoretically desirable.[33]

The real failure was on the part of the elite, particularly the non-Bolshevik socialists who won the elections. The sad fact is that it was their very virtues that undid them. They believed in democracy, due process and the rule of law. Confronted with the gangster tactics of the Bolsheviks they had no answer. Yes, they had the support of most of the people, but not with the degree of commitment that would have enabled them to take back the streets. Indeed, in the course of the 'July Days' six months earlier, when the Bolsheviks had come close to subverting the whole authority of the Soviet, the other socialists, unbelievably, had made real efforts to protect them in the subsequent clampdown. The SRs and Mensheviks had spent so many years battling the autocracy arm in arm with their Bolshevik comrades that they simply could not see them as the menace they really were – only beatable by turning their own ruthless tactics against them. In fact, following the suppression of the Assembly, the SR leadership rejected military offers of support; civil war was to be avoided at all costs. Accordingly, in Trotsky's famous phrase, they disappeared into the 'dustbin of history'. Maybe Anton Chekhov caught a deep truth in his portrayal of the ineffectuality of the Russian intelligentsia. Or maybe no civilised political class in whatever country could have stood up to the unexampled cynicism and ruthlessness of Lenin's Bolsheviks.

HISTORICALLY INEVITABLE?

Finally, we are left with one huge 'what if'. It took eight months from the February Revolution for the Assembly to be elected, and ten for it to be convened. By that time the Bolsheviks were in power and it was doomed. But in roughly comparable circumstances in France in 1848 it took two months to convene an assembly, and in Germany in 1918 four. We have seen the widespread understanding, after February, of the urgent need to convene the Assembly before it got bogged down in nitpicking arguments about electoral arrangements and all the rest. Suppose the Provisional Government had been able to maintain the momentum, and the elections for the Assembly had taken place either as originally hoped by June or as subsequently timetabled by September?

History would certainly have been different. The interesting question is by how much. Petrograd between April and July saw three Bolshevik-prompted insurrections on the streets. The first, in April, was suppressed by order of the Soviet executive – in effect the non-Bolshevik socialist parties who at this point also joined the Provisional Government, leaving the Bolsheviks as the only active opposition. The second, in June, was pre-empted by essentially the same forces. The third, the 'July Days', could in fact have taken control of Petrograd, but failed through a last-minute (and entirely uncharacteristic) loss of nerve by Lenin. So the Bolsheviks would certainly have had it in their power to take control of the city at the time the Constituent Assembly might have convened.

But the political circumstances would have been very different. The Assembly would, at least initially, have enjoyed a legitimacy and breadth of political support that the Provisional Government never achieved. The winners of the elections to the Assembly would certainly have been, as actually happened in November, the non-Bolshevik socialist parties, notably the SRs. This by itself would have sucked political vitality and support out of the Soviet, which had been the principal pretext for the mayhem the Bolsheviks had been able to cause over the period March to September (the key Bolshevik slogan from April on had been 'All power to the Soviets'). The Bolsheviks, not being in power, would not have been able to cripple and constrain the Assembly in the way they actually did in December/January. And those nice gentlemen who led the Mensheviks, SRs and so on, and who were astonishingly tolerant of the Bolsheviks even when faced with the outrages of the July Days, may well have been ready to be much tougher in support of the flagship institution for which they had all been working for decades. Lenin, for all his fanaticism, was a careful and shrewd reader of the odds. He would surely have held his hand for at least the first few weeks of the Assembly's existence.

A lot then depends on how the Assembly performs. This was a large (800 members) parliamentary body led by exactly the same ineffectual politicians who in February had submitted their authority to the whims of the Soviet, and, as actually happened in January, had gone quietly when faced with an armed Bolshevik mob. This was not the body, and these were not the men, to steer Russia through a destructive war, rural anarchy, imperial dissolution and a complete collapse of the apparatus of the state. Even countries with much stronger experience than Russia in 1917 of the give and take of representative politics have, when confronted with such crises, moved to some form of 'strong man' rule (Gaullist France, Civil War America, Second World War Britain, for example) with, at best, some form of democratic legitimation. And, as we have noted, Russia's historical experience up to that point was almost exclusively of rule by an autocrat. The bulk of the Russian governing class then, as now, were much more comfortable obeying orders than giving them.

Given his ruthless single-mindedness it is thus not impossible to imagine Lenin's moment coming in another form. He could, at least early on, take over the streets, and he controlled a quarter of the votes in the Assembly itself. Indeed, it is fair to ask why, given that in actuality he disposed of the Assembly with remarkably little difficulty, he should not have been able to do so in this alternative universe as well. The answer is that he might have done, but that the odds were worse. Lenin would not have been in even partial control of the formal machinery of the state. The Assembly would have had longer to establish itself. It might well have earned some credibility by taking on (as it tried to do in its aborted 5/6 January session) the key issues of 'land and peace', which the Provisional Government had not been able to tackle. The Assembly, or the government it appointed, would at the very least have had the time and standing to look for the military support which it entirely lacked in the short moment which history actually gave it. And the Assembly, particularly if it came into existence before the disastrous Kornilov affair in August, would have had a key ally in Alexander Kerensky, who for all his operatic faults was one of the most able and influential politicians of the age. Bolshevism remains a possible outcome, but a significantly less likely one.

What was the alternative? History suggests (as all the Russian revolutionaries were uncomfortably aware) that Russia's strong man was much less likely to come from the left than from the right – the wing of Russian politics with the bulk of effective armed force at its disposal. The next months could well have seen an Assembly unavailingly and wordily struggling to grapple with Russia's huge problems as real authority slid in the direction of a 'Russian Napoleon'. Right-wing dictatorship would undoubtedly have been a bitterly disappointing outcome to Russia's first genuine stab at democracy. It would also have materially affected European history outside Russia (one of the key factors driving Hitler's rise was his opposition to Soviet Communism). But it has to be questionable whether it could have been worse than what Russia actually experienced.

9

RESCUING THE TSAR
AND HIS FAMILY

July 1918

EDVARD RADZINSKY

T HE TSAR AND his family could have been saved.
The first time this could have happened was in Tobolsk.

The imperial family arrived in Tobolsk at the peak of their unpopularity. A weak tsar under the heel of his wife, with the illiterate peasant Rasputin controlling the royal couple – that was the people's portrait of the dynasty on the eve of the revolution. And if they despised the weak tsar, they hated the empress.

Through the whole course of the revolution it is impossible to overstate the impact of Alexandra Federovna. Against the background of the defeat of the Russian army – hundreds of thousands killed and maimed – there were consistent rumours of the treason of the 'German Tsaritsa' and of her lover Rasputin, most probably through the selling of military secrets. One of the leaders of the opposition, Milyukov, said in a widely reported speech to the state Duma 'from province to province creep torrid rumours of betrayal and treachery. These rumours climb high and spare no one … The name of the Empress is more and more repeated together with those of the adventurists who surround her … What is this – stupidity or treason?' Denikin wrote in his memoirs, 'Rumours of treason played a fatal role for the attitude of the army to the dynasty.' And one of the leaders of the Duma's monarchist faction, Purishkevich, to enthusiastic applause from the Duma, called the empress 'the evil genius of the Tsar and of Russia, an unalterable German on the Russian throne, alien to the country and its people'.

The dynasty, once it had lost all authority, fell unbelievably fast and easily. Nicholas's attempt to transfer the throne to the Grand Duke Michael would only have ended in bloodshed. Michael hastily refused the dangerous offer.

The country blew away its 300-year-old monarchy like fluff off a sleeve.

After Nicholas's abdication all that was left for the imperial family was to quit Russia and to do so as quickly as possible. To this end the Provisional Government opened contacts with the government of Great Britain. The British throne was occupied by the tsar's relative and friend, George V, who bore a striking resemblance to Nicholas (in the past they had swapped uniforms to fool those around them). After Nicholas's abdication George had sent sympathetic telegrams to his old friend. Nicholas was a true ally of the English to the point where, while the tsar in Russia bore the modest rank of colonel, in England he was an admiral and a field marshal. The tsar, having voluntarily abdicated, saw departure for England as entirely natural.

But the Soviet of Workers and Soldiers Deputies gathered in Petrograd, and, heavily dependent on the forces of the Petrograd garrison, demanded that the tsar be put on trial. The tsar was arrested. The Investigatory Commission of the Provisional Government started work. Was it possible for Britain, intending to continue the war in alliance with the new Russia, to accept the family which Russian society had rejected and which stood accused of treason? 'We truly hope that the British Government has no intention of giving asylum to the Tsar and his wife ... that would deeply and rightly offend the feelings of the Russians who have been compelled to make a great revolution because they have been repeatedly betrayed to our current enemy,' wrote the *Daily Telegraph*. Finally, George was compelled to refuse his hospitality.

The imperial family was now living under arrest in Tsarskoe Selo. The 'Citizen Colonel', as they dubbed yesterday's autocrat, was constantly exposed to the open hostility of the soldiers of the guard. Nor at this time could there even be talk of efforts to escape. During the French Revolution Louis XVI and Marie Antoinette had been in a similar situation, imprisoned in the Tuileries Palace. But then certain foreigners – Marie Antoinette's lover, the Swedish Count Fersen, and the Russian Baroness Korf – had risked organising the escape of the royal family. The attempt of course ended in failure because the whole country was against them. And the honorary president of the Russian Historical Society, Nicholas II, knew the whole story well.

But, three months after the abdication, on 4 July 1917, Zizi Nar-ishkin, former maid of honour to the empress, wrote in her diary 'Princess Palei [wife of the Grand Duke Paul Alexandrovich] has just left. She secretly told me that a group of young officers has put together a mad project to take them in an automobile by night to one of the ports, where an English ship would be waiting. I felt unbeliev-able alarm...'

Why such alarm? Because the project was 'mad'? Both Zizi and Palei knew that, given present attitudes to the family, if they didn't get to the port they would be seized and killed on the road. Moreover, there was of course no English ship, nor any plot. There was just the drunken boastfulness of young officers.

At this time influence in the capital was shifting in the direction of radicals demanding the punishment of the tsar and tsarista. The great poet Alexander Blok wrote, 'the tragedy has not yet begun. Either it will never begin or it will be terrible when they [the family] stand face to face with the enraged people.' But Kerensky, now the leader of the Pro-visional Government, did not want to become the executioner of the unfortunate family who were more and more becoming a dangerous card in the struggle between the Soviet and his weakening Provisional Government. So he tried to rid himself of them.

Such was Kerensky's fear that the Soviet would refuse permission for their departure that it was in circumstances of unusual secrecy, at dawn, under a Japanese flag, that a train with shuttered windows set off from Petrograd to take the family away. Some 330 riflemen under the command of Colonel Kobilinsky accompanied and guarded them.

In order to maintain popular calm the place chosen for exile was Siberia – the same place to which Russian tsars had previously exiled revolutionaries.

The city of Tobolsk lies lost in the vastness of Siberia. In this provincial capital the arrested family lived like Noah in his ark. Here resided the emperor and empress of a vanished empire, the Adjutant General of a vanished suite, and the Head Chamberlain of a vanished court, all addressing each other by vanished titles. But so far, the revolution had not come to Tobolsk. The spiritual leader in the region was Archbishop Hermogen. Once he had been a zealous supporter of Rasputin, and then his avowed enemy. At the initiative of the empress, the Synod had exiled him for this to a distant monastery. Now the Provisional Government had appointed him archbishop in Tobolsk.

But Hermogen had forgotten his oppressions, and was ready to serve the Anointed of God. He saw this service as his foreordained destiny. Indeed, the name 'Hermogen' went back to the very origin of the Romanov dynasty. In the 'time of troubles' in the seventeenth century, a patriarch called Hermogen had launched the call to drive the Poles out of Russia. For this he had suffered a martyr's death. And now, 300 years later, an archbishop with the same name, Hermogen, here in Tobolsk, could help the last Romanov regain his freedom. It was precisely of this that Nicholas's mother, the widowed empress, wrote to him – 'Your Worship ... you bear the name of the Saint Hermogen. This is predestined.' She expected fateful steps from the fateful archbishop.

At this time, in order finally to reconcile the revolutionary committee to the exile of the tsar, Kerensky sent Commissar Pankratov to Tobolsk. Pankratov was a revolutionary who had spent fourteen years as an imprisoned convict in the Shlisselburg Castle on the order of the overthrown tsar. He was thus an outstanding symbol and a guarantee of strict supervision. But Pankratov had forgiven the tsar for the lost years of his life. For him, the tsar was simply the father of a large family subjected to an incomprehensibly awful new life. He presented no real threat of escape. But the soldiers of the guard were suspicious of the good-natured State Commissar. So at this time they took orders only from their commandant, Colonel Kobilinsky.

Kobilinsky had been appointed to Tsarskoe Selo by General Kornilov. His chief qualification was as a committed supporter of the February Revolution. But over his time spent with the tsar the colonel had much changed. Nicholas's despair, his gentleness and delicacy; those delightful daughters; and the empress, defenceless in her unhappy arrogance, had together transformed Kobilinsky from the family's jailer to its friend. 'I surrendered to you, Your Highness, that most valuable thing, my honour,' he, entirely rightly, said afterwards to Nicholas.

Thus, in this quiet little town where the only military force is the 330 riflemen guarding the family, their commander becomes close to Nicholas. And the majority of the guard – 'good soldiers' as Nicholas calls them – receive endless presents from the family. And indeed at that time the guard could have helped them escape. Tatiana Botkina, daughter of the doctor Evgeny Botkin, who shared the family's captivity in Tobolsk, remembered 'in these months [that is from August to the October Revolution] the family could have escaped'. But where could they escape to?

Up until the Bolshevik seizure of power, as we have already said, there was no place for the tsar in Russian politics. In fact, the only people contending against the revolutionary power of the Provisional Government were the Jacobin Bolsheviks. The Whites, the movement to rebuild a strong sovereign power, had only just been born. If the tsar fled, all he could do was quit the country. But to do that he would have had to cross half of Russia. Nicholas couldn't risk the lives of those closest to him...

In the middle of November the terrible news reached Tobolsk of the storming of the Winter Palace, the sacking of the palace of the tsar's ancestors, and of the Bolshevik seizure of power. The tsar wrote in his diary on 17 November, 'it is sad to read the description in the newspapers of what happened two weeks ago in Petrograd and Moscow ... This is much worse and more shameful than the events in the time of troubles.'

It was not in vain that Nicholas in Tobolsk had read *Quatre-vingt-treize* by Victor Hugo, a book about the Jacobins. The tsar understood that that was what had come to power. And as Gilliard subsequently recalled 'Nicholas more and more regretted his abdication'.

The Civil War started. The White movement against Bolshevik power came into existence. Now Nicholas could contemplate fleeing to the Whites. And now the riflemen and their commander could help. But the most important factor was Hermogen. The powerful archbishop had in his control distant monasteries like fortresses, where it would be possible to stop peacefully by, rivers with hidden boats ... all of this could facilitate a successful escape.

But Alexandra hesitates. The whole thing depends on Hermogen. Alexandra cannot entrust the fate of her family to the avowed enemy of Rasputin.

Indeed, how happy it made Alexandra when a certain Boris Soloviev, married to the daughter of Rasputin, appeared in Tobolsk. Soloviev said that he had come to organise their escape. And Alexandra of course saw a great sign in this; the name of the 'Monk', as always, carried her into a familiar world of fantasy. Her Grigory, from beyond the grave, was bringing a 'Mighty Host' in order to help her. She believed in Soloviev with her whole soul. So the normally thrifty Alexandra generously pours out to him royal treasures and money for their liberation. All this time in St Petersburg the empress's friend Vyrubova is working on her behalf. She sends to Tobolsk both money and Sergei Markov, an officer of the Crimean cavalry regiment whose commander had been the empress herself. And again the romantic Alexandra believes this is a sign. The emissary of the Monk and the emissary of the valiant Russian officers had come together! After a regular communication from Soloviev she began to rave about '300 officers who have already gathered,' as Soloviev wrote to her, 'near Tiumen'. And Alexandra even more generously poured out tsarist treasures to Soloviev. In reply Soloviev writes to Alexandra with his notions on 'mobile groups of officers' that had already been set up all along the road from Tobolsk to Tiumen, where the railway started. They would hand the imperial family on from one to another at the time of the escape. He told her that he controlled the telephones of the Bolshevik Soviet itself. The time of liberation was approaching! Alexandra infects Nicholas with her belief. Even the heir's guardian, the sensible Swiss Gilliard, decides 'to hold himself ready for all possible events'.

Indeed, in March 1918 on Freedom Street the bells began to ring as armed men arrived in brave, tinkling troikas with whoops and whistles. Alexandra, looking out of her window, whispered with delight 'what good Russian faces'. They had come. The Mighty Russian Host, the '300 officers' about whom Soloviev, the emissary of the Monk, had just written to her. But in reality what arrived on that day was a detachment of Red Guards from Omsk, sent to establish Bolshevik power in Tobolsk. This was the day when the idyllic period of their detention came to an end. With tinkling, whoops and whistles a new world burst upon Tobolsk. Soon the Bolsheviks were to drown Archbishop Hermogen in the river, and flight from Tobolsk became impossible. In fact, as Tatiana Botkina wrote in her memoirs 'there were no groups of officers to liberate the imperial family'. Soloviev, 'Rasputin's emissary', turned out to be one of the many adventurers in which the revolutionary era was so rich.

Thus Rasputin, even after his death, brought destruction on the imperial family.

But every month of Bolshevik rule made life in the country less and less bearable. As happens with regimes that have seized power by force, everything began to disappear. Food disappeared, and fuel. Winter came. There was no heat in the cities. Apartments were transformed into caves. Broken lanterns didn't burn. The streets at night saw theft and murder. And by degrees people began to think back to the 'accursed tsarist regime'.

And now Bolshevik Russia found itself surrounded in a ring of intervention and revolt. The Civil War was under way.

The White movement was headed by tsarist generals. None of them drew attention to the unpopular tsar. But … but … could the tsarist idea rise again from the ashes? Especially since the act of abdication had been cunningly contrived. At the right moment it could be declared illegal. The tsar had no right to abdicate on behalf of his heir. His son did not belong to him. By law Alexis belonged to Russia.

These ideas crossed the Bolsheviks' minds as well. So they decided to speed matters up – to stamp out the smouldering fire. Trotsky, second in command of the revolution, planned to set up a People's Court for the tsar on the model of the courts of the French Revolution. He got Lenin's agreement to transfer the family to Moscow, now the capital of Bolshevik Russia.

Commissar Myachin (whose Bolshevik pseudonym was Yakovlev) was sent to Tobolsk. His job was to transfer the tsar to Moscow. But transferring the whole family was impossible – the heir was ill. So Moscow ordered Yakovlev to bring the tsar on his own. And despite all protests, leaving the heir in the care of three grand princesses, Yakovlev carried the tsar off to Moscow. The tsaritsa decided to go with her husband, as did their daughter Maria.

But Yakovlev's train was stopped in Omsk. In the Urals there were rumours that he had absolutely no intention of taking the imperial family to Moscow. The Ekaterinburg Bolsheviks agreed with the Omsk Bolsheviks to arrest Yakovlev, shoot him, and to hold the imperial family under strict guard in the capital of the Urals, Ekaterinburg. The commissar was only saved by a telegram from Moscow confirming his mission. But of course Moscow heard about the arguments concerning Yakovlev in Ekaterinburg. He was ordered to hand the family over to the Ekaterinburg Bolsheviks, and himself to return to the capital.

Myachin/Yakovlev, commissar and former bold Bolshevik fighter, was a dangerous man. His biography included assaults on banks, bombings and the killing of officials. 'A bullet, and noose around my neck, followed at my heels,' he proudly wrote in his memoirs. So when the uprising of the Czechoslovak legion broke out at the end of May, Yakovlev was placed in command of one of the Bolshevik armies in the Ufa and Orenburg regions. But then Commissar Yakovlev abruptly quit the Bolshevik forces and fled to Ufa, which was occupied by the Whites. Here he announced that he had 'abandoned the idea of Bolshevism', and moved over to the side of the Whites. He also appealed to his former colleagues themselves to join the Whites.

There will, further on, be many more sharp turns in the astonishing life of Yakovlev/Myachin. This was a high-risk gambler, playing complicated games throughout his life, pursuing the most unbelievable adventures. So it is perfectly possible that the story heard in Ekaterinburg – that Commissar Yakovlev had absolutely no intention of taking his train to Moscow – was true. In fact, on the whole trip he had been notably kind and respectful towards his prisoners. An interesting passage turns up in the diary of the tsaritsa:

'16 April on the train. The Omsk soviet of deputies is not letting us travel through Omsk because of fears that they want to take us on to Japan.'

Maybe there is truth in this half hint? Maybe it was only to her – the real head of the family – that the secretive commissar hinted at his true aim. If so, this was the first attempt that might have culminated in the liberation of the tsar and the tsaritsa.

So now the tsar, tsaritsa and Maria were held in Ekaterinburg in a house that had previously belonged to a merchant named Ipatiev. Soon the remainder of the family joined them there.

Even in Ekaterinburg the imperial family could have been saved.

In May 1918 the former Nikolaevsky General Staff College had been moved to Ekaterinburg. Up until June 1918 the college numbered 300 students, 14 professors and 22 state tutors. The senior class of the college comprised 216 students. Just 13 of these would subsequently fight on the side of the Bolsheviks. The overwhelming majority of the students considered the Brest-Litovsk Peace Treaty, which the Bolsheviks had just agreed with the Germans, as an act of treachery; and the Bolsheviks as German agents.

So the college, along with its students – professional tsarist officers who hated the Bolsheviks – was now situated right alongside the arrested imperial family. This worried the leadership of the Urals Soviet. The head of the Ekaterinburg Bolsheviks, Isai Goloshchekin, informed Moscow that the presence in Ekaterinburg 'of an organised nest of counter-revolutionaries under the name of a college' was entirely unacceptable.

At the end of May the situation in Ekaterinburg deteriorated sharply. On 28 May Nicholas wrote in his diary: 'Attitudes to us have changed in recent days. Our jailers are trying not to speak to us, as if they are not quite themselves, and as if they feel some kind of alarm or danger around them. Hard to understand!'

But outside the walls of the Ipatiev house there was no problem understanding. In the middle of May the Czechoslovak legion, formerly prisoners of war of the tsar, had risen up against the Bolsheviks. Cossack units then joined up with the Czechoslovaks. Chelyabinsk fell. The Czechoslovaks and the Cossacks were moving on Ekaterinburg. Kyshtym fell. Zlatoust fell – just 130 versts from Ekaterinburg. On 14 June all the Communists and workers from the Sysertovsky, Nizhny Tagilsky and Alapaevsky factories departed for the front.

The college nestling within Ekaterinburg now constituted a real threat to Bolshevik power. By Trotsky's order the college was swiftly transferred to Kazan. But its students declared themselves 'neutral'. Less than half of the complement in fact went to Kazan. So about 200 model professional soldiers remained in Ekaterinburg – a city now gripped by panic.

On 28 May there were street disorders in Ekaterinburg. On the eve of these, Ensign Arbatov, along with his unit, defected to the Whites. The only remaining support for the Bolsheviks left in the city was the Upper Isetsky Workers Detachment under the command of Pyotr Yermakov. Every other workers' detachment was at the front. A huge crowd of citizens shouting anti-Bolshevik slogans gathered on the cathedral square. Yermakov with his detachment, and Commissar Goloshchensky with the Chekists, with difficulty dispersed the mutinous crowd. They simply didn't have enough Red Guards. Meanwhile Red Guards fit for the front were guarding the 'tyrant' and his family. Louder and louder, voices were saying 'take them from their posts'. In other words, finish off the family.

The college was situated not far from the Tikhvinsky monastery at the heart of the city. It was from the Tikhvinsky monastery that milk, cream and eggs were delivered to the imperial family. It would not be difficult for the professional officers to establish links with the detainees. And the Ipatiev house was protected by men who, up until yesterday, had been workers, many of whom had never fired a gun. What about an attack? In the fear, panic and confusion that had seized the town such an attack had every prospect of success.

Meanwhile the Bolsheviks had decided to hasten matters. They already understood what the consequences of the Tsar's liberation could be in current circumstances. Trotsky wrote precisely of this straight after the execution of the imperial family. In his diary he quotes his discussion with Sverdlov – Lenin's right hand man.

Trotsky, just back from the front, asks Sverdlov;

- Where is the tsar?
- He has been shot of course, Sverdlov replies.
- And the family?
- The family with him.
- All of them?
- All of them.
- And who made the decision?
- We decided here. Ilyich reckoned that we should not leave them as a living symbol, especially in our difficult situation.

From the end of May the Bolsheviks were preparing to destroy the 'living symbol'.

Three days after the disturbances in the town Nicholas wrote:

31 May. Today, for some reason they didn't let us out into the garden. Avdeev came and had a long conversation with E. S. [that is, Botkin]. According to him, both he and the Regional Soviet fear the intervention of the anarchists. So we may have to make a rapid departure, probably to Moscow. He asked that preparations be made for departure. Packing quickly began, but, at Avdeev's particular request, quietly so as not to attract the attention of the guard. At about eleven o'clock in the evening he came back and said that we would

be staying for a few more days. Finally after dinner Avdeev, slightly tipsy, informed Botkin that the anarchists have been captured, the danger has passed, and our departure had been put off. After all these preparations it has now become very dull...

If only Nicholas, as he listened to the worried locals planning his journey to Moscow, had known what had happened the previous night; what 'journey' had already taken place. But up until his death he knew nothing.

At the beginning of that night, at a house previously belonging to the merchant Korolev in Perm, three unknown men had appeared. They showed a Cheka order and took the tsar's brother, the Grand Duke Michael, and his secretary Johnson away. In the forest attached to Motovilikhi village both were shot. The chairman of the Motovilikhi Soviet, Myasnikov, the chief of the militia, Ivanchikov, and three subordinates took part in the operation. The Bolsheviks announced that Michael and his valet had been 'seized by persons unknown and carried off in an unknown direction'.

In this way they eliminated the second in line to the throne, an important component of the 'living symbol'. Plainly such a 'journey' had also been prepared for the imperial family. Why had they decided to postpone it? Whereas it had been decided that Michael's disappearance was to be silent, that of Nicholas was to make more noise. The press were to be informed. But before doing this Moscow decided they needed proof that shooting him was unavoidable. They intended to obtain 'proof of a White Guard conspiracy aimed to free the Tsar'. Had there been such a conspiracy it would indeed have necessitated the swiftest possible execution of Nicholas II.

It was also decided to liquidate the remainder of the family, but to announce that they 'had been carried off to an unknown place'.

So the false conspiracy was put together in the Cheka. Half a century later the participants spoke about it. In it, the alleged conspirators were exactly those who might genuinely have conspired – the students of the Nikolaevsky College. Food was brought to the imperial family from the Novotikhvinsky monastery and with the milk in one of those monastery bottles the tsar began to find letters:

'The hour of liberation is approaching and the days of the usurpers are numbered. Whatever happens, the Slovak army is approaching closer and closer to Ekaterinburg. They are a few versts from the town ... Do not forget that the Bolsheviks even at the last moment will be ready to commit any crime. The time has come, it is vital to act ... An Officer.'

Nicholas enters into correspondence with this 'Officer'. He diligently describes the dispositions around him: how many guards, where the two machine guns are, and so on.

And finally he writes in his diary 'we prepared ourselves to be abducted by certain committed persons'.

Now the diary of the tsar, which the guards read while the prisoners were out walking, contained the words that were necessary. Now the Bolsheviks had proof of a conspiracy.

The imperial family was doomed, all of it.

Indeed, the question of the destruction of the whole imperial family was settled by Lenin, the Jacobin, even before the revolution.

In the journal *30 Days* (no. 1, 1934) Bonch-Bruevich recalled some words of the young Lenin. Lenin had been delighted by a successful answer given in Dostoyevsky's *The Devils* by the revolutionary Nechaev, the main hero, whom Lenin had dubbed 'a revolutionary titan' and 'one of the blazing revolutionaries'.

As recalled by Bonch-Bruevich, the answer of Nechaev that had so pleased the young Lenin was as follows. To the question 'who should be destroyed from the ruling house?' Nechaev gave the crisp reply 'All the Great Ektenia' (the prayer for the ruling family, which lists all its members). 'Yes, the whole Romanov House – so simple that it amounted to genius,' said the delighted Lenin of Nechaev's answer.

And Lenin accomplished Nechaev's dream; the list of Romanov martyrs destroyed by the Bolsheviks was to be long.

But the most brutal massacre was to be the shooting of the imperial family at the Ipatiev house. There, four unwed girls, a sick adolescent, their mother and their father, were all murdered, one with another.

On the eve of the killing of the imperial family a circle of advancing Czechoslovak and Cossack units was tightening around Ekaterinburg – but slowly, as if the attackers were waiting for something. How awful to write this – as if they were waiting while the imperial family was disposed of. Is it possible that the liberation of the former Supreme Commander together with the authoritarian empress could have been deeply uncomfortable for the Whites' current commanders?

As for the students of the college, in the aftermath there would be many stories of secret groups of officers organised to liberate the imperial family – stories put about by the Cheka.

'A certain N attracted 37 student officers but fearing that the Bolsheviks were on their trail they all fled to the advancing Czechoslovaks.' 'A certain Captain Bulyagin sent by the mother of the Tsar was arrested on the road to Ekaterinburg.' And so on.

These are all splendid post facto myths. The gentlemen officers had not forgiven the tsar and tsaritsa their failed war and the collapse of all order. The attitude of most officers towards the tsar is best of all characterised by an entry in the diary of Lt Gen. Baron Alexei Pavlovich von Buler (minister of war in the Russian government of Admiral A. V. Kolchak). He described the requiem mass that took place on 17 July 1919, a year after the murder of the imperial family:

> They held a requiem mass for the imperial family in the cathedral. The democratic choir refused to sing. Nuns from a neighbouring monastery were invited, and alone made possible the solemnity of the service. The Archpriest conducted the mass well, including the proclamation of titles.
>
> Opposite the cathedral was the Archbishop's house where about ten assorted senior clergy live having cast off their pastoral role. Of these, none dared to come and pray for the departed soul of the man who for them was not only Tsar but also the Anointed of God. Senior officials at the requiem included me, Rozanov, Khreshatitsky, and the Urals General Khorotkin. The remainder made an effort to forget

the requiem so as not to compromise their democratic credentials. After the requiem some elderly fellow looking over those gathered in the cathedral (a few dozen, mostly old officers) loudly declaimed 'Ha, there aren't many decent people in Omsk.'

Meanwhile the Bolsheviks were right. The tsar could have become a living symbol, and above all a unifying symbol. The White movement had become subject to a law originally formulated by the eighteenth-century aristocrat Artemy Volinsky: 'We Russians don't need bread. We eat one another and thus are satisfied.'

The White leaders, generals, determinedly hated one another; Vrangel, Denikin; Denikin, Vrangel; neither of them liked Yudenich, and none of them Kolchak.

There was just one person who had the right to stand above them: God's anointed tsar. Only he could bind the movement together, damp down the generals' haughtiness, and become that unifying symbol.

Dark semi-literate Russia, where peasants not too long ago were christened on the tsar's passing train, could well have seen a revival of the belief of which Archbishop Hermogen had written in 1918: 'According to the sacred writings, former Emperors, Kings and Tsars who have lost power in their country do not lose their rank. That is granted to them by God … Thus an abandoned church is still a church, an over-thrown idol is still God.'

The tsar did a lot of thinking in his captivity and humiliation. He saw with pain that the most important thing in the forthcoming blood and savagery was to be able to forgive it. His daughter wrote in one of her last letters 'the sovereign asks that he not be revenged. He forgives all.'

'Pray gently for your enemies.' This is the last line of a poem left in a book found after their murder in the Ipatiev house. It remained as their testament.

Such a tsar was necessary for a maddened nation washed in the blood of civil war.

But he was not needed by history.

So he was not saved.

10

FANNY KAPLAN'S ATTEMPT TO KILL LENIN

August 1918

MARTIN SIXSMITH

W HEN THE SLIM MARGINS of history's what-ifs are measured, the flight of a bullet is among the slimmest. An inch to the left and a man dies; to the right, he lives. And when the target is Vladimir Lenin, an assassin's aim can change the fate of the world.

Few in the West are aware that on 30 August 1918 a volley of bullets, fired at close range, came within inches of ending Lenin's life. Fewer still are aware that the plot may well have been staged by agents of British intelligence.

In 1918 Soviet Russia was in its infancy, fragile and struggling to survive. The Bolshevik regime was beset by enemies within and without. Western troops and White armies were battling to bring it to its knees; Soviet power hung in the balance.

If Lenin had died, depriving the socialist state of his iconic leadership, the whole enterprise could have foundered; the twentieth century would have taken a different course. Conversely, had the assassination attempt never happened, some of the worst excesses of the Red Terror might have been averted – hundreds of thousands of people might not have lost their lives in the horrors of the Gulag.

So, what are the facts? While much else might be in dispute, the medical bulletin is not.

On the evening of 30 August, Lenin was driven from the Kremlin to the Zamoskvorechie district of Moscow to address the assembled workers of the Mikhelson (Hammer and Sickle) engineering factory. It was a hotbed of revolutionary fervour and Lenin had already spoken there at least four times. Originally built in the mid nineteenth century by an Englishman called Hopper, the factory is nowadays known as the Vladimir Ilyich Electromechanical Plant. It has commemorative plaques recording the occasions on which Lenin visited the building. The plaques make no reference to the dramatic events of 1918, but when I turned up at the site in the dying days of the Soviet Union, the guards at the gate were happy to regale me with stories of 'the day Lenin nearly died'.

The Soviet leader, they said, had finished his speech and was leaving the building; they showed me the door from which he would have emerged into the factory's inner courtyard. His car was waiting nearby with the engine running, but Lenin paused to talk to some Bolshevik activists about the bread shortages that were plaguing the country. When a woman called out to him from the crowd he turned to face her, unaware she was clutching a Browning revolver under the folds of her cloak. Lenin had only a moment to glimpse his assailant's face before she fired three rapid shots. The first missed him, passing through the collar of his overcoat and wounding a bystander; the second lodged in his shoulder; the third punctured his left lung. Lenin's bodyguards rushed forward as he slumped to the ground, bundling him into the car and rushing him back to the Kremlin. He was unconscious and seemingly close to death. The woman was seized by angry members of the public, roughed up and handed over to the police.

The guards' stories were dramatic. They were told with genuine passion. But they were very much the product of official history, the version that decades of Soviet propaganda had inculcated in public opinion. Victors' history has held sway for nearly a century, but it hasn't removed the uncertainty that continues to cloud the events of autumn 1918.

I knew the guards' account was the official version because I had seen it in the cinema. *Lenin in 1918*, a black and white biopic from 1939, was one of the most widely viewed Soviet films, directed by Mikhail Romm, an artist feted by the Kremlin and a five-time winner of the Stalin Prize. It was the sequel to Romm's earlier *Lenin in October*, which told the story of the Bolshevik leader's role in the 1917 revolution, and it is undoubtedly the version the Kremlin wanted people to believe. It shows Lenin delivering a rousing speech to the factory workers, then stepping outside. Gunshots ring out and with a heroic look on his face Vladimir Ilyich clutches his chest. At this point the camera cuts to a menacing-looking woman skulking amid a crowd of people. Romm's movie shows the would-be assassin to be a disenchanted Socialist Revolutionary named Fanny Kaplan, who is arrested, tried and deservedly executed by an impartial Soviet judiciary.

But was this really how it all happened? Secrecy and doubt surrounded the aftermath of the assassination attempt; the regime was not slow to shape the story to its own political ends; and some historians now question whether Kaplan pulled – or was even capable of pulling – the trigger.

Fanny Kaplan was born Feyga Chaimovna Roitblat on 10 February 1890 in a Jewish settlement in what is now western Ukraine. Her childhood coincided with the upsurge in state sponsored anti-Semitism that sparked waves of deadly pogroms across the tsarist empire and prompted a mass exodus of Jews from Russia. Young Feyga didn't emigrate, but instead poured her resentment of the status quo into revolutionary activity, joining the Socialist Revolutionaries in her early teens.

Inspired by the socialist thinker Alexander Herzen, the SRs were the leading opposition force in the years before 1917. They were committed to toppling tsarism and were prepared to use violence to do so; but their aim was a democratic socialism that would enfranchise the peasantry and rely on the ballot box as well as the revolver and the bomb. In the maelstrom of competing factions that emerged among the revolutionaries as 1917 transformed the political landscape, the SRs were to be eclipsed and destroyed by the messianic zealots of

Bolshevism, who had no time for either the peasants or democracy. In 1906, when Feyga Roitblat adopted the revolutionary pseudonym of Fanya – or Fanny – Kaplan, that split was yet to happen; but it would ultimately seal her fate.

Fanny Kaplan's first revolutionary act had been to take part in a plot to blow up the tsarist governor of Kiev, Vladimir Sukhomlinov, who had used the military to put down strikes and demonstrations in the city. Still aged only sixteen, Kaplan was romantically involved with the anarchist Viktor Garsky, the driving force behind the plot. As they were preparing the bomb in their room at the Commercial Hotel on Voloshskaya Street, they dropped it and it exploded. Garsky was unscathed, but Kaplan received severe injuries to her hands and face, and for a time it seemed she would be permanently blind. In the ensuing chaos, Garsky ran away. Unable to see and barely able to walk, Kaplan was quickly arrested. At her trial on 5 January 1907 she was sentenced to death, but was spared execution because of her youth. Condemned instead to life in jail, she was transported later that year to the tsarist labour camps of Nerchinsk in Siberia. In the Maltsev prison she was stripped naked and flogged. With bomb fragments still lodged in her body, partially deaf and almost completely blind, she spent months in the prison hospital suffering constant pain. She recovered some of her sight, but she would experience excruciating headaches and extended periods of blindness for the rest of her days.

By early 1917, Kaplan had spent over a decade in captivity and the tsarist regime was falling apart at the seams. The February Revolution brought the socialists and liberals of the Provisional Government to power in Russia, committed to political reform and a democratically elected national parliament. The leader of the Provisional Government, Alexander Kerensky, had been a Socialist Revolutionary, just like Kaplan, and one of his first acts was to order the release of all political prisoners.

In early March Fanny Kaplan returned to Moscow. She benefited from the new government's generosity towards veterans of the revolutionary struggle with an official pass to stay at a health clinic in

Yevpatoria on the Crimean coast. While she was there she met Dmitry Ulyanov, the younger brother of Vladimir Lenin and a key Bolshevik official in the region. It was the summer of 1917 and the split between Kaplan's SRs and Lenin's Bolsheviks had not yet reached its bloody apotheosis. The two young people – Ulyanov was only six years older than Kaplan – evidently hit it off, and he gave orders for her to be admitted to a specialist eye clinic in Kharkov. Two complex operations succeeded in restoring some of her sight; she would never be able to distinguish fine detail, but she was now able to make out the silhouettes of people who were directly beside her and she no longer tripped over large objects.

There is some dispute over Kaplan's activities between the summer of 1917 and her re-emergence into the spotlight of history in August the following year. She was certainly back in Moscow by the spring of 1918 and she was again active in Socialist Revolutionary circles. But it is here that the official Soviet version takes over. Much of the information about Kaplan in the months leading up to the attempt on Lenin's life in August 1918 comes from later writings, Soviet accounts of her political affiliations, references to her interrogation, and – not surprisingly with such a high-profile case – they inevitably embody the party line.

The official story is that Kaplan immediately joined an anti-Bolshevik conspiracy under the leadership of the SR activist and military commander Grigory Semyonov, and that the group was engaged in planning a series of assassinations of Bolshevik leaders, including Lenin, Trotsky, Zinoviev, Uritsky, Volodarsky and others. Their plots were portrayed as a highly organised armed conspiracy, funded by reactionary groups and foreign powers, dedicated to overthrowing the legitimate power of the Bolshevik state. August 1918 was not a single episode, the line went, but part of a web of violent actions against the regime.

The aim of such allegations was to blacken the reputation of the Socialist Revolutionaries, who were by then regarded by the Bolsheviks as their sworn enemies. All evidence of SR treachery was grist to the regime's propaganda mill.

It is, nonetheless, completely understandable that Kaplan would have been disenchanted with Lenin and the Bolshevik party. After February 1917 the short-lived Provisional Government had begun to introduce the foundations of parliamentary democracy; and even after he seized control in October, Lenin continued to promise 'All Power to the Soviets', the directly elected local councils of workers, peasants and soldiers. To the surprise of his opponents and many of his own supporters, Lenin stood by the Provisional Government's promise of free elections to a national Constituent Assembly, a body that was intended to pave the way for a constitution and a parliament based on universal suffrage.

The millions who turned out to vote on 25 November 1917 probably believed that democracy in Russia was finally dawning. After a largely peaceful election, in which two thirds of the population voted, the Constituent Assembly convened in the Tauride Palace in St Petersburg on the afternoon of 5 January 1918. It was the first freely elected parliament in Russia's history, a historic moment by any standard.

But it was doomed to failure. The Bolsheviks had not done well in the elections and the Socialist Revolutionaries had secured a majority in the Assembly. With more than twice as many seats as the Bolsheviks, the SRs should have been the dominant force in Russia. But Lenin had already installed a government packed with Bolshevik ministers, and he wasn't about to let an election remove them from power.

'To relinquish the Soviet Republic won by the people, for the sake of the bourgeois parliamentary system of the Constituent Assembly, would now be a step backwards and would cause the collapse of the October workers' and peasants' revolution,' Lenin wrote. 'We must not be deceived by the election figures. Elections prove nothing. The Bolsheviks can and must take state power into our own hands...'

The Constituent Assembly was allowed to exist for just over twelve hours. The Bolsheviks walked out after the first votes went against them. The other parties carried on until four o'clock in the morning of 6 January and were then evicted by pro-Bolshevik guards fuelled with vodka and brandishing rifles. When the deputies came back the next day they found the Tauride Palace locked and surrounded by soldiers. Lenin's Bolsheviks had hijacked the embryonic institutions of freedom and democracy. Now they were about to impose a centralised dictatorship even harsher than the tsarist regime they had overthrown.

Given such treachery on the part of the Bolsheviks, Fanny Kaplan and the other disenfranchised SRs would undoubtedly have felt cheated and angry. But did she really pull the trigger that day in August? Would Semyonov really have selected Fanny Kaplan to carry out the attack? A woman who was nearly blind, had never shot a revolver in her life and had little or no experience of terrorist attacks? Her role up to then had seemingly been confined to intelligence gathering – finding out where Lenin would be at a specific time and reporting back to her colleagues.

It was nearly 10 p.m. by the time Lenin emerged from the Mikhelson factory; sundown in Moscow at that time of year is around 9 p.m. and Fanny could not see in the dark. When Kaplan was arrested, she was not even wearing glasses. Not one of the eighteen witnesses who were interviewed actually saw her firing. And the bullet removed from Lenin's neck, almost four years later, was found not to have come from the Browning pistol alleged to have been held by Kaplan.

In 1922, Semyonov would testify that the official version of events was true in all respects, despite the inconsistencies it contained. But by then he had renounced his Socialist Revolutionary allegiance and was almost certainly collaborating with the Bolsheviks as they prepared for a show trial of SR leaders designed to discredit the party once and for all.

What is undeniable is that Fanny made no attempt to exculpate herself. She was arrested either on the spot or at a tram stop on nearby Serpukhovka Street – the policeman who collared her changed his testimony – carrying a suitcase and making no effort to run away. Taken for questioning by the Cheka secret police, she allegedly made the following statement (although there is no way of verifying its authenticity, as she would be dead by the time the Cheka released it):

My name is Fanya Kaplan. Today I shot at Lenin. I did it on my own. I will give no details. I resolved to kill Lenin long ago. I consider him a traitor to the Revolution. I was exiled to Siberia for participating in an assassination attempt against a tsarist official in Kiev. I spent eleven years doing hard labour. After the [February] Revolution, I was freed. I supported free elections to the Constituent Assembly and I still support that. In October, the Bolsheviks seized power without the consent of the people. The Bolsheviks are conspirators who carried out a coup.

Another suspect arrested at the same time as Kaplan, a man named Alexander Prototipov, had been shot almost at once, so Fanny knew the fate that awaited her. Yet she refused to argue her innocence or to implicate any accomplices. Her silence has led to suggestions that she was the scapegoat for others, shielding her comrades who had done the deed. She would be presented by Soviet propaganda as a psychotic monster and her reputation has not been completely rehabilitated even now.

Guilty or innocent, Fanny Kaplan would, inevitably, be executed; but she would have one more appearance to make in our story before going to the firing squad.

While Kaplan was being bundled into the police van, Lenin was being rushed back to the Kremlin. Terrified that other assassins might be lying in wait for him, his security men refused to take the Soviet leader out of the safety of his fortified living quarters. They brought in doctors to treat his wounds, but the bullets were lodged in critical areas of his body and they decided not to remove them.

Lenin had come close to death; his injuries were severe, and although fate decreed that he would live, his health was badly undermined. The shooting almost certainly contributed to the series of strokes that would incapacitate and ultimately kill him in January 1924; but his survival – by the narrowest of margins – meant he would have five and a half more years to continue his work. In those five and half years, Lenin would succeed in consolidating a Soviet system that would endure for more than seven decades, bringing to fruition the greatest socialist experiment of all time. His survival would enable epochal changes in political and social thinking, changes that for better or worse would affect the lives of millions across the globe.

Lenin's injuries were grave, and blood from the wound to his neck had spilled into his lungs, making breathing difficult. But the Bolshevik media played down the seriousness of the situation, fearing it might engender public panic or encourage opposition forces plotting a coup against the regime. Official propaganda portrayed Lenin as brushing his injuries heroically aside, refusing to heed the warnings of the medical men. *Pravda's* headline read: 'Lenin, shot twice, refuses help. Next morning, he reads papers, listens; continues to guide the locomotive of global revolution.'

The Lenin myth was gathering momentum; the intimations of saintly stoicism and the extravagant personality cult that would attend him in life and in death are already evident in *Pravda's* words. Lenin was a holy martyr, saved by miraculous forces and insisting on carrying on working, Christ-like, for the good of the people. A party that had destroyed religion in a deeply Christian country needed something to replace it in the people's minds and holy Lenin – dedicated, self-denying and fanatical – was in tune with the times.

While Lenin was being very publicly heroic, Fanny Kaplan was pursuing her own concept of heroism in a considerably less glamorous setting. The police officer who arrested her reported her as saying, 'I have done my duty without fear, and now I shall die without fear.' But her courage was about to be tested.

Her interrogation, in the bowels of the Lubyanka, was rigorous. The Cheka were determined to make her reveal her fellow conspirators, and their methods were not renowned for subtlety. The sketchy record of her questioning, compiled later by Bolshevik sources, reflects the regime's insistence on creating its own version of what had happened.

Under examination by three investigators, named as Kursky, Skrypnik and Dyakonov, Kaplan is reported as being in possession of a Browning automatic with the serial number 150489. When the deputy head of the Cheka, Yakov Peters, questions her about this, Kaplan refuses to respond. Yakov Sverdlov, chairman of the Bolshevik Central Committee and de facto head of state, then joins the interrogation and is described as angered and exasperated by Kaplan's stubborn silence.

The Cheka's aim is to vilify Kaplan and establish her as an agent of the hated SRs. Her interrogation continued for three days and three nights, so the fact that they failed to make her talk is remarkable. Kaplan did not name Semyonov, or his fellow SR activist Lidia Konoplyova. She insisted that she had acted alone and not on the orders of any political party. She said she considered Lenin a traitor to the revolution, whose actions had put back the advent of socialism 'by decades'.

On 1 September, two days after the assassination attempt, the Socialist Revolutionary Party Central Committee denied having ordered the attack. According to Semyonov's 1922 testimony (by which time he had become a collaborator with the regime), this was a lie; the party leadership had promised him they would claim responsibility, but reneged in panic when they saw the scale of revulsion the shooting had caused.

Kaplan, it seemed, was of no further use to the Cheka; her firing squad was already being prepared. But there was one final twist still to come.

In August 1918, the Bolsheviks were fighting a vicious civil war against powerful military forces, led by former tsarist generals, whose aim was to topple the Soviet regime and restore the old order. The struggle between the Bolshevik Reds and the opposition Whites was at a critical stage, with the outcome hanging in the balance. Fearing that a Bolshevik victory would lead to world revolution and the spread of communist contagion throughout Europe, the Western powers had sent troops to support the White armies. British, French and American forces were landing in the Russian far north; Czech legions were seizing control of territory and communications in Siberia. With 40,000 troops on the ground, Britain had taken the lead in the campaign and the Kremlin leadership regarded London as the most dangerous of their enemies.

So it was little surprise that the Bolsheviks should suspect – or at least announce that they suspected – British involvement in the plot against Lenin. On the morning after the shooting, Yakov Sverdlov had issued a statement in the name of the Soviet government:

> A few hours ago there occurred an evil assassination attempt aimed at comrade Lenin. As he was leaving after a political meeting comrade Lenin was wounded. Two gunmen have been arrested. Their identities are now being established. We have no doubt that the fingerprints of the Right SRs will be discovered in this affair, along with those of the hirelings of the English and the French.

The British diplomat, Robert Bruce Lockhart, who had been acting consul general in Moscow before the 1917 revolution, was now serving as London's envoy to the Bolshevik regime. In his vivid, tendentious memoirs, he describes the backlash against Britain that followed the attack on Lenin:

> On the way home we had bought a paper. It was full of bulletins about Lenin's condition. He was still unconscious. There were, too, violent articles against the bourgeoisie and against the Allies ... There had been a terrible tragedy in St Petersburg. A band of Cheka agents had burst into our Embassy there. The gallant Cromie [Captain Francis Cromie, the British naval attaché – MS] had resisted the intrusion and, after killing a commissar, had been shot down at the top of the staircase. All British officials in St Petersburg had been arrested...

As well as fulfilling his diplomatic duties, however, Bruce Lockhart was also working for British intelligence – it is no coincidence that his autobiography is entitled *Memoirs of a British Agent* – and there are grounds to believe that he had a hand in, or at least knew about Kaplan's plans to murder Lenin. For their part, the Bolsheviks were certain of his guilt. Together with his fellow spy Sidney Reilly, Bruce Lockhart was publicly accused of masterminding the plot on behalf of the Western imperialists.

On the Tuesday we read the full tale of our iniquities in the Bolshevik Press, which excelled itself in a fantastic account of a so-called Lockhart Plot. We were accused of having conspired to murder Lenin and Trotsky, to set up a military dictatorship in Moscow, and by blowing up all the railway bridges to reduce the populations of Moscow and St Petersburg to starvation. The whole plot had been revealed by the loyalty of the Lettish garrison, whom the Allies had sought to suborn by lavish gifts of money ... An equally fantastic story described the events in St Petersburg. Cromie's murder was depicted as a measure of self-defence by the Bolshevik agents, who had been forced to return his fire. Huge headlines denounced the Allied representatives as 'Anglo-French Bandits,' and in their comments the leader-writers shrieked for the application of a wholesale terror and of the severest measures against the conspirators.

Bruce Lockhart was dragged from his bed and arrested. With the net closing in, Sidney Reilly fled north via Petrograd to Finland, finally reaching London on 8 November. Bruce Lockhart was interrogated by the Cheka in the Lubyanka prison. His memoirs are the epitome of British *sangfroid* under duress, but there is little doubt that his life was hanging by a thread:

My term of imprisonment lasted for exactly one month. It may be divided into two periods: the first, which lasted five days and was marked by discomfort and fear; the second, which lasted for twenty-four days and may be described as a period of comparative comfort accompanied by acute mental strain. My one comfort was the official Bolshevik newspapers, which my gaolers took a propagandist joy in supplying to me. Certainly, as far as my own case was concerned, they were far from reassuring. They were still full of the Lockhart Plot. They contained numerous resolutions, passed by workmen's committees, demanding my trial and execution ... From the first day of my captivity I had made up my mind that, if Lenin died, my own life would not be worth a moment's purchase.

Bruce Lockhart's first five days of 'discomfort and fear' coincided with the continuing interrogation of Fanny Kaplan. After refusing all demands to name her co-conspirators she had been consigned to a basement cell where, according to one of her guards, she spent the night pacing back and forth, then sitting forlornly on a wooden stool. In the morning she refused breakfast. As the sun rose she was taken into Bruce Lockhart's room and confronted with the man the Bolsheviks believed had sponsored her act of terror. He was careful to give no sign of recognition:

> At six in the morning a woman was brought into the room. She was dressed in black. Her hair was black, and her eyes, set in a fixed stare, had great black rings under them. Her face was colourless. Her features, strongly Jewish, were unattractive. She might have been any age between twenty and thirty-five. We guessed it was Kaplan. Doubtless, the Bolsheviks hoped that she would give us some sign of recognition. Her composure was unnatural. She went to the window and, leaning her chin upon her hand, looked out into the daylight. And there she remained, motionless, speechless, apparently resigned to her fate, until presently the sentries came and took her away. She was shot before she knew if her attempt to alter history had failed or succeeded.

At 4 p.m. on 3 September Fanny Kaplan was taken to an underground garage and executed with a single bullet to the back of the head. There had been no trial and no verdict. Pavel Malkov, the Kremlin commandant who did the deed, wrote later that he had no hesitation in despatching a 'traitor' such as Kaplan:

> I knew at that moment that there must be no mercy shown to the enemies of the revolution. Retribution was complete; the sentence carried out. I, Pavel Dmitrievich Malkov, Bolshevik party member, sailor of the Baltic Fleet and commander of the Kremlin, carried it out personally. If history were to repeat itself and another piece of

work such as she, someone who had lifted her hand against Vladimir Ilych, were to appear before the barrel of my pistol, my hand would not tremble as I pulled the trigger, just as it did not tremble back then.

Malkov says he received orders from Yakov Sverdlov that Kaplan should have no grave; no physical trace should be allowed to remain of a woman who might become a counter-revolutionary martyr. So Malkov soaked Kaplan's corpse in petrol and burned it in a steel barrel in the Alexandrov Gardens beneath the Kremlin wall. The whole gruesome process was witnessed by the Bolshevik regime's poet laureate, the proletarian hack Demyan Bedny, in order 'to fuel his socialist imagination'.

Bruce Lockhart was considerably luckier. After a month in the Lubyanka, London swapped him for a high-ranking Soviet diplomat. On his return, the British media were quick to portray him and Sidney Reilly as heroic Western agents nobly trying to smash the communist menace. A radio play starring Errol Flynn, and a Warner Brothers movie with Leslie Howard, entitled *British Agent*, took a resolutely anti-Bolshevik stance, portraying our plucky 'diplomats' as the prime movers in a daring operation sanctioned by London.

Bruce Lockhart's claims that Britain had nothing to do with the attack on Lenin are contradicted by the Cheka's records of the affair. They suggest he confessed to being part of a plot to overthrow the Bolshevik regime and that Sidney Reilly was also involved. Bruce Lockhart's own son, Robin, wrote in 1967, 'Once intervention in Russia had been decided on in 1918, he gave his active support to the counter-revolutionary movement, with which Reilly was actively working. My father has himself made it clear to me that he worked much more closely with Reilly than he had publicly indicated.'

Recently released telegrams between Bruce Lockhart and his Foreign Office bosses lend credence to this. In late summer 1918, shortly before Fanny Kaplan's attack on Lenin, he reported on a meeting he had held with the former leader of the SRs' Fighting

Committee, also known as the Terror Brigade, the anti-Bolshevik plotter Boris Savinkov. One telegram states: 'Savinkov's proposals for counter-revolution. Plan is how Bolshevik barons will be murdered and military dictatorship formed.'

In a handwritten note at the bottom of Bruce Lockhart's message, the foreign secretary Lord Curzon comments, 'Savinkov's methods are drastic, though if successful probably effective.'

The evidence remains inconclusive, but if Britain were indeed behind the assassination attempt, Bruce Lockhart was extremely fortunate to be released. Before he left the Lubyanka, he caught a chilling glimpse of the consequences that the plot against Lenin would have for those who fell foul of Bolshevik power:

> As we were talking, a motor van – a kind of 'Black Maria' – pulled up in the courtyard below, and a squad of men, armed with rifles and bandoliers, got out and took up their places in the yard. Presently, a door opened just below us, and three men with bowed heads walked slowly forward to the van. I recognised them instantly. They were Sheglovitoff, Khvostoff, and Bieletsky, three ex-Ministers of the Tsarist régime, who had been in prison since the revolution. There was a pause, followed by a scream. Then through the door the fat figure of a priest was half-pushed, half-carried, to the 'Black Maria.' His terror was pitiful. Tears rolled down his face. His knees rocked, and he fell like a great ball of fat on the ground. I felt sick and turned away. 'Where are they going?' I asked. 'They are going to another world,' said Peters drily ... the first batch of the several hundred victims of the Terror who were shot at that time as a reprisal for the attempted assassination of Lenin.

The day after Fanny Kaplan's execution, Sverdlov announced the opening of a campaign of reprisals that would be known as the Red Terror. It would be uncompromising and brutal, and it was the direct result of the assassination attempt on 30 August:

Moscow Kremlin, 5 September 1918.
The Council of People's Commissars of the Russian Soviet Federal
Socialist Republic.
DECREE: 'On Red Terror'
Having considered the report of the Chairman of the Cheka commission on the struggle against counterrevolution ... the Council
of People's Commissars finds that in the current situation the use of
political terror to secure the non-militarised areas of the country is
an absolute necessity; ... that it is necessary to safeguard the Soviet
Republic from class enemies by confining them to concentration
camps; that all persons participating in White Guard organisations,
conspiracies and rebellions must be executed by shooting, and that
the names of those executed and the reason for their execution must
be made public.

The decree gave free rein to the bloodthirsty fanatics of the Cheka.
From now on they would arrest and eliminate anyone they suspected of
harbouring the slightest reservations about the Bolshevik regime, and
many others who simply got in their way. The rule of law and judicial
oversight were suspended; executions could be ordered by a 'troika' of
three secret policemen, sitting in private, and with no right of appeal.

As paranoia became the norm, the Bolsheviks relied more and
more on their murderous henchmen. The Cheka's methods, cynically
acknowledged by its leader, 'Iron' Felix Dzerzhinsky, were simple: confessions extracted by torture, followed by immediate execution. 'We
stand for organized terror,' Dzerzhinsky said. 'This should be frankly
admitted. Terror is an absolute necessity during times of revolution.
Our aim is to fight against the enemies of the Soviet Government and
of the new order of life. We judge quickly ... Do not think that I seek
forms of revolutionary justice; we are not in need of justice now – this
is war.'

The shooting on 30 August had plunged the Bolsheviks into panic
and fear. In the throes of civil war and surrounded by enemies, the
fragile regime saw threats everywhere. There was an absolute and

immediate assumption that this was an enemy conspiracy. News came in of another attack, this time fatal, on the head of the Petrograd secret police, Moisei Uritsky. Scores of suspects were rounded up, tortured and shot.

Exact figures for the number of deaths are hard to establish. The 'first batch' of victims referred to by Bruce Lockhart seems to have claimed the lives of around 800 Socialist Revolutionaries and other political opponents of the regime, most of whom had been arrested after the October revolution. Since then they had been held as hostages, whose lives would be forfeit in the event of enemy action against Bolshevik interests. Even the officially admitted figures make startling reading. In Petrograd alone, 512 political prisoners – none of them connected in any way with Fanny Kaplan – were murdered. Across the country, an estimated 14,000 executions were carried out.

The immediate effect of the August shootings was a terrible hardening in the Bolshevik mentality. In response to the attack on Lenin, so-called class enemies were rounded up and executed for no other crime than their social origin. In operations that foreshadowed the Gestapo, hostages were selected from former tsarist officials, landowners, priests, lawyers, bankers and merchants to be used as reprisals. The British journalist Morgan Philips Price recorded his horror at the Bolsheviks' methods:

> I shall never forget one of the Izvestia articles for Saturday, September 7th. There was no mistaking its meaning. It was proposed to take hostages from the former officers of the Tsar's army, from the Kadets and from the families of the Moscow and Petrograd middle-classes and to shoot ten for every Communist who fell to the White terror. Shortly after, a decree was issued by the central Soviet Executive ordering all officers of the old army within territories of the Republic to report on a certain day at certain places ... The reason given by the Bolshevik leaders for the Red terror was that conspirators could only be convinced that the Soviet Republic was powerful enough to be respected if it was able to punish its enemies, but nothing

would convince these enemies except the fear of death. All civilized restraints had gone...

Lenin himself signed the execution lists. It was he who initiated the Terror and he who pushed it ever further into bloody excess. He acknowledged the ruthlessness that drove him onwards when he confessed that he took the fanatical Rakhmetov in Chernyshevsky's novel *What Is To Be Done?* as a model and inspiration: 'I can't listen to music,' Lenin said, 'because it makes me want to say sweet, silly things, and pat people on the head ... but you have to beat people's heads, beat them mercilessly!'

That fanaticism, which would result in a lot of 'merciless beating' over the next five years, was undoubtedly intensified by the impact of the bullets he received in August 1918. Lenin's aim now seemed to be the physical annihilation of a whole social class. Being modestly well off made you guilty; soft hands unused to manual labour could get you shot. Martin Latsis, the head of the Cheka in Ukraine, revealed the real purpose of the Terror:

> Don't go looking in the evidence to see whether or not the accused fought against the Soviets with arms or words. Just ask him which class he belongs to, what is his background, his education, his profession. These are the questions that will determine the fate of the accused. That is the meaning and the very essence of the Red Terror.

In the name of Lenin's Utopia, an estimated half a million people were killed in the three years to 1921. The long-term legacy of Kaplan's three bullets in August 1918 would be to make terror a permanent feature of Soviet society. It would reach its apogee in Stalin's murderous purges of the late 1930s, but for the whole seven decades of its existence the USSR consistently relegated the rule of law to a secondary role. Even in the 1980s, Mikhail Gorbachev was lamenting that the Soviet Union had never been 'a law governed society'. The killings had stopped, but the lawlessness continued, and it continues in Russia today.

Would it all have been different if Fanny Kaplan had succeeded in killing Lenin? Or if she had never embarked on her mission in the first place? Counterfactual history is a thankless task; it leaves too much to the individual imagination, but there is evidence that Lenin's brush with death changed the whole tenor of Soviet politics.

The terror against 'class enemies' prompted an unprecedented flight of the brightest and best in Russian society. Members of the former middle class were denounced as *bourzhoui,* 'bourgeois parasites', and 'non-persons'. Their homes were confiscated, their furniture seized and their clothes requisitioned for the state. They were placed in the lowest category for food rations, on the border of starvation, and forced to do cruel, often deadly labour.

Of those intellectuals, scientists and artists who had not been mown down by the Cheka, between one and two million fled abroad. It was a brain drain that left the nation bereft. Shortly before he himself starved to death, the philosopher Vasily Rozanov wrote presciently:

> With a clank, a squeal and a groan, an iron curtain has descended over Russian history: the show is over, the audience has risen. It's time for people to put on their coats and go home. But when they look around they see there are no coats anymore, and no more homes…

The men and women who had made the country function – doctors, engineers, chemists, architects, inventors – were gone, dead or fled. Their absence hastened the economic collapse, industry stalled and factories closed. With wages losing 90 per cent of their value, even the proletariat began to desert the Bolsheviks. 'Down with Lenin and horsemeat,' scrawled the Petrograd graffiti, 'Give us the Tsar and pork!' When strikes broke out, the government turned its Red Terror on the workers, with mass firings, arrests and executions.

As his hold on power became ever more fragile, Lenin abandoned his promises of freedom, justice and self-determination. The rhetoric of liberation gave way to what came to be known as War Communism

– harsh, enslaving and repressive. Lenin had come to power promising 'Peace, Bread, Land and Workers Control'. But after 1918 the Bolsheviks would rescind every one of these promises.

Between 1918 and 1921, forced labour was imposed on the population, with breaches of discipline punishable by death. The labour camps began to fill up with 'anti-revolutionary elements'. A siege mentality informed the government's every act. Workers were no longer seen as agents of the revolution but as raw material, an expendable resource to be exploited in the great experiment of building socialism.

Instead of peace, Lenin had brought devastation. Instead of bread – starvation. Instead of land – requisitions. Instead of workers representation – terror. Winston Churchill commented tartly that 'Lenin's aim was to save the world, his method to blow it up'. The British consul in Petrograd, Colonel R. E. Kimens reported:

> The only work done by the Soviet authorities is the inciting of class hatred, requisitioning and confiscation of property, and destruction of absolutely everything. All freedom of word and action has been suppressed; the country is being ruled by an autocracy that is infinitely worse than that of the old regime. Justice does not exist and every act on the part of persons not belonging to the 'proletariat' is interpreted as counter revolutionary and punished by imprisonment and in many cases execution … The Soviet authorities' one object is to overthrow the existing order of things and capitalism, first in Russia and afterwards in all other countries, and to this end all methods are admissible.

Lenin seemed unmoved. In the years after he was shot by Fanny Kaplan, it is hard to find a word of human sympathy or concern anywhere in his collected works. Directives that he signed personally called for ever-greater repressions in the name of Bolshevism.

'If it is necessary for the realization of a specific political goal to perform a series of brutal actions, then it is necessary to perform them in the most energetic manner,' Lenin wrote to Molotov. 'We must …

put down all resistance with such brutality that they will not forget it for decades,' he wrote of those priests who were resisting his campaign to close the churches and confiscate church property. 'The greater the numbers of reactionary clergy and reactionary bourgeoisie we succeed in executing ... the better. Because these people must be taught a lesson in such a way that they will not dare to even think of further resistance for decades to come.'

Russia was slipping into anarchy. Strikes were crippling the towns, the countryside riven by revolt. And Lenin's response was still more terror.

When Grigory Zinoviev and Nikolai Bukharin tried to moderate the powers of the secret police Lenin overruled them. As late as 1921 he was still expanding the Cheka's powers of summary execution.

Even after the Khrushchev revelations of 1956, when Soviet historiography began to heap blame on Stalin for the murderous excesses of the century, it continued to exculpate Lenin as if his reputation were inviolable. But it was unequivocally Lenin who initiated and inculcated the reign of terror. It was he who ordered the repressions, the executions and the concentration camps. And he ordered them after he was shot by Fanny Kaplan.

The shooting in August 1918 had a dramatic impact on Lenin. If the Kaplan assassination attempt had never taken place, the intensity of the Red Terror would surely have been less; fewer people would have lost their liberty and their lives.

But if Kaplan hadn't been half blind, if her aim had been less uncertain, if Lenin had died that day in August, the impact on history could have been cataclysmic. Chaos theory's 'butterfly effect' – time's amplification of initially minor perturbations, a butterfly flapping or not flapping its wing, into the immense force of hurricanes – could have changed everything. The Bolshevik regime, already assailed by powerful enemies, could easily have foundered. And even if it had survived the loss of its inspirational leader, its subsequent development would have been dramatically different.

It is likely that Leon Trotsky, the cruel, mercurial minister of war, would have become leader in Lenin's place. His hatred of Stalin would almost certainly have precluded the Georgian monster's rise to ultimate power. But it is equally probable that Trotsky's insistence on exporting communism to the rest of the globe – he was the unbending proponent of world revolution – would have done for the USSR well before then. Whatever Stalin's other failings, it was his pragmatic abandonment of the pipe dream of world revolution in favour of retrenchment – 'socialism in one country' – that saved the USSR from almost certain annihilation in the crisis years of the 1920s.

As it turned out, the events of 1918 – the escalation of civil war, the ferocity of Bolshevism's opponents, the spiralling feuds within the ranks of the revolution and, not least, Fanny Kaplan's attempted assassination of its leader – hardened the Bolsheviks into a party of autocratic power, uninterested in debate or divergent opinions. Henceforth they would consider themselves a paramilitary fraternity surrounded by an untrustworthy population that must be re-educated to understand the new reality. To achieve their ends, the party's leaders would steel themselves to be austere, disciplined zealots, untroubled by human emotions. It was the end of all hopes for democracy in Russia; the beginning of seventy years of unbending communist autocracy.

SEA CHANGE IN THE CIVIL WAR

November 1918

EVAN MAWDSLEY

Two events in mid November 1918, separated by only a week, transformed the course of the Civil War in Russia. The first was the armistice between Germany and the Allies, signed in a railway carriage at Compiègne in France on Monday, 11 November. The second took place 2,900 miles away, at Omsk in central Siberia on the following Sunday night, 17 November. The Provisional All-Russian Government (PA-RG), a body claiming to be the legitimate government of Russia and led by a 'Directory' of five men, was overthrown in a coup d'état. The following morning a military dictator, Vice Admiral Alexander Kolchak, took the post of 'supreme ruler' (*verkhovnyi pravitel*) of Russia.

THE ARMISTICE AND RUSSIA

The terms of the Compiègne armistice included the withdrawal of German troops to within their own borders. While such forces in the west would move within fifteen days (Clause II), and most of those in the east should also do so 'immediately' (Clause XII), Russia was for the Allies something of a special case. Clause XII of the Armistice stipulated that while German troops 'in territories which before the war formed part of Russia' should also return home, this was to occur only 'as soon as the Allies shall think the moment suitable, having regard to the internal situation of these territories'. Also important was Clause XXV, which required the Germans to give Allied ships free access to the Baltic.[1]

The German military presence on Russian territory had developed over four years. Military defeats suffered under the Imperial Government and the 1917 'revolutionary' Provisional Government led to enemy occupation of Poland as well as parts of Belarus, Lithuania and Latvia. In November 1917 the Bolsheviks seized power, with the promise of bringing an end to the war. But negotiations, followed by an armistice and then renewed fighting, ended with the Treaty of Brest-Litovsk on 3 March 1918. Under this treaty the new Soviet government lost control of large swathes of territory in the west and south, notably in the Baltic and Ukraine, which were occupied by German (and Austro-Hungarian) troops.

The November 1918 armistice undid all this. The troops of the Central Powers in the Russian 'borderlands' were now concerned mainly with effecting their own rapid withdrawal. A temporary power vacuum was created, which could be filled by different forces. Nationalists among the ethnic minorities of the borderlands hoped to achieve genuine statehood. Ethnic Russians, opposed to both the Bolsheviks and the minority nationalists, wanted to regain control of these territories and use them as a base to strike against the Soviet zone. The Bolshevik central government prepared to reassert control over the borderlands by using its growing Red Army. At a grander level, the Bolsheviks hoped the borderlands would provide a bridge to central Europe, enabling them to extend socialism to Germany and the lands of Austria-Hungary. From the west the British and French wished to contain this expansion of Russian/Soviet power, by supporting anti-Soviet governments – minority nationalist or Russian anti-Bolshevik. The French, in particular, were eager to establish a cordon sanitaire around Bolshevik Russia. The Allies, like the Leninists, had a maximum programme: by isolating the Soviet zone and supporting local forces they would bring about the total destruction of Bolshevism.

On 23 October, two weeks before the Armistice and based on the already rapidly changing military situation, Premier Georges Clemenceau had signed a directive launching an active struggle against Soviet Russia. He made much of the danger of growing Bolshevik strength and put forward a policy of economic blockade. Troops would be landed in south Russia to cut the Soviet regime off from the grain and mineral resources of Ukraine and the Don region, and a military nucleus would be created, around which anti-Soviet forces could rally. Three days after the Armistice, on 14 November, the British War Cabinet met to approve the outlines of a post-war Russia policy. These included provision of military supplies to the anti-Bolshevik General Denikin in south Russia and to the governments of the Baltic States, 'if, and when, they have Governments ready to receive and utilise such material'. The small number of British troops already in north Russia and Siberia would remain there. In Siberia diplomatic support – de facto recognition – was to be offered to the local anti-Bolshevik government.[2]

In the weeks that immediately followed the 11 November armistice Allied fleets passed into the Baltic and Black seas. After the Mudros armistice with Turkey (signed on 30 October) British and French warships were finally able to enter the Dardanelles. On the morning of 13 November a large force anchored off Constantinople. Passing out of the Bosphorus and steaming north across the Black Sea, the main fleet arrived at Sevastopol on 25 November. Individual ships reached Novorossiisk in the north Caucasus on the 22nd and Odessa on the 27th. In the Baltic Sea, Allied naval vessels reached Libava (Liepāja) in Latvia on 9 December, and Revel (Tallinn) in Estonia on the 12th.

THE OMSK COUP

Meanwhile, on 5 November 1918 – six days before the Compiègne armistice – Vice Admiral Alexander Vasilyevich Kolchak had become the war and navy minister of the Provisional All-Russian Government, now based in Omsk in central Siberia. He had arrived in the city three weeks earlier, on 13 October.

The train carrying the leaders of the 'all-Russian' anti-Bolshevik government had only arrived in Omsk from the west on 9 October. The executive of the Provisional All-Russian Government was modelled on that of the French Revolution: supreme power was vested in a Directory of five men. (The French version, the *Directoire executif*, created by the Constitution of Year III, held office from 1795 to 1799, after the overthrow of the Jacobins.) An attempt had been made to give the Russian Directory (*Direktoriia*) a balanced membership. N. D. Avksentiev and V. M. Zenzinov were members of the Socialist Revolutionary Party (PSR); V. A. Vinogradov belonged to the non-socialist Kadet (Constitutional Democrat) party; P. V. Vologodsky was a Siberian 'regionalist'; and General V. G. Boldyrev commanded the local anti-Bolshevik armed forces.

The events of the coup are a matter of some historical dispute. The most likely sequence of events is that on Saturday afternoon (17 November) a meeting in Omsk of middle-level politicians and military leaders, all men of the right, made the final decision to take action against the Directory.[3] In the early hours of Sunday, a detachment of Cossack troops surrounded a block of flats in Omsk where the Socialist Revolutionary (SR) E. F. Rogovsky lived. Rogovsky was the deputy minister of internal affairs in the PA-RG. The Directors Avksentiev and Zenzinov, and a number of other SRs, were meeting in his flat. Cossack officers arrested those present and imprisoned them at the Agricultural Institute on the outskirts of Omsk. The barracks where a small pro-SR internal security unit was quartered was also surrounded, and the men there disarmed. There was no bloodshed.

Before dawn the following morning the PA-RG Council of Ministers, including now Admiral Kolchak, met in the former Governor-General's Palace.[4] A third Director, the Kadet Vinogradov, now resigned. A fourth man, Vologodsky, the Director most closely associated with Siberian interests, was evidently surprised by the coup, but not prepared to argue for a return to the status quo. General Boldyrev, the fifth and final Director was absent at the front.

The meeting then turned to the need for a replacement executive, and there was no opposition to replacing the Directory with one-man rule; civil and military power was to be concentrated in the hands of one individual as 'supreme ruler' (*verkhovnyi pravitel*). After some discussion a vote of those present voted nearly unanimously for Admiral Kolchak, who agreed to serve in this post. He issued, as 'Supreme Ruler Admiral Kolchak', the following proclamation:

> On 18 November 1918 the Provisional All-Russian Government collapsed [*raspalos*]. The Council of Ministers took all the power and invested it in me, Admiral Aleksandr Kolchak of the Russian Navy.
>
> Having assumed the burden [*krest*, literally 'cross'] of this power in the exceptionally difficult circumstances of the Civil War and the complete disruption of public life, I announce:
>
> I will go neither down the path of reaction, nor along the fatal path of party politics. My chief aims are the organisation of a combat-ready army, victory over Bolshevism, and the establishment of law and order, so that the people may be able to choose without hindrance a form of government to which they are suited, and to realise the great ideas of freedom which are now been proclaimed [*provozglashennye*] throughout the world.
>
> I call you, fellow citizens, to unity, to struggle with Bolshevism, to labour and sacrifice.[5]

To understand the political tensions that led to the Omsk coup, and why and how Kolchak emerged as a military dictator, some key events of the preceding year need to be outlined. While retreating from the Central Powers in western Russia in the winter of 1917–18, the Bolsheviks in Petrograd had succeeded in establishing their authority in many urban centres in the southern and eastern parts of the Russian Empire. Lenin's party took advantage of the lack of any effective rival authority in Petrograd, and of the revolutionary network of councils (soviets) of workers' and soldiers' deputies created in 1917. Detachments of pro-Bolshevik soldiers and armed workers were sent out along the railways to crush local resistance. In the city of Omsk a Bolshevik-dominated 'soviet' took charge from 30 November 1917.

Bolshevik hold on power was, however, extremely tenuous, especially in distant regions. It was weakened in the winter of 1917–18 by the rapid demobilisation of the radicalised wartime army and plummeting economic activity in the towns. The defeated political opponents of the Bolsheviks, both left and right of the political centre, were still active, in some cases in organised – and rival – political undergrounds. Some were agrarian socialists (especially the SRs) who felt that 'their' revolution had been hijacked by the Bolsheviks. Some were members of the former privileged groups; any enthusiasm for revolution that they might have had in the heady days of early 1917 had been dissipated by political anarchy, economic ruin and national humiliation. Some were 'patriotic' survivors of the pre-war and wartime officer corps, who dreamed of restoring Russian honour and international status.

It did not take much to shake the rickety Bolshevik hold on power. The main agent of this overthrow in eastern Russia took the extraordinary form of the Czech Corps. Some 50,000 men – eight regiments organised in two divisions – were numerically not a large force, but they were strung out in trains strategically positioned across the railway system. First raised in a spirit of Slav solidarity in 1914, by Czech and Slovak civilians living in Russia, the formation had been expanded rapidly in 1917, through recruitment of Austro-Hungarian POWs. In early 1918 the Soviet government in Petrograd agreed to let the corps depart to fight in France, but in May fighting broke out with local Soviet authorities. In the course of June and July the men of the corps took effective command of the 4,000-mile railway line from the Volga River to Vladivostok. So important was this transport artery that the Soviet government in Moscow suddenly lost control of all of Siberia, the southern Urals and part of the Middle Volga region. On 7 June, during this advance, power changed hands again in Omsk; the victors were the Czechoslovaks and the local Russian opposition to the Bolsheviks.

Some 950 miles to the west, the Volga town of Samara was taken by the Czechoslovaks on 8 June, and the first post-revolutionary government to rival the Bolshevik one in Moscow was formed. This body claimed its authority from the All-Russian Constituent Assembly (*Uchreditel noe sobranie*). The Assembly had been the result of national elections organised in the last days of the Provisional Government of Alexander Kerensky, and held in the first days of Soviet rule. Some forty-five million voters had taken part, and the result was a clear victory for the Socialist Revolutionaries. They were the peasant party, in a peasant country; they had a strong revolutionary heritage and they advocated policies of popular sovereignty and land reform. The elections gave the SRs 428 deputies out of 767; there were only 180 Bolshevik deputies (and very few from the political right and centre). The Assembly met in Petrograd early in January 1918, but was immediately dispersed by the Bolsheviks. Several SR deputies, however, were present in Samara and others joined them; their organisation named itself the 'Committee of Members of the Constituent Assembly', known in Russian by the abbreviation *Komuch*.

Komuch evolved, over several months, and through ill-tempered negotiations, into the PA-RG and the Directory. A 'State Conference' of the various local authorities that had sprung up under Czechoslovak protection was held in the town of Ufa in the southern Urals (between Samara and Omsk) in September. The SR leaders of Komuch accepted that they would have to broaden their base and, as we have seen, the Directory included, as well as two SRs, a Kadet and a leader of the former Siberian regional authority, as a well as progressive soldier.

The Samara government had raised a small 'People's Army', which fought alongside the Czech Corps. A few early successes were followed, however, by a Red Army counter-attack in late September, and the Komuch forces had to fall back from their original Volga base into the southern Urals and western Siberia.

Meanwhile, the European Allied powers, although obsessed with their life or death struggle with Germany on the western front, had maintained their presence on the fringes of Russia. Responding to the successes of the Central Powers before and after the Treaty of Brest-Litovsk, they had kept ships and landing parties in the two peripheral ports that they could reach and the Germans could not: Murmansk and Vladivostok. The 'rescue' of the Czech Corps provided a justification for further operations in Russia. In early August 1918 a small expeditionary force, led by the British, took control of the port of Arkhangelsk, south of Murmansk and 600 miles north of Moscow. Japan, a non-European ally, landed forces in some strength at Vladivostok, as did the British and the Americans. A minor British army unit, a reserve battalion of the Middlesex Regiment, was even sent 'up country' to Omsk.

Despite the Ufa State Conference and the involvement of the Allies, by the late summer of 1918 political opinion in the anti-Bolshevik camp, and especially in Omsk, had become more polarised. It was a conflict in multiple dimensions – between left and right, between soldiers and civilians, between locals (Siberians) and outsiders (refugees from European Russia). An especially important issue was the presence of the two Socialist Revolutionary members in the Directory. The SRs were bitter enemies of both the Bolsheviks and the Germans. Nevertheless, they were regarded by those on the right as little different from Lenin's party and certainly as part of Russia's humiliation as a great power in 1917; the Director Avksentiev had been minister of the interior in the Provisional Government of Alexander Kerensky. What also aroused ongoing hostility from other parties was the SR's claim to an exclusive and continuing legitimacy, as a result of their landslide success in the elections to the Constituent Assembly.[6]

For their part the SRs, who regarded themselves as the true heirs of the 1917 revolution, not its opponents, were increasing distrustful of their non-socialist political adversaries, and especially of the military officer corps. Etched in their collective memory was the struggle with the autocracy, especially in the failed revolution of 1905. In August 1917 there had been the attempt by General Kornilov to seize effective power in Petrograd. Most recently, in September 1918, conservative officers had briefly overthrown the government led by the veteran SR N. V. Chaikovsky, which had been created in Arkhangelsk (under

British protection). In Omsk there were violent incidents in which SR activists were killed by right-wing death squads.

These growing tensions prompted the national SR leader Viktor Chernov to draft a manifesto (*obrashchenie*) that made the struggle with 'counter-revolutionary intrigues' a main priority. The manifesto called on party members to be mobilised, trained and armed to resist such intrigues, and was issued by the PSR Central Committee (based in Ekaterinburg in the Urals) in late October 1918.[7] This act in turn further inflamed the right, and it was of special importance in motivating the imprisonment of the SR Directors in Omsk on 17–18 November.

The conflict was furthered by the political and institutional weakness of the Directory, which had been grafted on top of an existing non-socialist 'Siberian' government. Many of the individuals and institutions in that government continued in power within a 'Council of Ministers' (*Sovet ministrov*), formed on 4 November. Meanwhile, the prestige of the Directory suffered because the military campaign being conducted in its name was not going well; the anti-Bolshevik forces were having to give up ground to the growing Red Army on the Volga, and then in the southern Urals. The retreat made it seem to conservative soldiers – Russians and foreigners alike – that what was required was 'firm' authority, organised in the form of uncompromising military rule.[8]

Alexander Vasilyevich Kolchak was a remarkable – and ultimately tragic – figure.[9] In August 1916, at the age of only forty-two, he had been promoted to the rank of vice admiral, and made commander-in-chief of the Black Sea Fleet; this force was an important element of Russia's war effort against Turkey. Kolchak was already a much decorated war hero, having led daring offensive destroyer actions in both the Russo-Japanese War and in the Baltic in the First World War. In addition he had earned a reputation as an intrepid polar explorer, and an ocean-ographer. From his service in the Naval General Staff during the early 1910s he had made valuable political contacts. After the 1917 revolution Kolchak furthered his political reputation by opposing revolutionary change in the armed forces. At the Sevastopol naval base in early June 1917, when confronted by radical sailors who demanded that officers surrender their side arms, Kolchak threw his ceremonial sabre overboard and resigned his post.

The Provisional Government despatched the admiral with a naval mission to the United States, and he visited the British Admiralty en route. After his visit to America he departed from San Francisco on 25 October (New Style), aiming to return to Russia via the port of Vladivostok. By the time he reached Yokohama, Kerensky and the Provisional Government had been overthrown; unable and unwilling to return to Russia under the Bolshevik 'anarchy', Kolchak stayed in the Far East in the winter of 1917–18. A man of action, still committed to the defeat of the Central Powers, Kolchak offered his services to the British and was invited to take part in the Mesopotamia campaign. En route to the Persian Gulf, he had reached Singapore from Japan in March 1918, when he was recalled by the Russian (pre-Soviet) ambassador to China, and asked to raise forces for the Russian-owned Chinese-Eastern Railway. Based in Kharbin (Harbin), Kolchak held his post for three months in the spring and early summer of 1918; he achieved little and returned to Japan in late July.

During his summer in Japan Kolchak had talks with General Alfred Knox, the British Army's leading expert on Russia. General Knox was impressed by Kolchak's energy and his no-nonsense preference for military government; he reported to the War Office in late August 1918 that 'there is no doubt that he is the best Russian for our purposes in the Far East'.[10] In early September Kolchak and Knox sailed together across the Sea of Japan to Vladivostok, where they disembarked on the 8th. The two men set off by train into Siberia two weeks later. Of necessity the journey was a slow one, and a further three weeks would pass before Kolchak reached Omsk (on 13 October).

Kolchak's decision to travel deep into Siberia has intrigued historians. When on trial for his life at Irkutsk in January 1920, the admiral maintained that he had hoped to join his family in south Russia.[11] It is more likely that he was exploring various options, in the highly uncertain and rapidly developing political and military situation of September and October 1918. One possibility was a role with the anti-Bolshevik forces taking shape in the Urals and western Siberia. Another was making his way further west – if a route opened – to join the forces of General Alexeev and General Denikin; these two leading figures in the old army were reported to be waging an isolated but successful struggle to consolidate their position with their 'Volunteer Army' in the north Caucasus (south Russia) region. There is only circumstantial or *post factum* evidence that Kolchak journeyed with the intention of becoming – or being helped by the British Army to become – a regional military dictator, let alone an all-Russian one. The PA-RG and the Directory did not even exist when he left Vladivostok.[12]

It was not surprising that once he arrived in western Siberia Kolchak became involved with the new anti-Bolshevik authority and its armed forces; a figure of his known abilities, political stature and good relations with Allied benefactors was attractive. The admiral later claimed that he was invited to take part in the PA-RG Council of Ministers by General Boldyrev – the front-line commander of the Directory's military forces, and Boldyrev certainly did not want to overthrow the Directory.[13]

Lt General Boldyrev, although in late September 1918 styled as the 'Supreme Commander-in-Chief of all Russia Armed Forces', did not have the status of Kolchak among the Allied governments or their representatives in Russia. More important, he was genuinely much more sympathetic to the politicians of the centre-left. The son of a peasant, Boldyrev had risen in the tsarist army to become deputy chief of staff of the Northern Army Group, under General Ruzsky, in the winter of 1916–17; in the late autumn of 1917 he was briefly commander-in-chief of the Fifth Army. He had in early 1918 become a member of the Union for the Regeneration of Russia (*Soiuz vozrozhdeniia Rossii*), an influential underground organisation including activists on the left of the Kadet Party and on the right of the Socialist Revolutionaries; its leaders included Avksentiev and Zenzinov. It is highly unlikely that Boldyrev would have been offered the role of the military dictator by the rightist Siberian politicians, and unlikely, too, that he would have accepted it.[14]

On being made war and navy minister on 4 November, Admiral Kolchak immediately left Omsk for a twelve-day inspection tour of the forces fighting some 600 miles to the west, in the northern Urals. General Knox, for his part, took a train back towards Vladivostok on the 5th. Some writers accused Kolchak and Knox of absenting themselves from Omsk simply to avoid open complicity with a planned coup; the opposite case can be made – that if either man had contemplated the overthrow of the Directory in these weeks they would have wanted personal oversight. A diary entry for 5 November written by one of the main coup plotters (V. N. Pepeliaev) recalled Kolchak saying that he was not prepared, under present circumstances, to seize power. At the same time Knox informed the War Office that he had told Kolchak that it would 'at present be fatal' to follow the urgings of the right-wing officers around him and take supreme power.[15]

Kolchak's activities in the days (and hours) immediately before the morning of 18 November are clearly important. Was he actively conspiring to make himself a military dictator? Or was he genuinely surprised by events, and was it only after the fact that he agreed to 'assume the burden of this power'? He arrived back in Omsk just before the coup, on 16 or 17 November.[16] Kolchak claimed that he only learned of the night-time arrest of the SR Directors when he was woken at his apartment at 4 a.m. on the 18th; that is at least possible. Few historians have attempted to make the admiral a direct participant, and one of the best accounts, by the British historian Peter Fleming, rules out such involvement.[17]

Different views have also been put forward regarding the role of British military or diplomatic representatives. General Maurice Janin, who arrived in Omsk a few weeks after the coup as the senior French military representative, later maintained that the coup was supported and even organised by British military advisers.[18] There were two Russian-speaking British officers in Omsk at the time of the coup, Lt Colonel Neilson and Captain Steveni, who had some contact with Omsk politicians and officers. Neither of them was in favour of the Directory, and they may have given verbal support or assurances to some of the conspirators.[19] It seems unlikely, however, that they organised anything. Another British factor was the Middlesex battalion, which was still stationed in Omsk, and which at least had the potential to oppose a counter-coup. No one has suggested, however, that that battalion had been ordered to the city to carry out a strike against the Directory or that it took any active part in the events of 17–18 November.

The definitive account by Richard Ullman argued that the British government and the Foreign Office certainly played no part. The involvement of Knox, who was subordinate to the War Office, could not be determined, but he – in Ullman's view – was at most 'a warm sympathiser'; Ullman did not preclude the unauthorised encouragement (or lack of discouragement) by the junior British officers on the spot. General Knox, who had left Omsk nearly two weeks before the coup subsequently denied any involvement by Britain.[20] Above all, the British War Cabinet, in the important meetings on 13–14 November (described earlier), had in fact decided, among other elements of its post-war Russia policy, 'to recognise the Omsk Directorate [sic] as a *de facto* Government'.[21] Still, this important development in British policy was not publicly announced, and it was almost certainly not communicated to personnel in Siberia.

We are on less thin ice when considering the activities of the *known* conspirators, rather than the ultimate beneficiary, Admiral Kolchak.[22] The core leaders appear to have been the civilians V. N. Pepeliaev and I. A. Mikhailov, and the deputy chief of staff of the Siberian Army, Col. A. D. Syromiatnikov. What is most likely is that the conspirators acted on their own. Their motives were important. They had long been hostile to the SRs, and after the Chernov Manifesto ill feeling was heightened. Genrikh Ioffe's Soviet-era account plausibly put emphasis on the intrigues of the Kadet Party and the underground National Centre (*Natsionalnyi tsentr*) organisation, in both of which Pepeliaev played a major role.[23] They were ambitious 'Young Turks': Pepeliaev was thirty-four, Syromiatnikov thirty-one, and Mikhailov was only twenty-six. They may well have hoped to use Kolchak as a mere figurehead.

Also important was the acceptance of events by more senior (and cautious) members of the political and military leadership in Omsk. On the morning after the arrest of Avksentiev and Zenzinov they agreed to a fait accompli. In a private letter to Mikhailov written in April 1919, Syromiatnikov gave him the credit for making the higher-ups do something they would not have done otherwise.[24] There was no pressure from above in Omsk, or from outside (by the foreign governments), to restore the Directory.

As for Admiral Kolchak, he did not have to accept 'the burden of this power'. But, as he declared in his manifesto, he did not want to follow 'the fatal path of party politics'. During his 1920 trial Kolchak recalled one of his conversations with General Knox in Japan, when he (Kolchak) had stressed the importance of the armed forces:

[T]he organization of political power [vlast] at a time like the present was possible only under one condition: this power must rely on [opiratsia na] the armed force which it has at its disposal. This in turn determines the question of power, and it is necessary to solve the question of the creation of the armed force on which such a political power would rely, for without it political power will be a fiction, and anyone else who has such an armed force at his disposal will be able to take political power in his hands.

Kolchak certainly had no time for the SRs, and for the Constituent Assembly on which they based their authority. '[T]he Constituent Assembly which we got ... [he testified] and which when it met broke into singing the "Internationale" under Chernov's leadership, provoked an unfriendly attitude on the part of most of the people I met [in Siberia before the coup], it was considered to be artificial and partisan. This was also my opinion. I considered that although the Bolsheviks had few positive features, their dispersal of the Constituent Assembly was a service for which they should be given credit.'[25]

Finally, there is little to connect the Omsk coup with the Armistice. The penultimate sentence of Kolchak's 18 November announcement mentioned 'the great ideas of freedom which are now been proclaimed throughout the world', and this might be taken to refer to the Allied victory (paradoxically, Kolchak's announcement declared a military dictatorship). The War Cabinet's secret decision of 14 November to recognise de facto the Directory was part of a review of British policy brought about by the Armistice; the British historian and journalist Michael Kettle thought it likely that information about this had been secretly communicated to right-wing circles in Omsk and might have motivated a pre-emptive strike by the conspirators on the 17th.[26] Given the distances and the wobbly chain of events this seems unlikely (although it is not impossible). It is also improbable that the conspirators in Omsk feared or anticipated that the Armistice would mean that once the war ended the Allies would lose interest in Russia – although that was indeed the case.

CONSEQUENCES AND COUNTERFACTUALS

For a time Admiral Kolchak enjoyed military success. In December 1918 White Russian and Czechoslovak troops pushed the Red Army back in the Urals; at the end of the month they took the important industrial town of Perm. In March 1919 Kolchak's army began a general offensive in the southern Urals, which quickly recaptured Ufa. But by the summer the Siberian anti-Bolshevik forces were in retreat. There was some disorder in the rear, and the government made little attempt to rally popular support. Kolchak proved to be neither an effective military commander nor an astute politician. In November 1919 he was forced to abandon Omsk. He had not been able to secure the recognition of his government by the Allies, and he gave up the title of Supreme Ruler (in favour of General Denikin). In January 1920, during the admiral's retreat to the east, his train was stopped at Irkutsk (1,300 miles east of Omsk). Kolchak was arrested, tried and shot, and his body thrown through the ice of the Enisei River. He was the only one of the senior White leaders to be captured and killed during the Russian Civil War.[27]

We might consider some counterfactuals. The biggest of all would be if the Central Powers had not lost the war in the autumn of 1918. That is indeed a fascinating question but one well beyond the scope of this chapter; the present work is about the situation after the late summer of 1918, by which time the last German offensive had failed.

More narrowly, the Directory could have continued at least into 1919. This might well have happened had there not been a credible 'dictator' on hand, or if Admiral Kolchak had refused the post of 'supreme ruler'. He might have done this if the most 'senior' of potential all-Russian military leaders, General M. V. Alexeev, had not died unexpectedly in south Russia in October; Alexeev had been chief of staff to the tsar for much of the war, and Supreme Commander-in-Chief in part of 1917.

The Directory might also have survived if the inclination of the British Foreign Office to support the PA-RG had been followed through – and if more time had been available. General Boldyrev was an alternative leader; he might have followed a more sensible political course, and he could not have been any less effective as a military commander than Kolchak.

But the tension between left and right in Russia, and the unrestrained power of the reactionary armed gangs, precluded such a happy outcome for the anti-Bolsheviks. The real significance of the Omsk coup, whoever inspired it or carried it out, was that it demonstrated the unbridgeable and fatal gulf between 'party politics' and 'the path of reaction' (to use Kolchak's words) in the anti-Bolshevik movement.[28]

The Armistice ended the domination by Germany and her partners over the Russian western and southern borderlands and opened fierce civil war fighting there. The Allies, with large and successful forces at their disposal, now had unopposed access to the territory of Russia. Again, thinking counterfactually, could Britain, France, the United States and Japan have decided, in the winter of 1918–19, to intervene in strength in Russia?

That they did not do so had little to do with the character of Kolchak's government. Much more important was the fact that the overthrow of German military power in November 1918 meant that the Allies lost any serious motive to intervene, certainly on a large scale and with their own forces. Their armies and populations were war-weary and there was little domestic political appetite for action in Russia. The French did commit some military strength to an expedition to southern Ukraine in mid December 1918, but there was clear reluctance to fight on the part of their troops (and those of France's Balkan allies). The campaign culminated in a humiliating withdrawal – accompanied by mutinies – from Odessa in March 1919, and from Sevastopol in April. Meanwhile, no Allied ground forces, and few supplies, were committed to the Baltic region. The British could and did send surplus arms and other supplies to south Russia, from wartime munitions dumps in the Middle East and elsewhere, but supplies alone were not enough to defeat the Red Army.

Nevertheless, a fundamental problem for the Siberian Whites, although perhaps not the decisive one, was the opening of the Black Sea, which occurred simultaneously with the Omsk coup. The shorter length of the route to south Russia made General Denikin and the Volunteer Army a much more attractive recipient of Allied supplies than Kolchak's armies in remote Siberia. Because of this the events in Omsk were in the long run probably not of central importance. Denikin created an authoritarian government in south Russia, and would have done so in any event; there was no 'Directory' stage in the counter-revolutionary politics of the south.

The Provisional All-Russian Government probably could not have competed with the south Russian White generals for Allied military and diplomatic support. Nor, from faraway central Siberia, halfway around the world in terms of the practicalities of travel and communications, could the PA-RG have exercised control over the whole ('All-Russian') anti-Bolshevik movement. And a more democratic PA-RG probably could not have put a first military offensive together as fast as Kolchak did. Might a more democratic Siberian government have won more (or alienated less) popular support in Siberia in 1919? Perhaps, but the peasant-based Socialist Revolutionary Party did not have strong local roots in Siberia (where there was no history of serfdom, and land hunger was not a central issue). In the task of state building, it is hard to believe that the Directory would have had any more success than Kolchak.

Probably the fatal divisions in the anti-Bolshevik movement were unavoidable. Probably, too, it was inevitable that the Allies would not consider serious post-war military intervention in Russia. Nevertheless the events of mid November 1918 did divide the tragedy of the Russian Civil War into two distinct parts. Foreign involvement was always important, but the collapse of the Central Powers and the ascent of the Allies actually reduced the scale of foreign intervention. The troops of the Central Powers had physically occupied the Baltic region, Belarus, all Ukraine, and much of the Transcaucasus in 1918. The Allies attempted nothing on this scale in 1919 or 1920.

Likewise the triumph of the military elites in the anti-Bolshevik camp in November 1918, led by men like Kolchak and Denikin, changed the political nature of the conflict. The 'White' Russian forces, even after most of the Czechoslovaks returned home after 1918, and even without direct involvement of foreign military forces, were now more of a threat to the Red Army; they were superior in their leadership, mass and effectiveness to what had existed before November 1918. But on the other hand these armies had only rudimentary political programmes, compared even to Komuch and the PA-RG. A popular dictator (or tsar-substitute) could not gain mass support in Russia, at least not before the 1930s.

12

THE FATE OF THE SOVIET COUNTRYSIDE

March 1920

ERIK C. LANDIS

O F THE MANY CHALLENGES that faced the Soviet government in the Russian Civil War, none was greater than overcoming the breakdown in the supply of food that had started before the February Revolution of 1917, and had itself been a significant factor in the fall of the Russian autocracy. Procuring food from the farmers to feed the Red Army and the civilian population in the Soviet heartland of the urban, industrial centres of northern European Russia forced the ruling party into a number of policy changes and attempted innovations between 1918 and 1921. However, in the conditions of civil conflict, the procurement of food from the farming peasantry nearly always boiled down in practice to a reliance upon 'administrative measures' and 'taking grain'.[1] The challenge of securing food to meet the needs of the state generated almost continuous conflict in the Soviet countryside during the Civil War, pitting village farming communities against state procurement squads.

Throughout this period, agricultural production declined. On the eve of the harvest in the autumn of 1920, at a time when the outcome of the Civil War was all but settled, with the main forces of the White armies defeated and the Soviet government seeking a way out of its war with nationalist Poland, another round of grain requisitioning by armed procurement squads sparked a wave of unrest in the Soviet countryside that escalated to an unprecedented scale, with sustained anti-Soviet insurgencies occurring in a number of important regions of the Soviet Republic. Restoring control over the regions consumed by this violence required the deployment of hundreds of thousands of Red Army troops, and frequently this was only after hastily mobilised (and poorly armed) units of local Communist Party members had tried and failed, at great cost, to suppress the resistance in the provinces and regions they ostensibly 'controlled'. The Civil War, in effect, was extended by nearly a full year as the struggle for grain became an all-out war.

This 'second civil war', as one historian preferred to describe it,[2] was ended only after tens of thousands were killed in the course of the rebellions. In the language of the regime, the rebellions were the product of the machinations of subversive, counter-revolutionary 'kulaks', or rich peasants who were the inveterate enemies of Soviet power, working with the regime's socialist rivals, the Socialist Revolutionaries (PSR), and the 'international bourgeoisie'. And it was amid this wave of violence that significant parts of the republic suffered extensive harvest failures, bringing famine to areas such as the Middle Volga and the Urals region of western Siberia, in which several millions lost their lives. Yet it is difficult to avoid the conclusion that this was an avoidable coda to the era of revolution and civil war, and that it was the consequence of decisions taken by the Soviet leadership at the start of 1920.

The present essay concerns the end of the Russian Civil War, and describes the opportunities that were passed up to demobilise the Soviet state machinery that had been hothoused in the conditions of civil conflict over the previous two years. The year typically given for the conclusion of the Russian Civil War is 1921, and while armed clashes continued for several months across the former Russian Empire, the critical moment in this chronology is the introduction of the New Economic Policy (NEP) by the Communist Party leadership, initiated with the decision in March 1921 to end the practice of forced grain requisitioning – of 'taking grain' – a measure soon followed by decrees that, among other measures, partially decriminalised the market. Permitting the peasants to dispense (relatively) freely with their produce after a tax ('in kind', or in the form of foodstuffs) was assessed and collected, was a radical reversal of Soviet policy. It was adopted as a means of defusing the anger and desperation that had given rise to the rural violence of the previous several months, and which had also become the focus of urban protests and mutiny in the armed forces. This was the first, and most important, step taken in the process of reconstruction for the Soviet state, itself desperate to put an end to the years of continuous war-related strife that began in 1914.

In March 1920, a full year before Lenin introduced the reforms that would lay the foundation for the NEP, proposals were advanced by Leon Trotsky to end grain requisitioning and to seek an alternative that appealed to the individual incentives of farmers. In the course of a trip to the Urals in January and February 1920, the Commissar for War emerged of the opinion that the current approach to food procurement was unsustainable, detrimental both to the health of the agricultural economy and to relations with the rural population. In the spirit of post-war reconstruction, which the Soviet leadership was openly discussing at the start of 1920, Trotsky suggested a number of possibilities, including a return of market-driven exchanges between agricultural producers and manufacturers, to help incentivise the farmers to produce more grain and other foodstuffs. In germ form, Trotsky's ideas strongly resembled what would be adopted by the party, but only after several months of further violence and suffering linked with an ill-fated continuation of the wartime food procurement policy. Trotsky's ideas, however, were dismissed by his colleagues in the Soviet government.

The ramifications of this decision extend beyond the human suffering of the final phase of the Civil War. Less than a decade later, another senior Soviet official would make a hastily arranged trip to the Urals region, and in familiarising himself with the situation there, and with a concern for resolving a crisis of grain supply and political control in the countryside, would publicly advocate a return to compulsory surplus grain deliveries and confronting the menace of 'kulak' sabotage once and for all. Joseph Stalin's speech in Novosibirsk in January 1928 would set the USSR on the path towards full-scale collectivisation of agriculture, activating a militant strain within the Communist Party that had never been reconciled with the ignominious 'retreat' of March 1921, when the party was forced to yield to 'kulak' pressure and adopt the New Economic Policy. The speech in Novosibirsk in 1928 was a vital moment in the formation of what became Soviet socialism and in the creation of the Stalin dictatorship, and it is linked in revealing ways with the Civil War and the party's earlier efforts to manage the challenges of building socialism in a peasant country.

In December 1919, even though the armies of the White forces had not yet been completely defeated, the outcome of the Civil War in Russia appeared clear. Russia's former allies in the First World War had withdrawn their troops from the north and far east of the former empire, and with that their financial and material support of the White armies had been significantly scaled back all along the periphery of the future Soviet Union, from Murmansk to Vladivostok. The White forces of Admiral Kolchak in Siberia, whose offensive in the spring of 1919 momentarily appeared to be the greatest threat to the Soviet regime in Moscow, were in the final stage of the longest military retreat in modern history, and Kolchak himself was only weeks away from arrest and execution just east of Lake Baikal. The forces of General Yudenich, which had threatened to take Petrograd in October 1919, were definitively routed by November, and the White armies under General Denikin had seen their 'drive to Moscow' reach its height in the early autumn of 1919, retreating back to the Don and Kuban territories of southern Russia in the final weeks of that year as rapidly as they had advanced earlier in the summer.

Addressing the Eighth Conference of the Communist Party in early December 1919, Lenin spoke with confidence about the rapid turn of fortunes enjoyed by the Soviet regime:

We see opening before us the road of peaceful construction. Of course, we need to remember that the enemy will be lying in wait at every turn of the way, and will seek to throw us off course by any means necessary: violence, lies, bribery, conspiracy, and so on. Our task is to utilise all our experience and knowledge from the military front in addressing the challenges of peaceful construction.[3]

With his words on the immediate future of the republic, Lenin foreshadowed the controversial discussions that developed in the second half of December over the 'militarisation' of labour, stemming from an article published by Leon Trotsky in *Pravda* calling for the leadership to embrace the principles of compulsion in work. Trotsky, who was never shy to weigh in on any sphere of public policy, directed attentions to the model for economic construction provided by the successful organisation of the Red Army, particularly to the controversial embrace of conscription and hierarchies of command that he had championed in 1918. Seeing the demobilisation of the Red Army as a welcome consequence of victory in the Civil War, Trotsky advocated utilising the machinery of the army to conscript the labour force of the Soviet Republic, such that that force could be deployed strategically and efficiently in vital industries and in pursuits to rebuild the economy and expedite the transition to socialism. The obligation to work as a basic component of citizenship had been a part of Communist discourse since the very first days of the revolution. Civilians had been mobilised for trench digging, road maintenance and track clearing in an ad hoc fashion in both the cities and villages throughout the Civil War, much as they had been by the tsarist government before the revolution.[4] But the principle of labour obligation had never been openly embraced on such an ambitious scale by the regime until this point. Lenin proved enthusiastic about the ideas, championing Trotsky and his vision in the face of aggressive criticism from the trade union representation in the Communist Party. At the turn of the year, Lenin helped oversee the creation of a Commission of Labour Duty, to be chaired by Trotsky, on top of his responsibilities as Commissar for War.[5]

The challenges of economic revival were enormous. Industrial production had largely collapsed in the years that followed the fall of the tsar in February 1917, and the Soviet government's attempts to contain and reverse the decline had proven ineffective. By the start of 1920, the output of large-scale industry was less than a fifth of what it had been on the eve of the First World War. Output for small-scale industry was better, but still significantly less than 50 per cent of its pre-war levels.[6] Essential pursuits, such as mining and timber production, vital for both the transport system and industry, were in desperate need of revival, and when the project of mobilising the labour force assumed a more concrete form in 1920, it was to these pursuits that attention turned. The first test case for the creation of a 'labour army' deployed for urgent economic needs came in western Siberia, where the Revolutionary Military Council of the 3rd Red Army, whose soldiers had contributed significantly to reversing the advance of Kolchak's Siberian Army, placed itself at the disposal of Trotsky and his project. Not required for the further pursuit of Kolchak's dwindling forces, and at the time largely idle owing to the difficulties with the overloaded rail network, the opportunity was thus available to assign the men of the 3rd Red Army to work felling timber, clearing snow, repairing infrastructure, and other tasks in the region. This was not the conscription of civilian labour that had originally been proposed by Trotsky, and which had stirred such controversy among the trade unions, but it was a start that brought together the parallel processes of demobilisation and economic reconstruction.[7]

Setting off for Ekaterinburg on 8 February 1920 to oversee the processing of the soldiers of the 3rd Red Army and their redeployment to productive tasks, Trotsky's mind was clearly focused on economic challenges and looked towards peacetime. Having travelled throughout the country almost continuously during the previous two years, Trotsky's engagement with economic matters had been largely in connection with military challenges. But as he was among the most prominent of Soviet political leaders and in some respects the most visible to the wider public, Trotsky was regularly in receipt of letters and petitions from average civilians. As his personal train made its way to his destination in the Urals, he took considerable time to pen a reply to one such letter from a peasant named Ivan Sigunov of Penza province, who had written to express grievances over the shortages being endured in the countryside, and the seemingly endless demands placed upon the farmers by the agents of the state.

In his reply of 12 February, Trotsky explained the dilemmas currently facing the Soviet Republic, faithfully sticking to the party line, particularly as regards the razverstka. The razverstka was a policy introduced in 1919 that moved away from talk of 'surpluses', and instead defined the needs of the state and collected food from village communities on the basis of strictly defined targets. Whereas the Soviet state had previously requisitioned surpluses with the promise of equivalent exchange of manufactured goods and other items of basic necessity, it eventually had to recognise that such a system of goods exchange was a fiction, and that requisitioned grain would be forfeited by producers as a sort of 'loan' to the state, an investment in the victory of the revolution. 'The peasants currently hold many credit notes,' Trotsky wrote, acknowledging that the patience of people such as Sigunov was being tested.

> The current situation is not with that, however. What we need are goods, manufactured products, the kinds of things that a person requires both for himself and his household. We need to revive textile and metals production, lumber mills, chemicals, and so on, such that our people no longer suffer shortages … But currently we produce only little, as our country is all but destroyed, machines are worn out, factories are in disrepair, raw materials are in short supply, there is no fuel, and workers, mindful of their plight, have fled [the cities].

The first step towards resolving this problem, according to Trotsky, was to collect enough food to sustain a viable industrial workforce, which had shrunk considerably in the years of civil war as families went to the countryside to, in essence, be closer to the food:

The workers of Moscow, Petrograd, the Ivanovo-Voznesensk region, the Don Basin and even the Urals have suffered terrible food shortages, and at times have genuinely been starving. Moscow and Petrograd proletarians have gone hungry for a matter of years, not just for days. The railroad workers are going hungry. Hunger weakens not only the body, but the soul as well. The [worker's] arms drop, as does the will. It is difficult to rouse a hungry worker to perform disciplined, vigorous and organised work. The first job, therefore, is to feed the workers.[8]

Without the grain taken from the peasants, no revival in industry could be expected. (The title given by Trotsky to the letter, when it was published at the time, referred to the current state of ruin in Russia and the 'tasks' of the peasantry.) However, as Trotsky was aware, without non-agricultural goods to offer in exchange, grain would be secured from the peasants begrudgingly, at best.

In fact, the Soviet state's efforts at food procurement had been punctuated by violence. In 1918, after a failed attempt to work within a system of fixed prices for grain and the criminalisation of the market, the state sought to implant new institutions at the local level – the committees of the poor – that would empower the poor and landless peasants at the expense of the so-called 'kulaks' in the village. With a hope that class conflict could be fomented and harnessed to expedite grain procurement, the Soviet state promised that a portion of hidden 'kulak' surpluses revealed through the work of the committees would be redistributed among the poor in the community, as would any additional confiscations of property carried out as punishment for non-compliance. The committees proved ineffective in the second half of 1918, and in several provinces they provoked much violence, with village communities either closing ranks against perceived 'outsiders' who assumed prominent positions in the new committees, many of whom perished in a wave of violence that accompanied the procurement campaign, or clashing with state procurement agents with the insistence that there were neither kulaks nor surpluses to be found in their village.

Who was a kulak and who was not was clear to no one, and there were neither customary understandings nor legal definitions that enjoyed authority, either before the revolution or after. When the Soviet government sought to levy an 'Extraordinary Tax' on the rural population in late 1918, to be assessed on the village kulaks, communities that complied tended to distribute the financial burden evenly among the households, or protested to state authorities that there were no kulaks among them. Collection rates were disappointing, and local officials admitted that acceptable rates of collection could only truly be achieved at gunpoint.[9]

Waves of violence occurred in early 1919, with entire regions overrun by rural rebels who tried to form organised insurgencies, but these proved to be spectacular but short-lived flares of protest. Denounced by Soviet officials as evidence of the strength of kulak influence, such violent protests struggled to carve a space within the polarised context of revolution and civil war. In the Middle Volga region that encompassed the provinces of Samara and Simbirsk, a rebellion lasting just over two weeks rapidly dismantled rural state administration and sent Communist Party members into hiding as angry communities tried to exact revenge for what were viewed as unjust requisitions and confiscations of grain and livestock, and for the conduct of state agents in the countryside, popularly understood to be brutal and arbitrary.[10] With estimates placing the number of villagers to take up weapons as anywhere between fifty and one hundred and fifty thousand, it was the largest such rebellion in this region of Russia since the time of Emelian Pugachev in the 1770s. In attempting to clarify the situation on the ground near the epicentre of the rebellion, the Communist Party secretary for Simbirsk province, I. M. Vareikis, found himself speaking with the chairman of the district soviet in the village of Novodevich'e, a man by the name of Poruchikov. Assuming that Poruchikov was a loyal servant of the regime, Vareikis asked for information about the 'counter-revolutionary uprising', and about the number of 'kulaks and deserters' that were behind it. Unexpectedly, Poruchikov revealed himself to be unapologetically on the side of the rebels:

These are no kulak uprisings, nor have there ever been, and we have no counterrevolutionaries, [the people] are against the improper requisitioning of grain and livestock[;] we welcome the Bolshevik party and are not fighting against them, we are against the communists, but in general there are no counterrevolutionaries, we are opposed to the improper requisitioning of grain and livestock, there are no kulak uprisings, all the peasants are honest toilers. The number of rebels taking part – all the villages and hamlets. We would like it if you would come here yourself, and see who is rebelling... You see, comrade Vareikis, we are not saboteurs, we only want to have a chance to talk with you; you will see for yourself that we are right, and that the people here will listen to you.[11]

If anything, the violent protests against requisitioning only forced state officials to dig in, spurred on by the (valid) reports of hardship in the cities and 'grain-deficit' regions, and by the conviction that sufficient grain was out there, and that the only way to get it was by overcoming 'kulak' resistance.[12]

What was becoming clear, however, to some outside of the food supply bureaucracy of the Soviet state (Narkomprod), and particularly to those who witnessed the collection of grain by armed requisition squads, was that the razverstka was unsustainable. While the razverstka declared that the basic consumption needs of the household would be respected (in accordance with defined 'norms' of consumption), the achievement of collection targets always took priority. As one Narkomprod official in a central Russian province told his colleagues at the local Congress of Soviets: 'the kulak peasantry has learned to hide its grain much more effectively than we have learned to find it. That is why the razverstka must be pursued without regard for "norms".'[13] The image of the kulak justified many of the shortcomings of the razverstka system. While possessing a veneer of data-driven credibility, with its projections on harvests and its delineation of consumptions norms, the system was driven in practice by the desperate need to control as much of the available food in the country as was possible.[14]

Despite the fact that the logic of the razverstka policy held that produce not required by the state under its targets could be retained by farming households, without any legal means of disposing with this surplus, and precious few products available to exchange for grain, there was no incentive to produce above the basic needs of the household itself.[15] Official statistics and anecdotal reports strongly indicated that farming households were reducing their sown acreage, with yields similarly falling, in some areas by over one third.[16] There were many factors at play in creating this outcome. The number of households had increased since 1917, with the average size of those households going down. This made them less productive, both because of military mobilisation and because the productive capacity of those households was declining, with horses requisitioned for military purposes and agricultural implements falling into disrepair without available replacements.[17] For many of the most significant grain-growing regions, the shifting fronts of the Civil War itself was profound enough to significantly disrupt the agricultural cycle.

These circumstances were significant, but the voluntary factor – the lack of incentives to produce above subsistence – was much more controversial within Communist Party circles, unless it was expressed with reference to 'kulak sabotage'. The flourishing black market was obvious for all to see, and later studies would confirm that it was absolutely vital to the survival of the urban population in Soviet Russia, for whom the dwindling state rations could not cover their needs.[18] While the state procurement campaign in 1919 had been a success, close observers recognised that this was not the result of some sort of transformation (what the optimists in the Communist Party frequently called a *perelom*) in the relations between the farming peasantry and the Soviet regime. It was instead the result of procurement being conducted on an ever-larger scale, in territories 'liberated' by the Red Army (whose own fortunes had experienced a decisive *perelom*). Yet anxieties among the rural and town populations alike were quick to appear in those newly liberated territories, as the prospect of sweeps by armed requisition squads and by militia policing illegal trade activities acquired greater salience.[19]

In the days that followed the production of Trotsky's open letter to Ivan Sigunov, the Commissar for War spent time travelling through parts of the Urals region near Ekaterinburg. Simply put, little is known about Trotsky's movements during this time. (Unlike Stalin's trip later in the decade, Trotsky's journey to the Urals was not the subject of countless official reminiscences, and has not attracted the same level of detailed historical examination.) However, his observations of this region – one of those recently 'liberated', which had yet to feel the full weight of Soviet demands, but which had nevertheless suffered considerably under Kolchak – did produce a proposal that Trotsky submitted for consideration by the Communist Party's Central Committee when he returned to Moscow in March. In it, he provided an assessment of the current situation with food collection, in concise terms describing the critical importance of the state's policy to the overall economic prospects of the republic.

The essential problem, Trotsky noted, is that the peasant no longer had a reason 'to cultivate his land more than is required for his family's needs' if the state is determined to requisition everything he produces above that level.[20] With food scarce in the cities, increasing numbers of industrial workers were leaving for the countryside, and if they were able to secure land for cultivation, these households were also inclined to produce only for their own subsistence. Thus, the number of small-sized farming households was rising, legitimate 'surpluses' were declining, and the urban labour force was, likewise, dwindling. '[I]n general,' wrote Trotsky, 'the food resources of the country are threatened with exhaustion, and no improvement in the requisitioning apparatus will be able to remedy this fact.'[21]

What Trotsky proposed was far from identical to what would become the New Economic Policy, introduced over a year later. In his memo, Trotsky listed four basic principles for agricultural policy. First, he proposed replacing the razverstka with a (progressive) tax-in-kind, 'calculated in such a way that it will nevertheless be more profitable for the peasant to increase the acreage sown or to cultivate it better'. Second, he wanted a renewed commitment to the supply of manufactured and

other non-agricultural goods to the countryside – not only fertilis-
ers and ploughs, but salt and kerosene – which would be purchased
in-kind, with grain. He insisted that they should avoid the mistake
made in 1918–19, when the decree on goods exchange stipulated that
manufactured products be distributed to villages and districts upon
fulfilment of grain deliveries, and not to individual households. This
earlier disinclination to see individual households – potential 'kulak'
households – benefit from such exchanges had to be overcome, wrote
Trotsky, for such a system to succeed and provide incentives.

The memo's final two points, which were dropped from later ver-
sions of the text published by Trotsky himself, include a commitment
to investment and growth of the state and collective farm network,
which had by early 1920 become little more than an embarrassing
sideshow for party leaders, even though the fundamental principle of
state-sector, collectivised agriculture was central to everyone's vision of
full socialism in the future. Trotsky also described a basic reorientation
in the strategy guiding agricultural policy by concentrating state efforts
at the sowing stage of the agricultural calendar (and less on harvest-
ing), involving the party and soviets in the preparation and cultivation
of the fields as a means of ensuring that a greater area was sown. As
such, the Soviet regime would not be depending upon individualised
incentives alone to stimulate the expansion of production, but could
mobilise additional labour and oversight for agriculture in a way that
was consistent with Trotsky's own enthusiasm for labour conscription,
and which were already a part of the regime's current direction in economic policy.[22]

In Trotsky's proposal, he explained that he saw potential in the
regime treating regions of the republic differently, recognising that in
Siberia and parts of Ukraine the first two of his suggestions would be
most likely to succeed, while in central Russia and the Volga, where
rural population density was higher and communal land tenure
remained strong, emphasis on collectivisation and managed tillage
would be more appropriate. As could be expected, Trotsky had little to
say about the market, not referring to it specifically in the proposal at

all. However, in reference to his first two points – about a tax-in-kind and goods exchange – he wrote that it signified 'a certain slackening in the pressure on the kulak; we shall contain him within certain limits but not reduce him to the level of a peasant producing only for subsistence'. At the heart of Trotsky's proposal, then, there was a recognition that the obsession with kulaks, and with the food crisis being reducible to matters of class conflict, needed to end in order for economic recovery to achieve any traction. It is the same basic obsession that defenders of the NEP continued to struggle against within the party in the 1920s, after Lenin had died.

Trotsky was by no means the first to be critical of the razverstka. While the socialist rivals of the Communists, the Menshevik Party, had included the idea of a tax to replace the razverstka in their economic platform in the summer of 1919 (something echoed by the Socialist Revolutionaries in their own pronouncements on food policy), the impact of this was exceptionally limited, just as the Mensheviks were struggling to influence political discussions on the whole in the later months of the Civil War.[23] Then, shortly before Trotsky made his trip to Ekaterinburg, the Communist Party specialist on financial affairs, Yuri Larin, advanced proposals to the Third All-Russian Congress of Soviets of the People's Economy (institutions known at the time as *sovnarkhozy*) on 20 January 1920 that similarly called for the end of the razverstka methods of food collection. In its place he proposed a tax-in-kind, which would be introduced alongside a renewed commitment to the exchange of manufactured goods for food, to be overseen by the trade unions, and some measure of price regulation or even fixed prices on grain. Larin's main concern, like that of Trotsky, was for the state to incentivise food production above what was needed for the household alone.[24]

Larin was a member of the Soviet regime's highest economic body, the Supreme Council of the People's Economy (VSNKh), and his proposals were given serious consideration at the opening session of the Third Congress, although they were not formally adopted by the delegates, which chose instead to reaffirm the principles of centralisation in food procurement tasks. (Indeed, Larin's proposals, and the ensuing discussions, were not included in the published materials relating to the Congress of Sovnarkhozy at all.) Lenin was informed by the Commissar for Finance, Nikolai Krestinsky, of Larin's proposals the day after they had been presented to the Congress, adding his own judgement: 'I consider these to be impracticable and to be politically harmful.' Lenin concurred, replying to Krestinsky: 'Forbid Larin from any more such "blue sky" thinking (*prozhekterstvovat*).' Having intensified his condemnation of concessions to 'free trade' less than two months earlier, Lenin went further than demanding that Larin be rebuked. In fact, Lenin pushed for Larin's removal from his official post as member of the VSNKh presidium, and even sent a word of warning ('rein in Larin, or you might find your own career affected') to the chairman of that body, Alexei Rykov, another official known to be critical of the razverstka and food supply policy, more generally.[25]

Larin, whether consciously or not, had violated an instruction to all senior officials across a number of state bodies not to make independent statements on food policy, let alone critiques of the existing practices. Such was the level of dissatisfaction and dispute surrounding food supply at all levels of the system – collection, transport and distribution – that on 5 January 1920 the leading Collegium of Narkomprod, somewhat controversially, asked for all speeches and pronouncements on food supply issues to be vetted by the Central Committee of the Communist Party.[26] Less than a fortnight later, Larin had fallen foul of this principle, and been made to pay a price for confusing 'the young party members and non-party workers, who might regard you as an authority, a leader of the party who occupies a senior post in one of the most important state institutions'. So wrote the Central Committee in the letter to Larin informing him of his removal from the VSNKh.[27]

Trotsky's proposals, however, were discussed by the Communist Party Central Committee's Politburo in late March 1920. They were rejected by a vote of eleven to four.[28] Trotsky wrote before the meeting of the Politburo that the proposals were only a rough draft, and that the language would need to be reconsidered, even if he was satisfied with the core ideas. Still, despite the fact that there had been considerable discontent and discussion surrounding the current food supply policy both within the Communist Party and without, there was clearly no stomach for changing course on this, the most vital and problematic of state pursuits. At the Ninth Congress of the Communist Party, which opened shortly after the vote on Trotsky's proposals, the central tenets of the razverstka were reaffirmed, and Trotsky himself would move on from the subject of food policy and expand upon his project for the militarisation of labour, which was one of the major programmes endorsed by the Congress.[29] He would not revisit his proposals on food supply until one year later, in March 1921, when (in typically humble fashion) he chose to remind his colleagues in the party that the proposals for a tax-in-kind they were then adopting at Lenin's insistence, were fundamentally the same as those he had advanced earlier.

It is clear that there was insufficient political support for a radical reorientation of the food supply policy at the start of 1920. However, the political situation changed dramatically over the next twelve months, as the material costs of the continuation of the razverstka policy mounted in step with popular anxieties about the future, and gave rise to unprecedented levels of violence in the countryside when preparations were being made for another major grain procurement campaign in the autumn of that year.

When Trotsky was submitting his proposals to the Central Committee, Communist Party officials in the provinces were already engaged in a campaign of their own to try to arrest the degeneration of popular attitudes towards the party and Soviet government in the countryside. In Samara province, which had been the host of repeated outbreaks of violence between village communities and state agents, party activists received briefing papers on the most common anti-government slogans – number one on the list: 'Up with free trade!' – with instructions of how to counter these as they put across the party's message.[30] The officials charged with monitoring the correspondence to and from

Red Army soldiers produced numerous excerpts from letters they had opened and examined, which referred to the continuing requisitions that left households with less and less to eat, and diminishing levels of seed to sow the fields for the next harvest.[31] As the summer of 1920 progressed, anxieties grew as poor rainfall and high winds in certain regions produced early indications of drought and crop damage.[32] When the food requisition squads descended on the villages, protests by peasant farmers and local soviet officials were dismissed, taken only as evidence of 'kulak sabotage' and 'parochialism'.[33] Dismissing letters of appeal against the announced targets for grain collection sent by village communities and local (village and district) soviets in the weeks before the harvest was to commence, the county food commissar in Lebedian (Tambov province) declared to his colleagues in the county administration that these appeals 'only amount to pitiful kulak whining'. 'Is it not well known by now,' he explained,

> that the peasants continue to distil vodka, that they sell their grain on the black market, that they bury it in the ground? It is about time that you all understood that the requisitions are carried out according to the official razverstka target, which is established on the basis of government statistics. If the peasants do not have the necessary amount of grain, then that is their fault, and not ours.[34]

Such was the extent of the breakdown in relations between the central government and the periphery, broadly defined, that armed requisition squads expected resistance from locals and took it as confirmation of sabotage, carrying out the business as agents of the 'Centre', and bypassing local officials. The Cheka organisation in Penza province reported in August 1920 that

> [t]he peasants are protesting against the violence and humiliation they suffer at the hand of the requisitioning squads, which in some cases does occur on account of misunderstandings and misinterpretations of their orders from the centre. The centre is proposing to

extract grain surpluses to an inhuman degree, and some of the requisition squads do not spare the whip in trying to fulfil these orders. Amidst all of this there has been outright criminal behaviour by squads that behave as if they have some sort of axe to grind.[35]

Reports such as this indicate that the atmosphere that surrounded the grain procurement campaign, in which hundreds of armed squads descended upon the countryside to collect designated targets from villages, was one that combined a measure of desperation among the farming peasantry with a strong measure of despondence that characterised local administration and even many local Communist Party members.

The importance of this was most spectacularly demonstrated in Tambov, an agricultural province in central Russia that had been one of the main focal points of Soviet food supply efforts, having remained under Soviet control very nearly throughout the Civil War period. Like other provinces in Soviet Russia, Tambov had experienced waves of violent resistance from villagers as the state sought to collect grain and conscript men into the Red Army. When requisitioning began in August 1920 in Tambov, the anticipated clashes with farming households were dealt with firmly by the armed squads, but for the first time this violent defiance proved to be more durable. Making examples of individual villages that fought requisition squads – either by taking hostages, performing public executions, or even burning individual houses and even whole villages – proved ineffective, as it emerged that armed 'bandit' gangs were fighting alongside the villagers, working to sustain the resistance to requisition squads and state officials. Under the wave of violence, Communist Party members in the countryside rapidly took flight, fearing for their lives, and the soviet administration melted away as rebellion spread. Over the course of the next several weeks, the makings of a rebel army formed in the densely populated, agriculturally rich southern part of Tambov, effectively ending the campaign to requisition grain, and complicating the efforts of the Soviet state to secure food in the region, more generally, as important

rail lines connecting the cities of the north of Soviet Russia to the traditional grain-growing regions passed through the province. By the end
of the year, Soviet authority in Tambov was effectively isolated in the
provincial capital city, and the administrative centres of the counties,
while still holding out against the rebellion, were vulnerable and nearly
overcome by fatalism and panic. Over the winter months of 1920–21,
the 'Partisan Army' in Tambov took shape, incorporating a number
of regiments and keeping some 30,000 men under arms. At the same
time, the rebellion worked to implant an alternative government for
the territory creating its own civilian network of village-based 'unions
of the labouring peasantry', which numbered in the hundreds.[36]

The rebellion in Tambov at the time was unique in the Soviet Republic in its size and level of organisation. In several other regions, what
predominated was termed 'raiding banditry' – rebels who carried out
hit-and-run attacks targeting state agents and official institutions, but
who did not attempt to cultivate institutions of their own.[37] The disrup-
tion to the Soviet state, however, was considerable. Grain procurement
had virtually come to a halt in Tambov province by October/November
1920, but complications were experienced in several other agricultural
provinces, both contiguous to Tambov and further afield, that left the
regime facing a renewed crisis just as the formal military fronts of the
Civil War had all but disappeared. A survey of the situation produced
by the Cheka in mid December 1920 illustrated the manner in which
'banditry', such as that found in Tambov, was an extensive phenomenon, detailing its manifestation from western Ukraine and Belorussia
to the Caucasus and through to Kazakhstan and Siberia. Emphasising
the mainsprings of such disorder in each of these regions, the report
nevertheless underlined that the violence was a consequence of the
economic breakdown that the republic was suffering after so many
years of conflict, and as such could be understood as inevitable. In
that it threatened to form linkages across regions, however, the Cheka
report insisted that a coordinated strategy was required to end the wave
of banditry and bring the Civil War to an end.[38]

Facing great difficulties in central Russia, the Volga region and further south, the Soviet regime turned its attentions to the grain-growing regions of the Urals, the very places that Trotsky had visited at the start of 1920.[39] As in Tambov and the agricultural provinces of central Russia, the effort to procure grain in western Siberia was conducted like a military campaign, although in the case of the latter this was on account of its relatively recent 'liberation', rather than owing to a fundamental mistrust of 'localist' soviet administration.[40] Seeing in western Siberia a source of relief from the mounting crisis in food supply, procurement squads were despatched in great numbers (more than 25,000 were mobilised for procurement work in the vast region), with literally 'hungry' workers from the northern cities of European Russia deployed to ensure that the commitment to the task of procurement was beyond question.[41] Little had improved, however, in the state of agricultural production since Trotsky's diagnosis of the situation in the region one year earlier, and the demands for grain made at gunpoint inspired much the same resistance and violence as had been seen in regions of European Russia.

The province of Tiumen, which was the principal focus of grain collection efforts in Siberia, became the epicentre of a wider regional rebellion that took in parts of Ekaterinburg and Cheliabinsk provinces, as well as northern Kazakhstan. The resistance to the Soviet state there assumed a more organised character, as it had in Tambov. Requisition squads and other government agents found themselves under attack by units of the 'People's Insurgent Army', whose most important actors were former Red partisans who had been instrumental in sustaining grassroots resistance to Kolchak and the Whites in 1919. Now, in 1920–21, they emerged as the prime movers in defending the village population from what were perceived as unjust and threatening demands by state requisition squads. Although unable to create the same coherent organisation of command and administration as had been achieved in the much more compact space of southern Tambov province, the rebels in western Siberia mobilised tens of thousands of local men, occupied significant regional towns (even briefly issuing their own newspaper), and made Soviet state administration and grain requisitioning virtually impossible in the first three months of 1921. With their prominent slogan of 'Soviets without Communists!', the People's Insurgent Army of western Siberia, like its counterpart in Tambov, sought to project its struggle as one of regime change rather than 'merely' protest against the policies and practices of the ruling Communist Party.

Such ambitions aside, and in acknowledgement of the fact that many of these anti-Soviet rebels wanted – sometimes desperately – to believe that they were part of a wider movement that had a strong chance to topple the Soviet government, these rebellions stood little chance of success on those terms. While in the midst of preparations to begin demobilising the Red Army at the end of 1920 – an army that had grown to several million men by the end of the Civil War – the situation in the grain-growing regions of the republic necessitated the redeployment of hundreds of thousands of those soldiers for counter-insurgency operations against, for the most part, Russian peasants. By the summer of 1921, the territory most affected by the rebellion in Tambov would be occupied by more than 100,000 Red Army troops, a force that would stay in place until the end of the year to prevent a renewal of the 'banditry' that had raged in the province over the previous twelve months. In western Siberia, regular Red Army divisions were sent to suppress the insurgency, joined by special armed units of the Cheka and Communist Party.

At these particular fronts, and elsewhere in Soviet Russia, special camps were created to imprison captured rebels, as well as to intern the neighbours and family of suspected rebels, kept as hostages, under threat of execution, to encourage the surrender of anti-Soviet insurgents. Villages were bombarded with heavy artillery and from aircraft, the Red Army experimented with using poisonous gas to 'smoke out' rebels hiding in the forests, and 'troikas' of state, party and military officials moved from village to village and carried out hasty investigations of the locals' involvement in the resistance, carrying out swift justice

to demonstrate the resolve and power of the Soviet state. Throughout this process of mounting state repressions, villagers lived in fear
of reprisals, either from state forces or those of the remaining rebel
groups, both of which could be merciless in punishing collaboration.
It is impossible to know the number of victims of the wave of violence
that began in the autumn of 1920, and extended for well over a year in
certain parts of Soviet territory, but the count certainly runs into the
tens of thousands. As with any civil war, civilians were overwhelmingly
the largest group to fall victim in this final phase of the conflict.

The combined effect of the disturbances that infected the grain-
growing regions of the Soviet Republic, as well as the desperate
attempts by the state to requisition as much as possible of the farmers'
harvests over the course of 1920–21, left many of those same regions in
an exceptionally vulnerable position. Already subject to the pressures
identified by Trotsky and many other critics of the food supply policy
of the Soviet government, a harvest failure in the preceding year meant
that the seed grain of farmers fell subject to state requisitions, and the
ensuing harvest was nothing short of disastrous, leaving the communities of the Volga region, as well as the southern Urals and parts of
Ukraine, facing famine. While a massive relief effort was eventually
spearheaded by the American government in 1921, the famine claimed
the lives of more than five million persons between 1921 and 1923.[42] The
crisis in food supply in the Soviet Republic, then, left victims in the
cities and the villages, in the traditionally 'grain-deficit' regions of the
north of European Russia, and in the so-called 'grain-rich' provinces of
central Russia, Ukraine and western Siberia. 'I'll believe you are starving when I start to see mothers eating their children,' one Soviet official
was reported to have told a group of protesting villagers in the province
of Voronezh in early 1921. Such evidence was in abundance in the traditional grain-growing regions of Russia only a short time later.[43]

The decision to persist with the razverstka in 1920 – that is, with the
policy of the armed requisitioning of grain as per the needs of the state
– clearly had significant consequences for the Soviet Republic and
its people. At a time when the policy's justification as an emergency

wartime measure was being legitimately questioned in light of the increasingly favourable political and military situation, and with a growing appreciation within the Communist Party of the policy's political consequences and questionable sustainability, the dismissal of the opportunity to alter the path of official policy on food supply is a moment that effectively extended the Civil War and helped create the famine that claimed the lives of millions of Soviet citizens.

In March 1921, at the Tenth Congress of the Communist Party, Lenin spearheaded the move to abandon the razverstka, introducing in its place a progressive tax-in-kind system that would, in principle, be assessed on the basis of actual harvests. While the razverstka had been cancelled in the province of Tambov over one month earlier, the desire at that time had been to limit the knowledge of this concession to the insurgent countryside of that province alone, rather than for it to become policy nationwide. The obvious impossibility of this, however, placed the discontinuation of the razverstka campaign on the national agenda, and Lenin drafted proposals for the introduction of a tax that same month. Then, only days before the party congress was to convene, a mutiny at the Kronstadt naval base near Petrograd added additional urgency to the matter. The sailors taking up arms against the regime protested against the failing food supply policy and the treatment of the farmers, in particular. For them, the mutiny was an act of solidarity with the workers, who themselves demonstrated on the streets of Moscow and Petrograd against the shortages and repressions of the Soviet regime, and with the peasants, whose beleaguered villages were home for many of the mutinying sailors themselves. While the Red Army was storming the naval base at Kronstadt, putting down the mutiny at the cost of thousands of lives, the delegates to the Tenth Party Congress voted to approve Lenin's proposed abandonment of the current food supply policy.

Adopted under popular pressure, at a time when, in Lenin's own words, the party faced a challenge far more dangerous than 'all the Denikins, Kolchaks and Yudeniches' of the earlier period of the Civil War, the abandonment of the razverstka was now regarded as a necessity.

'Only agreement with the peasantry can save the socialist revolution in Russia,' Lenin told the delegates to the Tenth Congress.[44] Within months, the announcement of the tax-in-kind was reinforced with the decision to begin decriminalising the market, a necessary complement that helped provide agricultural producers with an outlet for the sale of surplus (after-tax) grain and, as Trotsky and others had emphasised, incentives to improve production. Trotsky, as well as other critics of food supply policy before 1921, did not speak openly of the market, nor were they, in truth, 'pro-peasant' in their political outlook. But, Trotsky himself, rather reasonably, pointed out in his autobiography that neither did Lenin consider the possibility of market decriminalisation in March 1921.[45] What became the New Economic Policy would take shape over a period of several months and even years, as the logic and consequences of the initial concessions at the Tenth Congress were worked out.[46] There is little reason to assume that this path would not have been similarly trodden had the decision to end the razverstka been taken one year earlier.

While Trotsky and Larin were not shy in reminding others of their advocacy of such measures, either at the time of the Tenth Congress or after, neither were as bold as to speak in terms of the costs that would have been avoided, especially in terms of human life, had their earlier advice been acted upon.[47] The tax-in-kind, though, was 'sold' to the wider party membership as a concession, as – in the words of the trade union activist, David Riazanov – the 'peasant Brest', a reference to the Treaty of Brest-Litovsk, which had secured Russia's withdrawal from the First World War in 1918 and had, in Lenin's own words at the time, forced Russia to 'the very bottom of that abyss of defeat, dismemberment, enslavement and humiliation'.[48] In the eyes of many, the NEP, from its very beginnings, was a perversion in the course of the socialist revolution. Lenin would devote much of his final months and years to rationalising the path upon which his decision in March 1921 had set the Soviet Republic. Even the advocates of the NEP, which had finally secured peace with the peasantry, defended its continuation in reference to the Civil War and the events of 1920–21. Stalin, at the time one such advocate, scolded his rivals at the Thirteenth Communist Party Conference in January 1924 (only days before Lenin's death) for claiming that the party had been slow to react to events: 'Were we late in abandoning the razverstka? Wasn't it the case that with such facts as the Tambov rebellion and Kronstadt we recognised that it was impossible to live any longer under war communism?'[49] Stalin's claim was that the party had saved the revolution with this change of course; his concern with the people who had lost their lives over the many months it had taken the party leadership to actually arrive at this decision was less in evidence.

How would the course of Soviet history have been different had the disaster of 1920–21 been avoided? Leaving aside the humanitarian considerations already discussed – the political violence and famine that would likely have been lessened, rather than avoided entirely – might there have been longer-term ramifications of the earlier adoption of the reforms and concessions that became the New Economic Policy? The short answer to such a question is no. The NEP, with its denationalisation and markets, its cultural pluralism and unsavoury 'Nep-men', proved untenable within the context of the Soviet revolution, and it proved unworkable in the hands of Soviet leaders, who had neither the will nor expertise to manage a mixed economy. A significant part of the drama that constitutes the history of the unravelling and abandonment of the NEP, however, brings us back to the troubled moment of its birth. For many in the wider Communist Party membership, the return of money and markets and the perceived toleration of kulaks and 'bourgeois specialists' under the NEP were inexcusable, and consideration of social and cultural problems, and not just macroeconomic ones, almost invariably came back to the 'peasant Brest' as a turning point.[50]

When Stalin himself changed his line on the sustainability of the NEP in 1927, when he demanded a return to 'extraordinary measures' in confronting the menace of the kulaks and the crime of market speculation, he tapped into that current within the Communist Party that had never reconciled itself to the capitulation of the Civil War and the perceived concessions that had been made to the peasantry.[51] While the overall trajectory in the development of Soviet socialism is unsurprising, with the long-term commitments to centralised economic planning and the creation of large-scale collective farms in the place of private, household farmsteads, it is insightful to consider the manner in which this transformation would have been achieved had the brief experiment of the NEP been initiated in different, more favourable, circumstances. At the very least, consideration of this issue highlights the connections that bridge these seemingly discrete eras in the development of Soviet socialism.

THE 'BOLSHEVIK REFORMATION'

February 1922

CATRIONA KELLY

O N 16 MARCH 1922, a crowd of more than 10,000 people packed Haymarket Square, at the centre of Dostoevsky's St Petersburg, renamed Petrograd in 1914. The mood was ugly. Shouts and jeers turned into scuffles; a policeman was badly beaten. The protestors were enraged by the attempt to remove from the Church of the Saviour, one of the largest and best loved in the city, items made of precious metals and gemstones that had devotional significance. The unrest was part of a wave of dissatisfaction stirred up by the Decree on the Confiscation of Church Valuables, passed a month earlier[1] – a central episode in what might be termed 'the Bolshevik Reformation'.[2]

The law passed on 16 February 1922 had represented the removal of church valuables as a measure *in extremis,* to relieve the suffering caused by the terrible famine in the Volga region after drought and crop failures the previous year. The Soviet press carried articles about the disaster throughout the autumn and winter of 1921–22. On 27 January 1922, for instance, a headline in *Petrograd Pravda* screamed: THE STARVING ARE DRAGGING CORPSES FROM GRAVEYARDS TO EAT THEM. Reporting the aid work carried out by Russian and foreign organisations, the press made clear that the efforts were totally inadequate.[3]

On 18 February, Father Alexander Vvedensky, star preacher and intelligentsia salon lion, exhorted the Orthodox faithful to help all they could with the drive to bring aid to the starving. 'In the crazed state caused by hunger, mothers are killing their own children and eating their little corpses,' he wrote. 'We weep over them, far off, dying, forgotten. Forgotten by whom? By the Christian world.'[4] An avalanche of Soviet press coverage over the next weeks pressed home the point. The first confiscations were reported in early March, and by the end of March, the propaganda pressure had been increased, with newspapers recording mass votes by factory assemblies demanding the surrender of church valuables.[5]

By this point, the Bolshevik leaders were preparing to use the confiscations as an excuse for an all-out assault upon what were officially known as 'religious associations'. An important plan, where the Orthodox Church was concerned, was 'to initiate a split in the clergy, seizing the initiative in a decisive way and taking under government protection the clergy who are openly advocating cooperation with the confiscations,' as Trotsky put it on 20 March 1922.[6]

The basis for this policy lay in a division about exactly what 'church property' was to be confiscated. The decree passed on 16 February had stated that only objects '*the removal of which cannot impact on the interests of a given cult*' were to be confiscated.[7] The issue was whether communion vessels and other 'sacred objects' (*svyatyni*), such as reliquaries, might be removed without bringing about such 'impact'. On 19 and 28 February, Patriarch Tikhon explicitly stated that the removal of these was improper. However, a month later, this policy was openly challenged. A letter signed by twelve reformist priests, including Vvedensky, published in *Petrograd Pravda* on 25 March, pointed to the justification in Christian practice for surrendering 'even the most sacred vessels', provided that the government would allow the Church to help in the relief effort. This rider was quickly forgotten, and cooperation with the state became the issue. On 18 May 1922, Vvedensky and other supporters of the confiscations created the Higher Board of Church Management, a body that began to act as a government-sanctioned alternative to the official church, promoting a self-declaredly progressive agenda of church reforms. For several years, the so-called 'Renovationist' (*Obnovlencheskoe*) movement enjoyed official favour, with traditionalists rehabilitated only in 1927, when, two years after Tikhon's death, the Patriarchal locum tenens, Sergii, made a statement of cooperation with the Soviet government.[8]

In terms of their declared rationale – to raise funds for aid to the starving – the confiscations produced disappointing results. Across Ukraine, only 2.6 metric tonnes of silver had been collected by 4 May 1922.[9] But the social change they brought about was enormous. The stripping of church valuables fatally weakened the institutional authority of Patriarch Tikhon and the official church hierarchy. It caused immense distress to believers and strife among them, leaving wounds – in particular a deep suspicion of attempts to reform Orthodoxy – that lasted into the twenty-first century.

The confiscations also underlined the pariah status of what Bolshevik terminology labelled 'religious cults'. From now on, religious associations, particularly the Orthodox Church, would be regarded by Soviet officials as bastions of privilege, milked for financial contributions (such as local taxes), and denied access to state resources for the repairs to buildings that were legally required by the terms of their contracts of use. Religious associations were under a pall of suspicion, their members pilloried as benighted (at best) and at worst, socially hostile. Over the spring and summer of 1922, a series of show trials, their results predictable from the denunciatory style of the prosecutors' orations, ended with the execution of clergy and laymen who had supposedly resisted confiscation, including, among others, Metropolitan Veniamin of Petrograd. Veniamin and his co-defendants were charged under Article 62 of the 1922 Criminal Code, which dealt with counter-revolutionary activity. Court discourse and press reporting alike underlined the political threat posed by church leaders and their links with the ancien régime.[10]

The confiscations were more than just an episode in the history of church-state relations. The drive to seize church property was also a pioneering example of all-out mass mobilisation, the harnessing of media and organisational resources to achieve immediate political ends. By participating in it, minor officials and members of the population learned (more accurately, invented) the rules of 'campaign justice'.[11] 'Vengeance is not the purpose of justice,' Professor Alexander Zhizhilenko remarked in his summing-up for the defence at the trial of Metropolitan Veniamin. But the mockery in the press of the defence team – 'their conclusions are ridiculous' – betrayed the obsolescence of this view.[12] A particularly clear indicator of change was the attribution of seditious character to actions that had been sanctioned by the authorities when they actually happened. Petrograd churchmen who had read aloud a letter from Metropolitan Veniamin about the need to cooperate with the confiscations were retrospectively accused of taking part in a political plot.[13]

The conduct of the confiscations also predicted later social and political campaigns more broadly. The hysterical, authoritarian insistence on high-speed achievement of arbitrarily imposed targets (in this case, insistence that ever larger and more impressive quantities of precious metals, jewels and other valuables be located and handed over); the assumption that shortfalls were caused by subterfuge and ill will on the part of opponents (in this case, believers); the vituperative stigmatisation of actual and supposed enemies (in this case, top clergy) – all this established the new paradigms. The later confrontations with 'bourgeois specialists', 'wreckers' and 'kulaks' were rehearsed and perfected at this point.[14]

In the context of attitudes to heritage as well as church-state relations, the effects of the 16 February 1922 law were epoch-making. By 22 August 1922, more than 160 house churches in Petrograd alone had been closed, including 157 Orthodox house churches.[15] On 25 October 1922, a local official in Petrograd expressed ungrammatical bewilderment about what to do with the residuum of church property after liquidation had taken place:

We offered icons kiots and iconostases free of charge to Parish Councils of Parish churches that are still open but they refused because of not having no spare funds for transport and proper packing. On the basis of the above we request you to issue the appropriate order of what we are to do with the icons and kiots. If we take them into storage then they might as well be firewood or should we sell them to private icon shops or destroy them on the spot.[16]

In 1918, hundreds of churches in Petrograd had been issued with 'certificates of protection' that guaranteed the inviolability of buildings and their contents. In 1922, most of these were ignored. Preservation officials, racing desperately against time, attempted to salvage paintings and applied art, only to find themselves branded as 'not acting in a Soviet way' (a dangerously small step from 'anti-Soviet'). As the 25 October report suggests, much of the property, rather than being decorously disposed of to raise funds, simply ended up as trash. Objects that did make it to museums were often damaged, and almost always arrived without detailed descriptions of provenance. Plans to set up 'church museums' had at best limited results.[17] Damage to the historical heritage was incalculable. A sure sign of the authorities' bad conscience was an article published in May 1922 by Grigory Yatmanov, head of the Petrograd Museums Department, who solemnly listed the sterling work being done under the new government in order to protect historic buildings and objects, concentrating exclusively on the former royal palaces.[18] In fact, the boot was on the other foot: the confiscation of church property provided a model for the systematic liquidation, from 1927, of marketable assets held in other state collections, in particular the 'museums of daily life' set up in former aristocratic mansions during the first post-revolutionary years.[19] While much private property had been seized during and immediately after the revolution (so widespread were expropriations that Russian children even began playing a game called 'Search and Requisition'), the predation upon *already* nationalised property opened a new chapter.

All in all, the confiscations were a turning point in political, social and cultural terms simultaneously. But were they 'historically inevitable'?

For many historians and eyewitness observers, such a question would seem not just badly posed, but frivolous and indeed offensive. The church confiscations are almost always regarded as a manifestation of Bolshevism's abiding hostility to organised religion and its purposive, sustained efforts to eradicate alternative belief systems. As the Scottish-Canadian journalist Frederick Arthur Mackenzie observed in 1927, 'The persecution is not occasional, incidental or limited. It is carried out as a carefully planned campaign throughout the land and its aim is to destroy faith, if needs be by force.'[20] Similar arguments were made in the earliest historical account of Bolshevik action against religious societies, *The Black Book* of 1925. As Peter Struve wrote in the Foreword, Soviet power had 'a peculiar historical achievement to its credit – the resurrection of the Inquisition under an atheistic flag'. It aimed not to create a new religion, but a radically anti-religious new order, in which there was no middle ground.[21]

Indeed, the confiscations did not come out of nowhere. A series of decrees that indirectly affected the church – the Decree on Land of 26 October 1917, the Decree on Civil Marriage of 18 December 1917, the decree 'On the Recognition as Counter-Revolutionary of All Attempts to Arrogate the Functions of Government' of 3 January 1918 – were followed by the Decree on the Separation of Church and State and Church and School (20 January 1918). An Instruction of 24 August 1918 consequent upon the 20 January 1918 decree required the authorities to remove 'all and any religious images (icons, pictures, statues of a religious character etc.)' from public buildings – a measure already perceived as sacrilegious by the adherents of Orthodoxy.[22]

The legal changes fostered and sustained enmity at the political grassroots. As early as November 1917, Red Guards on duty at the funeral of Father Ioann Kochurov, a priest at the Catherine Cathedral in Tsarskoe Selo, gestured at the church's golden domes and speculated, 'If you chop those down, might god jump out?'[23] Kochurov himself had been summarily executed on 31 October 1917, after he attempted to calm anti-Bolshevik unrest in Tsarskoe. This was one of many cases where church property was removed or destroyed, and clerics assaulted and killed, sometimes after torture and mutilation.[24] On 19 January 1918, Patriarch Tikhon consigned to anathema those who engaged in persecutions of clergy and destroyed church property, an indication of how prevalent such events were.[25]

While this violence took place in areas affected by uprisings and civil war, and so might not be seen as 'purposive', there were also assaults on Orthodox property that had the sanction of central government. These included, for example, the dissolution of monasteries, and the drive, from late 1918, to organise the exposure of saints' relics. This latter strategy was held to be especially useful in enlightening ignorant believers who, once the contents of the precious caskets had been revealed as half-rotting corpses, dried-up bones, or indeed waxen dolls, were expected to dismiss religion itself as 'a con'.[26] The removal of church valuables, the forcible closure of churches, the stripping of the altars known as 'liquidation' when a church was closed, and the demolition of the building itself, could be understood, from this point of view, as steps on a continuum.

Yet in part this impression of a 'grand plan' comes from what happened from 1922 onwards. It is notable that the compiler of *The Black Book*, setting out 'the basic views and aims' of the Bolshevik government with regard to religion, adduced mainly evidence from 1922 and later.[27] Certainly, anti-clerical and anti-religious rhetoric had been widespread from the beginning; any self-respecting agitational sketch or celebration of a revolutionary anniversary was bound to include a fat priest alongside an obese banker or two. But only in February 1922 did the Bolshevik leadership openly throw its weight behind a national anti-religious campaign. The exposure of relics, though sanctioned at the top, had been the responsibility of a sub-ministerial agency, the Eighth Section of the Commissariat of Justice. As a journalist pointed out in 1922, exposure had affected sixty-three sites, rather than the 40,000 affected by requisitioning.[28] Now ordinary parish churches were under assault, for all the previously widespread commentary emphasising the lay believer's right to worship.

In the first years after the Bolsheviks took power, pronouncements at the centre suggested the possibility of at least limited conciliation, following Lenin's 1905 article, 'Socialism and Religion', which had suggested that direct confrontation with the masses was not advisable. As the lead article in the journal *Revolution and the Church* had put it in 1919: 'Despite the blatant counter-revolutionary stance of the church in general, the Soviet government considers it appropriate to maintain a defensive position, at least where faith itself is concerned. The full force of political repression is unleashed on the adherents of the church only where they engage in counter-revolutionary activity.'[29]

Proclamations of this kind are often, understandably, seen by church historians as mere hypocrisy. Yet Soviet officials did make some effort to ensure freedom of worship in the first months and years after the 20 January 1918 decree was published. The so-called 'house churches', or chapels, in public buildings should have been closed down automatically after the decree was passed, since they clearly maintained an alien religious presence in secular space. But in fact they often remained open, expediently reclassified as 'parish churches'. This arrangement was supported or encouraged by state preservation bodies, since some of the most important architectural constructions of major cities (essentially, all official buildings) contained such 'house churches'. It was not until late 1922 and 1923 that there was a concerted drive to shut them – in other words, this drive followed the 16 February 1922 decree, rather than acting as a prompt to it. The decree also marked a watershed in terms of implementing the strict letter of the law relating to 'cults'. Though on paper, religious groups had not been juridical subjects since 20 January 1918, in practice they were often treated as though they were.[30] The encrustation of religious practice in pettifogging dirigisme, like the systematic employment of counter-revolutionary legislation, marked the start of a new phase of church-state relations.

All in all, the 16 February 1922 decree heralded important changes in the legal treatment of cults (as opposed to extra-legal impositions of repression upon them).[31] These changes do not seem to have been part of a carefully premeditated plan. Over the course of late summer to winter 1921, Soviet leaders havered about whether to accept offers of aid to the starving from religious groups in Russia. By the terms of the 20 January 1918 decree, such groups were not allowed to raise funds or to engage in political or philanthropic activity – yet the Soviet government had accepted aid from foreign religious groups.[32] The need for cash vied with a fear of allowing the Church too prominent a role. On 8 December 1921, the government and the Church eventually reached agreement on joint action. Yet less than three weeks later, on 27 December, another decree stipulated that property in churches was to be surveyed and assigned to three categories (of museum value, of monetary value and everyday), and this was followed by a third decree, on 2 January 1922, ordering the removal of all objects of 'museum value'. Trotsky, the coordinator of famine relief, was pressing hard for action against the Church, and had moved to expedite confiscation (with the piquant detail that his wife, Natalia Sedova, in charge of government heritage policy, had apparently been able to lobby on her own agency's behalf). Yet the sense that the Church had particular or exclusive responsibility for funding famine relief had not yet taken general hold. Rather, in January and February 1922, the press rammed home the responsibility of all Soviet citizens to surrender valuables, reporting tales of party members who had handed over their own gold objects.[33]

Into January, February, and even March, some officials and clerics, in some places at least, were still trying to thrash out a compromise.[34] On 14 February 1922, *Petrograd Pravda* published an article, 'The Contribution of the Orthodox Clergy to Aid for the Starving', which reported Church-led initiatives and used a neutral or even approbatory tone. Even after the 16 February decree was passed, Metropolitan Veniamin and the Petrograd Soviet engaged in dialogue, holding a meeting on 5 March to review the situation. Efforts were, reportedly, halted by an order from central government. At a second meeting 'a few days later', the officials from the Petrograd Soviet retreated to a hard-line position.[35] Within the country's ruling group, there were also divisions, as well as a general sense of uncertainty. The secret police chief, Felix Dzerzhinsky, mainly pushed for a hard line against the Church leadership, and mocked a December 1921 proposal by Anatoly

Lunacharsky to attempt cooperation with liberal clergy. Yet even Dzerzhinsky could waver: in April 1923, he expressed concern that undue use of force against Patriarch Tikhon might threaten international relations. At times, ideological rectitude was less important than pragmatic considerations.[36]

There was no question of sympathy for believers. Rather, the fear of goading them into outright rebellion (and losing political capital with the working classes generally) was offset by the fear of encouraging 'reactionary forces'.[37] What finally resolved the situation against compromise was a serious riot in the textile town of Shuya, just over 150 miles from Moscow. Both the effects (four deaths, as opposed to minor injuries) and the closeness to the capital rattled the authorities badly. A famous letter by Lenin, penned on 19 March, just after news from Shuya had reached the centre, claimed that 'the clerical black hundreds' were plotting 'a decisive confrontation'. Referring obliquely to Machiavelli's words, 'For injuries ought to be done all at one time, so as being tasted less, they offend less', Lenin called for all-out action to crush religious resistance. Published as an isolated document in a Russian émigré journal in 1970, this letter seemed to bespeak the existence of a master plan.[38] But in broader context, preceded as it was by lengthy wrangling in the Politburo, it is clear that the shift to the hard line was a rush decision; Lenin's politics were of a less reflective and methodical kind than those of the thinker he suggested emulating.[39]

It was, however, this letter that precipitated the marked acceleration of action against religious groups, and surge of anti-clerical rhetoric in the press, that became palpable in the last ten days of March 1922, and lasted until the early summer. If Lenin's letter about Shuya immediately preceded the start of the all-out anti-church campaign, then the scaling-down of this campaign in the early summer immediately followed another important event in Lenin's biography – his first fully incapacitating stroke, on the night of 26–27 May. Had this stroke, requiring intensive rehabilitation, happened just two or three months earlier, no other member of the Politburo would have had the personal authority to push through the hard line.[40]

Throughout late March and April, the Soviet press was in a condition of hysteria. Reports of outrages by 'Black Hundred' groups, supposedly orchestrated by 'the princes of the church', vied with indignant letters from members of the public about the slowness in surrendering valuables. Action by the clergy was now uniformly represented as 'too little, too late', where it was not actually obstructive, and the show trials against them were lovingly detailed.[41] In the wake of the confiscations, Soviet Russia for the first time acquired a properly organised (though still small and limited) atheistic establishment, with the founding of the League of the Militant Godless, whose newspaper, *Bezbozhnik* (*The Militant Atheist*), began publishing in December 1922. The famous Communist rituals – Red Christenings and funerals, celebrations of Communist Christmas and Easter – also date from the post-confiscation period, 1923–24, rather than characterising the post-revolutionary years in a broad sense.[42]

All-out strife against religious groups in February–June 1922 was not, therefore, the culmination of a well-planned policy. Confrontation with the Church was at some level predetermined, in that the Bolsheviks were radical atheists, and that attitudes to the status of church buildings and church vessels were irreconcilably different (on the one hand they were material objects best put to some more practical purpose, on the other, earthly symbols of the heavenly kingdom).[43] But it did not have to happen at this precise point. So, what if some kind of compromise with a church leader who enjoyed respect both among reformists and among traditionalists, such as Metropolitan Veniamin, *had* been reached?

There were formidable obstacles to any such compromise, to begin with on the church side. With Patriarch Tikhon set against confiscation of communion vessels, there was limited room for manoeuvre by any senior cleric who wished to remain in the patriarchal system, given that action without the 'blessing' of a superior was entirely unacceptable.[44] For their part, many believers, even those sympathetic to Bolshevism, had a profound attachment to church property. While the Soviet press constantly dredged up cases of 'Christians' who wrote in to urge rapid surrender of communion vessels, verbatim records of public meetings sometimes give a different picture. At a meeting of the Petrograd Soviet on 20 March, one speaker vehemently opposed the confiscation policy. 'Right before the Sebastopol campaign, Nicholas I forced the Kiev Cave Monasteries to hand over 20 million worth of stuff like that,' he recalled. But given the consequences of the Crimean War, 'it didn't do him any good'. As this speaker concluded: 'I'm the son of a former serf, I'm not going against Soviet power, I wish it well, but I keep saying: don't go against God...'[45]

For many ordinary members of the public, the line that church property was theirs, to do what they liked with because it was made by them, resonated loudly. This kind of attitude underpinned the arguments used by working-class congregations against the closure of churches and seizures of their contents. The faithful of St Pitirim's Church, Kievskaia ulitsa, Petrograd, felt able to assert, in summer 1922, 'Our church is little, and was made not by the efforts and capital of the *burzhui*, but by our calloused hands alone, and we have collected the essential vessels as and when we could.'[46] Yet there was also sympathy for the plight of the starving and uncertainty about what might properly be surrendered. The swithering of an ordinary member of the clergy recorded in the reports of the Petrograd trial of churchmen – first he had thought that removing church property was intolerable, later that it might in fact be tolerated – was a natural response, given the way in which religious believers were hectored by advocates within the church itself who held polarised views.[47] After all, in 1918 the Local Council (Pomestnyi Sobor) of the Orthodox Church had concluded that 'the sacred vessels may be quite without decoration, and the vestments of plain cloth', since 'the Orthodox Church treasures its sacred things not for their material worth'.[48] The fact that there were disturbances at a mere thirteen of the hundreds of churches still open in Petrograd during March and April 1922 suggests the lack of a 'general line'.[49] A governing desire was to keep out of conflict: in the words of Veniamin after his election as Metropolitan in 1918, 'I stand for church freedom. The church should keep clear of politics, since previously politics caused her much suffering.'[50]

As the reaction to the advice, 'don't go against God', from the speaker at the Petrograd Soviet suggested (shouts of 'Enough!' and general uproar), compromise with the clergy would have been extremely unpopular with many members of the Bolshevik rank and file. But as the hesitation over whether to close house churches shows, vehement anti-religious (as opposed to anti-clerical) feeling was by no means universal. The participation of believers in the confiscations might have been swallowed by many officials if a command to allow this had come down from above.

The possibility of an alternative path may be suggested by the aftermath of the legislation on which the Bolsheviks based the 20 January 1918 decree – the December 1905 law on the division of church and state passed by a socialist-majority French government under Clemenceau. This law was divisive in much the same way as the Soviet decree imitating it was to prove. In 1902, an official of the Department of Religious Affairs told the lawyer Louis Méjan, one of the architects of the 1905 law, that 'to separate Church and State would be as foolish an act as to release wild beasts from their cages in the Place de la Concorde to pounce on pedestrians', since there would no longer be a moral restraint upon governance and social relations.[51] In France too, virulent anti-clericalism in some sections of society – among the urban working class, for instance – was offset by tenacious attachment to religion and to the material fabric of church life, and there was a sturdy tradition of often foul-mouthed anti-clericalism. Congregations in France were far from delighted with the state property grab for 'their' churches, and bitterly resented the interruption to their life rituals.[52] Conversely, some of the ground on which compromise was enacted in France did exist in Russia – for instance, there too, a substantial proportion of churchgoers and clergy saw disestablishment as a chance to concentrate on spiritual matters and to assign more control in the parishes to the laity.[53]

There were of course significant differences. France had more fully developed property rights (so that *cultes* given access to historic buildings had better defined rights of usage) and a much better established history of heritage preservation. There was no question of using congregations as a cheap way of paying for the upkeep of historic buildings, as in Soviet Russia, and congregations were not cast into a comparable legal and economic limbo. But the most crucial difference may lie in the fact that the measures in France always anticipated a gradual transition to the new order, permitting an intervention of the unanticipated. With the nation swept by patriotism once the First World War began, hostility to the Church diminished, and much of the impetus behind the new legislation ebbed away.

Soviet history in the first years after the revolution, on the other hand, offered no counterbalancing event of this kind. Rather, the narrowly won civil war of 1918–21 had left a sense that the country was beleaguered by precisely the kind of reactionary forces that the Church was held to represent. With concessions made to other representatives of the old order, such as industrialists and traders, under the New Economic Policy, it was vital for the Bolshevik leaders to show their supporters that they had not 'sold out' to every kind of 'former person'.[54] It was only two decades later, during the so-called 'Great Patriotic War', that an alternative and far more life-threatening conflict brought about a full rehabilitation of nation-state patriotism. With this came a softening in attitude to religious practice, and particularly Orthodoxy, as manifested in the concordat contracted between Stalin and the Church's Moscow leadership in 1943.

Even this concordat offered the Church only limited concessions, mainly to do with property management, greater autonomy for parishes, and an approved procedure for the opening of closed churches. Without the stimulus of an external threat (the 1943 concordat was primarily a response to the widespread opening of churches in areas held by the Nazis), any compromise enacted in 1922 would certainly have been still more circumscribed. And it would at most have led to a slowing of pace in the assault on the Church, not to an abandonment of hostilities. In the wildest counterfactual dream, it is impossible to imagine a rehabilitation of the majority faith akin to that which took place under Franco (or, indeed, in post-Soviet Russia), with, say, Stalin watching proudly as his daughter Svetlana and her betrothed stood under the bridal crowns at the Cathedral of Christ Redeemer.

As a non-Soviet organisation, the Church would anyway have been subject to more and more stifling regulation in the mid 1920s, and to intense pressure in the years of cultural centralisation (one can compare the dissolution of independent literary organisations and the formation of the Union of Writers in 1932). In conditions of mass industrialisation and urbanisation, church closures would hardly have been avoidable, both because any useable buildings were pressed into service to house workspace and storage, and because they were alien to the landscape of the 'model socialist city' assiduously propagandised in the planning of the day. The most one can say is that the process of resolving demolition proposals might have worked differently, with congregations induced to believe that they themselves were exercising an important social role, and 'helping' society and the Church by moving from church A to church B. One might compare the way in which the Soviet government reached accommodation, during the early 1930s, with 'bourgeois specialists' in academia and with the literary and artistic establishment, after which a mildly antagonistic, but also mutually advantageous, relationship resulted. Professionals were aware that the receipt of state funding required that government agendas were honoured; party leaders withdrew backing from militant lobby groups such as Proletkul't and from the 'Red Professorate'.[55] This alternative path is not at all fantastic: in the post-war years, believers proved willing to use official channels to get churches open, and they rapidly acquired a sense of how to operate in the relevant bureaucracies.[56]

In some respects, this was an opportunity missed. A more 'docile' church would also have been – as some Soviet leaders had argued in 1922 – a more manageable one. Part of this lesson seems to have got through: 1922 was the last time that religious believers were subjected to show trials, and where the equation of religious belief and counter-revolutionary sympathies was openly made in procuratorial and press disquisitions. Thereafter, local soviet officials and the police, while working assiduously to enforce the laws on secularisation, did all they could to emphasise that clerics who happened to be arrested were guilty of ordinary 'civil' crimes (including political offences such as spying). As a pro-Soviet pamphlet published in London in the early 1930s put it: 'It is in the capitalist countries that religious persecution must be sought.' The followers of the Holy Name movement (*Imya-slavtsy*) had got into trouble 'because of an unnatural vice too revolting to be mentioned', while the Feodorovskoe Concord of Old Believers was comprised of 'former gendarmes, white guards etc.'. Catholic priests had been arrested solely because they were spies of 'fascist Poland'.[57] This gambit – to pass off victimisation as legal reprisal – was partly aimed at the outside world. Just as in the 1920s, Soviet politicians were aware that the treatment of religious believers was a major stumbling block to diplomatic relations with the Western countries whose goodwill was essential for technology transfer and trading relations. But the accusations were meant to have a home audience as well.

The extent to which they had traction in this context may be doubted. While campaigning atheists regularly pilloried believers as political subversives (as well as reactionaries, ignoramuses, etc., etc.), a majority of the pre-war Soviet population self-identified as religious, even in the forbidding context of the official Soviet census of 1937.[58] Certainly, there was a strong inverse correlation between belief (or readiness to admit this to census officials) and levels of literacy, as well as a weaker positive one with advancing age.[59] But this did not necessarily go with an overall social tendency to regard believers as 'the enemy'.

For their part, though, church congregations themselves were prepared to espouse the propaganda images of 'enemies'. However, they employed these for their own ends. In the words of a group of believers from St John Baptist Church on Mokhovaya Street, writing in March 1938: 'We firmly believe it is enemies who are closing the churches, in order to excite dissatisfaction with the Government. The elections to the Supreme Soviet are approaching and the enemy is doing his ghastly work[,] he is playing on people's sacred feelings.'[60] As this example suggests, a Soviet Union where believers were more fully integrated into society would not necessarily have been a more democratic and tolerant place. More likely, it would have been one in which fear of 'outsiders' was differently configured, resting on a traditionalist, rather than universalist, model of national identity. It would probably have been something like the émigré circles guyed in Vladimir Nabokov's novel *Pnin*, 'for whom an ideal Russia consisted of the Red Army, an anointed monarch, collective farms, anthroposophy, the Russian Church, and the Hydro-Electric Dam'.[61] The animus of the late 1930s would then have been directed against 'foreign' religions, in particular Lutheranism and Catholicism, seen as the havens of spies and subversives.[62]

The struggle with religion was about cultural, as well as political, cohesion. 'Soviet values' were supposed to exclude benighted religious belief, which was uniformly presented as a sign of ignorance and lack of 'culturedness', and a key form of social 'backwardness'. This type of perception was far more widespread than the view that all churchmen were spies. For instance, the confiscation of church goods was given a guarded welcome by heritage officials, since it removed them (supposedly) from the category of 'cultic objects' to the category of 'art', and made it possible to strip out items that were aesthetically unpleasing. The official polarisation of 'science' (more broadly, 'science and scholarship', *nauka*) and 'religion' as manifestations of 'enlightenment' versus 'backwardness' had plenty of adherents.

But representing science as enlightened to an at best semi-literate population would have been far more effective if objects had been removed from their church settings in a less vandalistic way. Through their actions in 1922, members of the Soviet government obligingly supplied the Orthodox Church, and indeed all the main 'cults' operating on Soviet territory, with an entire cohort of suffering saints, the so-called 'new martyrs' (*novomucheniki*). Even some non-believers, such as the famous scientist Ivan Pavlov, were thoroughly alienated by the hounding of the Orthodox Church.[63] In turn, the moral authority leant by social and political stigmatisation (a sign of glory in

Christian tradition) persisted through the late Soviet period – indeed, was enhanced as the history of Soviet oppression became familiar to a wider audience. Thus, while winning a decisive short-term victory in 1922, the Soviet government also stored up long-term defeat. For, had a church-state concordat – the sacrifice of communion vessels as the price of lighter regulation – actually taken place that year, it would have done much to strip the oppositional lustre of Orthodoxy. The faith could, in due course, have been integrated in the 'National Bolshevism' of the late 1930s, which recuperated for modern Soviet culture many artists and cultural forms previously considered 'reactionary'. In actual fact, even once judicial murder ceased, repression continued, and it always remained uncertain how 'Soviet' the Orthodox Church actually was – a fact that could only increase its appeal as a moral alternative among those who were hostile to Soviet power.[64]

At the same time, a failure to confront the Church would have left the Bolshevik government significantly weakened in terms of its central political project as of 1922. The long-term consequences of persecution were hardly of moment compared with the necessity of pushing through policy with 'implacability' (*neprimirimost*) and dealing with immediate political threats. In turn, this first successful assault on traditional Russia provided a vital lesson for the later campaign to collectivise Russian villages. Disaffection among the regime's opponents was a fact of life, but such disaffection was ephemeral, and it could be contained. Would Stalin, without the all-out campaign of 1922, have so confidently approached the question of how to impose his will on the Soviet countryside? The confiscation of church goods, after all, had not just shown how to conduct an effective campaign of mobilisation and use this as an instrument of social solidarity. It had also illustrated that the ruthless suppression of potential subversion and of social difference, a process believed to be essential to the construction of a socialist future, might be a near and achievable objective, rather than one lying on the far horizon.

14

THE RISE OF LENINISM: THE DEATH OF POLITICAL PLURALISM IN THE POST-REVOLUTIONARY BOLSHEVIK PARTY

1917–1922

RICHARD SAKWA

IN 1917, EVEN AS VLADIMIR LENIN sought to consolidate power after 25 October, a group emerged that warned of the consequences of the premature attempt to build socialism in a relatively backward country. The 'coalitionists' were made up of leading figures in the party, including Lev Kamenev, one of Vladimir Lenin's long-standing associates. Their worries re-emerged in various forms in later years, notably in the arguments of the Democratic Centralists in 1919 and the Ignatov movement and the Workers' Opposition in 1920. The central concern of these groups was the defence of some sort of pluralism *within* the revolution, although they were only marginally less harsh than mainstream Leninists in repressing opposition *to* the revolution. The defeat of these early attempts to establish some form of pluralist democracy within the party set the country on a course that was to endure to the very end, and which peaked in the Stalinist repressions of the 1930s. Nevertheless, the aspirations of those in favour of intra-party pluralism periodically resurfaced, notably in the attempts to establish 'socialism with a human face' during the Prague Spring in 1968, and Mikhail Gorbachev's struggle to create what he called a 'humane and democratic socialism' twenty years later.

The centre of this relatively more pluralistic form of Bolshevism was Moscow. The strength of the movement for Bolshevik pluralism, if we may use this term, reflected the city's distinctive social character, something that had become apparent in the late tsarist period. Moscow provided fertile soil for pluralistic Bolshevism, as opposed to the monist Leninism that provided the framework for the later Stalinist consolidation. Here opposition to the Bolshevik seizure of power was particularly strong, and a deep undercurrent of resistance persisted all the way into the 1920s. For our purposes, it was here also that the inner-party debates were not only pervasive, but also suggested an awareness of the dangers of trying to hold on to power in a society that had not yet 'matured' for socialism. The fundamental argument of the coalitionists and their successors was that although Russian society was backward, the more progressive elements could nevertheless be a partner in the struggle to achieve socialism.

In broader terms, throughout the Soviet period the tension between Moscow and what became Leningrad persisted. Party programmes alternated between a 'Moscow line', somewhat nativist and neo-populist, accompanied by stability in the state system (espoused by Nikolai Bukharin, Georgy Malenkov and Alexei Kosygin); and a 'Leningrad line', advocating a harsh revolutionary internationalism (whose advocates included Grigory Zinoviev, Andrei Zhdanov, Frol Kozlov and Grigory Romanov).[1] It was the Moscow line that triumphed in Gorbachev's perestroika between 1985 and 1991. This was not simply the 'reform of communism', which suggests mainly an attempt to make the system work better, but a far more profound attempt to achieve the 'reform communism' that was espoused by some of the party reformers in the Civil War years and by the Prague reformers in 1968. Although the early oppositionists would not have dared to talk about a 'humane and democratic socialism', certainly not within earshot of Lenin, the struggle for pluralism *within* the revolution was a theme taken up by proponents of 'socialism with a human face' in the 1960s, the Euro-communists in the 1970s and by Gorbachev in the 1980s. Gorbachev appealed for a return to Leninist principles, but in fact, as his critics so vigorously pointed out to him, it was these 'Leningrad' principles that had facilitated the rise of Stalin. If he had been more sophisticated theoretically, he would have talked about a return to the latent plural-ism within the Bolshevik party in the early years of Soviet power.

THE SPECIFICITY OF MOSCOW

In recent years there has been a spate of books describing the diversity of late tsarist society. These in particular focus on the development of liberalism and civil society, and thus reject the traditional idea that the autocracy was monolithic and effectively suppressed the development of a pluralistic public sphere. Indeed, the picture that overwhelmingly emerges is that late tsarist society was developing on 'Western' lines, with a vibrant environment for cultural and intellectual life, all of which was cut short by the Bolsheviks in their first months in power.[2] A notable example of this is Fedyashin's study of 'Liberals under Autocracy', an examination of the thick journal *Herald of Europe* (*Vestnik Evropy*), which gradually gained in stature from its foundation in 1866 until its peak in 1904, and continued to publish until its demise under the Bolshe-viks in 1918. The journal was at the centre of debates over the potential of local government, notably in the form of the zemstvo assemblies intro-duced into the thirty-four provinces (*guberniya*) of old Russia in 1864 as part of the great liberal reforms of Alexander II, to foster participation and citizen development in Russia from the grass roots. In keeping with Alexander Solzhenitsyn's view that Russia needed to develop authentic forms of democracy, the zemstvo movement in this reading was a form of liberal praxis that did not borrow from the West.[3]

Numerous studies have demonstrated the extensive development of civil society before 1917. Joseph Bradley describes the development of various professional associations and philanthropic organisa-tions.[4] The ten years from 1905 were marked by astonishing economic progress, with extensions to the railway system and the doubling of its traffic and revenue. Consumption statistics show great improvements in the standard of living, and the production of consumer goods was higher than in Germany. The industrial sector represented not so much an enclave, as is common in developing countries, but was organically linked to the rest of the economy through market and financial ties. By 1914 the vigorous social and economic developments of the past half century had closed the gap between Russia and the more developed countries and had elevated it to fifth place in the league of industrial powers. Above all, hegemonic strategies of rule were being devised that sought to bridge the gulf between state and society, the privileged and the outcast, with developments in the old capital of Moscow standing in sharp contrast to the polarisation in St Petersburg.[5] Moscow became a more inclusive city than Petersburg. In contrast to the northern capital, there was extensive development of public transport, social insurance and workers' housing.[6] However, while socio-economic progress was encouraged the autocracy tried to retain its political pre-eminence, provoking multiple contradictions. These may well have been resolved organically, but the First World War in the end provoked a revolutionary breakdown.

There are numerous differences between Moscow and Petrograd. Moscow was far more based on native capital, which developed the textile industry, whereas the metallurgical industry in the northern capital relied on foreign capital, above all from France. Moscow was a city of the Old Believers, whereas St Petersburg was a city of the administrative classes and the ruling elite. Moscow was more 'peasant', yet this suggested deeper organic ties with its hinterland and the country as a whole, less receptive to the revolutionary socialism that in the end triumphed in the north. In short, when it came to Moscow, Antonio Gramsci's observation that in Russia civil society was 'primordial and gelatinous' applied with less force. As Gramsci puts it:

In Russia, the State was everything, civil society was primordial and gelatinous; in the West, there was a proper relation between State and civil society, and when the State trembled a sturdy structure of civil society was at once revealed. The State was only an outer ditch, behind which there stood a powerful system of fortresses and earthworks.[7]

What he called Jacobinism was able to impose itself on society with relative ease in Petrograd, but in Moscow there was spirited resistance from the ramparts of civil society against the imposition of a monist form of revolutionary power.

THE MULTIPLICITY OF RUSSIAN REVOLUTIONS

Georgy Plekhanov, the founder of the social democratic movement in Russia, condemned the development of what was to become democratic centralism in the Bolshevik party, and he denounced Lenin's seizure of power in October 1917. His most famous book, published in 1895, was called *The Development of the Monist View of History*, and defended the materialist conception of social development.[8] In practice, although Plekhanov was a committed Marxist, he defended a pluralistic conception of politics, and it this tradition that inspired the opposition to Bolshevik monism.

The October Revolution turned out to be a number of revolutions, all rolled into one. There was the mass social revolution, in which peasants sought land, soldiers (peasants in another guise) struggled for peace, and workers struggled for greater recognition in the labour process. At the same time, there was a democratic revolution, expressing aspirations for the development of political accountability and popular representation, although not necessarily in classic liberal democratic forms. Above all, the democratic revolution sought a constitution, which would both define and constrain political power. This was reinforced by the liberal revolution, in which the nascent bourgeoisie repudiated the absolutist claims of divine rule by the monarchy and fought to apply what they considered to be more enlightened forms of constitutional government and secure property rights. This was accompanied by the national revolution, which confirmed the independence of Poland and Finland, and saw the rapid fragmentation of the Russian Empire. For Marxists, there was also the revolution of internationalism, which suggested that the old-style nation-state was redundant. As capitalism became a global system, so social classes would gradually lose their national characteristics and become part of a single social revolution. Then there was the revolution within the revolution. As the most extreme wing of the Russian Revolution, the Bolsheviks usurped the agenda of the moderate socialists, and mobilised workers and revolutionary idealists (such as the anarchists) to establish their own political dictatorship. The Bolsheviks were the most ruthless and effective advocates of the radical emancipation of the people in the name of a new set of social ideals.[9]

Such disparate sources of the revolution were reflected in the Bolshevik struggle to take Moscow.[10] The initial seizure of power in Petrograd was relatively easy, but in Moscow there was both social and political resistance. It took ten days for the Bolsheviks to break the resistance, including heavy fighting in and around the Kremlin, accompanied by significant loss of life. Victory was only achieved when Lenin drafted in the Latvian Riflemen and the Kronstadt sailors. In other words, Moscow entered the Communist era as a defeated city, with revolutionary socialism of the Petrograd type imposed on the city. This was an occupation regime, with all of the consequences that follow from the attempt to impose a political system on a reluctant population.[11] Strong resistance among the print workers and some other sections of the working class continued until spring 1918, and indeed a deep current of resistance lasted into the 1920s.[12] The Mensheviks were particularly deeply rooted in Moscow, and maintained a persistent critique of Bolshevik policy from their footholds in the trade unions and local soviets until they were finally extirpated in the 1920s.[13] This was rooted in the hostility of the traditional intelligentsia to the coercive radicalism of the Bolshevik administration.

OPPOSITION WITHIN THE BOLSHEVIK REVOLUTION

Not surprisingly, the struggle for pluralism within the revolution was reflected in the Bolshevik party itself. The Bolshevik party had grown from a small group of about 25,000 in February 1917 to something around 300,000 in October, and once in power the ranks continued to swell. The problem of managing this mass was achieved through various purges and discipline campaigns. Within the leadership the first major debate was over the organisation of Soviet power. The creation of an exclusively Bolshevik government in the form of the Council of People's Commissars (Sovnarkom) headed by Lenin on 25 October disappointed those who believed that power would be transferred to the soviets. The creation of Sovnarkom took power away from the Central Executive Committee (VTsIK) of the soviets, in whose name the revolution had been made, and was consolidated in a body responsible to no one but the Bolshevik party itself. In other words, the fateful step towards the 'substitution' of the popular power, as represented by the soviets, to unaccountable party committees was taken, as Leon Trotsky had warned earlier. Trotsky by now had joined the radicals, in keeping with his theory of the 'permanent' (uninterrupted) revolution, but this was countered by the moderates within the Bolshevik party, who in effect endorsed the logic that allowed the new government created after the February Revolution to be called 'provisional'.

They objected to Lenin's coup, arguing that the manner of seizing power meant that the only way the Bolsheviks could remain pre-eminent was through violence and civil war. For them, the revolution was indeed to be 'interrupted', if not impermanent. The coalitionists called for the broadening of the government to include all parties represented in the soviets. A group including Lev Kamenev, Grigory Zinoviev and Alexei Rykov insisted on the formation of a coalition government encompassing anti-war moderate socialists and envisaged a role for some organisations in addition to the soviets in the new system. They felt so strongly over the issue that they resigned from the new government, warning that Lenin's policies would lead to civil war.[14] Lenin in

November agreed to share power with the Left Socialist Revolutionaries (LSRs), which constituted itself as a separate party at that time, an arrangement that lasted to March 1918, but following an alleged attempt at an uprising on 6 July the LSRs were severely persecuted. After a bitter struggle the coalitionists were defeated. This was the first instance of a major debate in a revolutionary party in power. The warnings of the coalitionists turned out to be entirely prescient, with the coercive power of the regime confirmed by the creation of the Cheka (secret police) in December 1917, and the institution of the Red Terror from August 1918. Lev Kamenev at the head of the Moscow Soviet would go on to become the most consistent critic of secret police power.

Lenin refused to accept that Bolshevik authority was in any way 'provisional', and instead established the tradition that once a revolutionary socialist group came to power, the change of system was irreversible. From the teleological perspective that underlay Marx's view of history, why allow a reversion to a retrograde form of social organisation once a more advanced model had been established? Obviously, the Bolshevik moderates were not ready to give up power either, but they did defend a more inclusive version of that power. This meant that when it came to the long-awaited Constituent Assembly, they agreed with Lenin that this was a remnant of the 'bourgeois' phase of the revolution, and put up no resistance to its dissolution after only one day on 5 January 1918. Nikolai Bukharin announced that the Bolsheviks 'declare war without mercy against the bourgeois parliamentary republic'. Russia's experiment with accountable constitutional governance ended before it had begun. Lenin claimed that soviet power and the dictatorship of the proletariat was a far higher form of democracy, but the shooting of workers demonstrating in favour of the Assembly, in Petrograd and elsewhere, revealed the fate of those who disagreed.

THE LENINIST CONSOLIDATION

The imposition of a particularly narrow and intolerant version of revolutionary socialism elicited a hostile reaction from some of the leading lights of the movement abroad. Rosa Luxemburg, on the internationalist wing of German social democracy, initially welcomed the Bolshevik revolution as having 'put socialism on the agenda', but she soon condemned the methods of Leninist rule, above all its suppression of democracy. She insisted that socialism should mean the deepening and not the limitation of democracy, although she understood the need for temporary restrictions. In a famous formulation in 1918 she stressed that 'Freedom only for the supporters of the government, only for members of one party – however numerous they may be – is no freedom at all. Freedom is always and exclusively freedom for the one who thinks differently.'[15] Karl Kautsky, one of the leading figures of the German socialist movement, reaffirmed the commitment of social democracy to parliamentary forms of revolutionary transformation. He insisted that democracy was more than an instrument in the struggle but an inherent component of socialism itself. As he put it, 'For us, therefore, socialism without democracy is unthinkable. We understand by modern socialism not merely social organisation of production, but democratic organisation of society as well.'[16] Echoing Gramsci's view of Russia, Kautsky considered the Bolshevik revolution as something alien to the international revolutionary struggle. For him, it was the outcome of specific Russian conditions, notably the strains of war and relative social underdevelopment, a view that provoked Lenin's fury.

Lenin was no less agitated by the emergence of the Left Opposition in early 1918. This movement focused on two crucial issues: the question of war and peace (the Great War was still raging); and the emergence of bureaucratic authoritarianism within the party. As far as they were concerned, the two were connected. They advocated a revolutionary war against Germany that would then link up with the more advanced working class in the West and allow socialist Russia to break out from its isolation. The Left Communists came together as a faction in December 1917, and the peak of their activity was in January and February 1918 as the peace negotiations with Germany dragged on at Brest-Litovsk. They gained the support of some top party leaders, including Bukharin, N. Osinsky, Yevgeny Preobrazhensky and Karl

Radek, as well as the majority of grass roots organisations. Their stance quickly crumbled in the face of the renewed German onslaught from 18 February after the collapse of the peace talks. The Treaty of Brest-Litovsk of 3 March gave up land for peace. At the Seventh Party Congress on 7 March Lenin's hard-headed realism won the vote to accept the draconian terms imposed by Germany. Lenin refused to accept the Left Communist gamble that the Western working class would come to Russia's aid, and in the end Germany's collapse later that year proved him tactically correct.[17] Revolutionary élan was no match for the German war machine.

Equally, the social critique of the revolution advanced by the Left Communists, denouncing the 'petty bourgeois' degeneration of the revolution, warning in particular against the danger represented by the great mass of the peasantry, failed to engage with the fundamental political question of the accountability of the new authorities to the nominal subjects of the revolution, the working class. Their critique of Lenin's model of state capitalism, however, was more on target, with Osinsky calling for the 'construction of proletarian socialism by the class creativity of the workers themselves, not by orders on high issued by the "captains of industry".[18]

The Left Communists, however, were not so keen on the self-expression of the working class as embodied in the 'plenipotentiary' resistance campaign in spring 1918. This was a spontaneous movement to create 'plenipotentiary assemblies' (*Sobranie Upolnomochennykh*) of workers from the major plants in Petrograd, and the upsurge was also strong in Moscow. The aim was to 'create a broad working class organisation that could lead the masses from the dead end into which the policies of the new authorities have driven them.'[19] The word 'soviet' was studiously avoided, having now become tainted, and indeed, by late June the movement had been crushed by the Soviet authorities. Shortly afterwards Russia was embroiled in full-scale domestic conflict.

The Civil War years were accompanied by a series of 'oppositions' within the Bolshevik party, renamed the Russian Communist Party (Bolsheviks) (the RKP(b)) in 1918. Four key issues were raised that were at the heart of the new polity: the role of the soviets; the rise of the bureaucracy; the problem of democracy within the party; and relations with workers. The soviets became the foundation stone of the new polity, and in December 1922 lent their name to the new state when it became the Union of Soviet Socialist Republics, but since the soviets contained non-Bolsheviks as well as peasants they were treated with suspicion by the Leninist leadership. Soviet democracy quickly became managed democracy, but the question remained about how the party's 'leading role' could be reconciled with meaningful political functions for the soviets.

It was this question that was taken up by the Democratic Centralists from late 1918. They were largely based in Moscow, although their arguments did find support elsewhere. Many of the former Left Communists now moved on to join the critique of the alleged bureaucratic degeneration of the revolution, arguing against the imposition of one-man management, the use of bourgeois 'specialists' (the despised *spetsy*, in other words, the old technical intelligentsia) and in general 'to end bureaucratic methods of soviet construction'.[20] The Democratic Centralists argued that the relationship should be based on a division of labour: the party would provide ideological leadership, but the soviets should be integrated as institutions representing the working class. The first Soviet constitution of 10 July 1918 was long on declarations of principle, but left the institutional arrangements for the actual organisation of power vague. Although Sovnarkom was to 'notify' the All-Russian Central Executive Committee (VTsIK) of its decisions (Article 39), and the latter had the right to 'revoke or suspend' decisions (Article 40), Sovnarkom was granted a range of emergency powers that in the end voided VTsIK of effective supervisory authority, and this was repeated at all levels.[21]

The Democratic Centralists hoped to remedy the situation by revising the constitution to safeguard the rights of lower-level bodies from the encroachments of the centre. The Democratic Centralists demanded the introduction of what could be characterised as a type of 'separation of powers' within the regime itself. They called for greater autonomy for local soviets and lower-level party committees. In other words, in keeping with the original aspirations of the Russian Revolution to bring the polity within the ambit of constitutional constraints, they sought to 'constitutionalise' Soviet power. This would mean that the Soviet system really would have a genuine element of independent soviet power, with substantive powers for the soviets. The Eighth Party Congress in March 1919 agreed that the party should 'guide' the soviets, and not 'replace' them, though this formulation left the details vague and the problem of 'substitution' (*podmena*) remained to the end of Communist rule. A novel form of dual power was established which retained a revolutionary potential. It was therefore not surprising that when Gorbachev began to reform the system during perestroika in the late 1980s, he immediately returned to this idea by reviving the slogan of 'power to the soviets'.[22] Party leaders had to reinvent themselves as state leaders by taking up posts in municipal and regional soviets, while Gorbachev himself ultimately shifted the basis of the legitimacy of his rule from the party to the soviets when he was elected president by the newly created USSR Congress of People's Deputies on 15 March 1990. Both during the Civil War and during perestroika the idea of the 'withering away of the state' was postponed to some indefinite future.

The emergence of a rampant bureaucracy took the early Soviet state by surprise. Lenin's *The State and Revolution* in mid 1917 had suggested that 'any cook' could manage the affairs of state, a view reiterated by Bukharin and Yevgeny Preobrazhensky in their *ABC of Communism* in 1919: 'There will be no need for special ministers of state, for police and prisons, for laws and decrees ... The bureaucracy, the permanent officialdom, will disappear. The State will die out.'[23] As Polan notes, this strand in Lenin's thinking stands in contrast to the rest of his works, which are mostly practical, instrumental and timely. This element is used to restore Lenin's credentials as a 'revolutionary humanist' with a 'fundamentally emancipatory intent'.[24] In fact, as Polan demonstrates, the text was replete with authoritarian implications because of its negation of politics as the praxis of contestation over meaningful alternatives. Such a space in the end was denied as much for the adherents of the revolution as for its opponents. More specifically, the problem of unbridled bureaucracy was soon identified, but no coherent response was ever found within the logic of soviet power. The theory of commune democracy held that bureaucracy would disappear of its own accord, as outlined by Marx in his study of the Paris Commune of 1870–71, *The Civil War in France*, while Lenin insisted it was a social problem and reflected the lack of political culture in Russia. Others argued that it was a legacy of the tsarist regime that would be overcome in time. In fact, the problem was systemic: the attempt to run the whole life of the country from a single centre gave rise to the bureaucracy and its associated stifling bureaucratism. In his *Socialism: Utopian and Scientific* Friedrich Engels had argued that under socialism 'the government of persons is replaced by administration of things', but this turned out to be rather more problematic than the revolutionary socialists anticipated.

As the Civil War came to an end in 1920, two interrelated but separate debates challenged the Leninist structure of power. The 'party debate' focused on inner-party democracy and covered such issues as free speech within the party, the rights of party cells, the functions of the committees, and the role of leadership. The polarisation of society between the *verkhi* (upper tier) and the *nizy* (the masses) had been internalised within the party, with the *verkhi* now represented by higher party officials, and the *nizy* by the party's rank and file. As one of the eyewitnesses to the period, Alfred Rosmer, put it, 'The regime which bore the name "war communism" had been born with the war and should have died with it. It survived because there were hesitations as to the sort of organisation which ought to replace it.'[25] The trade union debate focused on the proper relationship between the party and the trade unions, and in general the role of the organised working class under socialism.

Moscow activists made a fundamental contribution to both the 'party' and trade union debates. The party debate raised some fundamental questions about participation and democracy within the party. It balanced 'party revivalism' with some of the themes of the

Democratic Centralists, notably more trust in the soviets. Through the summer of 1920 the criticism of the RKP(b) Moscow Committee gathered strength, with the party revivalists accusing it of bureaucratism and lack of leadership, whereas the trade union debaters were more concerned with maintaining the party's class hegemony over all other political institutions. The Moscow party revivalists were led by E. N. Ignatov, a veteran of the various Democratic Centralist oppositions. He denounced the party's 'pettifogging supervision' over the district committees and condemned the repression visited upon party activists with independent views.[26] By late 1920 the whole party organisation in Moscow was involved in vigorous debates in the belief that the end of the Civil War would finally provide an opportunity to return to what they believed to be the genuine principles of revolutionary socialism. In other words, they appealed to some sort of idealised Bolshevism against the harsh strictures of Leninist practices as they had developed since the party had come to power. The spirit of reform affected all social organisations. The Moscow Soviet took to meeting in factories to overcome the gulf that had opened up with workers, and the trade unions also sought to shed the bureaucratic spirit.

The welter of reform proposals in the end, however, did little to overcome the deadening practices of Leninist democratic centralism. Too often responses to political problems were sought in social measures, such as the appointment of workers to key posts. The myth of some innate worker purity did little to create the conditions for genuine party pluralism. In the end, the opposite effect was achieved. The party apparatus was strengthened and the independent grass-roots renewal movement quelled. Kamenev at the head of the Moscow Soviet was one of the most enthusiastic reformers. He had bravely condemned the excesses of the Cheka and the practices of the Red Terror, and he now sought to achieve an internal metamorphosis of the practices of Soviet power. He criticised the class analysis of bureaucracy, noting that even if all the 'bourgeois specialists' were sacked, the bureaucracy would not disappear. Against such superficial views, he stressed the gulf between the poverty and backwardness of the country and the creation of a complex and ramified system of state management in the absence of the existence of the basic elements able to sustain such a structure.[27]

However, all Kamenev's well-meaning innovations were caught in the systemic traps of the Leninist power system. As the veteran Menshevik politician Boris Dvinov puts it, in conformity with the classic Menshevik argument that the attempt to impose 'utopian socialism' in a backward country with a tiny proletariat inevitably created a monstrous bureaucratic mechanism:

> The problem for Kamenev, and some of the other Bolsheviks who at this stage wavered in favour of 'proletarian freedom', was how to preserve the soviets as meaningful political institutions given the fact that decisions were taken elsewhere. How could serious debate take place without opposition and with the soviet simply a party fraction. Hence Kamenev's attempts to breathe some life into the soviet by creating sections, the idea of non-party deputies, and the closer links with the factories.[28]

A rather different take on the problems of socialist governance was reflected in the 'trade union' debate. This focused on the role of worker organisations and advanced plans to curb the power of the bureaucracy. The Workers' Opposition led by Alexander Shlyapnikov and Alexandra Kollontai insisted that more rights should be vested in the direct expression of workers' organisation. They called for a national congress of producers to take direct control of economic management. Kollontai criticised the bureaucratic regulation of all aspects of social existence, which even included attempts to instil *partiinost* (the 'party spirit') in dog-lovers' clubs. She urged the initiative of the workers to be encouraged, and insisted that 'wide publicity, freedom of opinion and discussion, the right to criticise within the party and among the members of the trade unions – such are the decisive steps that can put an end to the prevailing system of bureaucracy'. The proposed remedy was catastrophically simplistic: 'In order to do away with the bureaucracy that is finding its shelter in the soviet institutions we must first get rid of all bureaucracy in the party itself', and that could be achieved by 'the expulsion from the Party of all non-proletarian elements', while the democratisation of the party would be achieved through the 'elimination of all non-working class elements from all administrative positions'.[29] Trotsky adopted the opposite tack, and argued that War Communist practices should be taken to their logical conclusion. He called for the unions to be incorporated into the economic apparatus. Lenin ultimately took a middle path: the unions were to remain independent and act as 'transmission belts' for party policy and as educators of the working class rather than the organisers of production.

The 'party democracy' debate in the autumn of 1920 represented the last serious discussion about the need for some sort of public sphere within the party to avoid the bureaucratisation of the revolutionary government. It was rapidly, and possibly deliberately, eclipsed by the trade union debate launched by the Workers' Opposition. Although the latter raised some similar concerns to the party democratisers, above all the condemnation of bureaucracy, the addition of anti-intelligentsia (anti-specialist) themes and above all the claim that workers should run industry roused Lenin's hostility. While the party democratisers sought solutions at the level of political institutions, the Workers' Opposition reduced the question of political reform to the class dimension. As the Democratic Centralists had argued earlier, and reiterated in the party debate, the poor functioning of Soviet institutions derived more from problems (as we would now put it) of institutional design than of petty bourgeois elements worming their way in to the ruling system in order to advance their own careers. The portrayal of political issues as a matter of class played into the hands of the Leninists, and allowed the new regime to avoid a serious self-analysis of what it had become, and certainly inhibited the creation of some sort of more pluralistic Bolshevism. When the question was couched in class terms, Lenin was unequalled; it was to political problems of autonomous representation and participation that he had no solution.

War Communism was in crisis by early 1921, with peasant revolts against forced requisitioning in the countryside and urban protests against the continuation of harsh restrictions against markets. The protests climaxed in March 1921 with the revolt of workers and sailors at the Kronstadt naval fortress in the Gulf of Finland, earlier one of the strongholds of Bolshevism. The insurgents rallied under the slogan of 'soviets without Bolsheviks', denouncing the Bolshevik usurpation of the rights of the soviets. They were savagely crushed, in a military operation led by Trotsky.[30] Lenin now argued that the Civil War had effectively destroyed the 'conscious' working class, reinforcing his belief that the party had to take up the burden of defending socialism and insulate itself from the degradation prevalent in society. In fact, there remained an active and engaged Moscow proletariat with its own ideas on how to build socialism.[31] At the Tenth Party Congress in that month, economic concessions were balanced by the intensification of War Communist political processes. The first measures that were to lead to the New Economic Policy (NEP) were launched, and in particular forced requisitioning from the peasantry was replaced by a fixed tax-in-kind. Lenin admitted that the attempt to continue the organisation of the economy by wartime means had been a mistake. War Communism, he insisted, had been necessitated by the war and dislocation but it was not a viable long-term policy. Lenin hoped both to justify the necessity of War Communism and its repeal.

The party debate was as such never resolved. A cosmetic programme of reform under the label of 'workers' democracy' was instituted, but its effect was only to consolidate the powers of the committees and the party leadership in a process which first saw the use of the term *perestroika* (restructuring) in the Soviet context. The challenge to War Communist political relationships was met not by compromise but by repression. At the Tenth Congress two decrees condemned the oppositional groupings and imposed a 'ban on factions', a 'temporary' measure that placed sharp limits on inner-party discussion which long remained a cardinal principle of Soviet rule. The NEP was not accompanied by a new political policy, and instead Lenin insisted that during a retreat discipline was at a premium to avoid a rout.

In the early 1920s the vestiges of non-Bolshevik parties were effectively eliminated. The trial of a group of leading Socialist Revolutionaries in mid 1922 presaged the show trials of the 1930s. To compensate for the real and imaginary threats to Bolshevik rule the mystique and power of the party were enhanced all the more. The NEP-style perestroika saw Bolshevik committees tighten their administrative control over local party organisations. Centralisation and conformity within the party were intensified just as they were being relaxed in the economy. In April 1922 Stalin became General Secretary of the party, a post at the time regarded as no more than that of a glorified filing clerk. In a consummate manner he consolidated the party machine and his own power over that machine. His ability to appoint, dismiss and transfer party officials prefigured the ubiquitous *nomenklatura* mechanism of later years and gave him a powerful weapon in the inner-party debates. A 'circular flow of power' was established whereby Stalin's appointments became beholden to him for their positions.[32] The Bolshevik tradition of open contestation was over, and in its place the deadening grip of the Leninist-Stalinist bureaucracy was intensified.

BOLSHEVIK PLURALISM IN PERSPECTIVE

This chapter has examined whether within the Bolshevik variety of revolutionary communism there was the potential for a more pluralistic institutionalisation of revolutionary power, as opposed to the strict monism of the Leninist type. Solzhenitsyn of course always argued against such a proposition, and indeed fundamentally rejected even the liberal revolution of February 1917. For Solzhenitsyn, the overthrow of the monarchy in what was effectively a coup d'état in the February Revolution set in train a series of consequences whose inevitable denouement was the seizure of power by the most radical wing of the revolutionary movement. This is a powerful argument and it has a deep resonance to this day. However, this chapter has demonstrated that although Solzhenitsyn's overall argument may be valid, we should nevertheless not overlook the diversity within the revolutionary movement. It is dangerously teleological to read back from history an inevitability that in practice may have been shaped by various contingencies. Above all, the story of Moscow suggests that in a different social and political environment, and with a different set of leaders, revolutionary socialism may have assumed more pluralistic forms, at least for its supporters.[33]

A radical form of the argument would suggest that there was the potential for a more pluralistic form of Bolshevism against Leninist monism. The various oppositions have been described as the 'conscience of the revolution', surviving to challenge orthodoxy and dogmatism all the way up to the final crushing of pluralism within the party in 1929.[34] They inherited the tradition established by Plekhanov in his critique of developments in what was to become the Bolshevik party from its establishment in 1903. The dynamic and contentious character of inner-party life in this period demonstrates that it was far from homogeneous and monolithic. It was the peculiarly narrow 'Leninist' version not only of organisational forms but above all of political practice that in the end squeezed the life out of the party, and indeed imposed this narrow and intolerant form on the country as a whole. The virulence and violence of Lenin's character became all the more evident when some of the secret archives were opened after 1991. The new documents expose in gory detail Lenin's 'terror practices'. For example, Lenin admonished the trade union leaders in May 1920 when they called for the administration of unions to be decentralised and for affairs to be run collegially. He mocked the idea but in the end conceded: 'We shall resort sometimes to the collegiate principle, sometimes to individual management', but the next sentence revealed his real views: 'We shall leave collegiality to the weak, the inferior, the backward, the undeveloped. Let them chatter, get sick of it, and stop talking.' As Richard Pipes comments: 'Lenin rarely expressed more bluntly his contempt for democratic procedures.'[35]

Even then a degree of debate continued. In the 1920s there was more to the choices facing the Soviet Union than the struggle between Trotsky and Stalin. Nikolai Bukharin offered a considered and substantive alternative, defending the New Economic Policy as an evolutionary path towards socialism by allowing the creativity and entrepreneurialism of the masses to be unharnessed within the framework of Soviet power. By the 1930s Bukharin had become 'the last Bolshevik'. However attenuated, the Bolshevik tradition of debate continued even in this period, until Bukharin was finally put to death in 1938.[36] The political trajectory of Bukharin, and even to a degree of Kamenev, suggests that a deterministic view of Soviet history is misplaced. In the final period of Soviet power the Gorbachev variant once again took up some Bukharinite themes in order to reinvigorate the tradition of reform communism.[37]

Thus the question of alternatives and the role of Bolshevik pluralism remains a live one to this day. The root of the question is whether Marxism itself contains the potential for more diverse political practices. In other words, was Marx responsible for Soviet authoritarianism? The question can be posed as 'whether Soviet authoritarianism was a necessary or inevitable consequence of Lenin's attempt to fulfil what he understood as Marx's project'.[38] In other words, does the Marxist understanding of the transition from capitalism to socialism inevitably involve a degree of coercion? The Leninist 'dictatorship of the proletariat' subordinated law to power and ruthlessly crushed all opposition, and in the end gave way to the Stalinist dictatorship. This was challenged by Antonio Gramsci's emphasis on hegemony rather than coercion, an idea that was fruitfully developed in the Eurocommunist challenge to Soviet-style authoritarian communism. In the 1970s Eurocommunists sought to achieve a socialist transformation of society through democratic means, in a manner reminiscent of the earlier critiques of Lenin by Luxemburg and Kautsky. It is questionable whether Eurocommunists achieved a fundamental break with 'the authoritarian traditions of Leninism'.[39] The Eurocommunists held the Russian context as chiefly responsible for the degeneration of the revolutionary communist ideal, just as the Left Communists and the Workers' Opposition had held social factors responsible, whereas the problem is far deeper than that. Equally, the 'Bolshevik' critics of Leninist policies had a no less ambivalent attitude towards democracy than did Lenin himself. Even Bukharin is notorious for his statement that under socialism there would be two parties, one in government and the other in jail, and he was zealous in defending the coercive aspects of the 'dictatorship of the proletariat'.[40] Opposition was denigrated as 'bourgeois', which became a malleable concept to describe any opponent. Marxism lacked a sustained theory of the complexity of the modern state, and instead it was reduced to an instrument of coercion. Although Marx was careful to delineate an independent sphere for politics, in the end for him it was an element of the 'superstructure' that was ultimately derived from the material sphere of the means of production. The Marxian tradition of revolutionary socialism lacked a developed concept of the autonomy of politics where agency and decisions can decisively shape historical outcomes.[41]

The existence of pluralistic alternatives to dogmatic and coercive Leninism repudiates the cultural determinism that suggests that communism could have taken no other path than the one it did because of the character of Russia. Equally, it rejects the ideological determinism, prevalent in totalitarian approaches, that suggests a straight line from Marxism to Stalinism. However, although undoubtedly the Russian Revolution was far broader than its Bolshevik instantiation, and in its turn Bolshevism in the early years of Soviet power was broader than the illiberal Leninism that predominated, they all shared a social reductionist understanding of political contestation and lacked a developed theory of the role of opposition and pluralism within the revolutionary communist movement. Instead, they all shared a view of the politics of transition to socialism that was sharply at odds with the end state of freedom that they sought to achieve. The 'myth of human self-identity' in socialist thought collapsed the distinction between civil and political society. The Marxian ideal of unity was not only unattainable but it opened the way to what came to be known as totalitarianism.[42]

The Bolshevik challenges to proto-Stalinist features of Soviet rule did not represent a considered theoretical platform that questioned the *theory* of Leninist dictatorship, but instead sought only to modify some of its *practices*. The coalition, party and trade union debates demonstrate that there were alternative paths not only in the revolution but also within the Bolshevik party. However, the logic of Leninism tended towards the destruction of socialist diversity and pluralism, although the rationale of that logic adapted to circumstances. In 1917–18 Lenin justified exclusivity because of the logic of political struggle; in 1919–20 because of the exigencies of the Civil War; and from 1920 because of the alleged social determinism prompted by the destruction of the working class and the economic imperative of implementing a strategy of economic development. Lenin's assertion that the working class was destroyed by the end of the Civil War, which justified the intensification of top-down managerialism within the party, was greatly exaggerated. A conscious workers' movement remained, with a sense of purpose and leadership.[43] Finally, in conditions of the 'retreat' of the NEP, Lenin tightened discipline within the party and with the ban on factions put an end to a whole era of debate.

Thus Bolshevik pluralism is a contradiction in terms. As long as the Soviet system remained recognisably Leninist, it would lack the conceptual basis for genuine inner-party democracy. Debates and controversies over leadership and policy continued into the 1930s, and were revived after Stalin's death, but only with Gorbachev's perestroika did the fundamental problem of pluralist democracy and civil society in the Soviet system once again come to the fore. By the early 1920s, ideas of democratic socialism and social emancipation gave way to a bureaucratised and violent reality. Compulsion in external interactions and suppression within the party became mutually reinforcing, giving rise to the ferociously coercive Stalinist system. This was not something visited upon the Bolsheviks from outside, as the opposition within the party pointed out, but was part of an intrinsic political process. The potential existence of alternatives only demonstrates the narrowness of the path actually taken.

AFTERWORD

LENIN AND YESTERDAY'S UTOPIA

TONY BRENTON

T HE SHADOW OF THE 1917 REVOLUTION still looms large.
Every Russian town still has its memorial to Lenin. In Moscow
his mausoleum still presides over Red Square and serves as the review-
ing stand for the leadership on great national occasions. Stalin, in fact
a Georgian, regularly tops or almost tops national polls on who was
'the greatest Russian'. The FSB, lineal successor to the KGB and Lenin's
Cheka, still occupies its former insurance building on Lubyanka Square
(and there is regular talk of re-erecting the statue of Dzerzhinsky, the
Cheka's founder, in front of it). Russia's ruined agriculture and largely
obsolescent heavy industry testify to the brutal lunacies of Communist planning. Russia's almost instinctive grab at Ukraine in 2014, with
the spate of Western sanctions that followed, testify to the survival of
imperial and Cold War instincts that many had hoped were buried in
1991. And, raising our eyes from Russia itself, it is noteworthy that the
world's fast rising second superpower, China, is still ruled by exactly
the secretive, repressive, single-party system that it inherited from the
Soviet Union and ultimately from the 1917 revolution.

And yet. Since 1917 Russia has seen what in many ways was another
revolution. In 1991 the USSR collapsed, taking most of the Communist
project with it. It is striking to compare the vainglorious speeches made
in the Soviet Union in 1967, on the fiftieth anniversary of what was then
called the 'Great October Revolution', with the present Russian mood
of uncertainty about what the whole experience has meant. Should

the Dzerzhinsky statue be re-erected, or should Lenin's mausoleum be razed? Was Stalin indeed Russia's greatest man, or could it have been the leading dissident, Andrei Sakharov?

So what, if anything, does the 1917 revolution still have to teach us? In this afterword I approach this question first by asking whether we can indeed say anything sensible about what in the revolution was inevitable, and what was not. This leads, via consideration of the very particular role of Lenin, to a discussion of the impact of the revolution in history over the next seventy years – bringing us to 1991. While the two upheavals were of course very different there are also some telling points of comparison. And then, finally, after 1991 how much is left?

I: WHAT WAS INEVITABLE, AND WHAT WASN'T?

The chapters of this book have examined in detail a number of moments during the revolution when things might have gone differently. Some contributors have identified points where a small change of circumstances could have led to a large change in trajectory. Others have concluded that at the moment they are examining there was not much that was likely to shift. Against this background, is there anything sensible we can say about what was, and was not, inevitable in the overall course of the revolution?

Let me focus on two key questions. Could the tsarist regime in some form have survived? And, if not, how inevitable was the Leninist regime that succeeded it?

On the first of these questions it is useful, as Dominic Lieven points out, that we have international comparators. It was not just Russia. By about 1910 all three of the great European land empires – Romanov, Habsburg and Ottoman – faced pressures that they were visibly ill-equipped to meet. The Ottomans, dubbed by an earlier Russian tsar the 'sick man of Europe', were seeing their empire erode as more vigorous powers and upstart local nationalisms were dismembering it piece by piece. The Habsburgs, similarly, were having increasing difficulty holding their ramshackle empire together in the face of growing demands for independence from a range of subject nationalities, notably Slavs. And, as we have seen, the Romanovs were struggling with the combined effects of military defeat in Japan, the destabilising impact of economic modernisation (as the others were too), and widespread economic discontent.

The crucible where all this came together was the Balkan peninsula. Here all three empires had vital, and competing, interests. And the moment was the start of the First World War. As Dominic Lieven says, far too much attention has been paid to the supposed conjuncturality of the First World War. What if Gavrilo Princip had missed? And so on. In fact, the final breakdown of August 1914 was simply the culmination of a century of accelerating Balkan crises. There was near-war in 1909 between Russia and Austro-Hungary, and two actual Balkan wars in 1912 and 1913, into both of which the great powers were very nearly drawn. A couple of decades earlier, one of the most perceptive readers of European politics, Otto von Bismarck, had predicted that the next great European conflagration would be the result of 'some damned fool thing in the Balkans'. To the extent that anything in history is inevitable it is hard to avoid the conclusion that some final showdown in the Balkans involving Russia, Austro-Hungary and Turkey – with Germany almost certainly being pulled in – was it.

The war destroyed all three empires. These were pre-modern polities, enjoying limited loyalty from large swathes of their populations and grappling with the unprecedented economic and mass mobilisation challenges of modern war. It is possible to imagine the war coming in another form, but without some stroke of good luck (a much shorter war – unlikely given the technological superiority of defence over offence; or greater political good sense – made harder by the new phenomenon of aroused public opinion drowning out the subtle calculations of the diplomats) it is hard to see the political outcome being very different. At the risk of sounding deterministic (and to adapt Ian Fleming), the fall of one empire could have been happenstance, two could have been coincidence, but all three makes it look like a law of nature.

As for Russia itself, with the benefit of hindsight we can see that the signs of imperial morbidity were there in abundance. Educated and propertied Russians made clear through those they elected to the Duma their diminishing sympathy for incompetent, backward-looking tsarism. The supposedly more loyal 'dark people' voted when they could for expropriation of the rich, increasingly took the law into their own hands against landowners and capitalists, and served with less and less willingness and discipline in Russia's armed forces. Much of the urban proletariat was frankly revolutionary. And the revolutionary movement itself can only be compared in fanaticism and propensity to violence to today's extreme Islamists. The most able servants of the regime, Witte and Stolypin, were both driven by fears for its survival. The tsar himself was weak, petulant, mistakenly believed that he was loved by the Russian people, and was quite unrealistically attached to his own autocratic prerogatives. The weird and utterly Russian figure of Rasputin, embraced by the Romanov family in the face of the clearest need to get rid of him, finally says it all. Literary theorists would say that the final collapse was overdetermined. The First World War merely gave the last kick to a deeply rotten edifice.

But if the fall of the old regime was indeed overdetermined, it is hard to argue that that was also true of what succeeded it. Russia between the fall of the monarchy in February 1917 and the effective imposition of Bolshevik rule in early 1918 (with, even then, a civil war still to win) feels like a rudderless vessel pushed this way and that by the winds and the tides. The Provisional Government that notionally took over from the monarchy was able to exercise significant authority in some ways (it launched a serious military offensive against the Central Powers in June). But it lacked legitimacy, faced growing chaos in the countryside, a revolutionary working class in Petrograd and other cities, and an increasingly mutinous military. It operated in uneasy tandem with the Petrograd (and other) soviets, which were deeply hostile to the old order and controlled the streets and barracks of Petrograd. The traditional Soviet narrative of the period is of power ineluctably slipping into the hands of the soviets, and ultimately the Bolsheviks. In fact, while the Bolsheviks undoubtedly exploited the chaos of these months to extend their grip in any way they could, there were a whole series of moments, as described in a number of the chapters above, where their advance could have stopped. What if the Duma had successfully imposed its authority in February, as Kerensky subsequently suggested, and the rising power of the soviets had been contained at that point? What if the Constituent Assembly, to which everyone was looking to take authority, had succeeded in convening before the Bolshevik October coup, and had thus not been instantly snuffed out? What if Kerensky had avoided his catastrophic misunderstanding with Kornilov in August, and had thus retained the support of the army to confront the Bolsheviks in October? What if Lenin had been arrested on the way to the Smolny on 24 October, in which case the takeover of power would have been by all the socialists not just the Bolsheviks?

II: LENIN'S ROLE

We should pause for a moment over Lenin. It has become unfashionable in modern history to credit much to individual personalities. It is nevertheless quite impossible to understand the course of events in these few months in Petrograd (and afterwards) without acknowledging the formidable impact of Vladimir Ilyich Lenin. This was the situation for which he was born. A driven revolutionary from his schooldays, his relationships with his wife, his family and all those around him were completely dominated by politics. And for him politics was Manichaean: he saw only acolytes or enemies – the latter to be brought down by whatever means came to hand. From very early on he dedicated himself to bringing an extreme version of Marxism first to Russia and then to the world. He saw clearly that this could not be done by popular consent; force and terror would be needed ('How can you make a revolution without firing squads?' he asked in 1917). His chosen instrument to gain power, devised by him in 1902, was a disciplined, tightly bound, 'vanguard' political party. Through intra-party intrigue he created exactly the faction he needed, the Bolsheviks, in 1903.

Unsurprisingly he spent most of his early life in exile, and expected to die there. It was the February Revolution that gave him his chance. As described by Sean McMeekin in his chapter, the Germans shipped Lenin back to Russia in the famous 'sealed train' in April 1917. He then overcame almost total opposition among his Bolshevik colleagues, and galvanised the local political scene, by setting out an extreme programme that included overthrow of the Provisional Government and an immediate end to the war. As other opposition parties gradually came to link themselves with the Provisional Government so the Bolsheviks by their very extremism became more and more conspicuous (and popular) as leaders of the opposition. In particular their demand for peace attracted the crucial support of the Petrograd military garrison. After two major breakdowns of public order (the so-called 'April' and 'July' days) in which the Bolsheviks played a significant role, Lenin was forced once more into exile (and concluded at the time that his hopes for revolution were over). He returned in October and, as described by Orlando Figes, again persuaded his unwilling Bolshevik comrades firstly to launch the October coup that finally placed them in power; and then three months later to repress the long-awaited Constituent Assembly, which was the only immediate challenge to that power.

Lenin's centrality to the events of these months underlines how contingent the outcome was. He of course had able associates, notably Trotsky, who were crucial to carrying the Bolshevik project through. But it is striking how regularly he turns his whole party round with his single-minded insistence on taking and holding power. As Sean McMeekin points out, if the Germans had not sent Lenin back, or any of half a dozen possible accidents had happened to him once he was back, a Bolshevik-dominated outcome in Russia becomes much less likely. Lenin himself after the July Days seemed ready to acknowledge that all was lost and to revert to overseas pamphleteering. It was only the Kornilov fiasco that put him back in the game. Even after the October coup, not many seasoned Petrograd political observers were betting on the long-term survival of the Bolshevik regime.

The true significance of Lenin is that, having got through to achieve power, he (unlike those who fleetingly took the limelight before him – Rodzyanko, Lvov, Kerensky and Chernov) held on to it. After January 1918, there are still moments of contingency, but, somehow, with Lenin's iron grip on the tiller, the course seems more firmly set. He had an unerring eye for the weaknesses of his opponents, and a ruthless readiness to exploit them. Martin Sixsmith underlines Lenin's centrality in his comments on how radically different things could have been if Fanny Kaplan had in fact killed him in August 1918. And I am struck by the doubts among our other commentators on this later period (notably Evan Mawdsley on the Civil War and Richard Sakwa on the possibility of 'Bolshevik democracy') as to whether events by this stage could have gone very differently from how they actually did.

III: LENIN'S LEGACY

Lenin gave the world a political approach, a system and a state, all of which have been among the key drivers of world history through the twentieth century.

His approach to political action was utterly functional and unsentimental. All that mattered was gaining and holding power. He created the Cheka and enthusiastically encouraged the mass (and, where possible, public) murder of his opponents. He bullied his fellow Bolsheviks in 1918 into ceding vast swathes of western Russia to the Germans rather than lose power. Patriotism, compassion, truth would all be abandoned when necessary. There is no sign in Lenin's mature writings of any compunction about this. His lapidary summary of the criterion to be brought to any political judgement was 'Kto, kovo?' – who gains, who loses? This of course was not new in human history; Machiavelli had lauded the brutalities of Cesare Borgia. But it was Lenin, encouraged by Marx's own dismissal of 'bourgeois morality', who gave the doctrine its first mass twentieth-century outing. And, as Richard Sakwa makes clear, it was Lenin who irretrievably injected into the Bolshevik party its contempt for democratic procedure. The chicanery of the road to power, the savagery of the Civil War, the Red Terror, the mendacity and mass propaganda which became his regime's mode of communication with its own people and the wider world; these all cleared the way for the murderous collectivisations and purges which his successors inflicted on Russia. Outside Russia his approach found apt pupils in Mussolini, Hitler, Mao ... right up to Pol Pot and Ceausescu. He popularised an approach to politics that lies like a great stain across the whole twentieth century.

Lenin's second legacy was organisational. Partly by accident he arrived at one of the twentieth century's great political innovations – the one-party state. He had already set out his plans for a vanguard *revolutionary* party to seize the reins of power in 1902. Having done exactly that in 1917, his revolutionary party, without subsuming the Russian state, then became a monopolistic *ruling* party, taking all the high offices, pulling all the strings, and squeezing out all political opposition. The reason for things going this way are various: there simply weren't enough Bolsheviks to replace the entire Russian bureaucracy; the Russian state at that stage was in any case seen as no more than an obsolescent structure on the way to world revolution; and it somehow suited the oblique revolutionary mentality to control the state without actually being it – so much more was deniable or blameable on somebody else.

Once invented this was a system that offered huge attractions to twentieth-century authoritarians and ideologues, and it proved immensely successful. It is no accident that the official creed of the Soviet Union became the clumsily double-barrelled 'Marxism/Leninism'. Marxism of course, whatever the inadequacies of its actual implementation, remained a powerful insurrectionary brand, deployed by twentieth-century revolutionaries from Mao to Mandela. But Leninism was at least as important both in managing the Soviet Union itself and in its wider repercussions. Within its first two decades Lenin's one-party state had provided an explicitly acknowledged model for Mussolini, Hitler and Franco. After the Second World War, apart from its imposition all across Eastern Europe, it spread like a plague through newly decolonised Africa, the Middle East and Asia. At its high point, from Turkey to Tanzania and from Syria to Singapore it was the system of governance of more than sixty nations.

IV: THE STATE LENIN CREATED

Lenin's third great contribution to history was the Soviet Union itself. This is not the place to run through the detailed history of the Communist superpower. Rather like the newly independent United States at the end of the eighteenth century, it saw itself as an unprecedentedly innovatory political order ('Novus Ordo Seclorum', as it says on US banknotes). But unlike the United States, which in fact retained most of the legal, social and economic arrangements of its colonial past, the Bolsheviks set out to wipe the slate entirely clean. In what may well have been the biggest politico-economic experiment in the history of mankind, all of society and the economy were made subject to, and in effect the possessions of, a small, ideologically driven, political clique. The population of Russia became no more than grist to the mills of those who were building socialism; and were chewed up in their tens of millions.

It is hard not to see something tragically Russian in this. Having abandoned early hopes of world revolution, the Soviet regime reverted to some deep Russian archetypes: Ivan the Terrible, who created an elite cadre, the Oprichnina, to repress and terrorise the wider boyar class; and Peter the Great, who turned the entire nobility into state servants, and built his new capital, St Petersburg, on the bones of tens of thousands of forced labourers. Indeed, Stalin revelled in comparisons with these earlier figures. And under him the Russian tradition of autocracy was back with a vengeance. The all-embracing system of classification and control of the Soviet Union's people in the 1930s is comparable with nothing so much as the system imposed by Peter the Great 200 years earlier. Nicholas II looks positively liberal by comparison.

For a while it worked, though at an unimaginable cost in human lives. The economy was industrialised and society dragooned in time to defeat the genocidal Nazi invasion of 1941. That success, with the huge accretion in international power and influence it brought, made the Soviet Union the world's second superpower, leading a world communist movement which at its height governed one third of mankind. Even as late as 1956 the leader of the Soviet Communist Party, Nikita Khrushchev, was able to point to Soviet technological and economic successes and say, plausibly, to the West 'We will bury you.' But stagnation set in. The state-run economy simply couldn't compete in terms of dynamism or innovation with late twentieth-century capitalism. And the Communist Party, as long-serving elites do, became corrupt, sclerotic and conservative. Fitful efforts at reform failed until the final reformer, Mikhail Gorbachev, inadvertently and unexpectedly brought the whole system down.

V: TWO REVOLUTIONS COMPARED

The comparison between Gorbachev's 1991 'revolution' and the 1917 revolution which is the subject of this book has a lot to say about what has and has not changed in Russia over the past century. There were of course huge differences. The 1917 revolution came from below, driven by an angry population and political class. The 1991 revolution came from above, driven by an elite effort to make the system work better. The 1917 revolution began with a dysfunctional autocracy and largely peasant economy; it ended with communist totalitarianism. The 1991 revolution began with a repressive and closed communist system; it ended with 'managed democracy' and a recognisably market economy. What then are the common features? Four leap to the eye.

A] THE FRAGILITY OF RULING RUSSIA

The first is that in both cases what looked like a well-established and enduring regime fell with remarkable speed, taking the vast majority of contemporaries by surprise. The Romanov regime, for all its retrospectively obvious weaknesses, had been in power for 300 years. The massive tercentenary celebrations in 1913 gave the strong impression (not least to Nicholas himself) of a nation united behind its sovereign. The patriotic displays at the start of the war in August 1914 seemed to carry the same message. Until the crisis was fully upon them, the tsar, most of the ruling class and most outside observers dismissed outbursts of peasant anger, worker indiscipline and intelligentsia disaffection as untypical of the mass of the Russian people.

Similarly, the Soviet regime of the early 1980s felt rock solid. Certainly it faced economic stagnation, a gerontocratic leadership and the loss of passionate revolutionary belief. But the tiny dissident movement was seen as unrepresentative of a Soviet people who if not enthusiastic were at least submissive. No serious commentator was predicting collapse. What seemed to be needed was evolutionary reform, and the agent chosen for that was a true Leninist believer, Mikhail Gorbachev. Within five years the modest stimuli he introduced, a little more market and a little less repression, ran wild and destroyed the entire system.

Plainly, one cannot draw too wide a lesson from these two examples of unexpected regime downfall. But they do suggest that, in Russia, with its particularly opaque and repressive tradition of public life, an impression of widespread public acquiescence in the way they are ruled can prove, when put to the test, startlingly shallow. Which may help to explain why Russia's present regime follows public opinion with very close attention.

B] THE INSTABILITY OF EMPIRE

The second feature common to the two revolutions is the destabilising role played by Russia's subject provinces – particularly Ukraine. In 1917 one of the immediate consequences of the fall of tsarism was an upsurge of nationalist demands, initially for autonomy but ultimately for independence, in Poland and Finland (then provinces of the empire) as well as Ukraine and the Baltic republics. These demands, backed as they were by the Germans, were among the factors that made a quick peace impossible and so broke the back of the Provisional Government. It was only by 1922, after the Germans had collapsed to defeat in the West and the Bolsheviks had won the Civil War, that Ukraine was reclaimed. But Poland, Finland and (until 1945) the Baltics became independent.

The story in 1991 was different, but the underlying centrifugal forces were the same. As Gorbachev's reforms weakened Moscow's power so, again, demands arose for more autonomy in a number of Soviet republics, most particularly the Baltics and Ukraine. It was Gorbachev's efforts to meet these demands that provoked the fateful coup of August 1991 (conducted by hardliners intent on stopping the breakup of the Soviet Union). Even though the coup failed, it marginalised Gorbachev and so enabled the president of Russia (Boris Yeltsin) to do the deal with the president of Ukraine and others that broke the Soviet Union up into independent states.

Again, it would be a mistake to draw too wide a conclusion from these two particular cases. But plainly, and unsurprisingly, Russia's grip on its subject nationalities diminishes at a time of domestic political turmoil. This generates demands for autonomy/independence, which can add fatally to the pressures that the centre is already under. It is notable that even in post-1991 Russia one of the key challenges for Moscow has been Chechnya's demand for independence, and the destructive impact that has had on domestic security and governance.

C] THE CHALLENGE OF THE WEST

Tsarist Russia's relationship with the Western powers, even when polite, was never entirely comfortable. Many in the West saw Russia as alien and threatening. For its part, Russia, while hungry for Western modernity, mostly remembered regular Western invasions (Poles, Swedes and French, at roughly hundred-year intervals – each with the ambition of destroying Russia), and saw itself as leader of an alternative, and superior, Orthodox and Slavic tradition. Nicholas II was personally sympathetic to some of the most extreme exponents of this view, and it helped lead Russia into the First World War.

The revolution of 1917 was intended to end the old international politics. Russia was now just a station on the road to world communism, and Soviet foreign relations were initially subordinate to that objective. But by the mid 1920s hopes of world revolution had been replaced by the grey reality of 'Socialism in One Country'. The messianism of communism accordingly mutated into the straightforward pursuit of Russian national interest (two conspicuous examples: the subjugation of Soviet policy towards the Chinese communists between the wars to concerns about the Japanese threat to the USSR; and the 1939 somersault, again prompted by Soviet security concerns, from total ideological hostility to Nazi Germany to effective alliance with it). The Soviet Union until the end of its days certainly emphasised its role as leader of world communism (as Nicholas II had as leader of Orthodoxy), but pursued a very traditional Russian foreign policy agenda: protection from the threat of Western invasion by extending as wide a sphere of influence as possible, and expansion of Soviet/Communist influence wherever opportunity offered.

In 1991, policy evolved from a different starting point, but ended up in the same place. The economic and political models that the 1991 reformers set about introducing, market economics and liberal democracy, were Western models. The intention was explicitly for Russia to join the West. Gorbachev regularly spoke of the 'Common European Home'.

But again Russian patterns reimposed themselves. In the chaotic and demoralised circumstances of the 1990s, liberal democracy in Russia couldn't be made to work, and the transition to market economics was accompanied by social and material catastrophe. The result, accentuated by a series of Western 'humiliations' of Russia (most notably the expansion of NATO), was a sharp resurgence of Russian nationalism. The regime searched for a 'Russian' response to these pressures. It revived Orthodoxy, emphasised patriotism, and stood increasingly firmly (most notably in Georgia and Ukraine) against what it now saw as the predatory aims of the West.

Both revolutions, of 1917 and of 1991, were on behalf of universal values that ended up taking on some very traditional Russian features. In both cases Russia's foreign policy after an initial radical disturbance reverted to its familiar form. The key drivers have again become intense nationalism, fear of Western dominance and determination to protect a Russian sphere of influence. After the high hopes of 1991 the West has had some difficulty adjusting to this. One wonders if the outcome could ever have been different.

D) THE AUTHORITARIAN IMPULSE

The fourth obvious parallel between 1917 and 1991 is that in both cases a powerful social movement intent on democratising Russia led the country, via a period of chaos, back to authoritarianism. The story of 1917 has been traced in detail in the above chapters. As I have argued here, while Bolshevism was not the inevitable outcome of the chaos around 1917, the most likely alternative was not democracy but some other (probably right-wing) authoritarian regime. Russia's democratic tradition was too weak, and its democratic politicians too feeble, to be able to surmount the crisis. The perceived need for dictatorship (already being plotted even before Nicholas II fell) would almost certainly have become irresistible.

In the years after 1991, like the second act of a Beckett play, the same drama played itself out in paler form. The dissolution of the Soviet Union left a truncated Russia in a state of social disorder, economic collapse, civil war (in Chechnya), and with entirely untested governmental institutions. One key difference from 1917 was that Yeltsin, as directly elected president, had the democratic legitimacy that the 1917 Provisional Government had lacked. But even so he was forced into an increasingly dubious set of expedients (sending the tanks in against the Russian Parliament in 1993, 'buying' the election of 1996) in order to maintain power. The way was thus paved for the installation at the end of 1999 of Vladimir Putin (chosen in the expectation that he would be 'Russia's Pinochet') as Yeltsin's successor. What followed was the imposition of an increasingly 'managed' system of government in which the press is muffled, opposition activity hampered and elections manipulated.

One particular common feature between the 1917 and 1991 experiences is worth underlining. In both cases, after the upheaval the security organs of the state took on a central role in the way Russia was subsequently run. Critics of the 1991 revolution have argued that it was the lack of any 'lustration' – clean-out of the old guard – that made the eventual authoritarian outcome significantly harder to avoid. They may be right. But it is worth noting that in 1917 the lustration could not have been more thorough, and authoritarianism (to put it mildly) nevertheless followed.

It would of course be wildly premature to conclude from the 1917 and 1991 cases that Russia is in some sense doomed to authoritarianism. But it is clear that Russia's size, unmanageability and lack of democratic traditions make it peculiarly difficult for representational government to take root and function there. Given recent Russian history, the strong Russian popular preference (regularly reiterated in opinion polls) for 'order' over 'freedom' is not hard to understand.

VI: WHAT HAVE WE LEARNT?

The 1991 revolution was a massive rejection of the inheritance of 1917. Two of its most symbolic moments were the felling by a large crowd outside the headquarters of the KGB in Moscow of the Dzerzhinsky statue, and the unexpected decision by the inhabitants of what since 1924 had been Leningrad to change the name of their city back to St Petersburg. Lenin seemed dead. The next few years, famously, saw the 'End of history' with the United States dominating world affairs, and even the handful of countries which continued to describe themselves as communist in fact beginning to liberalise their economic systems – with the expectation in many minds that political liberalisation would follow. It was possible to see the 1917 revolution as profoundly important in the events it gave rise to, but, finally, one of history's great dead ends, like the Inca Empire.

Indeed, one of the key inheritances of the revolution has been negative. It has taught us what does not work. It is hard to see Marxism making any sort of comeback. As a theory of history the revolution tested it, and it failed. The dictatorship of the proletariat did not lead to the communist Utopia, but merely to more dictatorship. It also failed as a prescription for economic governance. No serious economist today is advocating total state ownership as the route to prosperity. While market economics undoubtedly has its problems, and the 2008 global crash did briefly raise Karl Marx to the top of France's non-fiction bestseller list, not the least of the lessons of the Russian Revolution is that for most economic purposes the market works much better than the state. The rush away from socialism since 1991 has been Gadarene.

The verdict on political Leninism is less definitive. Certainly the one-party state is past its prime. Following the stagnation and collapse of Soviet Communism, Western-style free market democracy looked like the only show in town. Starting in the late 1970s, and sharply accelerating after 1989, more than forty countries divested themselves of their single ruling parties. About two thirds of the world's nations are now democracies. And, in a world of vertiginously growing communication, trade and travel, there can be little prospect of resurrecting the sort of hermetically closed economy and society that underpinned the Soviet system. Even North Korea is now on the internet.

Nevertheless there is a real question about how much further the deLeninisation of the world will run. The rising tide of democracy shows signs of having reached its peak. In places (notably Russia itself) it has in fact begun to recede as regimes find ways of controlling their internal political processes while still forming part of a highly interconnected world. The most conspicuous case is of course China, still an explicitly Leninist single-party state, which, having junked Marx for the market, is now well on the way to becoming the world's largest economy and the greatest single challenge to the West's global dominance. Given the key role the USSR played in creating and shaping Chinese communist rule it is hard not to see today's China as by far the world's most significant inheritance from the 1917 revolution.

Seekers of predictability in history will note that both yesterday's and today's Leninist superpowers, Russia and China, are nations with exceptionally long histories of centralised and autocratic government. But, suggestive as such parallels may be, surely one of the key lessons of the 1917 revolution is the need to view grand theories of historical inevitability, and their purveyors, with immense caution. As the chapters above show, the history of the revolution is littered with ironies. Even the clearest sighted and best intentioned could be blown off course by accident or misfortune. Witte's Duma became a cockpit for opposition that helped bring down the very regime it was intended to save. Nicholas's patriotic feeling that he could best serve his people at the battlefront left St Petersburg in the disastrous hands of Alexandra and Rasputin. Rodzyanko's efforts to get Nicholas to abdicate in favour of his son produced the unintended end of the whole dynasty. The German General Staff, by sending Lenin back in 1917, gained a temporary advantage in the First World War, but also created the communist menace that loomed over Germany for the next seventy years. The non-Bolshevik opposition, by their willingness to tolerate Bolshevik excesses in the interests of revolutionary unity, swiftly found themselves in the 'dustbin of history'. And even Lenin, for all his amoral extremism, was driven by the Marxist vision of a fairer, gentler world. He and his successors produced exactly the opposite. They did so essentially by trying to bend reality to their ideas, rather than adjusting their ideas to reality.

All of this messy, bloody, unpredictable drama took place in Russia, and it is there that this book should end. Not only are individual personalities at a discount among the historical profession, but so too is national character. Theorists of revolution tend to overlook the inescapable Russianness that flavoured, and occasionally drove, much of what happened around 1917. The fanatical intelligentsia, driven to revolutionary excess by abstract theory, is laceratingly described in Dostoyevsky, just as the ineffectual bourgeoisie, unable to face up to necessary hard decisions, is portrayed by Chekhov. Nicholas II as 'Little Father' of his people, believing in a mystical bond that obviated any need for popular representation by rascally politicians, simply reflected the way Russia's rulers had always seen themselves. Rasputin is recognisably in the Russian tradition of the 'yurodiviy', the holy man who speaks truth to power.

And Russia was always an extraordinarily riven society. On one side stood her sparse, westernised, ruling class. On the other was the great mass of the 'dark people', serfs until 1861, focused on their own communities, suspicious and resentful of any interference from outside. It was Pushkin who wrote of the 'Russian revolt; mindless and merciless' – the mass uprising which, coming out of nowhere, sporadically through history burned and massacred entire Russian provinces. One picture of 1917 is that it was just such an uprising that consumed the whole country, and whose shadow then hung over world history for the next seventy years. We surely owe it to the many, many victims to ask whether we could have found another way.

NOTES

CHAPTER 1. FOREIGN INTERVENTION: THE LONG VIEW

A. A. Kireev: Dnevnik 1905–1910 (Moscow: 1910), p. 150.
Readers interested in further exploring these themes and the evidence on which my counterfactual arguments are based should consult my new book: Dominic Lieven, *Towards the Flame: Empire, War and the End of Tsarist Russia* (London: Allen Lane, 2015).

CHAPTER 2. THE ASSASSINATION OF STOLYPIN

1. Charles Moore, *Margaret Thatcher: The Authorized Biography, vol. 2: Everything She Wants* (London: Allen Lane, 2015), p. 617.
2. In the context of this chapter, see especially, V. S. Diakin, *Byl li shans u Stolypina? Sbornik statei* (St Petersburg: LISS, 2002).
3. S. G. Kara-Murza, *Stolypin: Otets russkoi revoliutsii* (Moscow: Algoritm, 2002); Kara-Murza, *Oshibka Stolypina: Prem'er, perevernuvshii Rossiiu* (Moscow: Eksmo, Algoritm, 2011).
4. Monakh Lazar' (Afanas'ev), *Stavka na sil'nykh: Zhizn' Petra Arkad'evicha Stolypina* (Moscow: Russkii Palomnik, 2013), p. 3.
5. Richard S. Wortman, *Scenarios of Power: Myth and Ceremony in Russian Monarchy, vol. 2: From Alexander II to the Death of Nicholas II* (Princeton, NJ: Princeton University Press, 2000), pp. 377–9, 380.
6. Abraham Ascher, *P. A. Stolypin: The Search for Stability in Late Imperial Russia* (Stanford, CA: Stanford University Press, 2001), pp. 13–33.
7. Already by late 1909, their relationship had been damaged by the Tsar's refusal to ease the legal position of Jews and by a crisis over the budget for the Naval General Staff. See Dominic Lieven, *Nicholas II: Emperor of All the Russias* (London: John Murray, 1993), pp. 174–6.
8. On *obshchestvennost'*, see Geoffrey A. Hosking, *Russia: People and Empire, 1552–1917* (London: HarperCollins, 1997), pp. 325, 332, 400–402.
9. Faith Hillis, *Children of Rus': Right-Bank Ukraine and the Invention of a Russian Nation* (Ithaca, NY: Cornell University Press, 2013), pp. 249–50.
10. P. A. Pozhigailo, ed. *Taina ubiistva Stolypina* (Moscow: ROSSPEN, 2003).

11. Here I follow Richard Pipes, *Revolutionary Russia, 1899–1919* (London: Collins, 1990), pp. 188–90, and Ascher, *P. A. Stolypin*, pp. 363–89. The leading advocate of the conspiracy theory is A.Ia. Avrekh, *Stolypin i tret'ia duma* (Moscow: Nauka, 1968), pp. 367–406.

12. Ascher, *P. A. Stolypin*, pp. 393–4.

13. From an extensive (and deeply riven) literature, see Judith Pallot, *Land Reform in Russia, 1906–1917: Peasant Responses to Stolypin's Project of Rural Transformation* (Oxford: Oxford University Press, 1999).

14. Geoffrey A. Hosking, *The Russian Constitutional Experiment: Government and Duma 1907–1914* (Cambridge: Cambridge University Press, 1973), pp. 41–55.

15. Peter Waldron, *Between Two Revolutions: Stolypin and the Politics of Renewal* (London: UCL Press, 1998), pp. 115–46.

16. V. V. Rozanov, *Russkaia gosudarstvennost' i obshchestvo: Stat'I 1906-1907 gg.*, ed. A. N. Nikoliukin (Moscow: Respublika, 2003), p. 336, describing Stolypin's speech in the second Duma on 6 March 1907. This article appeared in the liberal newspaper *Russkoe slovo* under Rozanov's widely-known pseudonym, V. Varvarin. He was more complimentary when writing for the conservative *Novoe vremia*. See, for example, Rozanov, *Staraia i molodaia Rossiia: Stat'I i ocherki 1909 g.*, ed. A. N. Nikoliukin (Moscow: Respublika, 2004), pp. 138–40, unsigned, praising Stolypin's determination to stand above party.

17. Simon Dixon, 'The "Mad Monk" Iliodor in Tsaritsyn', *Slavonic and East European Review*, 88, 1–2 (2010), pp. 377–415.

18. *I. I. Tolstoi: Dnevnik*, ed. B. V. Ananich et al., 2 vols (St Petersburg: Liki Rossii, 2010), vol. II: pp. 207–208, 6 September 1911.

19. A. Bogdanovich, *Tri poslednikh samoderzhtsa* (Moscow: Novosti, 1990), pp. 385, 387.

20. *A. A. Kireev: Dnevnik 1905–1910*, ed. K. A. Solov'ev (Moscow: ROSSPEN, 2010), p. 145, 22 May 1906.

21. Ibid., pp. 177–78, 5 November 1906; 'gentleman' in English in the original. For a wide range of contemporary responses to Stolypin, see *P. A. Stolypin, Pro et Contra*, ed. I.V. Lukoianov, 2nd ed. (St Petersburg: Izdatel'stvo Russkoi khristianskoi gumanitarnoi akademii, 2014).

22. *Osobye zhurnaly Soveta ministrov Rossiiskoi imperii: 1911 god*, ed. B.D. Gal'perina (Moscow: ROSSPEN, 2002), pp. 371–72, 13 September 1911. 'I mourn the untimely decease of my faithful servant, state-secretary Stolypin', the tsar scribbled disingenuously on 22 September.

CHAPTER 3. GRIGORY RASPUTIN AND THE OUTBREAK OF THE FIRST WORLD WAR

1. The chapter on Guseva's attack and the subsequent investigation draws chiefly on the police files in two Siberian archives: The State Budgetary Institution of the Tiumen' Region: 'The State Archive in the City of Tobolsk', Collection I-164, Inventory 1, Files 436, 437, 439; and The State Institution of the Omsk Region: 'The Historical Archive of the Omsk Region', Collection 190, Inventory 1, 1881–1917 gg., File 332. These important though little-studied files are produced in full in Sergei Fomin, 'Strast' kak bol'no, a vyzhevu … (Moscow: 2011), pp. 378–826. Additional information is from Oleg Platonov, Zhizn' za tsaria. Pravda o Grigorii Rasputine (St Petersburg: 1996), p. 111; V. L. and M. Iu. Smirnov, Neizvestnoe o Rasputine (Tiumen: 2010), p. 66; Fomin, 'Strast'', pp. 85–87, 101–05, 204; State Archive of the Russian Federation (hereafter GARF), 102.242.1912.297, ch. 2, p. 1.

2. Smirnov, Neizvestnoe, p. 66; Fomin, 'Strast'', pp. 117–18; Russian State Historical Archive, 472.2 (195/2683), pp. 7, 8–9.

3. Joseph T. Fuhrmann, Rasputin: The Untold Story (Hoboken, NJ: 2013), p. 126; Fomin, 'Strast'', pp. 161–62, 701–02; Platonov, Zhizn', pp. 136–37.

4. Fomin, 'Strast'', p. 136.

5. GARF, 1467.1.710, p. 24.

6. The most authoritative and judicious of the many biographies of Rasputin are Fuhrmann, Rasputin; and Aleksei Varlamov, Grigorii Rasputin-Novyi (Moscow: 2012).

7. See the clippings in GARF, 102.242.1912, ch. 2; New York Times, 14 July 1914, p. 1; 15 July, p. 4; 16 July, p. 4; 17 July, p. 4.

8. The suggestion of some international plot involving the assassination of Jaurès is absurd, but not uncommon among contemporary nationalist Russian historians. On his murder, see Harvey Goldberg, The Life of Jean Jaurès (Madison, WI: 1962), pp. 458–74. As Goldberg notes, Jaurès fought up to the end for peace in Europe, although he stood little chance of success.

9. Colin Wilson, Rasputin and the Fall of the Romanovs (New York: 1964), p. 156; Varlamov, Rasputin-Novyi, pp. 426–28; T. Groian, Muchenik za Khrista i za Tsaria. Chelovek Bozhii Grigorii. Molitvennik za Sviatuiu Rus' i Eia Presvetlago Otroka (Moscow: 2001), pp. 95–96; Iurii Rassulin, ed., Vernaia Bogu, Tsariu i Otechestvu. Anna Aleksandrovna Taneeva (Vyrubova) – monakhinia Mariia (St Petersburg: 2005).

10. Fuhrmann, Rasputin, p. 118; Varlamov, Rasputin-Novyi, pp. 422–23.

11. Fuhrmann, Rasputin, p. 115; Varlamov, Rasputin-Novyi, p. 423.

12. *Grigorii Rasputin v vospominaniiakh sovremennikov* (Moscow: 1990), pp. 71–73.

13. Varlamov, *Rasputin-Novyi*, p. 377.

14. Ibid., pp. 377–8.

15. Edvard Radzinsky, *The Rasputin File* (New York: 2000), pp. 188–89; W. Bruce Lincoln, *In War's Dark Shadow: The Russians Before the Great War* (New York: 1983), pp. 408–13; Orlando Figes, *A People's Tragedy: The Russian Revolution, 1891–1924* (New York: 1997), p. 248.

16. Varlamov, *Rasputin-Novyi*, p. 376.

17. Fuhrmann, *Rasputin*, p. 115.

18. Fomin, 'Strast'', p. 318.

19. Clipping of the *Frankfurter Zeitung*, 1 March 1913. Das Politische Archiv des Auswärtigen Amts (Berlin), R.10897.

20. V. Semennikov, *Romanovy i germanskie vliianiia, 1914–1917 gg.* (Leningrad: 1929), pp. 29–30.

21. Lincoln, *War's Dark Shadow*, pp. 409–11.

22. Semennikov, *Romanovy*, pp. 28–31; Fuhrmann, *Rasputin*, pp. 114–15.

23. GARF, 1467.1.710, pp. 151–55.

24. GARF, 102.242.1912.297, ch. 1, p. 94.

25. Iurii Rassulin, Sergei Astakhov, and Elena Dushenova, eds, *Khronika velikoi druzhby: Tsarstvennye mucheniki i chelovek Bozhii Grigorii Rasputin-Novyi* (hereafter KVD) (St Petersburg: 2007), pp. 140–41.

26. N. A. Sokolov, *Ubiistvo tsarskoi sem'i* (Berlin: 1922; reprint Moscow: 1990), p. 94.

27. KVD, p. 136.

28. GARF, 640.1.323, p. 2.

29. GARF, 1467.1.710, p. 159.

30. GARF, 1467.1.710, pp. 161–63. Akulina Laptinskaya (not Lapshinskaya) was a devoted follower and secretary to Rasputin. She stayed at his bedside during his recovery.

31. Fuhrmann, *Rasputin*, p. 129; Andrei Maylunas and Sergei Mironenko, eds, *A Lifelong Passion: Nicholas and Alexandra: Their Own Story* (New York: 1997), p. 397; Rassulin, ed., *Vernaia Bogu*, pp. 73–74.

32. Yale University, Beinecke Library, Romanov Collection, GEN MSS 313, Series 1, Box 1, Folder 100.

33. Yale University, Beinecke Library, Romanov Collection, GEN MSS 313, Series 1, Box 1, Folder 100; and GEN MSS 313, Box 8, Folder 111; Varlamov, *Rasputin-Novyi*, pp. 424–25; Fomin, 'Strast'', pp. 279–81. S. V. Markov, who

was with Soloviev in Tobolsk in 1918, saw the letter then, though in his memoirs he implies that the empress had given it and other letters from Rasputin to him earlier for safekeeping. *Pokinutaia tsarskaia sem'ia, 1917–1918* (Moscow: 2002), p. 54.

34. [A. A. Belling], *Iz nedavnego proshlogo: Vstrechi s Grigoriem Rasputinym* (Petrograd: 1917), p. 11; Varlamov, *Rasputin-Novyi*, pp. 425–26.

35. Fuhrmann, *Rasputin*, pp. 128–29.

36. R. R. von Raupakh, *Facies Hippocratica (Lik umiraiushchego): Vospominaniia chlena Chrezvychainoi Sledstvennoi Komissii 1917 goda*, ed. S. A. Man'kov (St Petersburg: 2007), p. 141; Fomin, 'Strast'', pp. 272–75, 313n1; Fomin, *Nakazanie pravdoi* (Moscow: 2007), p. 493; A. Amal'rik, *Rasputin: Dokumental'naia povest'* (Moscow: 1992), pp. 163–64, 185; Dominic Lieven, *Nicholas II: Emperor of All the Russias* (London: 1993), p. 205.

37. *Peterburgskii kur'er*, 16 July 1914, p. 1. Austria declared war on 15/28 July.

38. GARF, 102.242.1912.297, ch. 1, p. 69.

39. GARF, 102.242.1912.297, ch. 2, pp. 83–84.

40. GARF, 102.242.1912.297, ch. 2, pp. 82, 204, 206–06 ob.

41. Lieven, *Nicholas II*, pp. 198–203; Robert D. Warth, *Nicholas II: The Life and Reign of Russia's Last Monarch* (Westport, CT: 1997), pp. 191–96; Rassulin, ed., *Vernaia Bogu*, pp. 73–74.

42. KVD, p. 141.

43. GARF, 640.1.323, p. 3.

44. GARF, 640.1.323, 3 ob.

45. Varlamov, *Rasputin-Novyi*, pp. 429–31.

46. KVD, p. 144.

47. KVD, p. 147.

48. Fuhrmann, *Rasputin*, p. 132.

49. Varlamov, *Rasputin-Novyi*, pp. 428–29.

50. *Peterburgskii kur'er*, 16 August 1914, p. 4; 18 August, p. 2.

51. GARF, 1467.1.710, pp. 208–09.

52. See, for example, KVD, pp. 147, 157, 165, 194, 219, 223, 224, 225, 240, 259, 370, 417, 427.

53. See the excellent William C. Fuller, Jr., *The Foe Within: Fantasies of Treason and the End of Imperial Russia* (Ithaca, New York: 2006).

54. Joseph T. Fuhrmann, ed., *The Complete Wartime Correspondence of Tsar Nicholas II and the Empress Alexandra: April 1914–March 1917* (Westport, CT: 1999), pp. 373, 582–83, 593–94, 631–32, 636, 638–39; Maylunas and Mironenko, eds, *Lifelong Passion*, p. 473; and Rasputin's letters to the

minister of agriculture Count A. A. Bobrinsky in the Russian State Archive of Ancient Documents, 1412.3.1593.

55. See Varlamov, *Rasputin-Novyi*, p. 681; Hoover Institution Archives, Vasilii Maklakov Collection, 15–16, pp. 1–9.

56. Z. I. Peregudova, ed., *'Okhranka': vospominaniia rukovoditelei politicheskogo syska* (Moscow: 2004), vol. 2, pp. 123–24.

57. Varlamov, *Rasputin-Novyi*, p. 699; Raupakh, *Facies*, pp. 193–94; P. N. Miliukov, *Vospominaniia*, p. 447; the diary of P. I. Korzhenevsky in the Russian State Library, Scientific Research Division of Manuscripts, 436.11.1, 72 ob-73.

58. Sergey von Markow, *Wie ich die Zarin befreien wollte* (Zürich: 1929), p. 145.

59. *Poslednie dni imperatorskoi vlasti* (Moscow: 2005), p. 8.

CHAPTER 5. ENTER LENIN

1. Winston Churchill, *World Crisis* (London: T. Butterworth, 1923–31), vol. 5, p. 73.

2. Richard Pipes, *The Russian Revolution* (New York: Vintage, 1990), pp. 377–78.

3. Lenin, *Socialism and War: The Attitude of the Russian Social-Democratic Labor Party Towards the War* (Geneva: Sotsia-Democrat, 1915).

4. Lyrics by Eugène Pottier.

5. V. I. Lenin, *Collected Works, Volume 23 (August 1916–March 1917)* (Moscow: Progress Publishers, 1964), p. 253. On Münzenberg and Lenin in Zurich, see Sean McMeekin, *The Red Millionaire: A Political Biography of Willi Münzenberg, Moscow's Secret Propaganda Tsar in the West* (New Haven: Yale University Press, 2003), chapter 2.

6. The best documentary account is Werner Hahlweg, ed., *Lenins Rückkehr nach Russland 1917: Die deutschen Akten* (Leiden: Brill, 1957) and, for the middleman between Lenin and the Germans, Z. A. B. Zerman and W. B. Scharlau, *The Merchant of Revolution: The Life of Alexander Israel Helphand (Parvus) 1867–1924*.

7. Münzenberg, *Die dritte Front*, p. 236, and 'Mit Lenin in der Schweiz', in *Internationale Presse Korrespondenz* 6 (27 August 1926): 1838.

8. Cited in Pipes, *Russian Revolution*, p. 393. Pipes's translation.

9. Cited in James Bunyan and H. H. Fisher, eds, *The Bolshevik Revolution 1917–1918* (Stanford: Stanford University Press, 1934), p. 7.

10. Cited in ibid.

11. Cited in Leonard Shapiro, *The Russian Revolutions of 1917: The Origins of Modern Communism* (New York: Basic Books, 1984), p. 59.

12. Winfried Baumgart, *Deutsche Ostpolitik*, 21.

13. As recalled in paraphrase by Chernov in *The Great Russian Revolution*, trans. Philip E. Mosely (New York: Russell & Russell, 1966), p. 194.

14. Cited by Richard Stites in 'Miliukov and the Russian Revolution', foreword to Miliukov, *The Russian Revolution*, p. xii.

15. Pipes, *Russian Revolution*, pp. 257–58.

16. Citations in Chernov, *The Great Russian Revolution*, pp. 193, 200.

17. Oleg Airapetov, 'Na Vostochnom napravlenii. Sud'ba Bosforskoi ekspeditsii v pravlenie imperatora Nikolaia II', *Poslednaia voina imperatorskoi Rossii: sbornik statei* (Moscow: Tri kvadrata, 2002), pp. 241–43.

18. Bazili to N. N. Pokrovskii, from Stavka, 26 February / 11 March 1917, in the Archive of the Foreign Policy of the Russian Empire in Moscow (AVPRI), fond 138, opis' 467, del' 493/515, list' 1 (and back).

19. Bazili to N. N. Pokrovskii, from Stavka, 26 February / 11 March 1917, in AVPRI, fond 138, opis' 467, del' 493/515, list' 1 (and back).

20. Cited in C. Jay Smith, Jr., *The Russian Struggle for Power, 1914–1917* (New York: Philosophical Library, 1956), p. 465.

21. Usedom to Kaiser Wilhelm II, 16 April 1917, in the German Admiralty files in Freiburg, BA/MA, RM 40–4. Seven seaplanes: René Greger, *Russische Flotte im ersten Weltkrieg, 1914–1917* (Munich: J. F. Lehmann, 1970), p. 61.

22. Bazili to Miliukov, 23 March / 5 April 1917, in the AVPRI, fond 138, opis' 467, del' 493/515, list' 4–6 (and backs).

23. Cited in C. Jay Smith, *Russian Struggle for Power*, 472.

24. M. Philips Price, 'Russia's Control of the Straits,' published in the *Manchester Guardian*, 26 April 1917. Republished in Price, *Dispatches from the Revolution. Russia 1915–1918* (Durham, NC: Duke University Press, 1998).

25. Lenin, 'The War and the Provisional Government,' first published in *Pravda* on 13/26 April 1917, in *Collected Works (April–June 1917)*, vol. 24, p. 114.

26. As noted by Chernov, still fuming with rage over this 'mockery,' in *The Great Russian Revolution*, p. 200.

27. 'Resolution on the Attitude Towards the Provisional Government,' 18 April / 1 May 1917, in Lenin, *Collected Works*, vol. 24, pp. 154–55; and 'Draft Resolution on the War,' 'written between 15 April and 22 April 1917,' pp. 161–66.

28. Citations in Pipes, *Russian Revolution*, pp. 403–04.

29. Cited in ibid., p. 413.

30. 'Rukovodiashchiia ukazaniia General'Komissaru oblastei Turtsii, zanyatyikh' po pravu voinyi,' adjusted to comply with the Soviet's 'peace without annexations' declaration, 15/28 May 1917, in AVPRI, fond 151, opis' 482, del' 3481, list' 81–82.

31. Cited in Kazemzadeh, *Struggle for Transcaucasia*, p. 61. See also Allan Wildman, *The End of the Russian Imperial Army*, 2 vols (Princeton: Princeton University Press, 1980/1987), vol. 2, p. 141.

32. G. W. Le Page to Captain H. G. Grenfell from aboard the *Almaz* at Sevastopol, 29 April 1917, in The National Archives of the United Kingdom (PRO), ADM 137 / 940.

33. G. W. Le Page to Captain H. G. Grenfell from aboard the *Almaz* at Sevastopol, 23 May 1917, in PRO, ADM 137 / 940.

34. René Greger, *Russische Flotte im ersten Weltkrieg*, p. 63.

35. Report of Captain-Lieutenant Nusret from Constantinople after his tour of Russia's Black Sea ports, 14 April 1918, in the German Military Archive in Freiburg (BA / MA), RM 40–252.

36. Figures cited in A. K. Wildman, *The End of the Russian Imperial Army* (Princeton: Princeton University Press, 1980), vol. 1, pp. 364–65.

37. Pipes, *Russian Revolution*, p. 410.

38. Sean McMeekin, *History's Greatest Heist. The Looting of Russia by the Bolsheviks* (New Haven: Yale University Press, 2008), esp. chapter 5 ('Brest-Litovsk and the Diplomatic Bag').

39. Wildman, *End of the Russian Imperial Army*, vol. 1, p. 372.

40. William G. Rosenberg, 'Reading Soldiers' Moods: Russian Military Censorship and the Configuration of Feeling in World War I', in *The American Historical Review* vol. 119 no. 3, 2014, 714–40, esp. fn46.

41. 'Russian Soldiers Fleeing Germans on the Galician Front, July 1917,' from *Mirrorpix* (the photo archive of the London *Daily Mirror*).

42. In this account of the July Days, I have followed mostly Shapiro, *Russian Revolutions of 1917*, pp. 80–85, and Pipes, *Russian Revolution*, pp. 422–31.

43. Ibid., p. 431 and *passim*.

44. Citations in ibid., p. 433.

45. See Lucius von Stoedten from Stockholm, 20 July 1917, in the Political Archive of the German Foreign Office (PAAA), R 10080. On the Romanov treasure and Bolshevik efforts to sell it, see McMeekin, *History's Greatest Heist*, chapters 2 and 8.

CHAPTER 6. THE KORNILOV AFFAIR: A TRAGEDY OF ERRORS

1. Alexander Kerensky, *The Catastrophe* (New York, London: 1927), p. 318.
2. Ibid., *passim*.
3. E. I. Martynov, *Kornilov* (Leningrad: 1927), pp. 33–34.
4. D. A. Chugaev, ed., *Revoliutsionnoe dvizhenie v Rossii v avcruste 1917 q: Razqrom kornilovskoao miatezha* (Moscow: 1959), p. 429. This book is an excellent source of documents dealing with the Kornilov affair.
5. B. Savinkov, *K delu Kornilova* (Paris: 1919), p. 15.
6. A. F. Kerenskii, *Delo Kornilova* (Moscow: 1918), p. 81.
7. N. Avdeev et al., *Revoliutsiia 1917 qoda: Khronika sobvtii*, vol. 4 (Moscow: 1923–1930), p. 85.
8. Chugaev, *Revoliutsionnoe dvizhenie*, p. 421.
9. P. N. Miliukov, *Istoriia Vtoroi Russkoi Revoliutsiii*, vol. 1, part 2 (Sofia: 1921), p. 178.
10. Ibid., vol. 1, part 2, p. 202.
11. Rossiia. XX vek Dokumenty, *Delo Generala L.G. Kornilova*, vol. 2 (Moscow: 2003), p. 195.
12. Chugaev, *Revoliutsionnoe dvizhenie*, p. 428.
13. Rossiia. XX vek, *Delo Generala L. G. Kornilova*, vol. 2, pp. 196–98.
14. Chugaev, *Revoliutsionnoe dvizhenie*, p. 442.
15. Ibid., p. 443.
16. Savinkov, *K delu Kornilova*, p. 25.
17. Avdeev, *Revoliutsiia*, vol. 4, p. 98.
18. Chugaev, *Revoliutsionnoe dvizhenie*, pp. 445–46; Avdeev, *Revoliutsiia*, vol. 4, pp. 101–02.
19. Chugaev, *Revoliutsionnoe dvizhenie*, p. 446.
20. Ibid., p. 464.
21. Rossiia. XX vek, *Delo Generala L. G. Kornilova*, vol. 2, p. 156. Kerensky's testimony is available in English in his *The Prelude to Bolshevism: The Kornilov Rising* (New York: 1919).
22. *Novaia zhizn'*, no. 107/322 (4 June 1918), p. 3; *Nash Vek*, no. 96/120 (19 June 1918), p. 3.
23. E. H. Wilcox, *Russia's Ruin* (New York: 1919), p. 276.
24. *Russkaia Mvsl*, Book III–V (Moscow: 1923), pp. 278–79.

CHAPTER 7. THE 'HARMLESS DRUNK': LENIN AND THE OCTOBER INSURRECTION

1. S. P. Melgunov, *The Bolshevik Seizure of Power* (Oxford: 1972), p. 81.

2. Z. Gippius, *Siniaia kniga* (Belgrade: 1929), p. 210.

3. A. Rabinowitch, *The Bolsheviks Come to Power: The Revolution of 1917 in Petrograd* (New York: 1978), pp. 253–54.

4. V. Lenin, *Collected Works*, vol. 25 (Moscow: 1964), pp. 172–73.

5. Ibid., p. 310.

6. Ibid., vol. 26, pp. 19–21.

7. Ibid., pp. 74–85.

8. RTsKhIDNI, f. 17, op. 1, d. 33.

9. Rabinowitch, *The Bolsheviks Come to Power*.

10. RTsKhIDNI, f. 17, op. 1, d. 34, 1. 1–15.

11. *Novaia zhizn'*, 18 October 1917; Lenin, *Collected Works*, vol. 26, pp. 216–19.

12. Rabinowitch, *The Bolsheviks Come to Power*, pp. 290–91.

13. N. Sukhanov, *The Russian Revolution: A Personal Record*, ed. J. Carmichael (Princeton: 1984), p. 635.

14. Ibid., p. 294.

15. *Vtoroi vserossiiskii s'ezd sovetov rabochikh i soldatskikh deputatov* (Moscow: 1957), pp. 43–44.

16. RTsKhIDNI, f. 17, op. 1, d. 39.

CHAPTER 8. THE SHORT LIFE AND EARLY DEATH OF RUSSIAN DEMOCRACY: THE DUMA AND THE CONSTITUENT ASSEMBLY

1. *Oxford Dictionary of Political Quotations* (Oxford University Press, Oxford: 2001).

2. Dominic Lieven, *Nicholas II* (St Martin's Griffin, New York: 1993), p. 105.

3. Nikolai N. Smirnov, 'The Constituent Assembly', in William Acton, Vladimir Cherniaev and G. Rosenberg, eds, *Critical Companion to the Russian Revolution* (London: Hodder Arnold, 1997), p. 323.

4. Orlando Figes, *A People's Tragedy* (Jonathan Cape, London: 1996), p. 173.

5. Abraham Ascher, *The Revolution of 1905* (Stanford: Stanford University Press, 2004), p. 27.

6. Richard Pipes, *The Russian Revolution* (New York: Vintage, 1991), p. 34.

7. Ibid., p. 162.

8. G. A. Hosking, *The Russian Constitutional Experiment* (Cambridge: Cambridge University Press, 1973), p. 41.

9. Abraham Ascher, *P. A. Stolypin: The Search for Stability in Late Imperial Russia* (Stanford: Stanford University Press, 2001).

10. Orlando Figes, *Revolutionary Russia 1891–1991* (London: Pelican Books, 2014), p. 73.
11. Pipes, *The Russian Revolution*, p. 223ff.
12. Figes, *A People's Tragedy*, p. 178.
13. Pipes, *The Russian Revolution*, p. 255.
14. Kerensky in R. P. Browder and A. F. Kerensky, eds, *The Russian Provisional Government 1917, Documents* (Stanford: Stanford University Press, 1961), p. 43.
15. Figes, *A People's Tragedy*, p. 341.
16. V. D. Medlin and S. L. Parsons, eds, *V. D. Nabokov and the Russian Provisional Government* (New Haven: Yale University Press, 1976), p. 137.
17. Rodzyanko in Browder and Kerensky, *The Russian Provisional Government 1917*, p. 138.
18. Figes, *A People's Tragedy*, p. 336.
19. Pipes, *The Russian Revolution*, p. 297.
20. Lvov in Browder and Kerensky, *The Russian Provisional Government 1917*, p. 159.
21. Smirnov in Acton, Cherniaev and Rosenberg, *Critical Companion to the Russian Revolution*, p. 324.
22. Russkia Vedomosti in Browder and Kerensky, *The Russian Provisional Government 1917*, p. 447.
23. Rech' in Browder and Kerensky, *The Russian Provisional Government 1917*, p. 448.
24. Russkia Vedomosti in Browder and Kerensky, *The Russian Provisional Government 1917*, p. 450.
25. Rech' in Browder and Kerensky, *The Russian Provisional Government 1917*, p. 451.
26. Figes, *Revolutionary Russia 1891–1991*, p. 135.
27. Pipes, *The Russian Revolution*, p. 537.
28. Smirnov in Acton, Cherniaev and Rosenberg, *Critical Companion to the Russian Revolution*, p. 329
29. Pipes, *The Russian Revolution*, p. 551.
30. Ibid., p. 553.
31. Ibid., p. 556.
32. Smirnov in Acton, Cherniaev and Rosenberg, *Critical Companion to the Russian Revolution*, p. 328.
33. Figes, *A People's Tragedy*, p. 518.

CHAPTER 9. RESCUING THE TSAR AND HIS FAMILY

Emperor Nicholas II; Dnevniki, 1882–1918, GARF, f 601, op 1, ed khr 217–66.

The telegrams of V Yakovlev transferring the Tsar from Tobolsk to Moscow; GARF collection.

Alikina N; Rasskaz zaveduyushchei Permskym partarkhivom o vstrechakh s Markovym I prieme Leninym Markova posle ubiistva Mikhaila; 'Vechernyaya Perm', 3 Feb 1990.

Blok A. A.; Zapisnye knizhki; Moscow 1965.

Budberg A.; Dnevnik belogvardeitsa, Leningrad 1929.

Budberg; Dnevnik; Arkhiv russkoi revolyutsii, Vol. XIV, pp. 324–5, Berlin 1924.

Burtsev V. L.; Istinnye ubiitsi Nikolaya II – Lenin i evo tovarishchi; 'Obshchee Delo', Paris 1921.

Bykov P. M.; Poslednie dni Romanovykh; Sverdlovsk 1926.

Voinov V. M.; Iz istorii Nikolaevskoi Akadamii; Ural 1992.

Gilliard P., Tragicheskaya sudba russkoi imperatorskoi familii; Revel 1921.

Kavtaradze A G; Voennie spetsalisti na sluzhbe Sovetov 1917-20; Moscow 1988.

Lermontov M; 'Ya ne lyublyu tebya'.

Matveev P; Vospominaniya o Tobolskom zaklyuchenii tsarskoi semyi; 'Uralskii rabochii', 16 Sept 1990.

Markov A; Vospominaniya o rastrele velikovo knyazya Mikhaila; 'Sovershenno sekretno' No 9, 1990.

Markov S; Pokinutaya tsarskaya semya; Vienna 1926.

Melnik-Botkina T; Vospominaniya o tsarskoi semye i eyo zhizni do i posle revolyutsii; Belgrade 1921.

Pankratov V S; S tsarem v Tobolske; 'Byloe' No 25-26, 1924.

Plotnikov I F; Ekaterinburgskii etap deyatelnosti Akademii Generalnovo Shtaba; Kostroma 1988.

Entsiklopediya Ekaterinburga.

CHAPTER 11. SEA CHANGE IN THE CIVIL WAR

1. http://mjp.univ-perp.fr/traites/1918armistice.htm.

2. Michael Carley, *Revolution and Intervention: The French Government and the Russian Civil War, 1917–1919* (Kingston, ON: McGill-Queen's University Press, 1983), pp. 108, 111; Richard Ullman, *Intervention and the War* (Princeton: Princeton University Press, 1961), pp. 258–84. The high-level British discussion in November 1918 is in TNA (Kew), CAB 23/8 <http://filestore.nationalarchives.gov.uk/pdfs/large/cab-23–8.pdf>.

3. For the mechanics of the coup: G. Z. Ioffe, *Kolchakovskaia avantiura i ee krakh* (Moscow; Mysl', 1983), pp. 141–46; Jonathan Smele, *Civil War in Siberia: The Anti-Bolshevik Government of Admiral Kolchak 1918–1920* (Cambridge: Cambridge University Press, 1996), pp. 104–07; Scott B. Smith, *Captives of Revolution: The Socialist Revolutionaries and the Bolshevik Dictatorship, 1918–1923* (Pittsburgh: University of Pittsburgh Press, 2011), p. 159.

4. The relevant documents have been recently published in V. I. Shishkin, ed., *Vremennoe Vserossiiskoe pravitel'stvo, 23 sentiabria – 18 noiabria 1918 g. Sbornik dokumentov i materialov*, (Novosibirsk: RITs NGU, 2010), pp. 338–44.

5. V. G. Khandorin, *Admiral Kolchak: Pravda i mify* (Tomsk: Izd. Tomskogo Universiteta, 2007), p. 81.

6. Much the best treatment of the SRs and their policies is Smith, *Captives*.

7. Ibid., p. 155.

8. On the underlying factors behind the coup see also Evan Mawdsley, *The Russian Civil War* (Edinburgh: Birlinn, 2008 [1987]), pp. 143–51.

9. Smele, *Civil War*, pp. 62–71, provides the basic biographical background for Kolchak. The admiral has aroused much interest in post-Soviet Russia, and recent biographies include Khandorin, *Kolchak*, and I. F. Plotnikov, *Aleksandr Vasil'evich Kolchak: Issledovatel', admiral, Verkhovnyi pravitel' Rossii* (Moscow: Tsentropoligraf, 2002). Kolchak was the subject of a feature film directed by A. Iu. Kravchuk, *Admiral* (2008); a version of this was broadcast in the Russian Federation in 2009 as a ten-part television series.

10. TNA (Kew), WO 33 962/186 (31 August 1918).

11. K. A. Popova, ed., *Dopros Kolchaka* (Leningrad: GIZ, 1925), pp. 143–44 (30 January 1920).

12. Jonathan Smele noted Kolchak's relationship with another Russian woman in the Far East, suggesting this lowered the priority of his return to his family in south Russia (*Civil War*, pp. 76–77). Smele's argument that there was, in September 1918, a better route to the Alekseev/Denikin forces than the Trans-Siberian route (p. 76) is less convincing; the Black Sea was still blocked. Smele's reference to the admiral as 'the dictator elect' already during his journey from Vladivostok to Omsk (p. 79) is difficult to substantiate.

13. Popova, *Dopros Kolchaka*, pp. 152–53. Kolchak was formally attached to Boldyrev on 30 October (Shishkin, *VVP*, p. 190).

14. Boldyrev left his command post once Kolchak came to power. At the end of the Civil War he decided to remain in Soviet Russia (where he was arrested and executed in 1933).

15. Smele, *Civil War*, pp. 92–93; TNA (Kew), WO 33/962, Knox to War Office, 7 November 1918.

16. Kolchak himself testified that he arrived on the 16th, the day before the coup ([*Ia*] *pribyl* [*v Omsk*] *primerno chisla 16-go noiabria, za den' do perevorota*). He also said that between the time of his return and the coup 'many officers from headquarters and representatives from the cossacks' had time to come to see him to complain about the Directory and urge him to take power – urgings that he maintained were steadfastly rejected (Popova, *Dopros Kolchaka*, p. 167). One authoritative Soviet-era historian stated that the admiral returned to Omsk only at 5.30 p.m. on the 17th which, he sarcastically suggested, could hardly have been a coincidence (Ioffe, *Avantiura*, p. 140); this was also the hour and date given by Colonel John Ward, who accompanied Kolchak on his inspection tour (*With the 'Die-Hards' in Siberia*, London: Cassell, 1920, p. 125). Smele has the admiral returning to Omsk at 5.30 p.m. on the *16th* but remaining aboard his train at Omsk station, two and a half miles from the town centre (Smele, *Civil War*, pp. 100, 120).

17. Popova, *Dopros Kolchaka*, p. 169; Peter Fleming, *The Fate of Admiral Kolchak* (Edinburgh: Birlina, 2001 (1963)), p. 112: 'It does seem safe … to assume that Kolchak himself was neither involved in nor aware of the plot.' Smele, in other respects a very full account, does not raise the issue of Kolchak's direct involvement on 17–18 November (*Civil War*, pp. 102–07).

18. Maurice Janin, *Ma Mission en Sibérie* (Paris: Payot, 1933), pp. 30–31. See the discussion in Ullman, *Intervention*, pp. 280–81.

19. Ullman, *Britain*, p. 34. On J. F. Neilson and Leo Steveni, see especially Michael Kettle, *Churchill and the Archangel Fiasco: November 1918 – July 1919* (London: Routledge, 1992), pp. 11–15. Kettle quoted a 24 January 1919 typescript note, in Neilson's papers, where he apparently admitted 'having moved slightly in advance of the very halting policy, or rather lack of policy of our Government'. Peter Fleming, for his part, concluded that the two British officers 'had no part in the *coup d'état*', although it is worth noting that the sexagenarian Steveni provided help in writing Fleming's book (*Fate*, pp. 113–16).

20. Ullman, *Intervention*, p. 281; Ullman, *Britain*, pp. 33–35. See Knox's brief review of an early version of Janin's memoir; this appeared in *Slavonic*

Review, 3:9 (1925), p. 724. Knox noted that Janin had not been present when the coup occurred. It had also taken place 'without the previous knowledge, and without in any sense the connivance of Great Britain'. He pointed out that Janin also blamed the British for the overthrow of Nicholas II in March 1917. On the other hand Knox stated in his review, misleadingly, that the November 1918 coup was 'carried out by the Siberian Government'.

21. TNA (Kew), CAB 23/8.

22. For the conspirators see especially Smele, *Civil War*, pp. 90–104.

23. Ioffe, *Avantiura*, pp. 104–21. See also William G. Rosenberg, *Liberals in the Russian Revolution: The Constitutional Democratic Party, 1917–1921* (Princeton: Princeton University Press, 1974), pp. 392–95.

24. The Syromiatnikov letter is cited in Norman Pereira, *White Siberia: The Politics of Civil War* (Montreal: McGill-Queen's University Press, 1996), p. 106: 'If it were not for you [i.e. Mikhailov], the Council of Ministers would never have decided to give full authority to Admiral Kolchak ...'

25. Popova, *Dopros Kolchaka*, pp. 104 (27 January 1920), 140 (30 January 1920).

26. Kettle, *Fiasco*, p. 13; Pereira, *White Siberia*, p. 102, is more cautious, but considers such communication possible.

27. The best sources on Kolchak in power remain Smele, *Civil War*, pp. 108–677, and Pereira, *White Siberia*. See also Mawdsley, *Civil War*, pp. 181–215, 317–24.

28. For a perceptive discussion of the failure of conservative elites in Russia, including the officer corps, see Matthew Rendle, *Defending the Motherland: The Tsarist Elite in the Revolutionary Period* (Oxford: Oxford University Press, 2010).

CHAPTER 12. THE FATE OF THE SOVIET COUNTRYSIDE

1. This is taken from Moshe Lewin, 'Taking Grain: Soviet Policies of Agricultural Procurements before the War', reproduced in his *The Making of the Soviet System: Essays in the Social History of Interwar Russia* (London: Methuen & Co., 1985), pp. 142–77.

2. Oliver Radkey, *The Unknown Civil War in Soviet Russia: A Study of the Green Movement in the Tambov Region, 1920–1921* (Palo Alto, CA: Hoover Institution Press, 1976).

3. Quoted in A. K. Sokolov, ed., *Protokoly Prezidiuma Vysshego Soveta Narodnogo Khoziaistva. 1920 god: sbornik dokumentov* (Moscow: ROSSPEN, 2000), p. 3.

4. On the conscription of civilian labour before 1917, see Joshua Sanborn, *Imperial Apocalypse: The Great War and the Destruction of the Russian Empire* (Oxford: Oxford University Press, 2014), pp. 139–41.

5. Isaac Deutscher, *The Prophet Armed: Trotsky, 1879–1921* (Oxford: Oxford University Press, 1954), pp. 490–91. See also Leon Trotsky, *The Defence of Terrorism (Terrorism and Communism): A Reply to Karl Kautsky* (London: Labour Publishing Co., 1921), pp. 127–63.

6. Sylvana Malle, *The Economic Organization of War Communism, 1918–1921* (Cambridge: Cambridge University Press, 1985), pp. 84–85.

7. See Leon Trotsky, *Sochineniia*, 21 vols (Moscow-Leningrad: Gosudarstvennoe izdatel'stvo, 1927), vol. 15: pp. 27–51.

8. See 'Vserossiiskoe razorenie i trudovye zadachie krest'ianstva (pi'smo k Sigunovu),' in Trotsky, *Sochineniia*, vol. 15, pp. 14–26.

9. Viktor Kondrashin, *Krest'ianstvo Rossii v grazhdanskoi voine: k voprosu ob istokakh stalinizma* (Moscow: ROSSPEN, 2009), pp. 286–87.

10. See V. K. Vorob'ev, *'Chapannaia voina' v Simbirskoi gubernii: mify i real'nost'* (Ulianovsk: Vektor –S, 2008); Kondrashin, *Krest'ianstvo Rossii*, pp. 127–43.

11. The entire exchange can be found in Viktor Danilov and Teodor Shanin, eds, *Krest'ianskoe dvizhenie v Povolzh'e, 1919–1922: Dokumenty i materialy* (Moscow: ROSSPEN, 2002), pp. 127–28.

12. Trotsky later wrote that his travel to this region in 1919 was the true start of his misgivings of the regime's food procurement methods. See Leon Trotsky, *Novyi kurs* (Moscow: Krasnaia nov', 1924), pp. 52–53.

13. Ia. G. Gol'din, Commissar for Food in Tambov province, quoted in Erik Landis, 'Between Village and Kremlin: Confronting State Food Procurement in Civil War Tambov, 1919–1920', *Russian Review* 63 (January 2004), p. 77.

14. As the secretary of the Commissariat for Agriculture, V. N. Meshcheriakov, wrote: 'All that is important in the food supply commissariat is to get more grain.' Quoted in James Heinzen, *Inventing a Soviet Countryside: State Power and the Transformation of Rural Russia, 1917–1929* (Pittsburgh: University of Pittsburgh Press, 2004), p. 35.

15. On the razverstka policy and its antecedents, see Lars Lih, *Bread and Authority in Russia, 1914–1921* (Berkeley: University of California Press, 1990).

16. This comparison is against the standard set in 1913, after which declines were recorded. After 1917, however, the decline became much more severe. Malle, *Economic Organization*, pp. 426–31; Lih, *Bread and Authority*, pp. 261–62.

17. Iu. A. Poliakov, *Perekhod k NEPu i sovetskoe krest'ianstvo* (Moscow: Nauka, 1967), p. 88; Malle, *Economic Organization*, p. 468.

18. According to the Soviet economist Lev Kritsman, urban citizens depended upon the black market for up to 70 per cent of their food. See Alec Nove, *An Economic History of the USSR* (London: Allen Lane, 1969), pp. 61–62; Donald Raleigh, *Experiencing Russia's Civil War: Politics, Society and Revolutionary Culture in Saratov, 1917–1922* (Princeton: Princeton University Press, 2002), p. 296.

19. Igor' Narskii, *Zhizn' v katastrofe: Budni naseleniia Urala v 1917–1922 gg.* (Moscow: ROSSPEN, 2001), p. 280.

20. Translated passages are from John Channon, 'Trotsky, the Peasants, and Economic Policy,' *Economy and Society* 14, no. 4 (1984), pp. 518–20. The source document is in Trotsky, *Sochineniia*, vol. 17/2, pp. 543–44.

21. Lenin expressed the problem even more concisely, in specific reference to coal mining in the Donbass region: '[T]here is no bread because there is no coal, and there is no coal because there is no bread.' However, Lenin made his comments in late February 1921. See V. I. Lenin, *Polnoe Sobranie Sochenenii* (*PSS*), 55 vols (Moscow: Gos. izd. politliteratury, 1955–65), vol. 42, p. 364.

22. Two policy developments of note in this regard were the Communist Party *subbotniki* and the unrealised sowing committees project. See William Chase, 'Voluntarism, Mobilization and Coercion: Subbotniki, 1919–1921', *Soviet Studies* 41, no. 1 (1989), pp. 111–28; Lars Lih, 'The Bolshevik Sowing Committees of 1920: Apotheosis of War Communism?', *Carl Beck Papers in Russian and East European Studies*, no. 803 (1990).

23. Vladimir Brovkin, *Behind the Front Lines of the Civil War: Political Parties and Social Movements in Russia, 1918–1922* (Princeton: Princeton University Press, 1994), pp. 163–64.

24. Sergei Pavliuchenkov, 'S chego nachinalsia NEP?,' in N. N. Taranov and V. V. Zhuravlev, eds, *Trudnye vosprosy istorii: Poiski, razmyshlenii, novyi vzgliad na sobytii i fakty* (Moscow: Izd. polit-literatury, 1991), pp. 48–49; *Protokoly Prezidiuma Vysshego Soveta Narodnogo Khoziaistva*, p. 4.

25. Lenin, *PSS*, vol. 51, pp. 123, 405 fn. 128; Sergei Pavliuchenkov, *Krest'ianskii Brest, ili predistoriia bol'shevistskogo NEPa* (Moscow: Russkoe knigoizdatel'skoe tovarishchestvo, 1996), p. 143. For Lenin's earlier words on free trade, see his speech to the Seventh Congress of Soviets (5 December 1919) in *PSS*, vol. 39, pp. 407–08.

26. Pavliuchenkov, *Krest'ianskii Brest*, pp. 128–29.

27. Ibid., pp. 143–44.

28. Trotsky notes this outcome in his autobiography. See *My Life: The Rise and Fall of a Dictator* (London: Thornton Butterworth, 1930), p. 396.

29. *Deviatyi s'ezd RKP(b). Mart-Aprel' 1920* (Moscow: Partiinoe izdatel'stvo, 1934).

30. Danilov and Shanin, *Krest'ianskoe dvizhenie v Povolzh'e*, pp. 417–18.

31. For example, see Danilov and Shanin, *Krest'ianskoe dvizhenie v Povolzh'e*, pp. 468–72.

32. A. Berelowitch and V. Danilov, eds, *Sovetskaia derevnia glazami VChK-OGPU-NKVD, 1918–1939*, 4 vols (Moscow: ROSSPEN, 1998), vol. 1, p. 298.

33. This perspective was spelled out in clear terms by Soviet authorities in Moscow, warning regional and provincial authorities that they would be held personally responsible for shortfalls in procurement. See *Dekrety sovetskoi vlasti*, 13 vols (Moscow: Gos. izd. politliteratury, 1957–1989), vol. 9, p. 241; vol. 10, pp. 239–40.

34. Quoted in Landis, 'Between Village and Kremlin,' p. 83.

35. Berelowitch and Danilov, *Sovetskaia derevnia*, vol. 1, p. 283.

36. On Tambov, see Radkey, *The Unknown Civil War* and Erik Landis, *Bandits and Partisans: The Antonov Movement in the Russian Civil War* (Pittsburgh: University of Pittsburgh Press, 2008).

37. Danilov and Shanin, *Krest'ianskoe dvizhenie v Povolzh'e*, p. 760.

38. Berelowitch and Danilov, *Sovetskaia derevnia*, vol. 1, pp. 363–79.

39. V. I. Shishkin, ed., *Sibirskaia Vandeia*, 2 vols (Moscow: 'Demokratiia', 2000), vol. 2, pp. 9–11.

40. The official Sovnarkom instruction on preparations for the razverstka campaign in Siberia set the targets for 1920–21, and because these regions had not previously been under Soviet control, it also decreed that all surpluses from earlier harvests, before 1920, were to be delivered to state grain collection points. See Shishkin, L., *Sibirskaia Vandeia*, vol. 2, pp. 6–7.

41. Such were the words of the chairman of the Siberian Military Revolutionary Committee (I. N. Smirnov), the functioning Soviet authority in the extended region, although he was only echoing the language of the official Sovnarkom decree that announced the razverstka for Siberia in late July 1920. See *Sibirskaia Vandeia*, 2, pp. 6–7, 198, 241.

42. On the famine, see C. E. Bechhofer, *Through Starving Russia: Being a Record of a Journey to Moscow and the Volga Provinces in August and September 1921* (London: Metheun & Co., 1921); Bertrand Patenaude, *Big Show in Bololand: The American Relief Expedition to Soviet Russian in the Famine of 1921* (Palo

Alto: Stanford University Press, 2002); Marcus Wehner, 'Golod 1921–1922 gg. v Samarskoi gubernii i reaktsiia sovetskogo pravitel'stva', *Cahiers du Monde russe* 38, nos. 1–2 (1997), pp. 223–42; Narskii, *Zhizn' v katastrofe*, pp. 258–74.

43. Denis Borisov, *Kolesnikovshchina. Antikommunisticheskoe vosstanie voronezhskogo krest'ianstva v 1920–1921 gg.*(Moscow: Posev, 2012), p. 81; Narskii, *Zhizn' v katastrofe*, pp. 254–55.

44. Lenin, *PSS*, vol. 43, pp. 18, 59.

45. Trotsky, *My Life*, p. 395.

46. This is described in E. H. Carr, *The Bolshevik Revolution, 1917–1923*, 3 vols (London: W. W. Norton & Co., 1952), vol. 2, pp. 331–44.

47. Trotsky did note in his autobiography, written in 1930, that Lenin came round to the idea of the tax-in-kind only after '[t]he uprisings at Kronstadt and in the province of Tambov broke into the discussion as the last warning' (*My Life*, p. 397). Larin was a bit less politic with his public comments at the Communist Party Conference in May 1921, when he explained that his earlier proposals would have helped end the Civil War sooner. See Pavliuchenkov, *Krest'ianskii Brest*, p. 142; *Protokoly desiatoi vserossiiskoi konferentsii RKP (bol'shevikov). Mai 1921 g.* (Moscow: Partiinoe izd., 1933), p. 63.

48. Quoted in W. Bruce Lincoln, *Red Victory: A History of the Russian Civil War* (New York: Simon & Schuster, 1989), p. 90.

49. Joseph Stalin, *Sochineniia*, 13 vols (Moscow: Gos. izd. politliteratury, 1946–53), vol. 6, pp. 86–87.

50. The best recent literature on the NEP period is found in the fields of social and, particularly, cultural history. See Eric Naiman, *Sex in Public: The Incarnation of Early Soviet Ideology* (Princeton: Princeton University Press, 1997); Anne Gorsuch, *Youth in Revolutionary Russia: Enthusiasts, Bohemians, Delinquents* (Bloomington: Indiana University Press, 2000).

51. Stalin's trip to the Urals and abandonment of the NEP is most recently discussed in Stephen Kotkin, *Stalin. Volume 1: The Paradoxes of Power, 1878–1928* (New York: Penguin, 2014), pp. 662–76. On collectivisation and 'de-kulakisation', see Lynne Viola et al., eds, *The War Against the Peasantry* (New Haven: Yale University Press, 2005).

CHAPTER 13. THE 'BOLSHEVIK REFORMATION'

1. The decree was published in the central Soviet press only on 23 February; sources often give this date rather than the date when it was signed into law.

2. The parallels between Soviet religious iconoclasm and those in the Reformation of the Christian Church during the sixteenth and seventeenth centuries are in some ways striking (see e.g. Eamon Duffy, *The Stripping of the Altars: Traditional Religion in England, c. 1400–c. 1580* (New Haven: Yale University Press, 1992). However, the Soviet case involved a far more extreme rebellion against the architectural and artistic canons of the past, since the reformers hoped to negate religious belief in its entirety, not specific doctrines, social structures and practices within the Roman tradition of Christianity.

3. See e.g. the coverage in *Petrogradskaya pravda* (henceforth *PP*), 26 January 1922. While recent historical research has confirmed this picture of inadequate aid efforts, it has also challenged the Soviet-era causality: V. A. Polyakov's massive study, *Golod na Povolzh'e, 1919–1925* (Volgograd: Volgogradskoe nauchnoe izdatel'stvo, 2007), underlines that the famine began early in 1921, well before the drought itself, and that its devastating effects were attributable to the Bolsheviks' agricultural and food distribution policies rather than natural disaster. Indeed, the American Relief Administration began aid negotiations as early as 1919 (Harold H. Fisher, *The Famine in Soviet Russia, 1919–1923: The Operations of the American Relief Administration* (New York: The Macmillan Company, 1927)). At the same time, recent claims that agitation about the famine was simply an instrument of repression distort reality. The Scottish-Canadian journalist F. A. Mackenzie, a resolutely anti-Soviet observer who visited Buzuluk in 1921, recorded that 'thousands were flocking in from the country and people were dying in the streets', and that the cemetery warden 'took me to the further end of the cemetery and showed me the great pits full to the top with the naked bodies of the newly dead'. (*The Russian Crucifixion: The Full Story of the Persecution of Religion Under Bolshevism* (London: Jarrolds, 1927), p. 23; cf. Fisher, pp. 71–72).

4. *PP*, 18 February 1922, p. 2. Vvedensky was a figure both colourful and murky. As late as 1923, he was, according to a Finnish-Swedish visitor and qualified observer of the Soviet scene, swanking about Petrograd in a carriage drawn by two 'beautiful greys', accompanied by society ladies, while himself was elegantly dressed in white silk (Boris [Leonidovich] Cederholm, *In the Clutches of the Tcheka*, trans. F. H. Lyon (London: George Allen and Unwin

Ltd, 1929)). An informant of Cederholm's claimed that Vvedensky was 'a cynical, unprincipled voluptary, who believes neither in God nor the devil', ibid.

5. See e.g. *PP*, 30 March 1922, p. 2.

6. L. D. Trotsky, letter to the Politburo, 17 March 1922, *Arkhivy Kremlya*, vol. 1, *Politburo i tserkov', 1922–1925 gg.* (Moscow and Novosibirsk: ROSSPEN/ Sibirskii poligraf, 1997) (http://krotov.info/acts/20/1920/1922_0.htm), document no. 23: 14 (henceforth *AK* and by document no.) On high-level planning of the confiscations, see the archive-based discussion in Jonathan Daly, '"Storming the Last Citadel": The Bolshevik Assault on the Church, 1922', in Vladimir N. Brovkin, ed., *The Bolsheviks in Russian Society: The Revolution and Civil Wars* (New Haven: Yale University Press, 1997), pp. 236–59.

7. See e.g. the text of the law published in *Krasnaya gazeta* (henceforth *KG*), 23 February 1922, p. 3.

8. The history of the so-called 'Renovationist' movement went back to the 1900s, and particularly to the debates preceding the Orthodox Church's Local Council, eventually held in 1917–18, but widely discussed from 1905–6. 'Renovation' attained new energy under the Bolshevik regime, since the political context encouraged clergy's own hopes of reform, and there was support among some political agents for using the reformists as a 'Trojan horse' to weaken the official church. The complicated history of all this has been the subject of several book-length studies: see e.g. Edward Roslof, *Red Priests: Renovationism, Russian Orthodoxy, and Revolution, 1905–1946* (Bloomington, Indiana: Indiana University Press, 2002).

9. 160 poods, according to the traditional Russian system of weights and measures. *AK*, no. 23–42. That said, the Soviet government was under pressure from the US side to demonstrate willingness to expend its own gold resources on famine relief before external aid was provided. On 2 September 1921, President Hoover wrote to Colonel Haskell of the ARA: 'As you are aware, it is reported here that Soviet Government has still some resources in gold and metals, and it does seem to me fundamental that they should expend these sums at once in the purchase of breadstuffs from abroad. While even this will be insufficient to cover their necessities, they can scarcely expect the rest of the world to make sacrifices until they have exhausted their own resources' (Fisher, p. 155). The US administration certainly did not anticipate the confiscations from churches, but the frantic search for precious metal supplies in the autumn–winter of 1921–22 was

related to this determination that home resources should be called upon first. The later legend that the Soviet government had been required to 'pay' for aid (in fact, the Riga agreement of 20 August 1921 required only payment for transport, storage and administrative costs) probably derives from this pressure. (See Bertrand M. Patenaude, *The Big Show in Bololand: The American Relief Expedition to Soviet Russia in the Famine of 1921* (Stanford University Press, 2002), p. 741 for the rumour, p. 746ff. for the agreement).

10. For instance, the press emphasised that one of the accused in the Petrograd case, Father Anatoly Tolstopyatov, chaplain of the Petrograd Conservatoire, was a former lieutenant in the Russian navy, i.e. a member of the 'officer class' (*KG* 20 June 1922, p. 6).

11. For the term 'campaign justice', see Peter Solomon, *Soviet Criminal Justice under Stalin* (Cambridge: Cambridge University Press, 1996).

12. Zhizhilenko is quoted in the published resumé of the transcript from the trial of Veniamin and his supposed associates, *Delo mitropolita Veniamina*, ed. Anon (Moscow: TRITE-Rossiiskii arkhiv, 1991), http://www.krotov. info/acts/20/1920/1922_veniamin.htm. For the mockery of him, see Vysokushkin (no initials given), 'Ne tvorite muchenikov!', *KG* 4 July 1922, p. 5.

13. This can be traced in *KG*'s coverage over the first half of 1922. Cf. Jonathan Waterlow's account of how telling jokes that had been considered harmless at the time when they were originally narrated in the early 1930s was frequently adduced as evidence of seditious behaviour in 1937–8: 'Popular Humour in Stalin's 1930s: A Study of Popular Opinion and Adaptation', D.Phil Thesis, University of Oxford, 2012.

14. The show trial of the Socialist Revolutionaries, also orchestrated in spring 1922, was given far more prominent press coverage (front rather than inside pages), but this represented the end of the first phase of power consolidation by the Bolshevik leadership – the crackdown on alternative political parties, rather than the beginning of the second, the move against 'hostile' or 'alien' groups that did not necessarily intend to present themselves as oppositional in political terms.

15. These figures (157 Orthodox churches, 'two or three Catholic and Jewish' ones) were given in a letter from the Board of Management (Upravlenie) of the Petrograd Provincial Soviet responding to representations from Jewish communities against the closure of their 'house churches'. TsGA-SPb., f. 1001, op. 7, d. 1,l. 310.

16. TsGA-SPb., f. 1001, op. 7, d. 19,l. 24.

17. See my *Socialist Churches: Radical Secularization and the Preservation of Heritage in Petrograd-Leningrad, 1918–1988* (DeKalb, IL: Northern Illinois University Press, 2016), chapters 2–3.

18. G. S. Yatmanov, 'Okhrana khudozhestvennogo dostoyaniya', *PP* 25 May 1922, p. 3.

19. On Soviet monetisation of artistic resources generally, see N. Iu. Semenova and Nicolas V. Iline, *Selling Russia's Treasures: The Soviet Trade in Nationalized Art, 1917, 1938* (Paris: The M. T. Abraham Center for the Arts Foundation, 2013), including good discussions of religious art by Yuri Pyatnitsky.

20. Mackenzie, *Russian Crucifixion*, p. 27.

21. A. A. Valentinov, ed., *Chernaya kniga: Shturm nebes. Sbornik dokumental'nykh dannykh, kharakterizuyushchikh bor'bu sovetskoi kommunisticheskoi vlasti protiv vsyakoi religii, protiv vsekh ispovedanii i tserkvei* (Paris: izd. Russkogo natsional'nogo studencheskogo ob'edineniya, 1925). pp. 6–16, quotation p. 7.

22. 'O poriadke provedenii v zhizn' dekreta 'Ob otdelenii tserkvi ot gosudarstva i shkoly ot tserkvi' (Instruktsiia)', 24 August 1918, *Sbornik uzakonenii i rasporiazhenii RK RSFSR.* no. 62 (1918). Article 685, clause 29, p. 764. For objections to the removal of objects, see *Chernaya kniga*, pp. 26–9.

23. A. I. Vvedensky, 'Smert' religii', *Sobornyi razum* nos. 3–4 (1918), p. 5.

24. *Chernaya kniga*, pp. 35–44, details numerous cases, e.g. Andronik, Archimandrite of Perm and Solikamsk, who had his eyes put out and cheeks slashed before being murdered, as well as desecration of churches in areas hit by the War (pp. 29–30).

25. The letter later became known as 'Anathema to Soviet Power' but its original title, 'On the Unprecedented Oppression Unleashed upon the Russian Church', was less specific.

26. There is an enormous literature on the exposure of relics. Two excellent accounts in English are Steve Smith, 'Bones of Contention: Bolsheviks and the Exposure of Saints' Relics, 1918–30', *Past and Present* vol. 204 (August 2009), pp. 155–94; Robert Greene, *Bodies Like Bright Stars: Saints and Relics in Orthodox Russia* (DeKalb, IL: Northern Illinois University Press, 2010).

27. See *Chernaya kniga*, chapter 1.

28. Mikhail Gorev, 'Tserkovnoe zoloto – golodayushchim', *KG*, 25 February 1922, p. 2. On the Eighth Section, see Smith, 'Bones'.

29. 'Sovetskaya politika v religioznom voprose', *Revolyutsiya i tserkov'* no. 1 (1919), p. 2.

30. As reported in an article published in the journal of the reformist clergy, *Sobornyi razum*, no. 3–4 (1918), p. 1: 'Parishes have gradually won for themselves the right to act as juridical subjects, they have de facto exercised these rights, and no-one has dared challenge these.'

31. As James Ryan points out ('Cleansing NEP Russia: State Violence against the Russian Orthodox Church in 1922', *Europe-Asia Studies*, vol. 65, no. 9 (2013), pp. 1811–12), this was part of a general shift to legalism at this point.

32. For example, the American Jewish Joint Distribution Committee, Southern Baptist Convention, National Catholic Welfare Council, American Friends Service Committee (Fisher, p. 163). Direct aid was also accepted from the Vatican.

33. See e.g. *PP* 16 February 1922, p. 2, 17 February 1922, p. 2.

34. Regional variation and agency-by-agency variation in response to the confiscations campaign were important factors, too complicated to assess here. Daly, 'Storming the Last Citadel', emphasises that Cheka officials in Tatarstan, for example, began the confiscations before the 16 February 1922 decree; Gregory L. Freeze, 'Subversive Atheism: Soviet Antireligious Campaigns and the Religious Revival in Ukraine in the 1920s', in Catherine Wanner, ed., *State Secularism and Lived Religion in Soviet Russia and Ukraine* (New York: Oxford UP, 2012), pp. 27–62, underlines pockets of lassitude and resistance in this area.

35. See the account in *Chernaya kniga*, chapter 11, section 3. The meeting on 5 March (but not its sequel) was reported also in the official newspaper materials about the trial of Veniamin. The surmise about a directive from the centre seems to be borne out by the fact that, on 8 March, the Politburo held a meeting resolving to step up the confiscations campaign: *AK*, no. 23–2.

36. See the editors' introduction to *AK*, http://krotov.info/acts/20/1920/1922_1.html#_Toc491501082.

37. Compare the hesitation and division about whether to cooperate with Islamic leaders and groups in the Caucasus at exactly this period: Jeromin Petrović, 'Bolshevik Co-Optation Policy and the Case of Chechen Sheikh Ali Mitaev', *Kritika* vol. 15, no. 4, pp. 729–65.; or, on the other hand, the clear-cut ruthlessness with which, say, Socialist Revolutionaries and idealist philosophers were treated, also in 1922: '*Ochistim Rossiyu nadolgo*': *Repressii protiv inakomyslyashchikh* (Moscow: Mezhdunarodnyi fond 'Demokratiya'/ Izdatel'stvo 'Materik', 2008), e.g. docs. nos. 3, 11, 14, 75, 82.

38. The letter originally came out in *Vestnik russkogo studencheskogo khristianskogo dvizheniya*, no. 98 (1970), pp. 54–7. In the commentary

(p. 59), Nikita Struve refers explicitly to Lenin's game plan: 'Lenin himself took care that the Church had no opportunity at all to co-operate with the government in famine relief and did all he could to make sure that the removal of church valuables touched to the quick the essence of church life – the liturgy.'

39. Lenin alludes to Machiavelli as 'a certain clever commentator on matters of state', since the Italian political philosopher was a somewhat startling authority for a self-declared Marxist. See the text of his letter in *AK*, no. 23.16. This letter is invariably cited in accounts of the church confiscations, but usually as the document that initiated policy, rather than one that reflects its drift at a specific point. For an approach closer to my own, see Ryan, 'Cleansing NEP Russia'; Natalya Krivova, 'The Events in Shuia: A Turning Point in the Assault on the Church', *Russian Studies in History* vol. 46, no. 2, pp. 8–38. For a meticulous, archive-based study of the first period of Bolshevik governance that emphasises contingency, see Alexander Rabinowitch, *The Bolsheviks in Power: the First Year of Soviet Rule in Petrograd* (Bloomington: Indiana University Press, 2007).

40. At this stage, it was also already clear that the 1922 harvest would be abundant ('Prospect for the crop is now unusually favorable', wrote C. S. Gaskill on 12 May 1922 from Saratov; see Fisher, p. 297).

41. See e.g. *KG*, 23, 24, 28 March, 4 April, 9 April, 14 April, 11 May. On the Moscow show trial of clergy supposed to have resisted confiscation, see ibid. 10 May, on the Petrograd show trial, ibid., 10 June to 6 July, *passim*.

42. On the early history of militant atheism, see William Husband, *Godless Communists: Atheism and Society in Soviet Russia, 1917–1932* (DeKalb: Northern Illinois University Press, 2000). In fact, the militant atheist movement had limited usefulness to the central and local authorities, since its campaigns fostered social division and sometimes reproduced top-level policy and ideology in garbled form. For a detailed history, see Daniel Peris, *Storming the Heavens: The Soviet League of the Militant Godless* (Ithaca New York: Cornell University Press, 1998).

43. In comparable vein, *Chernaya kniga*, pp. 28–30, reported the secularisation of house churches as sacrilege, alongside defecation in church sanctuaries etc.

44. That said, the Church's Local Council of 1918 had conferred some limited regional powers on senior clergy, but in a context where communication with the centre was impossible because of the Civil War.

45. TsGA-SPb., f. 1000, op. 6, d. 266,1. 60.

46. TsGA-SPb, f. 1001, op. 7, d. 1,1. 333–5. On ordinary parishioners' defence of church treasures, see also Freeze, 'Subversive Atheism', pp. 31–3.

47. This case was reported in *KG*, 20 June 1922, p. 6. The person concerned is referred to here as 'Deacon Flerov', though Flerov was actually a priest (see *Delo mitropolita Veniamina*), so either the title or the surname is a slip.

48. See Point 11 of the 'Determination of the Holy Council of the Russian Church on the Preservation of Sacred Church Items from Sacrilegious Seizure and Disrespect', 30 August (12 September) 1918, *Svyashchennyi Sobor Pravoslavnoi Tserkvi: Sobranie opredelenii i postanovlenii*. Part 4 (Moscow: Svyashchennyi Sobor, 1918), p. 30.

49. The figure was mentioned by one of the lawyers, Yakov Gurovich, who is quoted in *KG* 4 July 1922, p. 5.

50. Quoted in M. V. Shkarovsky, *Peterburgskaya eparkhiya v gody gonenii I utrat, 1917–1945* (St Petersburg: Liki Rossii, 1995).

51. The story is cited here from John McManners, *Church and State in France, 1870–1914* (New York: Harper and Row, 1972), p. 141. There is a large literature on the history and consequences of the 1905 law. See, for example, Maurice Larkin, *Church and State after the Dreyfus Affair: The Separation Issue in France* (London: Macmillan, 1974), esp. pp. 133–226.

52. See Larkin, *Church and State*, p. 152.

53. This mood permeated the discussions at the Church's Local Council of 1917–18.

54. This is particularly emphasised in Ryan, 'Cleansing NEP Russia'.

55. A classic discussion is Sheila Fitzpatrick, *The Cultural Front: Power and Culture in Revolutionary Russia* (Ithaca New York: Cornell University Press, 1992).

56. There is now a significant body of work arguing that the Russian Orthodox Church's integration post-1943 was remarkably successful: see e.g. recent books and articles by Glennys Young, Tatiana A. Chumachenko, Natalia Shlikhta, Andrew Stone, and others.

57. Maxim Sherwood, *The Soviet War on Religion* (London: Modern Books n.d. [c. 1930]), p. 11, 14. The Holy Name movement was a mystical and charismatic grouping that included, for example, the distinguished Russian émigré theologian Father Sergei Bulgakov.

58. The figure self-identifying as believers was 56.7 per cent across the USSR, certainly an underestimate since census data was collected by means of face-to-face interview.

59. Zhiromskaya, 'Religioznost', ibid.

60. TsGA-SPb., f. 7834, op. 33, d. 50,1. 98.

61. Vladimir Nabokov, *Pnin* (1957) (London: Penguin, 1997), p. 59.

62. These denominations did come under all-out assault in 1935–8 in any case, as international relations worsened and members of ethnic minorities were increasingly targeted as 'foreign agents'.

63. As described in the authoritative biography by Daniel P. Todes, *Ivan Pavlov: A Russian Life in Science* (New York: Oxford University Press, 2014).

64. See Josephine von Zitzewitz, 'The 'Religious Renaissance' of the 1970s and its Repercussions on the Soviet Literary Process', D.Phil Thesis, University of Oxford, 2009.

CHAPTER 14. THE RISE OF LENINISM: THE DEATH OF POLITICAL PLURALISM IN THE POST-REVOLUTIONARY BOLSHEVIK PARTY

1. Anthony D'Agostino, *Soviet Succession Struggles, Kremlinology and the Russian Question from Lenin to Gorbachev* (London: Allen and Unwin, 1988), pp. 4–5 and *passim*.

2. Joseph Bradley, 'Subjects into Citizens: Societies, Civil Society, and Autocracy in Tsarist Russia', *The American Historical Review*, vol. 107, no. 4, October 2002, pp. 1094–1123.

3. Anton A. Fedyashin, *Liberals under Autocracy: Modernization and Civil Society in Russia, 1866–1904* (Madison, WI: University of Wisconsin Press, 2012).

4. Joseph Bradley, *Voluntary Associations in Tsarist Russia: Science, Patriotism and Civil Society* (Cambridge, MA: Harvard University Press, 2009).

5. For a critical analysis of these developments, see Thomas C. Owen, *Capitalism and Politics in Russia: A Social History of the Moscow Merchants, 1855–1905* (Cambridge: Cambridge University Press, 1981).

6. Robert W. Thurston, *Liberal City, Conservative State: Moscow and Russia's Urban Crisis, 1906–1914* (Oxford University Press, 1987).

7. Antonio Gramsci, *Selections from the Prison Notebooks*, edited and translated by Quintin Hoare and Geoffrey Nowell Smith (London: Lawrence & Wishart, 1971), p. 238.

8. G. V. Plekhanov, *The Development of the Monist View of History* (Moscow: Progress Publishers, 1974).

9. Richard Sakwa, *Communism in Russia: An Interpretive Essay* (Basingstoke: Palgrave Macmillan, 2010), pp. 43–4.

10. Diane P. Koenker, *Moscow Workers and the 1917 Revolution* (Princeton: Princeton University Press, 2014).

11. For an excellent comparative analysis, see S. A. Smith, *Revolution and the People in Russia and China: A Comparative History* (Cambridge: Cambridge University Press, 2008).

12. Diane P. Koenker, *Republic of Labor: Russian Printers and Soviet Socialism, 1880–1930* (Cornell, New York: Cornell University Press, 2005).

13. Vera Broido, *Lenin and the Mensheviks: The Persecution of Socialists under Bolshevism* (Aldershot: Gower, 1987).

14. *The Bolsheviks and the October Revolution: Central Committee Minutes of the Russian Social-Democratic Labour Party (Bolsheviks), August 1917 – February 1918* (London: Pluto Press, 1974), pp. 140–42.

15. Rosa Luxemburg, *The Russian Revolution* (Ann Arbor: University of Michigan Press, 1961), p. 69.

16. Karl Kautsky, *The Dictatorship of the Proletariat* (Michigan: Ann Arbor Paperback, 1964), p. 6.

17. For an evaluation of the emergence of Soviet foreign policy, see Richard K. Debo, *Revolution and Survival: The Foreign Policy of Soviet Russia 1917–18* (Liverpool: Liverpool University Press, 1979).

18. N. Osinskii, 'Stroitel'stvo sotsializma', *Kommunist*, no. 2, 1918, pp. 68–72, in Ronald Kowalski, *The Russian Revolution, 1917–1921* (London: Routledge, 1997), p. 200.

19. 'Sobranie upolnomochennykh fabric i zavodov petrograda k aprelyu 1918', a report in *Den'*, no. 7, Petrograd, 1918, in *Nezavisimoe rabochee dvizhenie v 1918 godu: Dokumenty i materialy* (Paris: YMCA-Press, 1981), p. 94.

20. Timofei Sapronov, *Devyataya konferentsiya RKP(b), sentyabr' 1920 goda: Protokoly* (Moscow: Izdatel'stvo politicheskoi literatura, 1972), pp. 156–61.

21. *1918 Constitution of the Russian Soviet Federated Socialist Republic*, 10 July 1918, https://www.marxists.org/history/ussr/government/constitution/1918/article3.htm.

22. Michael E. Urban, *More Power to the Soviets: The Democratic Revolution in the USSR* (Aldershot: Edward Elgar, 1990).

23. N. Bukharin and E. Preobrazhensky, *ABC of Communism*, introduction by E. H. Carr (Harmondsworth: Penguin Books, 1969), p. 118.

24. A. J. Polan, *Lenin and the End of Politics* (London: Methuen, 1984), p. 11.

25. Alfred Rosmer, *Lenin's Moscow*, translated by Ian H. Birchall (London: Pluto Press, 1971), p. 116.

26. Richard Sakwa, *Soviet Communists in Power: A Study of Moscow During the Civil War, 1918–21* (London: Macmillan, 1988), pp. 231–2.

27. *Kommunisticheskii Trud*, 19 February 1921.

28. B. L. Dvinov, *Moskovskii sovet rabochikh deputatov, 1917–1922: vospominaniya* (New York: 1961), p. 108.

29. Alexandra Kollontai, *The Workers' Opposition in Russia* (London: Dreadnought Publishers, 1923), pp. 20–21.

30. Paul Avrich, *Kronstadt 1921* (Princeton, NJ: Princeton University Press, 1970).

31. Simon Pirani, *The Russian Revolution in Retreat, 1920–24: Soviet Workers and the New Communist Elite* (London and New York: Routledge, 2008).

32. R. V. Daniels, 'Stalin's Rise to Dictatorship', in Alexander Dallin and Alan Westin, eds, *Politics in the Soviet Union* (New York: Harcourt, Brace and World, 1966).

33. For a discussion of alternatives, see Samuel Farber, *Before Stalinism: The Rise and Fall of Soviet Democracy* (London: Verso, 1990).

34. R. V. Daniels, *The Conscience of the Revolution: Communist Opposition in Soviet Russia* (New York: Simon & Schuster, 1969).

35. Richard Pipes, ed., *The Unknown Lenin: From the Secret Archive* (New Haven and London: Yale University Press, 1998), afterword to the paperback version, p. 179.

36. Stephen F. Cohen, *Bukharin and the Bolshevik Revolution: A Political Biography, 1888–1938* (New York: Vintage, 1975).

37. Stephen F. Cohen, *Soviet Fates and Lost Alternatives: From Stalinism to the New Cold War* (New York: Columbia University Press, 2009).

38. David W. Lovell, *From Marx to Lenin: An Evaluation of Marx's Responsibility for Soviet Authoritarianism* (Cambridge: Cambridge University Press, 1984), p. ix.

39. Lovell is sceptical about the possibility, *From Marx to Lenin*, p. 2.

40. Lovell, *From Marx to Lenin*, pp. 183–5.

41. For an exploration of this, see Jean L. Cohen, *Civil Society and Political Theory* (Boston, MA: MIT Press, 1994).

42. Leszek Kolakowski, 'The Myth of Human Self-Identity: Unity of Civil and Political Society in Socialist Thought', in Leszek Kolakowski and Stuart Hampshire, eds, *The Socialist Idea* (London: Weidenfeld & Nicolson, 1974), p. 18.

43. Pirani, *The Russian Revolution in Retreat, 1920–1924*.

DRAMATIS PERSONAE

Alexeev, Mikhail Vasilievich: General. Chief of Staff to Nicholas II from 1915. Advised Nicholas to abdicate February 1917. Served as Chief of Staff to Provisional Government. Arrested Kornilov on Kerensky's order. After October 1917 helped set up White army but died September 1918.

Avdeev, Alexander Dmitrievich: Bolshevik. Commandant of the Ipatiev House in Ekaterinburg during the detention of the imperial family.

Bogrov Dmitry Grigorievich: Anarchist revolutionary and police agent. Assassinated Pyotr Stolypin in Kiev, September 1911.

Bonch-Bruevich, Vladimir Dmitrievich: Leading Bolshevik. Personal secretary to Lenin after October 1917.

Botkin, Evgenii Sergeevich: Doctor to the imperial family. Assassinated with them, Ekaterinburg, July 1918.

Bukharin, Nikolai Ivanovich: Leading Bolshevik. Opposed treaty of Brest-Litovsk. Strongly backed NEP. Killed in Stalin's purges 1938.

Chernov, Viktor Mikhailovich: Leader of the Socialist revolutionaries. Member of the Duma. Minister in the Provisional Government. Chairman of the Constituent Assembly, and then leader of the anti-Bolshevik 'Komuch' in Samara. Died in exile.

Chkheidze, Nikolai Semyonovich: Leading Menshevik. President of the executive Committee of the Petrograd Soviet through the revolution in 1917. After October fled Russia.

Denikin Anton Ivanovich: General. Led White forces in Southern Russia during civil war. After defeat went into exile.

Durnovo, Pyotr Nikolaevich: Tsarist era politician and Minister of Interior 1905–6. Effectively repressed disturbances after Bloody Sunday. Accurately predicted social revolution would follow Russian war with Germany.

Dzerzhinsky, Felix Edmundovich: 'Iron Felix'. Polish by origin. Leading Bolshevik. Tasked by Lenin to establish the Cheka, December 1917. Headed the Bolshevik apparatus of terror from then until his death in 1926.

Gilliard, Pierre: Swiss tutor to the five children of Nicholas and Alexandra. Accompanied them into exile, but was not permitted to go on with them to Ekaterinburg.

Golitsyn, Nikolai Dmitrievich: Last Prime Minister of Imperial Russia, December 1916 to Feb 1917. Resigned following February revolution. Was then in and out of custody. Executed 1925.

Guchkov, Alexander Ivanovich: Conservative Russian politician and member of Duma. From 1916 on active in working for removal of Tsar. Sent to Pskov February 1917 to help persuade Tsar to abdicate. War minister in Provisional Government. Supported Whites in Civil War. Died in exile.

Guseva, Khionya Kuzminichna: Simbirsk peasant. Attempted to kill Rasputin June 1914. Declared insane. Later released on order of Kerensky.

Hermogen (Georgii Yefremovich Dolganyov): Orthodox priest and Bishop. Initially an ally of Rasputin, turned against him and on one occasion struck him. On the Tsar's instructions was accordingly expelled from his bishopric. Re-established contacts with the imperial family in Tobolsk. Drowned by the Bolsheviks 1918.

Iliodor (Sergei Mikhailovich Trufanov): Monk and charismatic preacher. Hostile to Stolypin (who tried to have him rusticated) but protected by Rasputin and the Tsar. Turned against Rasputin and spread rumours he was having an affair with the Empress. Eventually defrocked and died in the US.

Kamenev, Lev Borisovich: Leading Bolshevik. Opposed decision to seize power in October 1917, and sought coalition with non-Bolshevik socialists. Nevertheless held senior roles in early Soviet Union. Eventually opposed Stalin. Shot 1936.

Kaplan, Fanya Efimovna: Socialist revolutionary. Tried to assassinate Lenin August 1918. Injured but did not kill him. Shot September that year.

Kerensky, Alexander Fyodorovich: Leading socialist politician and brilliant orator. Member of fourth Duma, where he launched a major attack on Rasputin's links with the imperial family. After February 1917 vice-chairman of the Petrograd Soviet and minister in the Provisional Government. Became Prime Minister July 1917 and, after sacking Kornilov, also Chief of staff. Tried to fight back after the October revolution, was swiftly defeated. Died in exile 1970.

Kolchak, Alexander Vasilyevich: Admiral and military hero. Led the anti-Bolshevik cause in Siberia, eventually in effect as military dictator. Rigidly right wing and heavily dependent on Western support. After initial military success, he underwent a series of defeats, was handed over to the Bolsheviks in Irkutsk, and shot February 1920.

Kornilov, Lavr Georgievich: General. Appointed army Commander in Chief by Kerensky July 1917, but then suspected of planning a coup. Arrested September 1917 (fatally damaging Kerensky's credibility). Escaped after October to take charge of emerging White army. Killed in action April 1918.

Krupskaya, Nadezhda Konstantinovna: Lenin's wife, and a revolutionary in her own right. Accompanied him in exile and on his return in the 'sealed train'. Later Bolshevik deputy minister. Died 1939.

Lenin, Vladimir Ilyich: Lifetime revolutionary. Creator and leader of the Bolsheviks. After February 1917 returned to Russia with German help, persuaded Bolshevik party to take an ultraradical line which attracted growing public support and led to the seizure of power in October. Thereafter main author of all aspects of Bolshevik policy, including repressive terror. After a series of strokes died in 1924.

Lunacharsky Anatoly Vasilievich: Leading Bolshevik and supporter of Lenin. After revolution given charge of Soviet arts and education. Died 1933.

Lvov, Georgy Yevgenievich: Prince, moderate politician, Duma member, civic leader. Chosen as first head of Provisional Government February 1917. After a steady loss of support replaced by Kerensky July 1917. Arrested by Bolsheviks, escaped, died in exile 1925.

Lvov, Vladimir Nikolaevich: Conservative politician and Duma member. Misleadingly intervened between Kerensky and Kornilov precipitating the arrest of the latter and eventually the fall of the Provisional Government.

Martov, Yulii Osipovich: Leader of the Mensheviks. Precipitated the walkout from the Council of Soviets on 25 October 1917 which gave power to the Bolsheviks. Representative at the short lived Constituent assembly. Died in exile 1923.

Milyukov, Pavel Nikolaevich: Liberal politician. Leader of the Constitutional democrats (Kadets). Made devastating November 1916 'stupidity or treason' Duma speech attacking Tsarist regime. Foreign Minister of Provisional Government until forced out May 1917. After suppression of Kadets went into exile. Backed formation of White armies. Died 1945.

Yakovlev Vasily Vasilievich (aka Myachin, Konstantin Alexeevich): Violent revolutionary and saboteur. Member of Petrograd Soviet. Appointed March 1918 to transfer imperial family from Tobolsk to Moscow. May have intended rescue, but forced to surrender them to Ekaterinburg Bolsheviks. Later captured by Whites, fled to China, returned 1928, executed 1938.

Plekhanov, Georgy Valentinovich: Early Russian Marxist. Ideas, particularly on subordination of democracy to proletarian power, highly influential with Lenin. Nevertheless opposed the Bolsheviks and the October revolution. Died in exile 1918.

Protopopov, Alexander Dmitrievich: Politician and member of Duma. Close to Rasputin. Made Interior Minister at Empress' behest September 1916. Accused of mental instability. Survived repeated demands for his resignation. Badly mishandled popular anger in February 1917. Shot by Cheka.

Rasputin, Grigory Yefimovich: Mystic and monk. Gained deep influence with imperial family, particularly Empress, through apparent ability to cure Crown Prince's haemophiliac attacks. Fatally sapped credibility of regime as alleged co-ruler with, and lover of, Empress in Tsar's absence at front from August 1915. Murdered December 1916.

Romanova, Alexandra Feodorovna: Empress of Russia. Born a German princess. Married Nicholas II November 1894. Exercised great influence, particularly in her commitment to autocracy. Bore four daughters and a son. Fatally fell under the influence of Rasputin. Murdered, Ekaterinburg, July 1918.

Romanov, Alexis Nikolaevich: Heir to the Russian Empire. Born August 1904. Suffered from haemophilia which several times nearly killed him and which apparently only Rasputin could treat. Murdered, Ekaterinburg July 1918.

Romanov, Mikhail Alexandrovich: Grand Duke. Younger brother of Nicholas II and second in line to the throne (after Alexis). Military leader. Offered throne by Nicholas on his abdication. Put off acceptance. Arrested by Bolsheviks March 1918, transported to Siberia, murdered there June 1918.

Romanov, Nikolai Alexandrovich: Emperor of Russia 1894–1917. Mystically confident of his bond with the Russian people. Instinctively traditionalist. Unwaveringly committed to autocracy. Pliable, petulant and unreliable with his ministers. Caring family man, sometimes at public cost. Abdicated February 1917. Murdered, Ekaterinburg, July 1918.

Romanov, Nikolai Nikolaevich: Grand Duke, military leader, cousin of Nicholas II and influential with him. Persuaded him to accept Witte's reforms 1905. Russian supreme commander in first year of World War I until succeeded by Tsar himself. Among those who advised Nicholas to abdicate. Died in exile.

Rodzyanko, Mikhail Vladimirovich: Chairman of Duma 1911–17. Took centre stage in Petrograd in February 1917. Failed to persuade Tsar to make concessions in time. Persuaded military not to intervene. Chaired Duma committee which, with Soviet, gave birth to Provisional Government. After October joined Whites. Died in exile 1924.

Ruzsky, Nikolai Vladimirovich: General. Commander Northern Front 1916–17. The only senior figure with the Tsar in Pskov 1–2 March 1917. Helped persuade him to abdicate. Later joined Whites. Captured and killed September 1918.

Rykov, Alexei Ivanovich: Leading Bolshevik moderate. Opposed Lenin in aftermath of October revolution. Nevertheless took leading roles in regime thereafter. Executed in great purge 1938.

Sakhanov, Nikolai Nikolaevich: Menshevik member of Petrograd Soviet. Participated in (and later regretted) October 1917 walkout from Congress of Soviets which handed power to the Bolsheviks.

Sazonov, Sergei Dmitrievich: Russian statesman. Foreign Minister 1910–16. Sacked at behest of Empress. Backed Whites. Died in exile 1927.

Semyonov, Grigory Ivanovich: Socialist Revolutionary terrorist and assassin. Organised Fanny Kaplan's attempt to kill Lenin.

Shulgin, Vasily Vitalievich: Conservative member of Duma. Helped persuade Tsar to abdicate March 1917. Backed Whites, went into exile, but after imprisonment died in USSR 1976.

Soloviev, Boris: Son in Law of Rasputin. In Siberia, 1917, took valuables from imperial family to help them escape, apparently as a confidence trick. Died in exile 1926.

Savinkov, Boris Victorovich: Revolutionary and terrorist. Deputy War Minister to Kornilov July–August 1917. Planned assassination of Bolshevik leadership 1918. Killed, Moscow 1925.

Stalin, Joseph Vissarionovich: Top Bolshevik leader. Initially resisted Lenin's radical approach in April 1917, but quickly fell into line. After Lenin's death, 1924, manoeuvred himself into total control of USSR, and forced principal rival, Trotsky, into exile. Bloody, totalitarian dictator. Died 1953.

Stolypin, Pyotr Arkadievich: Russian statesman. Highly effective administrator. Appointed Prime minister 1906. Ruthless in suppression of disorder. Fixed franchise to ensure Duma support for his ambitious programme of reform, but lost support of Tsar. Assassinated, Kiev 1911.

Sukhomlinov, Vladimir Alexandrovich: General. Minister of War 1909–15. Sacked for military failure. Charged with treason March 1916 but released at demand of Rasputin and Empress, badly damaging reputation of regime.

Sverdlov, Yakov Mikhailovich: Leading Bolshevik. Close to Lenin. Deeply involved in decisions to close Constituent Assembly, sign Brest-Litovsk treaty and execute imperial family. Died 1919.

Tikhon (Vasily Ivanovich Bellavin): Patriarch of the Russian Church November 1917. Initially stood up to Bolshevik regime, for example over murder of imperial family, but came to take more conciliatory line. Protested at seizure of church property. Arrested 1922–3, and deposed. Died 1924.

Trotsky, Lev Davidovich: Bolshevik leader second only to Lenin in gaining and holding power. Played key role in October 1917 as Chairman of Petrograd Soviet. Led Red army to victory in Civil War. Endorsed and facilitated red terror. But outmanoeuvred by Stalin in power struggle after Lenin's death. Exiled 1929. Murdered 1940.

Veniamin (Vasily Pavlovich Kazansky): Metropolitan of Petrograd. Resisted state seizure of church property 1922. Tried as a counterrevolutionary and shot.

Vrangel, Pyotr, Nikolaevich: General. Led White army in Southern Russia. Disagreed sharply with fellow general Denikin. After defeat went into exile 1920. Died (perhaps poisoned) 1928.

Vyrubova, Anna Alexandrovna: Lady in waiting and probably closest confidante of Empress. Adherent of Rasputin and go-between between him and Alexandra. Arrested after revolution. Escaped to Finland. Died 1964.

Witte, Sergei Yulyevich: Count and key policymaker. Built trans-Siberian railway. Prime minister 1903–6. Negotiated end to Russo-Japanese war. Persuaded Tsar to accept political reform, including establishment of Duma, after Bloody Sunday. Resigned after losing trust of Tsar. Died 1915.

Yudenich, Nikolai Nikolaevich: General. Leader of White forces in NW Russia. Nearly took Petrograd before defeat in October 1919. Caught trying to escape with army funds. Died in exile.

Yusupov, Felix Felixovich: Prince. Rich, dissipated and married to Tsar's niece. Organised murder of Rasputin, December 1916. Despite wish of Empress that he be shot, merely confined to his estate. After revolution went into exile.

Zinoviev, Grigory Yevseevich: Leading Bolshevik. Opposed decision to seize power in October 1917, and sought coalition with non-Bolshevik socialists. Nevertheless held senior roles in early Soviet Union. Eventually opposed Stalin. Shot 1936.

CONTRIBUTORS

Dominic Lieven is a Senior Research Fellow of Trinity College, Cambridge, a Fellow of the British Academy and author of *Beyond the Flame: Empire, War and the End of Tsarist Russia*. His book *Russia against Napoleon* won the Wolfson Prize for History.

Simon Dixon is Sir Bernard Pares Professor of Russian History at UCL Chairman of the Literary Committee of the Russian Booker Prize. His critically acclaimed biography *Catherine the Great* was shortlisted for the Longman/ *History Today* Book of the Year Award.

Douglas Smith is an award-winning historian and translator, and the author of five books on Russia, including *Former People: The Last Days of the Russian Aristocracy* and *Rasputin: Faith, Power, and the Twilight of the Romanovs*.

Donald Crawford was for twenty years the publisher of *Parliamentary Brief*. He is the author of several books on Tsarist Russia, including *Michael & Natasha* (co-authored with his wife Rosemary Crawford and soon to become a film by Russian director Andrei Kravchuk) and *The Last Tsar: Emperor Michael II*.

Sean McMeekin is a Professor of History at Bard College. He is the author of several acclaimed works of history, including *The Ottoman Endgame*, which won the Arthur Goodzeit Book Award, and *The Russian Origins of the First World War*, which won the Norman B. Tomlinson Jr. Book Prize.

Richard Pipes is one of the world's best known historians of the Russian Revolution. He was Baird Professor of History at Harvard University and served as National Security Council adviser on Soviet and East European affairs.

Orlando Figes is Professor of History at Birkbeck, and the award-winning author of eight books, including the Wolfson Prize-winning *A People's Tragedy: The Russian Revolution 1891–1924*. His work has been translated into thirty-two languages.

Edvard Radzinsky is a Russian playwright, screenwriter, TV presenter and history writer. His books available in English include *The Last Tsar* and *Stalin*:

The First In-Depth Biography Based on Explosive Documents from Russia's Secret Archives.

Martin Sixsmith was the BBC's Moscow correspondent during the collapse of the Soviet Union, and is the author of several books, including the *Sunday Times* bestseller *Russia: A 1,000-Year Chronicle of the Wild East* and *Philomena*, the basis for the critically acclaimed movie of the same name.

Evan Mawdsley was Professor of International History at the University of Glasgow and is the author of several books, including *The Russian Civil War*.

Erik Landis is a Fellow at All Souls College, Oxford, and Senior Lecturer in Modern European History at Oxford Brookes. He is the author of *Bandits and Partisans: The Antonov Movement in the Russian Civil War.*

Catriona Kelly is Professor of Russian at the University of Oxford. She has published widely on Russian history, including *St Petersburg: Shadows of the Past* and *Socialist Churches*. She has also published translations of Mayakovsky, Tsvetaeva and others and reviews for the *TLS* and *Guardian*.

Richard Sakwa is Professor of Russian and European Politics at the University of Kent, an Associate Fellow at the Royal Institute of International Affairs and author of many scholarly works on Communist and post-Communist Russia, including *Frontline Ukraine* and *Putin: Russia's Choice*.

INDEX